CAROLINE MOOREHEAD

A Train in Winter

A Story of Resistance, Friendship
and Survival in Auschwitz

VINTAGE BOOKS
London

First published in Great Britain in 2011 by
Chatto & Windus

Vintage
Random House, 20 Vauxhall Bridge Road,
London SW1V 2SA

www.vintage-books.co.uk

Addresses for companies within The Random House Group Limited
can be found at: www.randomhouse.co.uk/offices.htm

The Random House Group Limited Reg. No. 954009

A CIP catalogue record for this book
is available from the British Library

ISBN 9780099523895

Jacket photographs: Women in Paris, December 1943 © (API/Roger Viollet)/
Getty Images; Arrival of Hungarian Jews in Auschwitz-Birkenau, Poland,
June 1944 © Galerie Bilderwelt/Getty. The photographs have been coloured.

Penguin Random House is committed to a sustainable future for
our business, our readers and our planet. This book is made from
Forest Stewardship Council® certified paper.

MIX
Paper from
responsible sources
FSC
www.fsc.org   FSC® C018179

Printed and bound in Great Britain by Clays Ltd, St Ives plc

Typeset by Palimpsest Book Production Limited, Falkirk, Stirlingshire

To Leo

Contents

The Routes taken through Wartime Europe

0   100   200 miles
0   100   200   300 km

North Sea

DENMARK
(Occupied)

Kiel

Neuengammen

Hamburg
(Zazel)

Bremen

ENGLAND

Amsterdam

Hanover

Beendor

London

Münster

NETHERLANDS
(Occupied)

R. Rhine

Calais

Brussels

Cologne

Erfur

Lille

BELGIUM
(Occupied)

E

Frankfurt

R. Seine

Compiègne

Würzburg

Metz

Nurember

G

Paris
(Romainville)

Châlons-
sur-Maine

Strasbourg

Stuttgart

Orleans

R. Danube

Tours

FRANCE
(Occupied)

Dijon

Basle

R. Loire

R. Saône

SWITZERLAND
(Neutral)

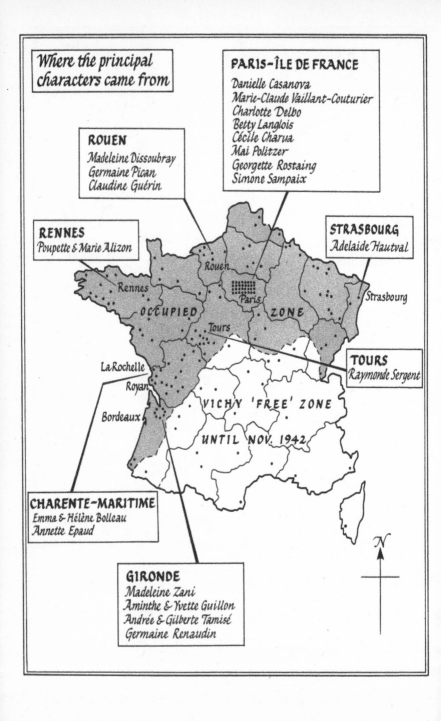

Where the principal characters came from

PARIS-ÎLE DE FRANCE
Danielle Casanova
Marie-Claude Vaillant-Couturier
Charlotte Delbo
Betty Langlois
Cécile Charua
Mai Politzer
Georgette Rostaing
Simone Sampaix

ROUEN
Madeleine Dissoubray
Germaine Pican
Claudine Guérin

RENNES
Poupette & Marie Alizon

STRASBOURG
Adelaide Hautval

TOURS
Raymonde Sergent

CHARENTE-MARITIME
Emma & Hélène Bolleau
Annette Epaud

GIRONDE
Madeleine Zani
Aminthe & Yvette Guillon
Andrée & Gilberte Tamisé
Germaine Renaudin

Rouen

Rennes

Paris

OCCUPIED   ZONE

Strasbourg

Tours

La Rochelle

Royan

VICHY 'FREE' ZONE

Bordeaux

UNTIL NOV. 1942

N

Preface

On 5 January 1942, a French police inspector named Rondeaux, stationed in the 10th arrondissement of Paris, caught sight of a man he believed to be a wanted member of the French Resistance. André Pican was a teacher, and he was indeed the head of the Front National of the Resistance in the Seine-Inférieure; there was a price of 30,000 francs on his head for the derailing of a train carrying requisitioned goods and war materiel to Germany.

Rondeaux's superior, a zealous anti-communist Frenchman and active collaborator of the Gestapo called Lucien Rottée, thought that Pican might lead them to other members of the Resistance. Eleven inspectors were detailed to follow, but not to arrest, him.

Over the next two weeks, they searched the streets of Paris in vain. Then, on 21 January, an inspector carrying out a surveillance of the Café du Rond-Point near the Porte d'Orléans thought he saw a man answering to Pican's description. He followed him and watched as he stopped to talk to a thickset man in his thirties, with a bony face and a large moustache. Rottée's men stayed close. On 11 February, Pican was seen standing outside a shop window, then, at '15.50' entering a shop in the company of a woman '28–30 years of age, 1.70m high, slender, with brown hair curling at the ends'; she was wearing a 'Prussian blue coat, with a black belt and light grey woollen stockings, *sans élégance*'. The policeman, not knowing who she was, christened her 'Femme Buisson-St-Louis' after a nearby métro station; Pican became 'Buisson'. After watching a film in Le Palais des Glaces cinema, Pican and Femme Buisson were seen to buy biscuits and oysters before parting on the rue Saint-Maur.

In the following days, Pican met 'Motte Piquet', 'Porte Souleau' and 'Femme No. 1 de Balard'. Not knowing who they were, the police officers gave them the names of the places where they were first seen.

On 12 February, Femme Buisson was seen to enter the Café au Balcon, where she was handed a small suitcase by 'Merilmontant' – a short woman in her mid-thirties, 'c. 1.55m, dark brown hair in a net, black coat, chic fauve leather bag, red belt'. By now, Pican had also met and exchanged packets with 'Femme Brunet St Lazare' ('34, 1.60m, very dark, pointed nose, beige coat, hood lined in a patterned red, yellow and green material'), and with 'Femme Claude Tillier' ('1.65m, 33, dark, somewhat corpulent, bulky cardigan and woollen socks'). 'Femme Vincennes' ('1.60m, 32, fair hair, glasses, brown sheepskin fur coat, beige wool stockings') was seen talking to 'Femme Jenna' and 'Femme Dorian'. One of the French police officers, Inspector Deprez, was particularly meticulous in his descriptions of the women he followed, noting on the buff rectangular report cards which each inspector filled out every evening that 'Femme République' had a small red mark on her right nostril and that her grey dress was made of angora wool.

By the middle of February, Pican and his contacts had become visibly nervous, constantly looking over their shoulders to see if they were being followed. Rottée began to fear that they might be planning to flee. The police inspectors themselves had also become uneasy, for by the spring of 1942 Paris was full of posters put up by the Resistance saying that the French police were no better than the German Gestapo, and should be shot in legitimate self-defence. On 14 February, Pican and Femme Brunet were seen buying tickets at the Gare Montparnasse for a train the following morning to Le Mans, and then arranging for three large suitcases to travel with them in the goods wagon. Rottée decided that the moment had come to move. At three o'clock on the morning of 15 February, sixty police inspectors set out across Paris to make their arrests.

Over the next forty-eight hours they banged on doors, forced their way into houses, shops, offices and storerooms, searched cellars and attics, pigsties and garden sheds, larders and cupboards. They came away with notebooks, addresses, false IDs, explosives, revolvers, tracts, expertly forged ration books and birth certificates, typewriters, blueprints for attacks on trains and dozens of torn postcards, train timetables and tickets, the missing halves destined to act as passwords when matched with those held by people whose names were in the notebooks. When Pican was picked up, he tried to swallow a piece of paper with a list of names; in his shoes were found addresses, an anti-German flyer and 5,000 francs. Others, when confronted by Rottée's men, shouted for help, struggled, and tried to run off; two women bit the inspectors.

As the days passed, each arrest led to others. The police picked up journalists and university lecturers, farmers and shopkeepers, concierges and electricians, chemists and postmen and teachers and secretaries. From Paris, the net widened, to take in Cherbourg, Tours, Nantes, Evreux, Saintes, Poitiers, Ruffec and Angoulême. Rottée's inspectors pulled in Pican's wife, Germaine, also a teacher and the mother of two small daughters; she was the liaison officer for the Communist Party in Rouen. They arrested Georges Politzer, a distinguished Hungarian philosopher who taught at the Sorbonne, and his wife Maï, 'Vincennes', a strikingly pretty midwife, who had dyed her blond hair black as a disguise for her work as courier and typist for the Underground, and not long afterwards, Charlotte Delbo, assistant to the well-known actor-manager Louis Jouvet.

Then there was Marie-Claude Vaillant-Couturier, 'Femme Tricanet', niece of the creator of the Babar stories and contributor to the clandestine edition of *L'Humanité*, and Danielle Casanova, 'Femme No. 1 de Balard', a dental surgeon from Corsica, a robust, forceful woman in her thirties, with bushy black eyebrows and a strong chin. Maï, Marie-Claude and Danielle were old friends.

When taken to Paris's central Prefecture and questioned, some of those arrested refused to speak, others were defiant, others scornful. They told their interrogators that they had no interest in politics, that they knew nothing about the Resistance, that they had been given packets and parcels by total strangers. Husbands said that they had no idea what their wives did all day, mothers that they had not seen their sons in months.

Day after day, Rottée and his men questioned the prisoners, brought them together in ones and twos, wrote their reports and then set out to arrest others. What they did not put down on paper was that the little they were able to discover was often the result of torture, of slapping around, punching, kicking, beating about the head and ears, and threats to families, particularly children. The detainees should be treated, read one note written in the margin of a report, *avec égard*, with consideration. The words were followed by a series of exclamation marks. Torture had become a joke.

When, towards the end of March, what was now known as *l'affaire Pican* was closed down, Rottée announced that the French police had dealt a 'decisive' blow to the Resistance. Their haul included three million anti-German and anti-Vichy tracts, three tons of paper, two typewriters, eight roneo machines, 1,000 stencils, 100 kilos of ink and 300,000 francs. One hundred and thirteen people were in detention, thirty-five of them women. The youngest of these was a 16-year-old schoolgirl called Rosa Floch, who was picked up as she was writing 'Vive les Anglais!' on the walls of her *lycée*. The eldest was a 44-year-old farmer's wife, Madeleine Normand, who told the police that the 39,500 francs in her handbag were there because she had recently sold a horse.

Nine months later on the snowy morning of 24 January 1943, thirty of these women joined two hundred others, arrested like them from all parts of occupied France, on the only train, during the entire four years of German occupation, to take women from the French Resistance to the Nazi death camps.

*   *   *

In the early 1960s, Charlotte Delbo, who had been one of the women on the train, sat down to write a play. She thought of herself as a messenger, bearing the story of her former companions. Twenty-three women, dressed in identical striped dresses, are talking about life in a Nazi camp. They are barely distinguishable one from another, all equally grey in their ragged and shapeless clothes, their hair and features purposefully unmemorable. 'The faces,' Delbo wrote in her stage instructions, 'do not count'; what counted was their common experience. As in a Greek tragedy, the violence is reported but not seen.

'There must be one of us who returns,' says one of the women. 'You or another, it doesn't matter. We have to fight, to stay alive, because we are fighters . . . Those who return will have won.' A second woman speaks up. 'What of those we'll leave behind?' Another replies: 'We won't leave them. We'll take them away with us.' And then someone asks: 'Why should you believe these stories of ghosts, ghosts who come back and who are not able to explain how?'

In 2008, I decide to go in search of the women who had left Paris, that freezing January dawn sixty-five years earlier. I wonder if any are still alive, to tell the story of what drew them into the Resistance, of how they came to fall into the hands of Rottée's men, and what battles they and their companions fought to survive, then and later.

Charlotte Delbo, I discover, died of cancer in 1985. But seven of the women are still alive. I find Betty Langlois, at 95 an emaciated but steely woman of immense charm, with the same sharp shining brown eyes that look quizzically out of her early photographs, living in a darkened flat in the centre of Paris, full of potted plants and mahogany furniture. She gives me brightly coloured macaroons to eat and a present of a small stuffed tortoiseshell toy cat, curled up in a brown cardboard box. Though she does not have a cat herself, she loves the way this one looks so lifelike and she gives them as presents to all her friends.

Betty sends me to Cécile Charua, in Guingamp in Brittany, who laughs at my formal French, and teaches me many words of bawdy slang. At 93, Cécile is sturdy, humorous and uncomplaining. I visit them both several times, and on each occasion they talk and talk, recounting scenes and episodes that seem too fresh and real in their minds to have taken place over half a century before. Neither one of them, in all this time, has spoken much about what happened to them. It is Cécile who tells me about Madeleine Dissoubray, 91 and a retired teacher of mathematics, living on her own in a little flat on the edge of Paris, surrounded by books; and later, at the annual gathering of survivors held every 24 January, I hear Madeleine, an angular, upright woman, with a firm, carrying voice, describe to a crowd of onlookers what surviving has meant. She is unsmiling and totally contained.

I have trouble finding Poupette Alizon, who has drifted away from the others and is estranged from her daughters. But then a lucky turn takes me to Rennes, where I trace her to a silent, elegant, impeccably furnished flat, full of paintings, overlooking a deserted park and some gardens. Poupette, at 83 somewhat younger than the others and in her long flowing lilac coat as elegant as her surroundings, seems troubled and a bit defiant. Poupette, too, talks and talks. She is lonely and life has not worked out well for her.

Lulu Thévenin, Gilberte Tamisé and Geneviève Pakula, all three alive in 2008, I cannot see: they are too frail to welcome visitors. But I meet Lulu's son Paul and her younger sister Christiane.

Betty dies, soon after my third visit, in the summer of 2009. She has had pancreatic cancer for seven years, and no one survives this kind of cancer for so long. The last time I see her, she tells me, in tones of pleasure and pride, that she has mystified all her doctors. Surviving, she says, is something that she is very good at.

Having spent many hours talking to the four surviving women, I decide to go in search of the families of those who did not return from the Nazi camps or who have since died. I find Madeleine Zani's son Pierre in a village near Metz; Germaine Renaudin's son Tony in a comfortable and pretty house in Termes d'Armagnac, not far from Bordeaux; Annette Epaud's son Claude convalescing from an operation in a nursing home in Charente; Raymonde Sergent's daughter Gisèle in Saint-Martin-le-Beau, the village near Tours in which her mother grew up. I meet Aminthe Guillon's grandson in a cafe in Paris. Each tells me their family stories and introduces me to other families. I travel up and down France, to remote farmhouses, retirement homes and apartment blocks, to villages and to the suburbs of France's principal cities. The children, some now in their seventies, produce letters, photographs, diaries. They talk about their mothers with admiration and a slight air of puzzlement, that they had been so brave and so little vainglorious about their own achievements. It makes these now elderly sons and daughters miss them all the more. When we talk about the past, their eyes sometimes fill with tears.

This is a book about friendship between women, and the importance that they attach to intimacy and to looking after each other, and about how, under conditions of acute hardship and danger, such mutual dependency can make the difference between living and dying. It is about courage, facing and surviving the worst that life can offer, with dignity and an unassailable determination not to be destroyed. Those who came back to France in 1945 owed their lives principally to chance, but they owed it too in no small measure to the tenacity with which they clung to one another, though separated by every division of class, age, religion, occupation, politics and education. They did not all, of course, like each other equally: some were far closer friends than others. But each watched out for the others with the same degree of attention and concern and minded every death with anguish. And what they all went through, month after month, lay at the very outer limits of human endurance.

This is their story, that of Cécile, Betty, Poupette, Madeleine and the 226 other women who were with them on what became known as *Le Convoi des 31000*.

Part One

CHAPTER ONE

An enormous toy full of subtleties

What surprised the Parisians, standing in little groups along the Champs-Elysées to watch the German soldiers take over their city in the early hours of 14 June 1940, was how youthful and healthy they looked. Tall, fair, clean shaven, the young men marching to the sounds of a military band to the Arc de Triomphe were observed to be wearing uniforms of good cloth and gleaming boots made of real leather. The coats of the horses pulling the cannons glowed. It seemed not an invasion but a spectacle. Paris itself was calm and almost totally silent. Other than the steady waves of tanks, motorised infantry and troops, nothing moved. Though it had rained hard on the 13th, the unseasonal great heat of early June had returned.

And when they had stopped staring, the Parisians returned to their homes and waited to see what would happen. A spirit of *attentisme*, of holding on, doing nothing, watching, settled over the city.

The speed of the German victory – the Panzers into Luxembourg on 10 May, the Dutch forces annihilated, the Meuse crossed on 13 May, the French army and airforce proved obsolete, ill-equipped, badly led and fossilised by tradition, the British Expeditionary Force obliged to fall back at Dunkirk, Paris bombed on 3 June – had been shocking. Few had been able to take in the fact that a nation whose military valour was epitomised by the battle of Verdun in the First World War and whose defences had been guaranteed by the supposedly impregnable Maginot line, had been reduced, in just six weeks, to a stage of vassalage. Just what the consequences would be were impossible to see; but they were not long in coming.

By midday on the 14th, General Stutnitz, military commandant of Paris, had set up his headquarters in the Hotel Crillon. Since Paris had been declared an open city there was no destruction. A German flag was hoisted over the Arc de Triomphe, and swastikas raised over the Hôtel de Ville, the Chamber of Deputies, the Senate and the various ministries. Edith Thomas, a young Marxist historian and novelist, said they made her think of 'huge spiders, glutted with blood'. The Grand Palais was turned into a garage for German lorries, the École Polytechnique into a barracks. The Luftwaffe took over the Grand Hotel in the Place de l'Opéra. French signposts came down; German ones went up. French time was advanced by one hour, to bring it into line with Berlin. The German mark was fixed at almost twice its pre-war level. In the hours after the arrival of the occupiers, sixteen people committed suicide, the best known of them Thierry de Martel, inventor in France of neurosurgery, who had fought at Gallipoli.

The first signs of German behaviour were, however, reassuring. All property was to be respected, providing people were obedient to German demands for law and order. Germans were to take control of the telephone exchange and, in due course, of the railways, but the utilities would remain in French hands. The burning of sackfuls of state archives and papers in the Ministry of Foreign Affairs, carried out as the Germans arrived, was inconvenient, but not excessively so, as much had been salvaged. General von Brauchtisch, commander-in-chief of the German troops, ordered his men to behave with 'perfect correctness'. When it became apparent that the Parisians were planning no revolt, the curfew, originally set for forty-eight hours, was lifted. The French, who had feared the savagery that had accompanied the invasion of Poland, were relieved. They handed in their weapons, as instructed, accepted that they would henceforth only be able to hunt rabbits with terriers or stoats, and registered their much-loved carrier pigeons. The Germans, for their part, were astonished by the French passivity.

When, over the next days and weeks, those who had fled south in a river of cars, bicycles, hay wagons, furniture vans, ice-cream carts, hearses and horse-drawn drays, dragging behind them prams, wheelbarrows and herds of animals, returned, they were amazed by how civilised the conquerors seemed to be. There was something a little shaming about this chain reaction of terror, so reminiscent of the *Grande Peur* that had driven the French from their homes in the early days of the revolution of 1789. In 1940 it was not, after all, so very terrible. The French were accustomed to occupation; they had endured it, after all, in 1814, 1870 and 1914, and then there had been chaos and looting. Now they found German soldiers in the newly reopened Galeries Lafayette, buying stockings and shoes and scent for which they scrupulously paid, sightseeing in Notre Dame, giving chocolates to small children and offering their seats to elderly women on the métro.

Soup kitchens had been set up by the Germans in various parts of Paris, and under the flowering chestnut trees in the Jardin des Tuileries, military bands played Beethoven. Paris remained eerily silent, not least because the oily black cloud that had enveloped the city after the bombardment of the huge petrol dumps in the Seine estuary had wiped out most of the bird population. Hitler, who paid a lightning visit on 28 June, was photographed slapping his knee in delight under the Eiffel Tower. As the painter and photographer Jacques Henri Lartigue remarked, the German conquerors were behaving as if they had just been presented with a wonderful new toy, 'an enormous toy full of subtleties which they do not suspect'.

On 16 June, Paul Reynaud, the Prime Minister who had presided over the French government's flight from Paris to Tours and then to Bordeaux, resigned, handing power to the much-loved hero of Verdun, Marshal Pétain. At 12.30 on the 17th, Pétain, his thin, crackling voice reminding Arthur Koestler of a 'skeleton with a chill', announced over the radio that he had agreed to head a new government and that he was asking Germany for an armistice. The French people, he said, were to 'cease fighting' and to co-operate with the German authorities. 'Have confidence in the German soldier!' read posters that soon appeared on every wall.

The terms of the armistice, signed after twenty-seven hours of negotiation in the clearing at Rethondes in the forest of Compiègne in which the German military defeat had been signed at the end of the First World War, twenty-two years before, were brutal. The geography of France was redrawn. Forty-nine of France's eighty-seven mainland departments – three-fifths of the country – were to be occupied by Germany. Alsace and Lorraine were to be annexed. The Germans would control the Atlantic and Channel coasts and all areas of important heavy industry, and have the right to large portions of French raw materials. A heavily guarded 1,200-kilometre demarcation line, cutting France in half and running from close to Geneva in the east, west to near Tours, then south to the Spanish border, was to separate the occupied zone in the north from the 'free zone' in the south, and there would be a 'forbidden zone' in the north and east, ruled by the German High Command in Brussels. An exorbitant daily sum was to be paid over by the French to cover the costs of occupation. Policing of a demilitarised zone along the Italian border was to be given to the Italians – who, not wishing to miss out on the spoils, had declared war on France on 10 June.

The French government came to rest in Vichy, a fashionable spa on the right bank of the river Allier in the Auvergne. Here, Pétain and his chief minister, the appeaser and pro-German Pierre Laval, set about putting in place a new French state. On paper at least, it was not a German puppet but a legal, sovereign state with diplomatic relations. During the rapid German advance, some 100,000 French soldiers had been killed in action, 200,000 wounded and 1.8 million others were now making their way into captivity in prisoner-of-war camps in Austria and Germany, but a new France was to rise out of the ashes of the old. 'Follow me,' declared Pétain: 'keep your faith in *La France Eternelle*'. Pétain was 84 years old. Those who preferred not to follow him scrambled to leave France – over the border into Spain and Switzerland or across the Channel – and began to group together as the Free French with French nationals from the African colonies who had argued against a negotiated surrender to Germany.

In this France envisaged by Pétain and his Catholic, conservative, authoritarian and often anti-Semitic followers, the country would be purged and purified, returned to a mythical golden age before the French revolution introduced perilous ideas about equality. The new French were to respect their superiors and the values of discipline, hard work and sacrifice and they were to shun the decadent individualism that had, together with Jews, Freemasons, trade unionists, immigrants, gypsies and communists, contributed to the military defeat of the country.

Returning from meeting Hitler at Montoire on 24 October, Pétain declared: 'With honour, and to maintain French unity . . . I am embarking today on the path of collaboration'. Relieved that they would not have to fight, disgusted by the British bombing of the French fleet at anchor in the Algerian port of Mers-el-Kebir, warmed by the thought of their heroic fatherly leader, most French people were happy to join him. But not, as it soon turned out, all of them.

* * *

Long before they reached Paris, the Germans had been preparing for the occupation of France.There would be no gauleiter – as in the newly annexed Alsace-Lorraine – but there would be military rule of a minute and highly bureaucratic kind. Everything from the censorship of the press to the running of the postal services was to be under tight German control. A thousand railway officials arrived to supervise the running of the trains. France was to be regarded as an enemy kept in *faiblesse inférieure*, a state of dependent weakness, and cut off from the reaches of all Allied forces. It was against this background of collaboration and occupation that the early Resistance began to take shape.

A former scoutmaster and reorganiser of the Luftwaffe, Otto von Stülpnagel, a disciplinarian Prussian with a monocle, was named chief of the Franco-German Armistice Commission. Moving into the Hotel Majestic, he set about organising the civilian administration of occupied France, with the assistance of German civil servants, rapidly drafted in from Berlin. Von Stülpnagel's powers included both the provisioning and security of the German soldiers and the direction of the French economy. Not far away, in the Hotel Crillon in the rue de Rivoli, General von Stutnitz was busy overseeing day to day life in the capital. In requisitioned hotels and town houses, men in gleaming boots were assisted by young German women secretaries, soon known to the French as 'little grey mice'.

There was, however, another side to the occupation, which was neither as straightforward, nor as reasonable; and nor was it as tightly under the German military command as von Stülpnagel and his men would have liked. This was the whole apparatus of the secret service, with its different branches across the military and the police.

After the protests of a number of his generals about the behaviour of the Gestapo in Poland, Hitler had agreed that no SS security police would accompany the invading troops into France. Police powers would be placed in the hands of the military administration alone. However Reichsführer Heinrich Himmler, the myopic, thin-lipped 40-year-old Chief of the German Police, who had long dreamt of breeding a master race of Nordic Ayrans, did not wish to see his black-shirted SS excluded. He decided to dispatch to Paris a bridgehead of his own, which he could later use to send in more of his men. Himmler ordered his deputy, Reinhard Heydrich, the cold-blooded head of the Geheime Staatspolizei or Gestapo, which he had built up into an instrument of terror, to include a small group of twenty men, wearing the uniform of the Abwehr's secret military police, and driving vehicles with military plates.

In charge of this party was a 30-year-old journalist with a doctorate in philosophy, called Helmut Knochen. Knochen was a specialist in Jewish repression and spoke some French. After commandeering a house on the avenue Foch with his team of experts in anti-terrorism and Jewish affairs, he called on the Paris Prefecture, where he demanded to be given the dossiers on all German émigrés, all Jews, and all known anti-Nazis. Asked by the military what he was doing, he said he was conducting research into dissidents.

Knochen and his men soon became extremely skilful at infiltration, the recruitment of informers and as interrogators. Under him, the German secret services would turn into the most feared German organisation in France, permeating every corner of the Nazi system.

Knochen was not, however, alone in his desire to police France. There were also the counter-terrorism men of the Abwehr, who reported back to Admiral Canaris in Berlin; the Einsatzstab Rosenberg which ferreted out Masonic lodges and secret societies and looted valuable art to be sent off to Germany, and Goebbels's propaganda specialists. Von Ribbentrop, the Minister for Foreign Affairs in Berlin, had also persuaded Hitler to let him send one of his own men to Paris, Otto Abetz, a Francophile who had courted the French during the 1930s with plans for Franco- German co-operation. Abetz was 37, a genial, somewhat stout man, who had once been an art master, and though recognised to be charming and to love France, was viewed by both French and Germans with suspicion, not least because his somewhat ambiguous instructions made him 'responsible for political questions in both occupied and unoccupied France'. From his sumptuous embassy in the rue de Lille, Abetz embarked on collaboration 'with a light touch'. Paris, as he saw it, was to become once again the *cité de lumière*, and at the same time would serve as the perfect place of delight and pleasure for its German conquerors. Not long after visiting Paris, Hitler had declared that every German soldier would be entitled to a visit to the city.

Despite the fact that all these separate forces were, in theory, subordinated to the German military command, in practice they had every intention of operating independently. And, when dissent and resistance began to grow, so the military command was increasingly happy to let the unofficial bodies of repression deal with any signs of rebellion. Paris would eventually become a little Berlin, with all the rivalries and clans and divisions of the Fatherland, the difference being that they shared a common goal: that of dominating, ruling, exploiting and spying on the country they were occupying.

Though the French police – of which there were some 100,000 throughout France in the summer of 1940 – had at first been ordered to surrender their weapons, they were soon instructed to take them back, as it was immediately clear that the Germans were desperately short of policemen. The 15,000 men originally working for the Paris police were told to resume their jobs, shadowed by men of the Feldkommandatur. A few resigned; most chose not to think, but just to obey orders; but there were others for whom the German occupation would prove a step to rapid promotion.

The only German police presence that the military were tacitly prepared to accept as independent of their control was that of the anti-Jewish service, sent by Eichmann, under a tall, thin, 27-year-old Bavarian called Theo Dannecker. By the end of September, Dannecker had also set himself up in the avenue Foch and was making plans for what would become the Institut d'Etudes des Questions Juives. His job was made infinitely easier when it became clear that Pétain and the Vichy government were eager to anticipate his wishes. At this stage in the war, the Germans were less interested in arresting the Jews in the occupied zone than in getting rid of them by sending them to the free zone, though Pétain was no less determined not to have them. According to a new census, there were around 330,000 Jews living in France in 1940, of which only half were French nationals, the others having arrived as a result of waves of persecution across Europe.

At the time of the 1789 revolution, France had been the first country to emancipate and integrate its Jews as French citizens. All through the 1920s and 1930s the country had never distinguished between its citizens on the basis of race or religion. Within weeks of the German invasion, posters were seen on Parisian walls with the words 'Our enemy is the Jew'. Since the Germans felt that it was important to maintain the illusion – if illusion it was – that anti-Jewish measures were the result of direct orders by the Vichy government and stemmed from innate French anti-Semitism, Dannecker began by merely 'prompting' a number of 'spontaneous' anti-Jewish demonstrations. 'Young guards' were secretly recruited to hang about in front of Jewish shops to scare customers away. In early August, they ransacked a number of Jewish shops. On the 20th, a *grande action* saw the windows of Jewish shops in the Champs-Elysées stoned. One of the Rothschilds' châteaux was stripped of its art, which gave Göring six Matisses, five Renoirs, twenty Braques, two Delacroix and twenty-one Picassos to add to his growing collection of looted paintings.

But it was not only the Jews who attracted the interest of von Stülpnagel and his men. France had rightly been proud of the welcome given to successive waves of refugees fleeing civil wars, political repression or acute poverty. Poles in particular had been coming to France since the eighteenth century, and the 1920s had brought thousands of men to replace the shortage of manpower caused by the immense French losses in the First World War. Many had become coal miners, settling in the north and east. More recently had come the German refugees, arriving in response to every Nazi crackdown, 35,000 of them in 1933 alone; Austrians escaping the *Anschluss*; Czechs in the wake of Munich; Italians, who had opposed Mussolini. Then there were the Spanish republicans, fleeing Franco at the end of the civil war, of whom some 100,000 were still in France, many of them living in appalling hardship behind barbed wire in camps near the Spanish border.

To these refugees the French had been generous, at least until the economic reversals of the 1930s pushed up unemployment and Prime Minister Daladier drafted measures to curtail their numbers and keep checks on 'spies and agitators' while opening camps for 'undesirable aliens'. France, under Daladier, had been the only Western democracy not to condemn Kristallnacht. The extreme right-wing leader of L'Action Française, Charles Maurras, spoke of 'these pathogenic political, social and moral microbes'. Watching a train of refugees leave France not long before the war, the writer Saint-Exupéry had remarked that they had become 'no more than half human beings, shunted from one end of Europe to the other by economic interests'. Despite the growing xenophobia, many foreigners remained in France; but now, in an atmosphere of uncertainty and hostility, they were stateless, without protection and extremely vulnerable. By late September 1940, many were on their way to internment camps, the German refugees among them branded 'enemies of the Reich' and handed over by the very French who not so long before had granted them asylum.

The treatment of the political exiles caused little protest. The French had other things on their mind. Initial relief at the politeness of the German occupiers was rapidly giving way to unease and a growing uncertainty about how, given that the war showed no signs of ending, they were going to survive economically. As more Germans arrived to run France, they commandeered houses, hotels, schools, even entire streets. They requisitioned furniture, cars, tyres, sheets, glasses and petrol, closed some restaurants and cinemas to all but German personnel, and reserved whole sections of hospitals for German patients. *Charcuterie* vanished from the shops, as Germans helped themselves to pigs, sheep and cattle.

What they had no immediate use for, they sent back to Germany, and packed goods wagons were soon to be seen leaving from the eastern Parisian stations, laden down with looted goods, along with raw materials and anything that might be useful to Germany's war effort. 'I dream of looting, and thoroughly,' wrote Göring to the military command in France. Just as Napoleon had once looted the territories he occupied of their art, now Germany was helping itself to everything that took the fancy of the occupiers. Soon, dressmakers in Paris were closing, because there was no cloth for them to work with; shoemakers were shutting, because there was no leather. Safe-deposit boxes and bank accounts were scrutinised and, if they were Jewish, plundered. Rapidly, French factories found themselves making planes, spare parts, ammunition, cars, tractors and radios for Germany.

In September 1940, the French were issued with ration books and told that in restaurants they could have no more than one hors d'oeuvre, one main dish, one vegetable and one piece of cheese. Coupons were needed for bread, soap, school supplies and meat, the quantities calculated according to the age and needs of the individual. Parisians were advised not to eat rats, which began emerging, starving, from the sewers, 'armies of enormous, long-whiskered, dark-coated, red-eyed rats', though cat fur, especially black, white and ginger, became popular to line winter clothes, since coal had disappeared and houses remained unheated. From November, a powerful black market in food, writing paper, electric wire, buttons and cigarettes operated in Les Halles.

The French were becoming resourceful. Everyone made do, mended, improvised. The word 'ersatz' entered the everyday vocabulary of Paris, housewives exchanging tips and recipes as they queued interminably for ever-dwindling supplies. They told each other how to make *gazogène*, fuel, out of wood and charcoal, how to crush grape pips for oil, and roll cigarettes from a mixture of scarce tobacco, Jerusalem artichokes, sunflowers and maize. As raw materials ceased to reach France from its colonies, and supplies of linen, cotton, wool, silk and jute dried up, women dyed their legs with iodine and wore ankle socks and carried handbags made of cloth. Soon, Paris clattered to the sound of clogs and horse-drawn carts. Vegetables were planted in the Tuileries and in window boxes. A first wind of resistance was beginning to blow. When the ashes of Napoleon's son, l'Aiglon, were returned from exile in Vienna on 15 December 1940 in a huge fanfare of military splendour to be buried again in Les Invalides in Paris, posters were seen with the words: 'Take back your little eagle, give us back our pigs'.

Nor was it easy to learn much about the outside world. On 25 June, a *Presse-Gruppe* had been set up to hold twice-weekly press briefings for those newspapers which, like *Le Matin* and *Paris Soir*, had been allowed to reappear. In theory, the Germans were to draw up the 'themes', while individual journalists decided on the actual content. In practice, editors had been issued with a long list of words and topics to avoid, from 'Anglo-Americans' to Alsace-Lorraine, while the words Austria, Poland, Yugoslavia and Czechoslovakia were never to be used at all, since as countries they no longer existed. Abetz had appointed a Dr Epting to 'diffuse German culture'. Publishers, meanwhile, had been given an 'Otto' list of banned books, which included anything written by a Jew, a communist, an Anglo-Saxon writer or a Freemason, the better to create a 'healthier attitude'. Malraux, Maurois and Aragon vanished from the bookshops, along with Heine, Freud, Einstein and H.G. Wells. In time, 2,242 tons of books would be pulped. By contrast, *Au Pilori*, a violently anti-Semitic paper based on Julius Streicher's *Stürmer*, was to be found all over the city.

Occupation, for the French, was turning out to be a miserable affair.

CHAPTER TWO

The flame of French resistance

Not many people living in France heard the celebrated call to arms of a relatively unknown French general, Charles de Gaulle, transmitted by the BBC on 18 June – four days after the fall of Paris. Some eight million of them were still on the roads to the south, though by now the traffic was crawling the other way, back towards their homes in the north. But the BBC had agreed to give the Free French a slot each evening, five minutes of it in French, and after his first *appel* to the French, de Gaulle spoke to them again, on the 19th, 22nd, 24th, 26th and 28th. With each day that passed, his stern, measured voice gained authority. His message did not vary. It was a crime, he said, for French men and women in occupied France to submit to their occupiers; it was an honour to defy them. One sentence in particular struck a chord with his listeners. 'Somewhere,' said de Gaulle, 'must shine and burn the flame of French resistance.'

Soon, the idea that it was actually possible not to give in to the Germans became an echo, picked up and repeated, written out and handed round, printed in Underground papers and flyers.

De Gaulle had said nothing about the reasons for the French defeat, simply that France was not beaten and would live to see another day. In the evenings, behind closed shutters, in darkness, defying German orders, those who owned radios gathered to listen as the first few chords of Beethoven's Fifth Symphony – chosen when someone pointed out that V, in Morse code, was three short taps – announced words that were quickly becoming famous: 'Içi Londres. Les Français parlent aux Français'. It had the effect of creating links between listeners. In the long food queues, housewives discussed what they had heard. Just at the time when the Germans seemed at their most invincible, it gave ordinary men and women the feeling that they, too, might participate in the ultimate defeat of their oppressors, even if that moment lay far in the future. And though they had little notion of what de Gaulle had in mind, beyond his call for volunteers to join him and the Free French in London, some of the French at least began to see in de Gaulle a future possible liberator and leader.

When the Prefect and future Resistance leader Jean Moulin visited Paris in November, come to see for himself whether there might be a possible *resistance Française*, he concluded that there was nothing much happening. But he was wrong.

The first acts of resistance were small, spontaneous and ill-co-ordinated, carried out by individuals acting out of personal feelings of rebellion and shame. The Free French's Croix de Lorraine – the symbol taken from Joan of Arc – and Vs for victory were scribbled in crayon, lipstick or paint on to walls, on to blackout paper, on to German cars, in the métro and at bus stops, and after the Germans co-opted the Vs, saying that they stood for Victoria, an ancient German word, the French wrote Hs instead, for *honneur*. Rosa Floch was only one of dozens of young girls who wrote 'Vive les Anglais' on their *lycée* walls. A few stones were thrown at the windows of restaurants requisitioned by the Germans. There were catcalls and whistles during German newsreels, until the order went out that the lights had to be kept on, after which the audience took to reading their books and coughing. A young man called Etienne Achavanne cut a German telephone cable.

Early in October, a music publisher called Raymond Deiss typed out two double sheets containing the daily bulletins of the BBC, printed them on linotype and called his news-sheet *Pantagruel*.* Tracts, posters, flyers, typed up and printed by journalists and university students, reminding women that a group of Parisian fishwives had marched on Versailles in 1789 demanding bread from Louis XVI, called on them to protest against rationing. In the Musée de l'Homme, a group of ethnographers and anthropologists joined forces to run off an anti-Vichy and anti-Nazi news-sheet on the museum's mimeograph machine.

Inspired by a mixture of patriotism and humanism, by a view

---

* Deiss would later be beheaded by axe in Cologne.

of France as the champion of individual liberties and the Germans as brutal conquerors, these early pamphlets and papers came from every class and every political ideology. Some extolled Catholicism and morality; others Marxism; others Tom Paine and the Rights of Man. All shared a conviction that to do nothing was wrong.

Faced by this outpouring of protest, the Germans acted swiftly and decisively. The writers and printers they were able to catch they tried and sent to prison. The naïve first resisters were no match for the Nazis, long accustomed to a harsh war of repression at home. The Germans took to putting up posters of their own, warning of the consequences of resistance and offering rewards to informers. Following close behind them, young boys ripped them off while they were still wet, or wrote the words 'Draw a line for de Gaulle', so that soon the German posters were covered in dozens of little lines.

*   *   *

There was, however, one political group in France which already knew a good deal about survival and the clandestine life. The Parti Communist Français, the PCF, born in the wake of the First World War from a schism of the left at Tours in 1920, had zig-zagged through the turbulent currents of French interwar years. Briefly in shared power as part of Léon Blum's coalition of radicals, socialists and communists in 1936 and again in 1938 as the Front Populaire, with a platform of better conditions for the workers and a banner of *Pain, Paix et Liberté*, the PCF had seen its numbers rise sharply in the mining towns of the north, in areas of heavy industry and in ports.

The party had attracted a wide sweep of followers, from the Stalinists, who believed in a revolution of the workers and were veterans of the early struggles with the socialists, to a whole generation of youthful idealists inspired by the PCF's vision of a more equal France. What united many of them was their support for the Spanish republicans after Franco launched his rebellion against the Frente Popular and invaded Spain in July 1936, and their disgust at France's decision to sign the non-intervention pact. Many of these younger communists had gone to Spain to fight in the International Brigades, while their families back in France collected money to help Spanish republican women and children. And, when the refugees fleeing Franco's soldiers began to cross the Pyrenees and into France, the French communists were the first to take in destitute Spanish families and to campaign on their behalf. To be young and active in France in the 1930s was to care passionately about politics.

One of these young idealists was Cécile Charua, a strong-minded, physically sturdy young woman who was born in Paris's *ceinture rouge,* the 'red' suburbs. As she saw it, to grow up French was to grow up communist, and if you did not fight injustice and xenophobia, well, then there was no point to life at all. Cécile's parents divorced when she was a small child, and her mother then married a painter, a man whose anarchist beliefs occupied more of his time than bringing in money for the family. Most of Cécile's considerably older brothers and sisters had long since moved away. Her mother left home before dawn in the early summer months to pick cornflowers in the fields to sell in the Gare Saint-Lazare on her way to work. She was a furrier by trade, but earned very little money.

Cécile Charua, 'le Cygne d'Enghien'

At the age of 13, Cécile was sent as apprentice to another furrier. She enjoyed working with fur, sewing it on to a lining, selecting the different pelts; she savoured their colours and the way the fur lay, making patterns. She particularly liked astrakhan, the fleece of central Asian lambs. Cécile saw herself as feisty and capable, and skilled at spotting the match between the different furs, but she was not much good at finer needlework. She could not afford a fur coat herself, and like all workers in the fur business, was laid off when the demand for fur dropped at the end of December. When she had money, she spent it on theatre tickets, going to the cheapest seats at the Comédie Française or to see Louis Jouvet perform at the Athenée; one day, her artist stepfather took her to meet Picasso.

Soon after her 16th birthday Cécile decided that she was sick of her mother's strictness and her stepfather's idle ways. Wanting, as she said later, a bit more to eat and a little freedom, she married a man who worked for the post office and was a keen trade union member. Nine years her senior, he took her along to political meetings, where she met anti-Fascists and learnt about what was happening to republican families in Spain. Soon she, too, began collecting money for milk for Spanish babies in Bilbao. Cécile had a daughter, and at weekends she put the baby into a sling on her back and went off camping in the forests around Paris with her friends.

In 1935, Cécile became a party member. What appealed to her about the PCF was that the communists wanted enough bread for everyone. Having had a hungry childhood, it made sense to her.

The Nazi–Soviet pact of non-aggression, signed by von Ribbentrop and Molotov on 24 August 1939, came as a shock, as it did to the entire French Communist Party. Overnight, communists were regarded by the new French centrist government, and its Prime Minister, Edouard Daladier, as being on the side of their old enemy, the Germans. After *L'Humanité*, the main PCF paper, published a long communiqué in praise of the pact, Daladier shut it down, along with its sister publication, *Ce Soir*. On clandestine presses, *L'Humanité* fought back, attacking the French and British governments as imperialists, waging war against the workers. In what they called an 'essential national purge', police raided party offices, arrested known militants, suspended communist mayors. The thirty-five communist deputies sitting in parliament were arrested and eventually sentenced to five years in prison for acting on behalf of the Comintern. By the autumn of 1939, there were said to be several thousand communists behind bars.

The party found itself bitterly divided. Outraged by the PCF's initial stand of support for the pact, feeling betrayed by Stalin, a number of members now left the party. But many more remained within, preferring to ignore a move that they either could not or did not want to understand, and as they watched comrades arrested and led away to internment camps, their sense of solidarity grew stronger.

With the German occupation in June 1940 came a further moment of confusion. Watching the troops march into Paris made Cécile feel physically ill. Standing near the Panthéon, she thought to herself, 'How terrible this is going to be.' After *L'Humanité* – still Underground but widely distributed and read – published an article saying that German soldiers were nothing but workers, just like French workers and should be treated with friendliness, communists felt optimistic that they might be allowed by the occupiers to return to the public arena. A number of prominent communists came out of hiding, which only made it easier to find them when Pétain and the French police suggested to the Gestapo that militant communists should be rounded up, along with Freemasons and foreign Jews, as 'enemies of the Reich'. Pétain's proposal was more than acceptable to the Germans, who praised the prefects and French police for their zeal and declared that the communists in detention would henceforth be regarded as 'hostages to guarantee the safety of German soldiers'. Pétain's internment camps were fast turning into holding depots for resisters and Jews.

By September 1940, what with all those who had been made prisoners of war and were in camps in Germany, and those now in custody, there were said to be barely 180–200 active Communist Party members left in the whole of the Paris area. But these were men and women who, like Cécile, now felt that they had a new goal, one more in keeping with the mood of much of the country: anti-Fascist, anti-Vichy and anti-occupier. Quickly, they set about regrouping, spurred on by Maurice Thorez, the PCF leader in exile in Moscow, who issued his own *appel* to the French: 'Never,' declared Thorez, 'will a great nation like ours become a nation of slaves.'

As Cécile saw it, she now had real work to do. She contacted a man she knew from the fur business, who was also a communist local councillor, and asked how she could help. She discovered that Raymond Losserand was running the military section of the communist resistance in Paris and that he had been forced to go underground, fearing arrest. He had grown a bushy moustache and wore a wide-brimmed hat. Losserand offered Cécile 1,500 francs a month for her expenses, and gave her half a métro ticket, telling her only to trust the person who contacted her if he presented her with the other half. Using two different names, sometimes Cécile, sometimes Andrée, she began to act as a liaison officer, and it became her job to pay the clandestine printers and to arrange for the collection of anti-German flyers and pamphlets and their distribution between printers and various depots. Sometimes her packets were so heavy that she could barely lift them, but she dreaded offers of help. Her main contact within the Resistance, the person who held the other half of her métro ticket, was a man called Maurice Grandcoing, a former printer with *L'Humanité*. Cécile would later admit that, despite her bravura, she was afraid, all the time. 'How could you do this work,' she said, 'and not be afraid?'

By now, Cécile was divorced from her husband and when she went off on missions for the PCF, she left her little girl with her mother in the 11th arrondissement. Increasingly at odds with her feckless stepfather, and fearing that what little food came into the household seldom reached her daughter, she decided to send the child to live with a foster family outside the city. She herself moved into a small flat in the centre of Paris, rented for her by the PCF. 'How can you do this work if you have a child?' asked her mother. 'It is because I have a child that I do it,' replied Cécile. 'This is not a world I wish her to grow up in.'

* * *

While Cécile was busy helping set up the Paris networks, another young woman, Madeleine Passot, known to her friends as Betty, took off to travel from one end of France to the other, to recruit new members for the communist Resistance. Betty was 26, the only child of a Parisian family of committed socialists; her mechanic father had served a prison sentence for opposing French involvement in the First World War. As a small child, Betty had appeared so interested in politics that her father had nicknamed her *la petite communiste*. Drawn into the PCF, like Cécile, by the fate of the Spanish republicans, Betty had abandoned her job as a secretary in a big firm and volunteered for resistance work as soon as war was declared. With so many of the men under arrest, she quickly became a crucial courier between Paris and the south.

Slender, fearless, elegant with her red nails and tailored suits, she was, she liked to say, the perfect candidate for 'life in the shadows'. Often, she chose to sit with Germans on the trains going south, rightly confident that they would gallantly protect her at checkpoints, though these journeys, with money hidden in the false bottom of her suitcase and papers in the lining of her handbag, were terrifying. She particularly dreaded passing through Marseilles, where the staircase was exposed and police stood watching the passengers arriving. Often, she was stopped and searched.

Betty Langlois, 'Ongles Rouges', and her companion Lucien Dorland

During the autumn of 1940, Betty was seldom not on the road; walking miles in her high-heeled shoes, with weapons concealed in baskets of grapes, she begged for lifts from farmers across the demarcation line. On her journeys, she was sometimes able to catch up with her companion Lucien Dorland, with whom she lived in a small flat in Paris, though he was busy setting up youth groups in the free zone. On her travels, Betty used other names, sometimes calling herself Madeleine, Odette or Gervaise and would say she sometimes had trouble remembering who she was meant to be. Lucien was also a communist and high up in the party hierarchy. She found the long separations hard, but, like Cécile, did not feel she had much choice in the matter.

By October 1940, the PCF in the Paris area had grown to over a thousand active members. Many were women, pressed into the fold by the absence of men, and, like Betty and Cécile, they were proving excellent as printers, distributors and liaison officers. The *Bulletin de la France Combattante* was run off by two women hidden in an abbey, while 84-year-old Mme Cumin worked a printing press in her launderette.

In November, after a wave of arrests, the number of PCF members fell to below three hundred, but a month later had passed the thousand mark again. Resilient, energetic and prepared to sacrifice themselves, the Communists shared a sense of solidarity and comradeship, and the courage with which they went about their work was not lost on possible new recruits. 'Those responsible for this war have fled,' the PCF announced. 'They have sown desolation and death. It is now up to us to rally the people and to save France.' As Heydrich reported to his superiors, the PCF was turning out to be the sole organisation 'in a position to rally those in search of a political cause'.

To avoid too many losses, the PCF was structured into tight three-person cells, so that no member knew the names of more than two others at any one time. For Cécile and Betty, the arrival of the Germans had had a galvanising effect. The long months of the phoney war had been a bleak and perplexing time and when Betty looked back on them she spoke of them as a 'void'. Now, she had a mission.

It was, however, getting more perilous all the time. One by one, highly conscious of the danger their work posed to their families, aware of the growing numbers of informers and the sophistication of the Gestapo, many of the activists – like Cécile – were leaving home and disappearing to work in other neighbourhoods and under other names. What many would later remember was how lonely they felt, constantly changing lodgings, seldom talking to anyone for more than a few minutes at a time.

* * *

Among the members of the pre-war PCF was a large number of university teachers and graduates from France's prestigious École Normale Supérieure. And it was from these men and women that now emerged the first serious, united, intellectual resistance to the occupiers.

In the 1930s, French intellectual life, epitomised by a small group of people – not all but most of them French – living and meeting on the Left Bank of Paris, had been at the centre of the European stage. This group read and wrote for the *Nouvelle Revue Française*, gathered in the art deco auditorium in the basement of the Palais de la Municipalité or in cafes in the Boulevard Saint-Germain. Though not all politically to the left, the mood was for the most part radical and socialist and there was much talk about the menace of Mussolini and Franco, about the need for peace and the importance of winning better working conditions for France's impoverished working classes. The cause of the Spanish republicans was supported passionately by many of them. André Gide, André Malraux, Henri Barbusse, Romain Rolland, Louis Aragon and his companion Elsa Triolet were among those whose voices were frequently heard in the pages of magazines with titles that perfectly expressed the longings for a better age: *Esprit, Combat* and *Ordre Nouveau*. When, in 1929, Marc Bloch and Lucien Febvre had launched their *Annales d'Histoire Economique et Sociale*, to look at society through a different lens, one that focused on the conditions in which ordinary people lived rather than on the deeds of politicians and rulers, it seemed perfectly to express the mood of the times.

Between 1933 and 1940, Paris became one of the only safe meeting places for intellectual exiles from Hitler, Mussolini and Franco and their dictatorships. One of the issues that exercised many of those sitting and arguing in the cafes was whether the proper role of the intellectual should be that of a seeker after truth, as the novelist and philosopher Julian Benda maintained, or whether on the contrary, it was important to become an *écrivain engagé*, one who got his hands dirty. In a decade of floundering political causes and alliances, with foreign, military and economic policy adrift from one end of the world to the other and French intellectuals defined by their attitude to communism, there were few easy answers. Some of the shrewdest critics of doctrinal rigidity had in fact even drifted into the neo-Fascist camp.

The sudden arrival of the Germans in Paris in the summer of 1940 caught the intellectuals, like everyone else, unprepared. Some fled abroad, some joined the exodus to the south, among them Aragon, Elsa Triolet and Jean Cocteau, and made their homes in the free zone. Others returned to occupied Paris. But while those on the far right quickly and pleasurably discovered a new popularity among the Nazis and their collaborators, those on the left were faced with the question of how they should react to occupation. Sartre, Simone de Beauvoir and François Mauriac soon decided that they would coexist with the enemy and let their own work go on appearing, even though the very fact that their articles were published alongside those of the pro-Germans and anti-Semites lent the Fascists a certain legitimacy. ('Alas!' remarked Jean Zay, who had been Minister of Education under Léon Blum, 'How much kneeling and renunciation there is in the world of French literature!') As Aragon saw it, the role of the man of letters was to speak out, to keep writing, since that was his métier, but to twist the words, giving them new, hidden meanings.

Other writers found this too shaming. Jean Guéhenno, appalled by the ease with which Pétain had made 'of dishonour a temptation', disgusted by those he referred to as an 'invasion of rats', had no difficulty in deciding what to do. Because he had effectively been made a prisoner, he would live like a prisoner; since he could not write what he wanted, he would write nothing at all. Before falling silent for the remainder of the war, Guéhenno wrote one final piece. 'Be proud,' he told his readers. 'Retreat into the depths of thought and morality' but do not, whatever else you do, 'descend into the servitude of imbeciles.' A socialist and trade unionist called Jean Texcier wrote what would later be called a 'manual of dignity', a list of thirty-three 'bits of advice to the occupied'. Husband your anger, he counselled, for you may need it. Don't feel you have to give the Germans the right directions when they ask you the way: these are not your walking companions. And above all, 'have no illusions: these men are not tourists'. His pamphlet was printed and reprinted, circulated from hand to hand, read and reread, and Texcier was soon a hero to the growing band of resisters. For Betty and Cécile, his jaunty defiance was infectious.

Along with being a writer, Guéhenno was also a student at the École Normale Supérieure. And it was here, as well as in the various faculties of the Sorbonne, that students, returning in the early autumn of 1940 to their classes, began to question their professors and each other about the extent to which they were prepared to accept the Nazi occupiers. They were angry that their Jewish teachers had been declared 'intellectually feeble' and 'undesirable' in the first anti-Semitic edict. When German officers began to drop in on their classes, they walked out. Some took to wearing a Croix de Lorraine, others to carrying a *gaule* – another word for a fishing rod.

Towards the end of October, Morais, the founder and president of a student group called Corpo des Lettres, began to talk to his friends about starting a poster campaign. Number 5 Place Saint-Michel was home to a number of student organisations and here, after office hours, Morais and his friends turned out anti-Vichy and anti-German flyers, distributed next day to *lycées* and faculties throughout Paris by students. In a rising mood of hostility and mockery, they went around repeating their favourite jokes. 'Collaborate with the Germans?' went one. 'Think of Voltaire . . . A true Aryan must be blond like Hitler, slender like Göring, tall like Goebbels, young like Pétain, and honest like Laval.' Another started with the question: 'Do you know what happened? At 9.20, a Jew killed a German soldier, opened his breast and ate his heart! Impossible! For three reasons. Germans have no hearts. Jews don't eat pork. And at 9.20 everyone is listening to the BBC.' When, in ones and twos, the student leaders were arrested, it only made their companions more resolute.

Then, on 30 October, a distinguished scientist in his late sixties called Paul Langevin was arrested in his office in the Faculty of

Physics and Industrial Chemistry. In the 1930s Langevin had been the founder of an anti-Fascist movement and he was much admired by his students. Professors and students alike decided to see in his arrest a Nazi attack on French intellectual life. Posters immediately appeared on the walls with the words 'Free Langevin'. And, since the professor held his classes on a Friday, a mass demonstration was called on Friday 8 November in front of the Collège de France where Langevin had his laboratory.

Despite the presence of German soldiers and French police, it passed off quietly. But the students now felt themselves to be at war. Meanwhile, in a message relayed over the BBC, the French in London had suggested that wreaths be laid at the Arc de Triomphe on the 11th, to mark Armistice Day. The Germans issued an order forbidding all such gatherings. The students decided to defy this. By 3 p.m. on the 11th, crowds of young people were collecting at the bottom of the Champs-Elysées and starting to walk towards the Étoile in small groups, singing the Marseillaise. One group of friends had produced a huge visiting card, over a metre long, with the words *Le Général de Gaulle*.

By mid-afternoon almost 10,000 people had gathered. The weather was fine and the mood was almost festive. But not for long. The Germans opened fire. A number of students were badly wounded, but none died since the soldiers had been ordered to shoot only at their legs. A hundred and fifty were arrested immediately; many more were picked up in the days that followed and sent, for brief periods, to prison. The university was closed. Paul Langevin remained in detention for thirty-seven days, during which time he went on with his research with the aid of some spent matches he found on the floor of his cell, before being sent to Troyes, under house arrest.

Professor Langevin had a 21-year-old daughter, a solemn, dark-haired young woman called Hélène. After her husband Jacques Solomon, a physicist working on quantum mechanics and cosmic rays, was demobilised from the medical services and returned home, Hélène suggested that they take a holiday cycling in the forests near Paris. As they cycled along, they discussed what they might do to oppose the German occupiers. Jacques said: 'We mustn't fool ourselves. Whatever we do will mean throwing ourselves in the lions' den.'

On the tracks in the forest they encountered two friends, a Hungarian Marxist philosopher called Georges Politzer and Maï, his wife. Maï, who was 25, was the only daughter of a celebrated cook, who had been chef to the Spanish court. Educated in a convent in Biarritz, she had studied to become a midwife and had met Politzer on a train in the Basque country. Through him, she discovered Marxism. The Politzers had a seven-year-old son, Michel. Maï was blond and strikingly pretty. Cycling along together, the two young couples talked about starting a paper, *L'Université Libre*, aimed at pulling together the entire sweep of intellectual resistance, regardless of political beliefs. It was, they agreed, to be a 'national front of all French writers'.

Maï Politzer, 'Femme Vincennes'

Hélène happened to be at lunch with her mother when the two German soldiers had come looking for her father. She quickly spread the word of his arrest. The Politzers and Solomons decided to rush the first issue of *L'Université Libre* out, 1,000 copies of four roneoed pages, in time for the demonstration on the 11th. By now they had joined forces with Daniel Decourdemanche, known as Jacques Decour, a scholar and teacher of German, a tall, thin, sporty young man who had spent the years before the war writing for various left-wing publications. The message of *L'Université Libre* was clear: words are themselves actions, and actions motivate; we have to say no to the occupier. The relationship between its founders was somewhat complicated by the fact that Decour and Maï were lovers.

Soon sought by the Gestapo, Jacques Solomon went into hiding in the house of a professor at the Lycée Fénelon, where he continued to work on the new paper. 'The French,' he repeated, 'must freely be able to read and think French in France.' In the evenings, Hélène took over the distribution of *L'Université Libre*, using the Café Wepler in the Place Clichy as a meeting place, or dropping off bags containing copies in the lockers of stations, later to be collected by others to distribute. Maï, who had good contacts inside the PCF, liaised with party members, while another friend, Viva, the daughter of Pietro Nenni, head of the Italian Socialist Party, offered to help print some of the issues on the presses that she and her husband ran. Viva, who was 25, had come to Paris with her father when he was forced by the attentions of Mussolini's secret police to seek refuge abroad, and she had finished her studies in France. She was also a striking looking young woman, with a mass of dark curly hair. Decour, who was teaching at the Lycée Rollin, cycled around Paris exclaiming: 'In the country of Descartes, reason will triumph.' It was still possible, in the winter of 1940, to be light-hearted about opposing the occupiers; the young resisters felt purposeful and elated.

In the weeks to come, *L'Université Libre* would comment on every arrest, every turn and step in the war, every Nazi edict and prohibition. In its wake soon came plans for other papers and magazines, designed to keep de Gaulle's flame of resistance alive by extolling all that was best and most important about French culture.

One by one, other young intellectuals were drawn into the fold. One of these was Charlotte Delbo, the 27-year-old daughter of a metalworker from the Seine-et-Oise who had risen to run his own shipyard. Charlotte was a tall, clever young woman with a long thin face and remarkable green-grey eyes. She was quick and funny and could be sharp. Both her parents – even her working-class Catholic Italian mother who had emigrated to France with her family before the First World War – were atheists, and it was from them that Charlotte, the eldest of four children, had picked up her strong anti-Fascist beliefs. There had been no money to send her to university, so Charlotte left school after taking her baccalaureate and trained as a secretary.

Charlotte Delbo, assistant to Louis Jouvet and a member of the
Jeunesse Communiste

In 1932, just as the PCF was entering its new phase of expansion
and recruitment, she joined its youth wing, Jeunesse Communiste.
Here, she was able to study at night under the Marxist philosopher
Henry Lefebvre. Maï and Georges Politzer were friends of Lefebvre.
The following year, working as a secretary by day, Charlotte began
to contribute articles to a paper put out by the young communists,
Jeunes Filles de France. Fascinated by the theatre, she was sent one
day to interview the director and actor Louis Jouvet, who had
recently taken over the Athenée theatre. Jouvet was captivated by
the intelligence of her questions and the speed with which she took
down his words in her neat, rapid shorthand.

Two days later, he offered her a job as one of his two assistants, taking notes for the course he gave in theatre at the university.
Charlotte, meanwhile, met and married Georges Dudach, the son
of a metalworker in an aeronautics firm. At the age of 12, Georges
had started as an apprentice in the business but when it became
clear that he was intelligent and studious he had left to work for
a union, and began to study law at night. In spite of his father's
opposition, Georges had joined the PCF in 1933 and when he
and Charlotte married he was working for one of the party's
other papers, L'Avant-Garde.

In the summer of 1939, Charlotte and Jouvet went walking
together in the countryside. When she got home, with a huge
bunch of mimosa she had picked, Charlotte sat down and recorded
in her diary what she remembered of their conversation, not

knowing what she might later need it for. Jouvet's attention to detail, and the way he analysed every aspect of a production appealed to her. She also had an excellent memory.

Because Charlotte spoke some German, along with English, Spanish and Italian, and because he could not bear to meet them himself, Jouvet asked her to handle most of the dealings between the Athenée theatre and the Germans. One day she was called to the rue de Saussaies and asked to report to the occupiers on individual members of the company, to say whether they were 'pure' or not. She felt outrage and contempt that she should be asked to spy. As the weeks passed, and the Germans moved steadily towards total control of the theatre in Paris, she observed with horror the growing exclusion of Jews from jobs and occupations. Charlotte herself was not Jewish, but her cast of mind was defiant, independent and humane. She had no time for the bullying and bureaucracy of the Nazis.

* * *

The winter of 1940 was exceptionally cold, the longest and coldest since meteorological records began. In Toulouse, temperatures dropped to minus 13 degrees. A metre of snow fell on Grenoble. In Paris, where it froze for sixty-six consecutive days, cold, hungry, angry women, unable to afford exorbitant black market ration cards, queued for hours for supplies that dwindled day by day. Though the integration of France into the Nazi war economy had dramatically cut unemployment, the French were beginning to understand that the shortages were the direct result of the enormous booty of clothing, food and raw materials leaving every day for the Reich. The Parisians were now obsessed with food and warmth, lining their clothes with newspapers, putting mustard in their socks and making muffs out of rabbit and cat skins. The extreme cold enabled the dissident young to dress in outrageous clothes – boys in vast enveloping overcoats, their hair slicked back with vegetable oil, girls in fur coats over very short skirts. They called themselves *zazous* and became a colourful sight on the streets of Paris; they reminded people of the exotic *merveilleuses* during the Directoire in 1795.

No longer the capital of France, without government or

embassies – apart from a US representative – French Paris had turned into a silent, still, anxious city, patrolled by enemy troops in uniform. The free press had gone underground, unions had been abolished and all gatherings of over five people were forbidden. German Paris, by contrast, was flourishing, its restaurants and cabarets full, its dress collections admired, its art shows well attended. The couturière Madeleine de Rauch had brought out a witty collection of winter clothes based on the theme of the métro. Solférino was a tailored red coat, Austerlitz a yellow jacket.

Paris had become a city of collaborators, both open and hidden, anti-Semites, anti-Freemasons, repentant communists and right-wing Catholics, who had hated Blum's Front Populaire and felt more than sneaking admiration for the German cult of youthful valour, orderliness and heroism. For the most part they were men, locked into an increasingly lucrative but dangerous relationship with the occupiers and effectively prisoners of their outwardly polite but inwardly ruthless German friends; but there were women among them too. Gabriel Péri, who worked on *L'Humanité*, called them *nazilous* and spoke of them as servants to the Germans. To the surprise of the occupiers, informers were coming forward in their hundreds, to denounce Jews, gypsies, black marketeers, and neighbours keeping pigs in their gardens. It would later be said that over half of the three million denunciations received during the years of occupation had been motivated because of the rewards offered, 40 per cent by politics and 10 per cent as acts of revenge.

A war of posters had been declared. For every message put up on the walls of Paris by resisters was to be seen a German counterpart, promising generous rewards to those who reported 'paid agents of foreign powers' and 'hidden Jews'. On Christmas Eve 1940, Parisians woke to a message, in bold red and black letters in both French and German, telling of the execution of a 28-year-old engineer called Bonsergent, shot for jostling a German officer in the street. The posters were soon torn down, and the places where they had hung were marked by little bunches of flowers. Daily, it was becoming harder to feel high spirited about defying the Germans.

In this battle of words, the French right, supported and nurtured by Abetz, was coming into its own. Jean Paulhan, the former editor of the prestigious *Nouvelle Revue Française*, at the centre of the French literary world for over three decades, had departed (and gone to help the Underground press). His job had been given to the Germanophile Nietzschean Drieu la Rochelle, who vowed to put an end to its 'Jewish and bellicose' tone. A pro-Vichy former philosopher and politician called Marcel Déat was running *L'Œuvre*, and the pro-Fascist Robert Brasillach was editing *Je Suis Partout*: both explored themes of decadence caused by Jews and Freemasons, and extolled the virility and adventurousness of the Nazis. Emerging from years of controversy, Jacques Doriot's virulently anti-communist Parti Populaire Français, and Colonel François de la Rocque's Croix de Feu were becoming popular with those young royalists and Catholics who liked these parties' Hitlerian style.

For all this, the resisters were holding their own. The months of relative tranquillity had allowed the PCF to regroup and the Underground magazines to flourish. Georges Politzer, who declared that he would henceforth regard writers in occupied France as belonging either to 'legal literature' or to the 'literature of treason', was hard at work on a reply to a particularly hateful speech given in Paris by Alfred Rosenberg, author of some of the main Nazi ideological creeds, on the subject of race and blood. *L'Université Libre*, in the hands of the Politzers, Hélène and Jacques Solomon and Charlotte and her husband, was doing well.

The Musée de l'Homme had brought out the first number of its new paper, *Résistance*, in which its energetic young editor, the polar ethnographer Boris Vildé, wrote: 'To resist, is already to preserve one's heart and one's brain. But above all, it must be to act, to do something concrete, to perform reasoned and useful actions.' There was only one goal, Vildé declared, a goal to be shared by all resisters, regardless of their political beliefs, and that was to bring about the 'rebirth of a pure and free France'. Here and there, as the freezing winter began to ease, the first acts of armed resistance, of the sabotage of trains and the blowing up of German depots, were being planned. What the occupiers most feared, the transformation of isolated and spontaneous gestures of rebellion into concerted acts of hostility, was just about to start. And in these, acting together or on their own, women of all ages and from all over France, such as Betty and Cécile, Charlotte, Hélène and Maï, generous-spirited and tough-minded, were about to play a crucial role.

Away from Paris, France itself was slowly turning into a police state, on the German model, a country of small internment camps, in Sarthe, Maine-et-Loire, Charente, Pyrénées-Atlantiques, Loiret and Doubs, dirty, unheated, unhealthy places in which, in the extreme cold of December, January and February, people were dying. Only slowly were the French learning the true nature of occupation. Avenue Foch, one of the most beautiful streets in Paris, had become the Gestapo's torture centre. The tensions between Germans and French, noted the communist critic and novelist Jean Richard Bloch, had become as taut as a violin string.

CHAPTER THREE

Daughters of the Enlightenment

One of the reasons given by Pétain for the defeat of France in 1940 was the severe lack of French children. Young women, he complained, had had their heads turned by seeing too many American films, and by being told by the Front Populaire that there was no reason why they could not study to become lawyers and doctors like their brothers. Under a law of 1938, French girls had been permitted to enrol in universities, open their own bank accounts, sign and receive cheques and have their own passports.*

Pétain intended to reverse this heady spirit of freedom, and, without an Assembly to hinder him, set about putting through a series of edicts and statutes aimed at strengthening what he saw as the degenerate moral fabric of France. Contraception had been declared illegal in the wake of the huge losses in the First World War, and would remain so, but now the penalties against abortion, and particularly abortionists, were strengthened to include the guillotine. Women who continued to breastfeed their babies beyond the age of one were given priority cards for queues (providing the baby was legitimate and French). Mothers of five children were presented a bronze medal, then a silver with the eighth and a gold with the tenth. Dozens of Vichy babies acquired Pétain as their godfather. Families were declared to be 'patriotic'; to remain single was to be decadent.

During the 1930s, the Front Populaire had poured money into popular culture and sport, into scouting, paid holidays and

---

* Though not to vote, a right the conservative French continued to find too threatening.

auberges de la jeunesse. While French intellectuals pondered modernism, socialism and peace, the young were encouraged to travel, discover the parts of France they had never visited, take cycling holidays. Sport, the Vichy government also now decided, would be particularly beneficial in forming 'young girls of robust beauty and well hardened character'. Since laxity of morals and seductive dress were indissolubly linked, designers were urged to tailor the new divided skirts – with the disappearance of the car, bicycles had become ubiquitous – in such a way that the division remained almost invisible. In Pétain's new France, girls were to be serious young women; not coquettes, but candid, fresh faced and without artifice.

As it happened, the move towards sport, the outdoors and independence had appealed greatly to young French women in the 1930s. For the first time, their parents allowed them to spend nights away from home with friends. They had become accustomed to cycling in groups through the French countryside, staying in the hundreds of newly opened hostels, sitting by the fireside late into the night discussing the issues of the day – activities that would for some now play into their roles in the resistance. For Cécile, her trips into the countryside with her baby daughter, sometimes the only young woman among a dozen or so boys, were times of talk and politics. It was pleasing to feel herself so much part of a group, sharing the same notions about equality and fairness.

In 1936, when the PCF was expanding and coming to power within the Front Populaire, a young dentist called Danielle Casanova was asked whether she would like to run a youth wing for girls, as a sister organisation to the Jeunesse Communiste, to be called L'Union des Jeunes Filles de France (JFdeF). Danielle, who was born in Corsica, was then 27, a forceful, high-spirited, tenacious young woman with a dark complexion, heavy eyebrows, a snub nose and very shiny black eyes, living with her husband Laurent just off the Boulevard Saint-Germain, where she had her practice. She was tall and somewhat overweight, and she liked to tease.

Arriving from Ajaccio to do her dental studies in Paris, Danielle became active in the various student associations. The Casanovas had no children and were ardent communists. Danielle had been to Moscow and returned more persuaded than ever of what communism might do for the impoverished French workers. In the evenings and at weekends, she wrote passionate articles calling on young women to rise up and engage in the great political debates of the day. She had no time for anyone who did not believe in absolute equality between men and women. She was, as Cécile would later say, as straight and honest as it was possible for a person to be.

The Jeunes Filles de France perfectly mirrored the healthy outdoor mood of the Front Populaire. When she found time, Danielle arranged to meet her friend Maï Politzer in a cafe and the two young women talked about how appalled they were by the squalor and poverty in which so many French working-class families lived. Sometimes they were joined by Marie-Claude, a handsome, strong-willed girl who had been married to Paul Vaillant-Couturier, editor of *L'Humanité*. Marie-Claude's father was a well-known newspaper editor and publisher, and her mother wrote on fashion and cooking. Marie-Claude was a reporter and photojournalist herself, and in the 1930s *Vu* magazine had published a series of her photographs on Dachau, the first concentration camp opened by Hitler, not far from Munich. Paul, who was much older, had left his wife for her. He had died in 1937.

Marie-Claude Vaillant-Couturier, 'Femme Tricanet'

In the offices of the JFdeF, near the Paris Opéra, where Danielle produced a newsletter calling on women to donate clothes and milk for Spanish war children, a team of similarly minded young women often gathered to talk. A few took evening classes in Russian. Though serious, they were not averse to having fun, and Danielle readily made people laugh. The fund-raising dances they gave proved very popular. By the outbreak of war, the JFdeF had over 20,000 members.

A gathering of the Jeunes Filles de France, shortly before the war

During the nine months of the phoney war, their torches dimmed by the blue paper used by French schoolchildren to cover their books, Danielle and her colleagues walked the streets writing messages about free speech and workers' rights on the walls. The blackout was very helpful for this kind of clandestine work. When issues of the magazine she edited for the JFdeF were ready, she gave them to students and schoolchildren to distribute. Danielle was a natural organiser.

The arrival of the Germans only served to spur her on to greater efforts. Everything in her revolted at the thought of occupation. Within hours she had prudently cleared her offices of all incriminating papers. During the long hot summer of 1940, Danielle and the other members of the JFdeF went bicycling in the forests around Paris, and after playing games of volleyball sat in the grass talking about what they could do to make the lives of the Germans harder. Some of the young men who went with them grew moustaches to make themselves look older; the girls took to wearing dark glasses. They were outraged when a friend reported that he had seen a poster in the local swimming pool with the words: 'No Negroes, Jews or dogs'.

In the autumn, when the schools and universities reopened, the members of the JFdeF volunteered to distribute the Underground copies of *L'Humanité*. There were angry scenes when parents discovered stashes of the paper hidden away in their daughters' bedrooms. Maroussia Naitchenko, who as a 14-year-old helped out in the offices by the Opéra, would later write that it sometimes seemed as if all these young people were 'playing at games of cops and robbers'.

Pétain's view of women as ideologically and politically inferior beings made Danielle's recruits extremely angry. Soon hundreds of new members were willingly tramping the streets of Paris with flyers in their rucksacks and, for a while at least, they were seldom stopped, neither the Gestapo nor the French police quite believing that such cheerful, healthy girls could have anything to do with the Resistance. As Danielle said, flirting a little with the Germans could yield excellent results. She was exceptionally good at inspiring others, making people feel that there was really no choice but to help.

It was when rationing started to bite into the lives of families that older women began to join her ranks in a new organisation, L'Union des Femmes Françaises. Watching the queues outside food shops grow ever longer, Danielle saw just how the women's discontent could effectively be harnessed to the cause. Astutely playing on their sympathies for hungry children, she persuaded some of them to contribute articles to her own clandestine paper – *La Voix des Femmes* – as well as to other women's magazines not banned by the Germans.

Women who had never before engaged in any activity outside their own homes were soon turning out angry articles about food shortages and the German expropriations. They wrote them in short, clear, declamatory sentences. While Vichy preached devotion, modesty and abnegation, Danielle called for activism and rebellion. The Germans became *les boches* and *les brutes nazies*. There were references to Joan of Arc, La Pasionaria and the women who stormed the Bastille in 1789. The first street demonstrations, organised by Danielle's local committees – women occupying food shops where the best produce was reserved for the Germans – passed off peacefully; but the women were getting angrier and more militant.

A student protest in Paris in the 1930s. Danielle Casanova is fourth from the left

From the first, the JFdeF had been naturally drawn to the world of clandestine printing. As secretaries and office workers, many of its members already knew all about stencils and roneo machines. The offices where some of them were employed proved the perfect place from which to steal dwindling stocks of paper and ink. Some of Danielle's colleagues were journalists and were happy to turn their hands to exhortatory flyers and posters. Under the library of the Sorbonne, the warren of cellars and corridors acted as storerooms for the university. Here, among the boxes and books, young university teachers printed news-sheets, laying the wet pages on the shelves to dry, later to be carried away by students in shopping baskets and knapsacks. Concierges in office buildings and apartment blocks, for whom the come and go of postmen was a daily occurrence, became letter drops. Queues turned out to be the perfect places for passing on orders and messages. Prams were ideal for hiding papers; and, later, weapons.

Danielle, meanwhile, had made efforts to lose some weight and to dress more fashionably, telling friends laughingly that the Germans were far less prone to stop women who looked pretty and well turned out. Her husband Laurent was a prisoner of war in Germany, and to cover her tracks she had taken to moving constantly round the city, seldom sleeping in the same place twice. Maï Politzer and Marie-Claude Vaillant-Couturier were naturally elegant and when the three met in the fashionable cafes of the Boulevard Saint-Germain to discuss strategy and pass on information, they looked like any group of high-spirited women friends, enjoying each other's company. Over tea in the Galeries Lafayette, Danielle recruited young women to run the JFdeF in other parts of the capital. By now she was working closely with both Betty, liaising through her with the PCF, and Cécile, who was turning out to be an extremely efficient courier. By the end of 1940, twenty-five of the thirty women on the national committee of the JFdeF were active members of the Resistance.

Not surprisingly, the *ceinture rouge*, the red belt of communist communes which surrounded Paris, home to many of the industrial workers, proved an excellent recruiting ground for new members. It was in Ivry, in the suburbs to the north of Paris, that Danielle found Madeleine Doiret, known to her friends as Mado, the daughter of a former groom who now ran a small lime and cement factory. Mado, who was the eldest of five children, interrupted her studies for the baccalaureate to learn shorthand and typing. With the declaration of war, however, so many male teachers had been mobilised that she became a temporary teacher in Yonne. Mado, like Cécile and Betty, had been drawn into politics by the Spanish Civil War. Having fled Paris in May 1940 during the great exodus to the south, she returned to Ivry and offered her services to the Jeunesse Communiste.

Delighted with her secretarial skills, they asked her to type texts on to stencils, which were then printed by her father at night in the hidden cellar of their house on an electric mimeograph. Both she and her father were immensely proud of their machine, which was one of the first of its kind in Paris. In the evenings, with the help of her brother Roger, who carried the packets in a rucksack, Mado dropped off the tracts at various distribution points in Ivry, ready to be picked up by other young resisters.

Early in 1941, Danielle asked Mado to go underground and work for her full time. So she moved out of her parents' house in Ivry and into a small flat in the 15th, where she lived under a false name, and composed articles calling on workers to engage in acts of resistance against Vichy and the occupiers, cast in the form of posthumous letters written by men executed by the Gestapo. Mado was just 20. Her work with the Resistance meant breaking off all contact with her family and her friends. At night, alone, having spoken to no one she knew all day, she sometimes lay on her bed and cried from loneliness.

Mado was not, of course, alone in believing that opposing Vichy and the Germans was worth making sacrifices for, even though at this stage of the war it was sometimes hard to see precisely what was being achieved. Nor was she alone in making these sacrifices. As the winter of 1940 wore on, several of the women working full time for the Resistance decided to send their children to live with grandparents or foster families, to keep them safe, and to feel freer themselves. Maï and Georges Politzer, constantly fretting about the dangers of their clandestine life, had already sent their son Michel to live with his grandparents away from Paris.

Not far from Mado in Ivry lived a good friend of hers, Georgette Rostaing, who had worked for the transport police before the war, and who now began to help her 18-year-old brother Pierre recruit members for the Jeunesse Communiste and the JFdeF. Georgette, too, had been drawn into the web by the civil war in Spain and she too knew Danielle and Marie-Claude, and helped out at the JFdeF. She was a single mother, not an easy position for a young woman in Pétain's France.

One day Pierre, who was on the wanted list of young

communists, fell into the hands of the police. Georgette did not hesitate. She left her little girl, Pierrette, who had just turned nine, with her mother and took over her brother's job as liaison officer and distributor of clandestine material; and, later, of explosives and detonators. She was a sunny, good-hearted young woman, like Danielle rather overweight, with a mass of dark hair and a fringe, and she could be seen tottering around Ivry on very high heels.

Georgette Rostaing, who loved to sing

Pierrette, Georgette's daughter

Even as a small child, Pierrette was taken to meetings of the JFdeF, to listen to Danielle and her friends make plans about acts of Resistance against the Germans and she was never sent out of the room when members of the Resistance came to the house. One of them taught her to tell the time. As Georgette would say, 'we are in this all together, as a family'. Instinctively, Pierrette knew that what she saw and heard were not things that should be repeated. From his prison camp, her uncle Pierre sent her letters covered with little drawings of birds; when he came home, he told her, he planned to become an artist in glass. Georgette loved to sing. One day she took Pierrette to hear Edith Piaf, whose songs she knew by heart and sang at the top of her cheerful voice. Living in a world of secrets and high spirits was exhilarating for the little girl.

Another household which decided to put a small child into care in order to work for the Resistance was that of the Serre sisters. Lucienne, known as Lulu, was the eldest, born in 1917; then came Jeanne – known as Carmen – in 1919, followed by Louis and Christiane. Their mother, a formidable Algerian woman who had left their Catalan father and moved from the Marseilles docks to Paris, taking all four children with her, kept the family by working as a cleaner in a concert hall. She was illiterate, having left school at the age of seven to work in the fields, but she spoke five languages fluently and she was a charming and devoted mother. She too loved music and singing, and in the evenings the little flat in rue de la Huchette rang with arias from Rossini and with flamenco dances. Madame Serre made couscous and *îles flottantes*, spun of egg whites and sugar, for them all.

Lulu found a job as a secretary; Carmen and Louis worked in a metal factory. Christiane, the youngest at 11, was still at school, and their mother was adamant that she do well at her studies, rewarding her efforts with presents of books of history and politics, which she could not read for herself but longed to understand. After school, the little girl would be told to read the books aloud to her mother, who would then explain their meaning to her.

On reaching Paris, Madame Serre had taken in as lodgers former fighters in the International Brigades in Spain and it was thought perfectly right and natural for Lulu and Carmen to join the JFdeF and Louis the Jeunesse Communiste. Indeed, to do anything else would have been unthinkable. As Mme Serre saw it, resistance was 'notre affaire', our business, and it didn't much matter who you joined as long as you did something.

Danielle Casanova

Lulu, who was married to a young communist, Georges Thévenin, who was now a prisoner of war, had a new baby called Paul, but since food and milk were so scarce and the baby was not thriving, she sent him to live with a foster family in the countryside. It gave her more time, in the evenings, to work for Danielle. Carmen had become a liaison officer with Viva Nenni's printing firm, and when the police seemed to be closing in, she could be seen hastening through the streets of Paris with a printing press, ink and paper loaded on to a wheelbarrow, searching for a better hiding place. When Mme Serre was arrested, the police having discovered boxes of clandestine papers in the flat, and sent by the Gestapo to the prison of the Cherche-Midi, Lulu and Carmen simply added her work for the Resistance to their own.

The Gestapo eventually decided that there was too little evidence against Mme Serre and let her go. After her release, she decided to take the two younger children down to Marseilles, paying a *passeur*, a guide, a kilo of dried bananas and 30 francs to take them across the demarcation line. In Marseilles, by now almost totally blind with glaucoma, she took a job with a grocer and used his horse and cart to distribute clandestine copies of *L'Humanité* to the dockers. For the Serres, resistance was more a state of mind than an activity. Surrounded by political convictions and a sense of duty, the four children, like Pierrette Rostaing, admired and loved their indomitable mother.

Throughout the cold winter of 1940 and early spring of 1941, more and more women of all ages were drawn into the Resistance, swelling ranks decimated by the early arrests of men, taking on tasks for which they found themselves admirably suited. There was as yet no very clear goal to their activities, beyond the constant harassment of the Germans, whose forces they hoped to keep in a state of perpetual uneasy alert. They also wanted to send a message to Vichy that collaboration was an odious affair, unacceptable to decent people, and that it would, when sanity and victory returned to France, be severely punished.

These schoolgirls, mothers, grandmothers, housewives and professional women were joining the Resistance because of their fathers and brothers who were already part of it; or because they had heard their grandfathers talking about the Dreyfus affair and Verdun; or because they had watched the Spanish refugee children struggle over the Pyrenees; or because, like Cécile, they did not want their children to grow up in a world run by Nazis; or, quite simply, because they were *frondeuses* – rebels against authority and dogmatism, true daughters of the French Enlightenment. As the Serre women saw it, they really had no choice.

What none of them knew, as they hurried around the streets of their villages and towns, carrying messages and tracts, feeling oddly safe in a country in which women were still not perceived to be active in the Resistance, was how lethal it was about to become.

*   *   *

The late spring of 1941 was marked throughout the German occupied zone of France by sporadic acts of sabotage, a continuing war of posters, and the arrests and internment of ever more 'enemies of the Reich'. A number of clandestine printing presses were discovered, and their operators tried and sent to prison. In May, hundreds of French policemen were dispatched into the traditionally Jewish quarters of Paris to 'invite' the residents to present themselves for an 'examination of their status'. Disoriented, stupefied to find that French laws would not protect them, 3,710 foreign-born Jews were subsequently interned. Posters offering rewards of 1,000 francs for information leading to the arrest of a militant communist went up on the walls of the capital. By June, 2,325 communists were in prisons or internment camps all over France. On the fête de Jeanne d'Arc, thousands of students gathered to sing patriotic songs and shout: 'Joan of Arc, deliver us from the barbarians!'

Since it had quickly become clear that the communists were not alone in backing the Resistance, but that all over France acts of rebellion were also being carried out by Catholics, Jews and Gaullists, it was decided, early in May, to try to co-ordinate their forces. On the 15th, a joint communiqué was issued to the entire Resistance, both in the occupied and in the free zones. All French men and women, regardless of their political affiliations, who 'thought French and wished to act French', were invited to unite under a National Front for the Independence of France. The idea was to set up little National Fronts all over the country, in factories, in mining areas, in villages. 'To live under defeat,' read one pamphlet, quoting Napoleon, 'is to die every day.' Even so, Otto von Stülpnagel and the occupying German forces continued to maintain that the state of France caused little alarm. The Communists, at this stage still the strongest element in the Resistance, continued to be regarded as pariahs by much of the public on account of the Nazi–Soviet pact.

Then, early on the morning of 22 June 1941, everything changed.

As dawn broke, two million German soldiers, 3,200 planes and 10,000 tanks invaded the Soviet Union along a 300-kilometre front. Overnight, among the worldwide opponents of Hitler, the Communists ceased to be perceived as in league with the enemy. Stalin redefined the war, from being one of imperialism to being a 'great anti-Fascist and patriotic war of liberation'. The Soviets – and the Communists – were now the allies. The message that went out to the communist parties across occupied Europe was clear: the German invaders were to be resisted, partisan groups were to be set up behind enemy lines, and acts of sabotage, the destruction of railway lines and telephone wires were to be carried out. The German occupiers, henceforth, were to be 'terrorised'. Resistance was to be racheted up to another, far more perilous, level.

The troubled PCF in France greeted the news of the invasion with immense relief. The months of ambiguity and doubt were over. Maï Politzer, her husband Georges and lover Decour, Hélène and Jacques Solomon, Danielle, Cécile and Betty were in from the cold. The clandestine *L'Humanité* responded with a call for armed combat.

*   *   *

For many months, talks had been going on about the need for fighters for an *Organisation Spéciale*, a group of armed men to protect militants and to punish traitors and informers, and also to collect weapons and plan acts of sabotage. These men were to be, said the resisters, the shock troops of the movement. But there had been considerable misgivings about progressing to armed attacks and the assassination of individual German soldiers, not least because so much of the French population, committed to *attentisme*, was anxious not to promote further repression and reprisals by the Germans. What was more, the guns that were available were antique and highly unreliable.

Now, in the wake of the invasion of the Soviet Union, a meeting was called in the Closerie des Montparnasse on the Boulevard Saint-Germain. To it came Danielle Casanova and a young man called Albert Ouzoulias, who had recently escaped from a prisoner of war camp in Austria. By the time they parted, Ouzoulias, who went by the Underground name of Zouzou, had agreed to set up what would be known as 'les Bataillons de la Jeunesse', an armed youth wing. To help him there was a 22-year-old veteran of the Spanish Civil War, Georges Pierre, who took the *nom de guerre* of Fabien or Fredo and was alone in having some combat experience. The two young men, who were inseparable friends, set out to find recruits; before long, they were a band of fifty-six. Not many were older than 20. They regarded Danielle, who was 31, as their big sister.

Among the first to come forward were 18-year-old Georges Tondelier, who had been running the Jeunesse Communiste in the 19th arrondissement, Isidore Grünenberger, who was Polish, and his school friend, a young cobbler called André Biver. Biver had a girlfriend, Simone Sampaix, an open-faced girl of 16 with a sweet smile and rosy cheeks. Her father, Lucien, was a former managing editor of *L'Humanité*, a distinguished looking man with thick grey hair cropped severely short. He was much admired within the Communist Party for writing a series of articles before the war linking the anti-Semitic Cagoule movement to French industrialists and the German secret services, for which he had been tried but acquitted. The Sampaix were friends of the Politzers and of Danielle, who was the family dentist, and as a young girl, Simone had attended the 'vin d'honneur' held for Fabien's wedding. Yvonne, Lucien's wife, worked in a textile factory and the family lived in a little house in the 19th, in the heartlands of the communist working class.

By the summer of 1941, Lucien was in prison, having been picked up by the French police during a crackdown on the Underground press. 'To think our grandfathers took the Bastille,' he wrote to his wife. 'How many Bastilles are still to be taken!' Simone visited him in prison, to tell him that she had joined the Bataillons de la Jeunesse and was already transporting material for them under her school books. With her innocent, childish looks, she was an improbable suspect. Lucien told her how proud he was of her, but warned her to be careful. The police were getting more resourceful, and the number of informers was growing. Women and girls would not be safe for long. Yvonne, only now learning of her daughter's activities, and both admiring of her and extremely fearful, sent her two younger children, Pierre and Jacques, to stay with friends in the country. The new young recruits to the Bataillons, some no more than 16 or 17, were often penniless, hungry, without money for the métro, and with nowhere to sleep. Their shoes leaked. In the little house in the 19th that looked more like a cottage than a city home, Yvonne often cooked for them.

All gatherings of more than half a dozen people were prohibited by the Germans, but Ouzoulias and Fabien, under the pretence of participating in one of Vichy's approved camping holidays, arranged to take twenty of the new recruits to the Bois de Lardy, in Seine-et-Oise. They left from the Gare d'Austerlitz, carrying knapsacks and wearing shorts. The youngest was André Kirschen, who had recently turned 15. In the woods they set up tents, cooked over open fires and discussed tactics. The boys were taught how to fire revolvers, throw grenades and make bombs out of empty tins, packed with dynamite, nails and little bits of wire; the girls did the cooking and washed the plates in the river. As Maroussia Naitchenko had rightly observed, there was a strong element of daredevil and bravura among the young resisters.

Simone Sampaix, on a camping holiday before the war, with her brothers

Simone and the few other girls were told that, as women, their roles would lie in 'logistics'. At night, they debated what they felt about shooting someone in cold blood, and Simone, far from certain that she would have the courage ever to do so, was relieved that she was not going to receive a gun. Fabien recounted the story of a hero of the First World War, an elderly peasant who, with only a pitchfork, attacked a platoon of heavily armed German soldiers. Like the Serre sisters, Carmen and Lulu, Simone would later remember thinking that there was nothing very heroic in what she was doing. What seemed to her strange was that others were not doing the same. From their exile in their farmhouse in the countryside, her younger brothers were envious of her good fortune.

Simone's father's fears, however, had been well placed. Confrontations between resisters and Germans were becoming daily more explosive. Among the first young people to join the Bataillons had been a number of Jews drawn from the large populations of Russians, Poles and Armenians who had settled in France in the 1920s and 1930s and set up their own association, the Main-d'Œuvre Immigrée. Many spoke Yiddish at home. Early in August, three friends, all under 20 – Samuel Tyszelman, Charles Wolmark and Elie Walach – raided a quarry in the Seine-et-Oise and came away with 25 kilos of dynamite. On 13 August, Tyszelman and another friend, Henri Gautherot, led a demonstration protesting against German restrictions. Thousands of people gathered, shouting 'Vive la France!' and 'à bas l'Occupant!' German soldiers opened fire. Tyszelman was hit in the leg, and he and Gautherot were arrested.

Simone and her young friends were appalled by this sudden violent turn of affairs and even more upset when they learnt that Tyszelman and Gautherot had been condemned to death by a German military tribunal. On the 19th, posters went up, in the usual bold red and black lettering, announcing that the two young men had been executed that morning by firing squad. As if to underline Vichy's attitude towards France's foreign Jews, a simultaneous round-up in the 11th arrondissement took 4,232 into custody, to join the other 30,000 Jews already held in French internment camps.

Two days later, early on the morning of 21 August, André Biver asked Simone to accompany him to the *grands boulevards*. He did not explain why. They had only just reached the Barbès métro stop when they heard shouts and Fabien and several members of the Bataillons raced up the stairs from the métro and scattered into the crowds. As he ran past them, Fabien called out, 'Titi and Henri have been avenged.' The killing that Simone had so feared to be part of had begun.

The attack had been minutely planned. Fabien had chosen the Barbès métro station, on line 4, because its platform curved in such a way that the controller could not see the entire train, while the first-class carriage, in which the Germans invariably travelled, stopped immediately by the stairs leading up to the Boulevard Rochechouart. Reconnoitring, Fabien had observed that between eight and 8.30 each morning a number of German officers caught the number 4 line.

That morning, there were some thirty people waiting for the train. One of them was a newly arrived officer of the Kriegsmarine, Alfons Moser, on his way to a depot at Montrouge. As he stepped on to the train, Fabien fired two bullets into his back. Moser died instantly. Isidore Grünenberger, who had been acting as lookout in the street, thanked Simone for transporting the gun that had made the attack possible. The play-acting was over; it had all become terrifyingly real.

The German response was instant. Hitler, hearing of Moser's death, demanded the immediate execution of one hundred hostages. All Frenchmen under arrest, it was announced, whether in French or German hands, were henceforth to be considered hostages, to be shot in response to any attack on the Germans. But von Stülpnagel was not yet prepared to abandon his satisfactory collaboration with the Vichy government, and so he informed Pétain, through his liaison officer Major Boemelburg, that the Kriegsmarine were asking for only ten hostages. Pierre Pucheu, newly elected Minister of the Interior, meanwhile ordered that the streets of Paris be combed for the assassins. A curfew was set for nine o'clock in the evening; restaurants and theatres had to close by eight. Within three hours, eight thousand IDs had been checked, but not one of the members of the Bataillons had been found.

There were already plans afoot for a special French tribunal to try resisters, with a tacit understanding that death penalties would be handed down. On 27 August, the hastily convened new body sentenced three communists to die, the fourth, Simone's father Lucien, having his sentence commuted to hard labour in perpetuity, after delivering a particularly eloquent and impassioned speech. He was sent to Caen prison, his hands and feet in manacles.

It was Vichy that now proposed to carry out the executions by guillotine, in public; the German military, fearing repercussions from the French public, agreed to the guillotine but insisted that it be used in private. On 28 August, the three communists went to the scaffold. For good measure, over the next few days, the Germans shot five other communists – for participating in Samuel

Tyszelman's demonstration – and then three Gaullists. French judges were now sending to their deaths Frenchmen, completely innocent of the crimes for which they were being punished, simply because they were assumed to be close in ideals to those presumed – but not proved – to be guilty.

Simone, training with the other teenagers under the beeches and oaks in the Bois de Lardy, had been right to question the implications of moving into armed attacks on German soldiers. The attack in the Barbès métro, the first public assassination of one of the German officers, marked a turning point. Ouzoulias would later say that this single act was the most important contribution made by the Bataillons, that of moving the Resistance into a higher gear. But, as the resisters turned to killing, so too would the penalties become more lethal.

No longer would it be possible for any member of the Resistance – even the women and girls, who had until now felt relatively secure in the shadows – to feel safe. Betty, Danielle, Cécile and the others, who were beginning to meet and forge links, were now living in a state of constant wariness. From now on, in an endlessly repeated cycle of attacks, reprisals, more attacks, more executions, it would be all-out war between occupiers and a growing number of the occupied, who, revolted by German brutality, would become gradually more sympathetic to the Resistance. As Pétain remarked, 'From various parts of France, I begin to feel an unpleasant wind getting up'.

CHAPTER FOUR

The hunt for resisters

Until the summer of 1941, the German soldiers stationed in France had felt relatively safe. The country they had overrun with such ease seemed to them for the most part to tolerate their presence, even to enjoy profiting from the occupation, though many ordinary people were increasingly looking away when walking past in the streets. But now, in the wake of the attack at the Barbès métro station, soldiers were advised not to go out after dark alone and never to leave their vehicles unattended. Von Stülpnagel, while continuing to argue that repression of all resistance should be left chiefly in the hands of the remarkably co-operative French police, at the same time sent out a secret communiqué to the German military commanders of the different occupied regions of France.

The war against the communists was reaching a critical stage, he said, and the job of the Germans was to make certain that the French operated against them with the utmost severity. 'Judge quickly, harshly and surely,' he instructed the Wehrmacht military tribunals. On 13 September, an old friend of Charlotte Delbo and Georges Dudach, the architect André Woog, was guillotined in the courtyard of the prison of La Santé, along with two other 'militant communists'. He had been picked up for distributing anti-German tracts. There had, to date, been thirty-three executions of communists and 'enemies of the Reich'; the youngest was a boy of 19, the eldest a man in his seventies.

From Berlin, Hitler continued to urge more frequent and tougher reprisals, not only in France but throughout the whole of occupied Europe, especially against the Communists, who continued to be widely blamed for the rising number of armed attacks. Though Germany had eight and a half million men under arms, more soldiers were needed to control France, Holland, Belgium, Denmark and the Balkans; there was heavy fighting in the western desert and along the eastern front. Acts of resistance could not be allowed to distract German soldiers who might otherwise be engaged in active service. On 28 September, in clear violation of Article 19 of the Third Tokyo Convention of 1934, which had spelt out without ambiguity that hostages should never, under any circumstances, be either physically punished or put to death, a Code of Hostages was issued to the French people. It breached both clauses.

'Pools' of Frenchmen, whether detained by the Germans or by the French for supposed communist or anarchist actions – espionage, treason, sabotage, armed attacks, assistance to foreign enemies, illegal possession of weapons – were to be held in readiness as hostages against attacks on German soldiers. In numbers proportionate to the crime, these hostages would be executed. Fifty to a hundred Frenchmen would be shot for every German killed. Since very few of these men were tried before a court, there could be no knowing whether they were guilty or not. Military commanders in the various regions were instructed to keep up-to-date lists of the names of those available. Where there were not enough, more were to be sought among university teachers and students, as well as among Gaullists, now also recognised as threats to the security of the German occupiers. *Notables*, prominent people, briefly regarded as suitable hostages, were discarded in favour of 'anti-Germans', principally communists, who remained the people most loathed by Vichy, and 'intellectuals', those who had used their pens to diffuse communist ideas. Fathers of large families were 'generally' to be spared.

Some members of the early Resistance had been troubled by the ferocity with which the Germans responded to their attacks, fearing that, by resorting to arms and assassinations, they would alienate the French public. But Danielle, Cécile and Maï were among those who argued passionately in favour of a 'national war of independence and liberation', with all the armed violence that the words implied. On the walls of Paris appeared posters with the words: 'For every one patriot shot, 10 Germans will be killed'. To back away from the tactic of armed attack launched at the Barbès métro, argued Ouzoulias, would spell 'capitulation and dishonour' and only lead to further and more terrible repression. Simone Sampaix and the young boys and girls of the Bataillons de la Jeunesse remained at home, waiting for further instructions. Simone's repugnance at the idea of shooting in cold blood had not altogether gone away, but she had no intention of abandoning the fight now.

When, earlier in the year, the united Front National of the Resistance had been set up, it was clear that some kind of military wing would follow. Around the time of the Barbès shooting, the Main-d'Œuvre Immigrée, the Opérations Spéciales of the PCF and the Batallions de le Jeunesse merged as the Francs-Tireurs et Partisans (FTP) under a former editor of *L'Humanité* called Pierre Villon. It was given four goals: to hit railway lines carrying men and materiel to the eastern front; to punish traitors and collaborators; to sabotage factories working for the Germans; and to excecute soldiers of the occupying forces, all actions whose symbolic value would go far beyond the actual damage caused.

A silent, dour, pipe-smoking former boilermaker at the Renault car factories, Arthur Dallidet, who was ferocious about discipline and prudence, and fanatical in his hatred of renegades and traitors, was put in charge of security. A librarian called Michel Bernstein became the master forger of false documents. And France Bloch, a young chemist with two science degrees, who as a Jew had lost her job in the Musée d'Histoire Naturelle, was given the task of making explosives. France was the daughter of the distinguished critic and historian, Jean-Richard Bloch, now in exile in Moscow. She was married to a metalworker, Frédo Sérazin, and had an 18-month-old son.

Ever since the mid-1930s, when they had attended anti-fascist rallies together, France had been close friends with a chemical engineer, Marie-Elisa Nordmann, a round-faced, somewhat plump young woman with a gentle manner. As a promising young researcher, she had spent a year in Germany and returned shocked by the spectacle of Hitler's rallies. She married young, and had a son, whom she doted on. But the marriage did not last and Marie-Elisa and the baby moved in with her widowed mother. In the evenings, she and France attended meetings of the newly founded Vigilance Committee of Intellectual Anti-fascists, of which Marie-Elisa became treasurer in the 5th arrondissement of Paris. Hélène

When André was arrested and sent to an internment camp in the summer of 1940, Germaine took over the job of liaising with the Francs-Tireurs et Partisans in Paris. She also knew all about printing, as her father had specialised in engraving the rollers used to print the calico for which Rouen was famous. She found a helper in Claudine Guérin, who at sixteen and a half was not much older than her own daughters. Claudine's mother Lucie, a fellow teacher and a good friend, had been sentenced to eight years' hard labour in Rennes prison for distributing tracts, and Germaine felt protective towards the young girl. Claudine was much liked; she was a pretty, talkative girl, always cheerful and uncomplaining, and she made people laugh. Together, Germaine and Claudine, and André before he was arrested, cycled out into the countryside to find chickens and butter to bring back to their comrades in the city.

In the early autumn of 1941, however, Germaine herself was in detention, suspected of running the Resistance in the Seine-Inférieure in the absence of her husband, and her two daughters were in hiding. Claudine's mother and Germaine were among the relatively few women resisters already in prison, the myth of the unpolitical, home-loving woman still prevailing across much of France. Germaine was held in a prison in Rouen, and Claudine came with her bicycle every day and the two exchanged news through an open window. In October, Claudine was sent to a boarding *lycée* in Paris, and from here she took over Germaine's job as liaison officer, transmitting messages from the capital to Rouen. She was a bright student, having already taken and passed her first baccalaureate.

Not far away and waiting to be allocated a task was 23-year-old Madeleine Dissoubray. Early in 1941, Madeleine had joined the Resistance and gone underground. She took a false name, Mme Duteurtre and under this she rented a room, though she occasionally went by the name of Thérèse Pasquier. Madeleine's mother was dead and her elder brother and sister were already in the Resistance; their father, an agricultural engineer and a socialist, had brought his children up to be politically active. A veteran of the First World War, he would say that Léon Blum and the Front Populaire had given him the first paid holidays of his life. During the Spanish Civil War, the Dissoubrays took in refugees from Spain.

Madeleine was studying to be a sports instructor, though she had thoughts of switching to mathematics. Among her sports-minded friends, there was much talk of trying to cross to England to join the Free French. They told each other that they would keep faith with the true France, even if it meant death. Death, they said, had to be 'tamed'. Seeing the German posters going up on the walls of Rouen, with their menaces and threats, Madeleine knew exactly what she was risking. It only made her feel greater solidarity with her friends. As she would later say, they were terrified, talking of what they could do, 'not only for ourselves but for each other'. Public dances had been forbidden by the Germans, but not dancing lessons, and it was in these classes, the boys with hair slicked back with vegetable oil, the girls with fashionable black and blond streaks in their hair, that they met and discussed their plans. 'How could you not resist?' Madeleine would later say. 'You couldn't live under the Nazis. You just couldn't accept it.' By the autumn of 1941, Madeleine was an important member of the communist secretariat for Rouen.

The attack on Rouen, set for 19 October, was to involve the derailment of a train just outside the station of Malaunay. Local engine drivers and railwaymen working for the Resistance had agreed to unscrew the heavy bolts holding the rails together, but it was noisy work and Madeleine, acting as a lookout for the frequent German patrols, was given a revolver in case of discovery. In the event, a number of rail tracks were successfully loosened without the Germans noticing, and a train carrying materiel for the eastern front slid off the tracks. There were no casualties, but considerable damage. Next day, the local French police chief arrested 150 people he suspected of belonging to the PCF. Madeleine managed to avoid capture.

The second attack, on the 20th, was more ambitious. Two young resisters, Gilbert Brustlein and Guisco Spartaco, sent from Paris to Nantes, where there was a large garrison of troops, spotted two German officers crossing the cathedral square. They followed them and drew out their revolvers. Spartico's jammed; Brustlein's worked. Lieutenant-Colonel Hotz, 'squealing like a pig', fell to the ground. Once again, the two attackers got away. 'What are they waiting for,' asked Robert Brasilliach in the newspaper *Je Suis Partout*, 'before they start shooting communists?'

The third attack, the shooting of a member of the German military command in Bordeaux called Reimers, on the night of 21 October, had not yet taken place when the Germans reacted against the attack on Hotz. Von Stülpnagel sent one of his officers to the internment camp at Châteaubriant in Brittany, to demand a list of detainees. A poster went up, announcing that since an officer had been murdered 'by cowardly criminals in the pay of England and Moscow', fifty hostages would be shot immediately, and fifty more if those responsible for the attacks were not in custody by midnight on the 23rd. A reward of 15 million francs was offered for information leading to the capture of the culprits. After the attack on Bordeaux and the death of Reimers, a further hundred men were earmarked to be shot. It was later said that the Minister of the Interior, Pucheu, when shown the list of names, exchanged those of '40 good Frenchmen', *anciens combattants* of the First World War, for those of the 'most dangerous communists'.

In the early afternoon of the 22nd, German soldiers driving lorries arrived to collect twenty-seven men from the camp at Châteaubriant to take them to a sandy quarry two kilometres away. They included a Communist deputy called Charles Michels, a number of prominent trade union leaders, a doctor and some teachers. The youngest was a schoolboy, Guy Môquet, the son of a Communist politician. Each of the men was given a sheet of paper, an envelope and a pencil with which to write a farewell letter. 'I am going to die!' Guy wrote to his mother, begging her to be brave, as he hoped to be, brave as those going with him. As the lorries drove out through the camp gates, onlookers removed their hats. The men were singing the Marseillaise, and they kept on singing even as they were led before the firing squad, in three batches. Not one accepted a blindfold. 'The victors that day,' noted one of the Germans present, 'were not us but those who died.'

Châteaubriant would not be the only site of mass reprisals; indeed, in the days that followed, other communist schoolteachers and trade unionists followed these first men to firing squads elsewhere. But the name Châteaubriant would enter the consciousness not only of the French, but of the Allies, as a symbol of German brutality. On the Sunday after the executions, though expressly forbidden to do so, the inhabitants of the town laid wreaths in the sand quarry. The bodies had carefully been scattered between nine different cemeteries, to avoid shrines of martyrdom.

Both Roosevelt and Churchill issued statements condemning the killings and warned that when the war ended, punishment would follow. De Gaulle, however, was more circumspect. It was perfectly right and proper, he declared, for Frenchmen to kill Germans. But wars involved tactics. And it was he personally, together with the National Committee, who was in charge of strategy. As fighters, the FTP should follow orders, and his orders were not to kill Germans, because it made it too easy for the enemy to massacre people who were 'momentarily disarmed'. The time would come for armed action, but it was still too soon. Danielle, Cécile, Madeleine, Maï and the Bataillons de la Jeunesse paid little attention to his words, but from Berlin Hitler ordered that the names of Gaullists be removed from the lists of hostages in the camps.

For the Germans occupying France, the assassinations at Nantes and Bordeaux marked another step on the road to ever more brutal repression. They wanted immediate, decisive retribution, and they intended to get it. But for the moment at least, von Stülpnagel continued to argue that the French must do their own policing, albeit greatly aided by the Wehrmacht and the Gestapo. Pétain, who had briefly thought of offering to take the place of one of the hostages until dissuaded by Pucheu, announced that Vichy was more committed to collaboration than ever, even if he personally bewailed the 'river of blood' caused by the mass executions. 'With a broken voice, I appeal to you,' he told the French, over the radio, 'do not let more harm come to France . . . With the armistice, we agreed to lay down our weapons. We have no right to take them up again in order to shoot Germans in the back.' He made no comment about the ratio of one hundred French lives for every one German one. Hostages, he reassured his listeners, would be taken only from among those 'whose guilt has definitely been proved'. Seventeen-year-old Guy Môquet was conveniently forgotten.

It was, however, becoming harder than ever for French collaborators to do the Germans' bidding. In order to fulfil fresh undertakings to redouble surveillance, discover the culprits and run to ground all Communist leaders, new forces were needed. Vichy was about to find them in a proliferation of specialised police groups, *polices d'occasion*, police for all occasions, devoted entirely to *la chasse*, the hunt, for resisters.

What no one expected was how tenaciously and bravely the resisters would fight back. In the weeks and months to come, more German soldiers and informers were shot, there were explosions on railway lines, grenades were rolled into German restaurants, bombs thrown at depots, at German libraries and German canteens. The industrial zone of the Seine-Inférieure, where Germaine Pican and Claudine Guérin were active, was the scene of constant attacks – railway lines cut, petrol bombs thrown, engines sabotaged by a collection of Gaullists, communists, Catholics and socialists working together, many of them students or railway workers. At one point, the attacks on the railways were so frequent that the Germans placed a number of French civilian hostages on board all trains carrying German soldiers. When the resisters ran out of money, they held up local *mairies*, and made off with whatever cash they could find.

For Betty, travelling up and down France as a courier, hearing herself and her companions described as terrorists, was to misunderstand the meaning of the word. Terrorists were people who shot innocent bystanders; she and her friends were fighters, engaged in war against the enemy. They felt elated.

*　　*　　*

In the early days of the occupation, the Germans had been wary of the French police, suspecting them of being ardent republicans at heart. A few, indeed, were, and these quickly resigned. But for the most part the 15,000 men who policed Paris and the department of the Seine stayed at their posts, and, as the months passed, were drawn ever deeper into a web of collaboration, into Primo Levi's 'grey zone', somewhere between occupier and occupied. Like many French people, they believed that Germany was bound to win the war. At best, they did what they could to mitigate the harshness of the occupiers; at worst, they became torturers.

A law had been passed in the summer of 1940 to the effect that any civil servant would be dismissed if he failed to give satisfaction. Infected by years of public hostility to the Communists, remembering the confrontations with 'Blum's creatures' of the left, frightened for their jobs, coerced by appeals to their sense of duty, many French policemen chose simply to try to survive the war years unscathed and uncompromised. By the summer of 1941, it was becoming increasingly hard for them to do so.

The assassination at the Barbès métro, as well as the attacks in Rouen, Nantes and Bordeaux, merely speeded up a process that was already under way. Since Pucheu, as Minister of the Interior, was determined to do everything possible to prevent the monopoly of repression passing solely into German hands, plans were already well advanced for a reorganised, reinvigorated French police force, committed both to Vichy's *révolution national* and to all-out attacks on the Resistance. All his best men, Pucheu promised von Stülpnagel, would be thrown against those guilty of the attacks. There was to be better pay for police officers, more training and new uniforms, but not, to their disappointment, new guns, for the Germans remained reluctant to see the French better armed.

Along with new sections dedicated to tracking down Jews, Freemasons and foreigners, run by their own 'specialists', came two new brigades, one for 'Communists', the other for 'terrorists'. There had been *brigades spéciales* before, under the office of the Renseignements Généraux, the intelligence service of the French police, whose job it had been to spy on possible troublemakers, but these would be more ruthless, more independent, more skilful.

In the summer of 1941, the new Prefect of Police, instructed to hunt down enemies of the Reich, appointed a senior French policeman called Lucien Rottée as head of the Renseignements Généraux. Rottée, a tall, thin man, wore three-piece suits and went everywhere accompanied by a large dog. He loathed communists, whom he regarded as agents of the Soviet Union. No sooner was he appointed than Rottée brought in his protégé Fernand David to head the anti-communist Brigades Spéciales, and, shortly afterwards, his own nephew, René Hénoque, as head of the anti-terrorist unit. David, who was in his early thirties, was arrogant and extremely ambitious; he would soon be known as the 'patriots' executioner'. Both brigades were to work closely with the Germans, particularly with the Gestapo.

There was no trouble finding recruits. Offered better pay, more freedom, plain clothes rather than uniforms, the promise of rapid promotion, and the chance to catch 'enemies' rather than persecute Jews and Freemasons, few of the young men refused. In other parts of occupied France, policemen, similarly seduced by ideas of power and promotion, hastened to volunteer for similar local Brigades Spéciales. The first were chosen from men who had already distinguished themselves as interrogators, but soon the new recruits were busy learning about surveillance, letter drops, safe houses, how to detect suspicious behaviour, all the telltale signs of the clandestine life. Rottée treated them well, inviting them to receptions, singling out those who performed particularly well and calming the doubts of the few who were troubled by the morality of spying on their fellow citizens. Soon they were perceived as an elite, with special privileges, generous expenses, access to many rationed items and even, occasionally, the possibility of securing the release of a relative who was a prisoner of war from a camp in Germany.

What Rottée had quickly understood was that everything depended on surveillance. His men worked in shifts, returning to the office to write up detailed reports. He taught them to develop their memory, to study minutely faces and gestures and clothes and to write down precisely what they observed. Some brought years of knowledge of the Communist Party to the job; others were skilled at deciphering codes. In the offices on the second floor of the Prefecture, on the Ile de la Cité in Paris, a card index was slowly assembled, of names, addresses, contacts, activities, pseudonyms, identifying characteristics, all greatly assisted by an army of informers, resentful neighbours, jealous friends and zealous bosses. Some of the tale-bearers sent in photographs with their denunciations. Every lead was followed up, every dossier of suspected communists picked over. Blackmail, bribes, promises, all brought in information.

Placing his men at strategic points around Paris, on bridges, by métros and train stations, and using old men, women and even children as extra spotters, Rottée's officers, all through the autumn of 1941, began to assemble a picture of clandestine Paris.

They watched, they followed – Rottée had arranged for them to have rubber rather than wooden soles to attract less attention – and they waited. Sometimes they disguised themselves as postmen, or electricity inspectors come to read the meter. When the people they were following appeared too anxious and too watchful, they backed away.

The moment would arrive when their card index would reveal the identity of entire networks of the Resistance; but not quite yet. And so, day by day, the inspectors returned to the Prefecture and filled in their report cards with minute descriptions. '1.80m, 30, moustache, slight limp, green overcoat' and '1.55m, 20s, elegant, white socks, hat with a feather', for among those they followed up and down the streets of Paris, along the banks of the Seine, through squares and over bridges, into parks and in and out of métro stations, were many women. The inspectors called Betty 'Ongles Rouges', because of her brightly painted red fingernails, and her stylish clothes.

Arthur Dallidet, attempting to instil in the resisters a proper sense of danger, kept telling them to vary their routes, wear different clothes, change the letter drops. Look elegant and coquettish, he told Danielle; Betty, with her stylish ways, did not need telling. In a booklet he issued to members of the Resistance, Dallidet counselled ceaseless vigilance and the need, always, to anticipate. Change your pseudonym from time to time. If someone misses a rendezvous, he urged, don't go home. And, he added, never, ever be late for an appointment.

*   *   *

It was not, however, only the communists and the different bands of resisters who were in growing danger. There was another group of people whose lives were about to be destroyed.

In the summer of 1940, observing the rapid advance of the German army, Langeron, the Paris police Prefect, had decided to evacuate the files held by the Service des Étrangers, the bureau that looked after foreigners, along with cabinet papers and political documents. Barges were brought to the quai des Orfèvres and several tons of paper passed from hand to hand along a chain of men, working in shifts for forty-eight hours. The barge with the political documents got through to the south before the Germans reached Paris, but the one with the dossiers on foreigners was blocked in the Seine when a boat carrying munitions exploded. In spite of feverish attempts by Langeron's civil servants to retrieve and hide them, most of the files were discovered by the Germans and carted back to the police Prefecture. And when, in October, a Bureau for Foreigners and Jewish Affairs was set up, the retrieved files, and particularly the 'fichiers Juifs', were very useful when the round-ups of 'undesirables' began.

The first anti-Semitic laws of the autumn of 1940 had excluded Jews from most forms of public office. Vichy, its definition of Jewishness rather more all-embracing than that of the Nazis, defined as Jewish anyone with three Jewish grandparents, or two Jewish grandparents and married to a Jew. Until that moment, some French Jewish families, who had for many generations been French citizens, and who remained secular, genuinely did not define themselves as Jewish. Both France Bloch and Marie-Elisa Nordmann, who had grown up without religion, saw themselves as essentially French rather than Jewish.

Even before any request was made by Vichy, the first anti-Jewish decrees had been floated. When required to do so, most of France's Jews – and especially the foreign Jews, anxious to demonstrate their allegiance to France – registered with the authorities, both because they feared the consequences of disobedience and because few realised what lay ahead. In any case, many who had decided not to declare themselves were soon denounced. Lawyers, doctors, bankers, shopkeepers, all hastened to denounce *Juifs camouflés*, camouflaged Jews, Jews living in 'luxury villas', Jewish women of 'loose morals', and Jews grown 'rich and greedy' at the expense of good Catholic families. With rationing and food shortages, the idea of Jews 'gorging' incensed these informers.

Arrests of Jews in Paris had begun in May 1941, not long after the setting up of a General Commissariat for Jewish Questions, under a right-wing member of parliament called Xavier Vallat. Vallat had lost an eye and a leg in the First World War, and was best known for the savagery of his attacks on Léon Blum in 1936. And it was in the summer of 1941 that the *chasse aux Juifs*, the hunt for Jews, began in earnest, so zealously pursued by the French collaborators that it was said that even the Nazis were impressed. Foreign Jews were to be interned; Jewish firms to be 'Aryanised'. 'To make our houses really clean,' read one poster for an exhibition, 'we must sweep up the Jews.'

The earlier arrests had been relatively restricted – of adult men who did not have French citizenship – but on 18 August, French policemen sealed off the 11th arrondissement of Paris. The initiative came from the Germans, while those carrying it out were, as usual, from Vichy. Checking papers at métro stations and in the streets, raiding flats, shops and offices, police took away every Jewish man aged between 18 and 50 that they identified. Raids continued until the 23rd, by which time there were 4,242 men in custody. They were taken to the newly opened camp of Drancy, on the outskirts of Paris, formerly used to intern British civilians. There were beds, but no mattresses; food, but no means of heating it. By now both Abetz, in the German embassy, and Dannecker, in the Jewish Affairs Department of the Gestapo offices in the rue de Saussaies, had already discussed interning Jews in various camps in the occupied zone until enough trains could be found to take them to the recently conquered lands in the east.

In mid-December, a moment of comparative tranquillity in the war on communists, another round-up of Jews took place and 743 were taken to a camp at Compiègne. Before long, together with three hundred Jews chosen from those at Drancy, they were on their way to the east. How many knew of Hitler's plans for the Final Solution? Radio Moscow had put out broadcasts on the German intention to exterminate the Jews, and pamphlets had been written and circulated throughout Paris, but who had read them?

*   *   *

In the early summer of 1941, Louis Jouvet left Paris for Buenos Aires, taking with him the scripts of eight plays, a cast of actors and Charlotte Delbo as his assistant. Increasingly disturbed by German censorship and rules forbidding him from employing Jews in his company, angry at being prevented from producing plays by Jewish playwrights, Jouvet had decided that he was no longer prepared to be part of a theatrical world that had become collaborationist. The choice of Buenos Aires as a city in which to sit out the German occupation had fallen in part to Charlotte, who had been given the task of exploring possibilities for foreign tours. Argentina had come up with the necessary invitation.

Georges Dudach, Charlotte's husband, had chosen to remain in Paris, where he was working closely with Georges and Maï Politzer, organising the Resistance in the various faculties of the Sorbonne, and recruiting students for the Francs-Tireurs et Partisans. In a flat that he rented in the rue de la Faisanderie, Dudach wrote and typed up tracts, calling on French patriots to become the new guardians of a 'spirit of liberty in a France whose face has been partially obscured by Hitler's lies'. There had to be a platform, Dudach insisted, for French writers who refused to be silenced.

In June 1941, soon after Charlotte's departure for South America, Dudach crossed the demarcation line to collect Louis Aragon and Elsa Triolet for a meeting in Paris to discuss starting a paper that would reflect the entire spectrum of the literary resistance. As with the new unified Front National of the Resistance, the moment seemed to have come to move beyond sectarian limitations. Returning across the demarcation line near La Haye-Descartes in Indre-et-Loire, 'in the grey and dangerous silence' of dawn as Triolet would describe it, Dudach was stopped and arrested by a German patrol. Aragon and Triolet got through.

Dudach was held in custody for three weeks but then released, his true identity not having been discovered. He was back in Paris in time to help plan a new National Committee of Writers, of all backgrounds and political beliefs, and a new paper, *Les Lettres Françaises*, with the remit of preserving the 'spiritual purity of man', and of reminding writers, scholars and poets of France's proud republican traditions. Just as the Enlightenment philosophers had once fought the supreme evil of obscurantism, so French intellectuals would again take up their pens to fight Hitler, who had extinguished the light of truth and freedom. *Les Lettres Françaises*, on which Politzer, Dudach and Decour started work, assisted by Maï Politzer and Hélène Solomon, was to publish book reviews, poems, work by writers banned in France and to provide lists of those executed as hostages.

In time would come a new version of an older paper, *La Pensée Libre*, as well as a clandestine publishing house, Les Editions de

Minuit, committed to the idea of challenging the draconian German domination of French culture. The novelist and engraver Jean Bruller, under the pen name Vercors, was soon at work on what would be the first book. *Le Silence de la mer* is the story of a German officer billeted with an uncle and his niece in Chartres who refuse to speak to him, and who becomes so appalled by what the Germans are doing to France that he volunteers for the war in the east. Though criticised for making his German too likeable, Vercors would say that such a man 'has to exist, for the sake of humanity'. Throughout France and abroad, *Le Silence de la mer* would soon become a metaphor for the silence of oppression and censorship, but also for the choice of saying no. And in the wake of these different publications came national committees for the other arts – music, film, theatre – extolling all that was French, and keeping in touch with artists exiled abroad or in the free zone.

There was indeed a great need to reassert French culture in German-occupied France. By late 1941, Paris was, as the Germans kept saying, 'shining culturally', but it shone for them alone. The theatres played to full houses, cabarets flourished, writers wrote, artists painted, musicians gave recitals, but all on condition that there was no Jew among them, that total censorship was accepted, that the list of banned books was observed. The list had recently been extended to include anything English or American written after 1870, which effectively meant that a writer such as George Meredith – one of the more surprising popular foreign writers in France – could be read only in part.

A clash between Goebbels and Ribbentrop over who should control German propaganda abroad had temporarily been won by Ribbentrop, and under Abetz's velvet paw a cultural atmosphere favourable to Germany, in which France appeared to be culturally independent but was in fact controlled, scrutinised and subverted, had been put in place. While at the German embassy Abetz seduced writers and artists with his glamorous receptions, Goebbels's men in the Propaganda-Abteilung quietly went on trying to destroy France's intellectual world, in order to replace it with a German one. Threatened with forced labour, or even death, if they listened to foreign radio broadcasts, many Parisians preferred not to engage with the whole question of collaboration and complicity, but instead went to the cinema to watch escapist movies. Collaboration had been something totally new, unknown, imposed by exceptional circumstances, and now it simply had to be survived.

What Maï and Georges Politzer, Decours and Charlotte's husband Dudach were determined to do was to counter, by all available means, this pervasive bad smell of complicity. For this they were reliant on printers and distributors. Maï, Cécile, Viva Nenni and Hélène Solomon had never worked harder, carrying proofs, lead, zinc and galleys from one end of Paris to the other for the new publications. Dallidet's orders about prudence and vigilance were becoming increasingly hard to obey: there was just too much to be done. And it was getting riskier every day.

These young women, known to the French police as *les militants techniques*, the technicians of the movement, had helped put in place a highly organised system. Fernand David and his men knew it existed, but had as yet failed to penetrate the network. One of the women would collect a manuscript from Politzer or Decours and take it to a typographer. From there it would travel, in the hands of another courier, to a photoengraver. After this, a third young woman would collect the pages and transport them to a printer.

There were by now a large number of separate clandestine printing studios around the city, some concealing the work they did for the Resistance behind legitimate jobs – like Viva Nenni and her husband in the Place de Clichy, who worked as ordinary printers for the public during the day, and for the Resistance at night, behind locked doors. Viva's husband, Henri Daubeuf, had been extremely reluctant to help the Resistance but Viva insisted, saying that her Italian socialist father would unhesitatingly have done so. What she did not know was that Daubeuf had insisted on being well paid for his pains.

There were then other agents, many of them also women, who delivered ink and paper, and those who collected the printed pages and took them to depots, from where still others handled the distribution. Never trust any stranger who approaches you, Dallidet told them, unless they give you the other half of a métro ticket I will give you.

One of the men in charge of the printing operation was a

29-year-old machine fitter called Arthur Tintelin, who had been a member of the Jeunesse Communiste before the war. Tintelin walked for miles around Paris every day, using the warren of little alleyways in the Marais and the 5th in which to cover his tracks, meeting up with Cécile, Lulu and Mado Doiret, Danielle's young protégée. By now another young woman had joined them. Jacqueline Quatremaire was a typist in her early twenties, who had lost her job at the Labour Exchange when the unions were closed down, and who liked to wear fashionable and brightly coloured clothes. Jacqueline's parents were both in internment camps. Mado and Jacqueline had become friends and, feeling increasingly lonely and isolated in their sparse lodgings, often going without food when their false ration cards arrived late, had taken to meeting and taking walks together. They were finding it hard to remember to destroy all incriminating names and addresses, having memorised them first, to find safe hiding places for false identity cards and ration coupons, to change their appearance and their routines every few days, and to make certain that, in the event of arrest, any codes in their keeping would not be decipherable.

* * *

The winter of 1941 was again unbearably cold. In Paris, it snowed thirty-one times, the temperature dropped to minus 20 and the Seine froze over. 'Paris a froid, Paris a faim,' wrote Paul Éluard in a poem called 'Courage'. 'Paris ne mange plus de marrons dans la rue . . ./ Paris tremblant comme une étoile'.* Factories were taking all the coal. An attempt to produce charcoal from leaves and pine needles failed.

Everything seemed to be rationed, even milk for children. Mothers longed for their babies to walk late, because there were no rations for shoes for children under the age of one. Well over half of all factories in the occupied zone were working for Germany, and it was said that what had been made and delivered to the occupiers during 1941 had enabled the Germans to assemble

---

* Paris is cold, Paris is hungry/ Paris no longer eats chestnuts in the streets/ Paris trembling like a star'.

and maintain eighteen armoured divisions and forty divisions of infantry, as well as to produce 2,500 planes and two-thirds of the winter equipment used by the Wehrmacht on the eastern front that winter. The black market was thriving, for those who had the money, like the informers, who were paid well and given a free hand to plunder in return for increasingly dirty work. As for Paris, the very fabric of the city was crumbling, its tramlines torn up for iron, its wooden paving stones taken for fuel, its sewers no longer properly maintained. Because there was no petrol for the lorries, rubbish piled up.

By the end of the year, 11,000 communists were in custody, in prisons and internment camps, of which there were over a thousand scattered around the country. They lived in constant fear of execution as hostages. And the mass executions continued, no culprit for the attacks on Nantes, Rouen and Bordeaux having come forward.

In December, a final group of hostages went before the firing squad in reprisal for the shooting of Hotz at Nantes. One of them was Lucien Sampaix, Simone's father. Sampaix, with his unshakeable courage and moral clarity, was something of a hero to the young resisters and plans had been under way for an operation to free him from his prison in Caen. It was to take place on 16 December and Simone and her young friends had been working feverishly to bribe guards and secure the escape route.

But on the 15th, Sampaix and twelve other men were taken to a nearby barracks and shot. Before he died, he told his friends that he was deeply relieved that he was not going to be guillotined. As a young journalist he had been forced to attend a guillotining, and the sight had always haunted him. Those who were about to be shot saw themselves as going on ahead, wrote one of Sampaix's friends, Gabriel Péri, who was executed with him. He used a phrase that quickly spread round France: they were going to prepare 'les lendemains qui chantent'.

No one had been warned. Simone heard of her father's death only some hours later, through the Underground networks. She tried to prepare her mother, but Yvonne was feeling happy, having just received a letter from Sampaix telling her that he would be spared. It was only when Fabien arrived with the official news of his execution that Yvonne took in what had happened. Saying nothing, she went to the cupboard, removed all her husband's clothes and handed them to Fabien for the young resisters; from this day on, Yvonne collected and concealed weapons for the Resistance in her shopping basket, hidden under the vegetables.

In his last letter to his children, written when he knew he was about to die, Sampaix urged Simone to work hard for 'the universal happiness that I so longed to see'. 'You are already grown up,' he told her. 'Cry, but be strong and resolute . . . Life is still ahead of you, it's yours, work for what it has to offer.' In Caen, his grave was soon covered in flowers. The Germans ordered them to be removed; more kept coming.

Simone had been devoted to her father; she was appalled and shocked by his death. Next day she decided to denounce his executioners, as publicly as she could. With the help of her friends in the Bataillons, she had printed black-edged posters and flyers accusing the Germans of murder, which she distributed throughout the whole neighbourhood. Assuming she was behind them, the police searched the Sampaix house, but found nothing. Simone would later say that her father's death had made her more resolute than ever to fight Vichy and the Germans; and that from that day her ties to her friends in the Resistance grew stronger. She was just seventeen and a half; but it was a very long time since she had been a child.

Between August and the end of 1941, there were sixty-eight serious attacks on the Germans in and around Paris. The brutality with which they were met, the mass executions of hostages, the growing shortages of food, were all at last combining to turn the French against their occupiers. Even von Stülpnagel and Abetz had begun to argue that the mass executions were becoming counter-productive. The days of almost universal *attentisme* were over. If in the early days, ordinary people, disapproving of the violence, had been willing to help catch the perpetrators, now witnesses turned their backs, walked away, said nothing, even sheltered those escaping into the crowds. The famous spirit of the seventeenth-century Fronde, rebellion, was revealing itself in go-slows, useless delays and the mislaying of documents. The most minor acts of disobedience restored a sense of dignity, lost with the collapse of France. Betty, Danielle, Charlotte and the other young women resisters felt the difference in the air, and worked harder than ever. And resistance was spreading and intensifying, among other women, in other parts of occupied France.

Never had so many false papers and forged stamps been so available: *Défense de la France*, which would become France's largest Underground newspaper, was said to be turning out two thousand separate false stamps and seals – from birth certificates to marriage licences, permits to ration books – in its workshops, and local grocers were distributing them hidden in empty packets of macaroni. The prefects, reporting from the provinces on the mood of the country, spoke of a 'veiled hatred' of the Germans, of growing resentment and pessimism. The people of France, they warned, were becoming anxious and 'unstable'.

CHAPTER FIVE

Waiting for the wolf

Under Article 2 of the Franco-German Armistice, fifty-three of France's eighty-seven departments were occupied by the Germans, forty-one of them in their entirety. The demarcation line divided the ostensibly free zone in the south from the occupied zone in the north and along the coastal areas. The line itself, however, was not nearly as neat as it sounded. In practice, it wiggled across the countryside and along the rivers, splitting in two farms, villages and even towns. Children were separated from their schools, doctors from their patients, farmers from their crops. At Clemenceau, it cut straight through the middle of the château: one half was occupied by German soldiers, the other by French nuns. At a certain spot on the Cher, a German patrol, perceiving what looked like an agreeable sandy beach on the other side of the river, shifted the line to take it in. There were occasional stretches of barbed wire, and even mines. All along the line, at the edge of forests, through fields and along roads, at crossroads and on bridges, were planted 1.5-metre-high poles, painted in the red, white and black of the German flag.

Immediately after the armistice all communication and movement between the two zones – whether of post, telegraph, trains, traffic or people – was halted. But soon Abetz agreed to special *laissez-passers*, 'for grave family matters', and, bit by bit, the demarcation line was breached. An inter-zone postal service of special pre-printed cards was set up; the telephone was restored; trains began to run. For the *frontaliers*, people living within five kilometres of the line on either side, it was possible to request a daily pass, provided that you crossed at prearranged times and visited the address listed on your pass. Children under 15 crossing to go to school did not need passes.

But for those coming from further afield it was considerably harder. A special central bureau opened in Paris to issue passes to those who had convincing business in the south; smaller offices followed in Vierzon and Bourges and later in Tours and Angoulême. For Jews, fleeing arrest in the occupied zone, for members of the Resistance liaising with contacts in the south, for Allied soldiers, shot down in the north and trying to regain their countries, crossing the demarcation line became a terrifying business. As the Resistance leader Rémy would later say, the line became a place of heroism, but also one of shame.

For the first eight months of occupation, German soldiers and German military police – known as *vaches de choix*, prize-winning cows, after the medallions they wore around their necks – supervised the occupied side of the line. But after Hitler's invasion of the USSR and the need for more troops for the war in the east, their places were taken by German frontier guards. Patrolling in groups of four, either on horseback or with motorcycles and sidecars, often with dogs, they had no hesitation in scouring the countryside far back from the line for would-be illegal crossers, nor in raiding houses where they suspected there might be people hiding. On the French side, it was left to the ill-equipped French *armée d'armistice* and the police to patrol. Vichy was constantly trying to make of the demarcation line a buffer zone, the better to protect its supposed sovereignty.

In the early days of divided France, the *frontaliers*, like the French generally, pursued a policy of *attentisme*, while grumbling about the inconvenience posed by checkpoints and passes. But as the occupation moved into its second year and the German soldiers proved cavalier and destructive of the countryside, holding their military exercises in the middle of newly planted fields, requisitioning the dwindling number of horses, and helping themselves to ever scarcer supplies of animal feed and fresh vegetables, so a spirit of rebellion developed along the demarcation line. Like pasting the anti-German posters on the walls of Paris, helping people cross clandestinely became an act of defiance against the occupier. And, as with the couriers in Paris and the liaison officers in the Charente, the role of *passeur* was one often taken by women.

It began slowly, individual farmers smuggling travellers across by night. But then it built up in response to a growing desperation among people in the occupied zone, whether because they were Jewish, or because they were involved in Resistance activities, or because they had become suspect in the eyes of the occupiers. The first *passeurs*, smugglers across the line, were often doctors, or priests, or peasants who knew the tracks through the wooded countryside, or train drivers, who hid people in their cabs or behind coal supplies then dropped them off once they had reached the free zone, by slowing down the trains and letting out belches of steam to conceal those climbing down.

Later grew up networks of *passeurs*, handing on people from safe house to safe house, often knowing nothing of the men and women they were helping. For the most part, the *passeurs* were both brave and generous, refusing all payment for their services. But, as Rémy noted, there were also unscrupulous traffickers, who made fortunes out of the money they extorted from terrified people, sometimes blackmailing them for more at the last minute. And it was not just the actual clandestine crossing – usually at night, on foot through the countryside or by boat across the river – that had to be negotiated, but stays in safe houses near the line, while waiting for a *passeur* or a night without a moon. In December 1941, the Vichy government instructed police in both zones to pay particular attention to trains, hotels and railway stations, after which it was essential not to be seen wandering uncertainly around the streets of any of the towns near the line.

Punishment for those caught trying to cross illegally started with a fine, or short spells in prison, but could in theory include permanent detention. For the *passeur*, as time went by and the Germans became conscious of the thousands of people crossing clandestinely every day, arrest meant prison, torture, possible deportation, or incarceration in the pool of hostages held to be shot in eventual reprisals.

Along the river Loire and its tributaries, the Lot, Cher, Creuse and Vienne, where the demarcation line fell sometimes on one side, sometimes on the other, and often down the middle of the water, the countryside was wooded, hilly and for long stretches sparsely populated. The riverbanks were sandy, the rivers themselves often broad, dotted with islands and planted with overhanging poplars and willow trees. Vineyards stretched away into the distance. The famous châteaux were surrounded by forests, once the hunting grounds of the nobility. These valleys were perfect *passeur* country.

*   *   *

It was early in July 1940 that the Germans reached Saint-Martin-le-Beau, a small village on the Cher, not far from Tours. Gisèle Sergent was then 10, and she and her mother and grandfather were hiding in the cellar. Hearing shouts and banging above, they emerged to find soldiers demanding beer and wine.

Raymonde, Gisèle's mother, ran a cafe in the village. One of five daughters in a family of Catholic farmers, she had grown up optimistic and strong minded, refusing to accompany her sisters to church on Sundays and choosing for herself as husband a woodcutter called Paul Sergent from nearby Bléré. During the 1930s, the couple moved politically to the left. They went to Paris to earn enough money washing up and serving in restaurants to buy a place of their own, and when they heard that the old Café de l'Union in Saint-Martin-le-Beau was for sale, they pooled all they had saved and came home to buy it.

It was a good life. Paul played football for a local team. The village had an active communist group and Gisèle would always remember the day when they marched from the station to the cafe, with everyone singing the Internationale at the top of their voices. The Front Populaire's provision of paid holidays for workers brought families from Paris to stay in the rooms above the cafe, arriving on the tram from Amboise, or cycling along the banks of the Cher. At night, the guests ate together at a big table, helping themselves from dishes laid out in the middle. There was singing, and often dancing, after dinner. Gisèle and her many cousins played together. Raymonde was strict with her only child, and Gisèle was painfully conscious that her mother longed for a son; but she was also very loving.

In 1940 Paul was taken prisoner on the Maginot line and sent to a Stalag in Germany. Raymonde joined the Resistance and became a *passeur*. There was an internment camp not far from Saint-Martin-le-Beau at Amboise and some of the prisoners who were able to escape made their way to the Café de l'Union, where she hid them in the cellar or sent them to sleep in the stables of one of her sisters' farms, while she arranged for them to cross the demarcation line. Although Saint-Martin-le-Beau lay in the occupied zone, Athée-sur-Cher, just across the river, was in Vichy France. The curé of Athée, the abbé Marcel Lacour, was also a *résistant*, and between them, using the services of a man called Pelé, who owned an illicit boat, they spirited countless numbers of people from the occupied to the free zone all through 1940 and 1941.

Raymonde had a *nom de guerre*, Denise, and a password – 'Bonjour, ma cousine' – known up and down the line by the *passeurs*. A warning – 'Le temps est bouché à l'horizon' (the weather is overcast on the horizon) – meant that police patrols were out on the banks of the Cher, or that there was no one available to guide people over the water. No boats were permitted to circulate on the rivers, but Pelé and his three young sons took it in turns to ferry people over the water. When news came that Germans were in the area, Raymonde led those trying to escape out of the cafe by a back entrance and down the passage to her neighbour, who hid them in his cellar behind bags of cement.

While waiting, her guests lived much as her lodgers had lived in the 1930s, sharing meals around a big communal table. A bookseller called André Wahl, having killed a guard and escaped from a prisoner of war camp in Germany, arrived in Saint-Martin-le-Beau early in 1941 with his wife, desperate to reach the south. Later he would say that Raymonde treated them as friends, comforting and calming his very anxious wife, and that she refused to take any money until he convinced her that it would not leave them short. Wahl's last sight of Raymonde, as he and his wife were rowed across the river, was of her standing on the path, her arm raised in a fraternal salute. She told him that she dreamt of finding a way to help Paul escape from his prison camp in Germany.

The abbé Lacour, a genial man who spoke good German and was careful to keep on friendly terms with the soldiers stationed in the nearby Château de la Chesnaye, was often so busy that he did not have time to change his boots to say mass. He had his own method for helping people cross the line. A funeral would leave the occupied zone, followed by grieving mourners, cross a bridge over the Cher with passes issued by the Germans and process to his church in Athée. There the coffin would be opened, a living person released, while some of the mourners quickly faded away into the countryside. The remaining mourners, setting off back into occupied France, were a much diminished group.

After the Gestapo descended unexpectedly one night on the Café de l'Union, where two exhausted North African soldiers were snoring loudly in the attic, and Raymonde only managed by great good fortune and quick thinking to conceal their presence, she decided that it was no longer safe for Gisèle to live at home. She sent her as a weekly boarder to a school in Tours, the little girl cycling home every weekend along the river to see her mother. If anyone asks you anything about us, Raymonde said to her, 'say that you know nothing and have seen nothing'.

Gisèle was home with her mother in the cafe when the French police came to arrest her on 6 June 1941. 'Don't cry,' Raymonde told her. 'Be brave. I'll be back.' She was taken to Paris, to the prison of the Cherche-Midi, used by both the French and the Germans to house resisters. From here she wrote long letters to Gisèle, in a tiny, neat hand. 'Little Gisèle, you who I love best of all . . . Papa told me to watch over you and to make you good and brave. Because I can't be there, be grown up and obedient . . . I will be home soon to cherish you as you deserve.' Not wanting Paul to discover what had happened to her, she got one of her sisters to let him know that she had bruised her hand badly, and so could not write to him for a while.

Raymonde was released in August. She resumed her work as *passeur*. She abandoned the name Denise and become Rossignol, nightingale. She remained just as bold, planning, with the abbé Lacour and the Pelé family, the best escape routes. To Gisèle's terror, when, one day, a Frenchman they all knew came into the café dressed in a German uniform, her mother slapped him in the face and told him to leave. 'You'll hear more of this,' the man shouted.

The Café de l'Union was always full. Raymonde took to holding dances to raise money for the families of prisoners of war. But some of the villagers were envious, and when the police came to arrest Raymonde for a second time, she knew that she had been denounced by the proprietor of a less successful café. Once again, Gisèle was at home and stood watching as her mother was led away.

Raymonde Sergent, a *passeur* across the demarcation line,
and her daughter Gisèle

This time, Raymonde was taken to the prison of La Santé in
Paris, like the Cherche-Midi a jail where the resisters were held
while the Germans worked out what to do with them. 'Don't leave
school,' she wrote to Gisèle, 'work hard, go to your music lesson
and to the dentist.' She said that she had been put into a cell on
her own, and that she needed a needle and some cotton. What she
did not say was that solitary confinement in La Santé was a grim
and desolate experience. 'Look after your grandfather. All my love
to you, whom I love so dearly.' Gisèle made up parcels of jam and
tinned meat and sent them to Paris. To her father, who was a heavy
drinker, Raymonde wrote sternly that he should eat properly, and
'above all, don't drink'. Three months later, Raymonde was released.

Even now, she refused to turn away people who came to her
for help in crossing to the free zone. As ever increasing numbers
of Jews were rounded up in fresh *rafles* in Paris, so ever greater
numbers of frantic Jewish families arrived in Saint-Martin-le-Beau,
begging for assistance in getting away. The German patrols inten-
sified. Now, Raymonde kept a suitcase packed by the front door.
The danger to known *passeurs* like her was now so great that
a sympathetic member of the French secret services came to

Saint-Martin-le-Beau to warn her that she was under constant surveillance by the Germans and their French colleagues. Gisèle lived in a permanent state of anguish; nothing that her mother could do or say reassured her. But still Raymonde and abbé Lacour went on with their work. Who was to run the cafe, Raymonde would say, if she went underground? Who hide the Jews? Who help the desperate people to escape? To anyone who asked whether she was frightened, she would reply: 'I feel like a goat, attached to a stake. I am waiting for the wolf to come and get me.'

The wolf came. One day, Raymonde's luck ran out. Together with the abbé Lacour, she was denounced by two other *passeurs* on the demarcation line. By then, most of the people she had been helping to cross clandestinely were Jews, fleeing the round-ups in the occupied zone. 'Be brave,' she told 11-year-old Gisèle, who watched silently as her mother was led away. 'It will be all right.'

*　*　*

The first escape lines out of France for Allied soldiers had been set up in 1940 to save the survivors of Dunkirk from being taken prisoner by the Germans. But in their wake came volunteers trying to join de Gaulle and the Free French, and then Allied airmen shot down over occupied Europe and who were hoping to make it home across the Channel. All along the western coast of France networks of resisters had come together, at first to provide safe houses and false identification papers, but soon also to gather information on German military installations, camps and weapons depots, to transmit to London and the Allies.

SOE, the Special Operations Executive, inspired by Churchill's enthusiasm for guerrilla warfare, but opposed by those who doubted that guerrilla tactics could achieve very much, was created in July 1940, when Hitler's march across Europe appeared unstoppable. The idea was to organise armies of resisters throughout the occupied countries. But there was another rival Resistance project, masterminded in London and run by a top secret section of MI9 in the War Office. Section 1.S.9 (d) dealt with France, Belgium and Holland. Its function was to supply money and radios, to drop supplies and to arrange for pickups by air or sea from the coast of France.

Having very few operatives of their own, M19 relied on local Resistance groups, formed in 1940 and 1941 throughout the rural parts of Brittany. One of these was called Johnny, started by an archivist from Quimper called Alaterre, whose *nom de guerre* was André. Johnny specialised in information, though it also protected those trying to escape by hiding them in châteaux, farmhouses and cafes. It was the first such network to transmit regular military information about Brittany to British intelligence. Johnny, like all similar groups, was extremely vulnerable to infiltration and betrayal; and both the Gestapo and the Brigades Spéciales were determined to break it.

As a child, Simone Alizon, always known as Poupette, was sickly and fragile. Her parents owned a hotel, the Arvor, an old *relai de poste* opposite the main railway station in Rennes. It had eighteen guest rooms above, a cafe below and a garage and workshops behind, converted from the stables once filled with the horses kept for France's travellers. Until she was six, Poupette spent much of her life with a farmer's family, out in the countryside, where good air and healthy food were thought to strengthen her. Though she missed her sister Marie, older by four years, she was not unhappy. Her mother, mourning a son lost at the age of two, had become morose and pious, and the atmosphere at home was often bleak. Life on the farm, Poupette would later say, gave her a taste for solitude and a certain independence of spirit.

It was in 1938, when Poupette was 13, that Spanish refugees first arrived in Rennes, and both she and Marie were struck by their misery. Poupette loved and idolised her sister, an affectionate, good-tempered and very pretty girl, with strong views about right and wrong. 'It was,' she would later say, 'a pleasure just to see her live.' During the great French exodus south in June 1940, when Rennes had been overwhelmed by terrified families fleeing the advancing Germans, the town was bombed and a train carrying munitions blown up. For Poupette, these were days of political awakening, made sharper by observing the shame and fury of the inhabitants of Rennes when they learnt of the terms of Pétain's armistice. Seeing the first German poster, of a smiling soldier with a small French child in his arms, and its caption, 'Have confidence in German soldiers', she and Marie felt outraged. Wondering what they could do to protest, they collected the postage-stamp sized pictures of de Gaulle, printed and distributed by his niece, Geneviève.

Not long after, a group of German airmen, attached to a nearby military aerodrome, was billeted on a hotel opposite the Arvor. They were bomber pilots and in the evenings they came to drink in the bar of the hotel, their aviator's furry boots folded down over their ankles. Poupette thought they looked magnificent, with their healthy, blond good looks. The Alizons successfully fought off an attempt by the German authorities to requisition the Arvor as a brothel, but there was no avoiding the nightly visits of the German troops who came to drink there. Mme Alizon, ill with what would become stomach cancer, did not bother to conceal her distaste for them.

One evening, as Mme Alizon was complaining about the Germans to a friend in the cafe, there happened to be sitting at one of the tables a young man who was the local head of the Johnny network. He was in Rennes to find a safe house for his radio operators. Next day, he sent back two colleagues to observe the hotel more closely. Talking to Marie and Poupette, they decided that the attics of the Arvor would be the perfect place to instal transmitters. The sisters agreed; Monsieur and Madame Alizon talked it over and said that although they personally wanted no part in it, they would not oppose the idea. The war was no longer their war, they said, but something fought by others far away; but as Poupette saw it, you could not ignore the bad things that happened around you.

Anchored in Brest harbour not far away were three German boats. The young resisters came back often to the Arvor, to receive and transmit messages about their movements. One of them fell in love with Marie, and she began to talk of getting married. Poupette thought that her sister had never looked more beautiful or happier. This was in the early winter of 1941. Life in the *réseau Johnny* was becoming precarious. Often, now, German cars with monitoring receivers patrolled the streets of Rennes, hoping to pick up signals from clandestine radio transmitters. A young Bavarian pilot, who had become attached to the girls, took Marie aside one evening and warned her that he had heard rumours that there were about to be a number of arrests. 'You don't know what the Nazis are capable of,' he said to her. Not long afterwards, Marie suddenly said to Poupette that they should have their photograph taken, 'because you never know what might happen to us'. The picture showed two smiling, pretty, bold young girls.

Marie and Poupette Alizon, the last picture of them taken together

By now the Alizons had been warned that Johnny had been infiltrated. Marie's boyfriend, breaking his ankle while trying to escape arrest by jumping through a second-floor window in Quimper, was said to be in detention. There were rumours of torture and confessions. On 13 March 1942, the Feldgendarmerie arrived to arrest Marie, while Poupette was at school. Marie was taken to Rennes central prison and held for three days before being sent to La Santé in Paris.

Poupette waited. She stopped going to school. She could have gone into hiding, but was worried about her parents. Five days later, at eleven o'clock in the morning, two German officers arrived at the Arvor to arrest her. They took her to Rennes prison, questioned her, slapped her about, and told her that they were putting her on a train for Paris where she would be questioned further. Her parents, notified that she would be leaving by train, went to the station and stood all day, hoping to speak to her. When the car bringing her to the station reached the forecourt, Poupette tried to seem nonchalant and cheerful; she was, she kept telling herself, just a schoolgirl, and they would surely not keep her for long. She was almost proud that the Germans had sent three armed soldiers to guard a teenager who had only just celebrated her 17th birthday and who still looked like a child. Her parents appeared grey with misery.

Along with Raymonde Sergent, Marie and Poupette were among the first women arrested. The others, one by one and in little groups, in Paris, on the demarcation line, on the farms of Brittany and Normandy, in their homes in Bordeaux, were all about to fall into German hands.

CHAPTER SIX

Indulgent towards women

The late winter of 1941 was terrible for the resisters. The group from the Musée de l'Homme went on trial and all seven of the men – anthropologists, ethnographers, social scientists – were sentenced to death for writing and distributing anti-German material. While an icy wind gripped most of France, and people shivered inside their unheated houses, the Brigades Spéciales in Paris, under David and Hénoque, prepared to score their first major success. Their operation was like an immense ball of wool and as it unravelled, one discovery at a time, one name, one letter drop, one informer, each led to another; sometimes the French police officers must have thought they would never get to the end.

In Paris, the clandestine journalists, publishers, printers and distributors worked without pause. *Le Silence de la Mer* was being copied and roneoed and bound by hand ready for distribution. All over Paris, groups of writers, doctors, artists, scientists, actors and teachers were at work on their own committees and their own news-sheets. It had become hard to find supplies of paper, which had been rationed by the Germans. Marie-Claude, Danielle and Maï continued to meet, elegantly dressed and passing as old friends out shopping, but covertly exchanging edited pages and planning future strategy. Cécile and Betty were still travelling from one end of Paris to the other, and one end of France to the other, carrying orders and distributing money.

What none of them knew was that bit by bit, item by item, David's men were preparing dossiers. Often, the police still had no names for the men and women they were following. Betty was still 'Ongles Rouges', Danielle 'Femme No. 1 de Balard'. But their doggedness and meticulous note-taking was about to pay off. It was not the carelessness of the resisters, well schooled by Dallidet, that was about to let them down, but the single-mindedness of their opponents.

The first to fall into Commissioner David's hands was Marie-Claude; and that was almost by accident. The Brigades Spéciales had been laying a *sourcière*, a trap, for another suspect when one of the inspectors noticed her visiting the same house. He did not know who she was, but he thought he remembered her face from following André Pican. He went back to the office and checked the records: the description matched. On 4 February, David decided to arrest her; his policeman picked her up as she was carrying a pound of butter to the family of a prisoner of war. Taken to the police station and questioned, she would give only her name.

David's next move was one of the only errors he would make in the entire operation. He put a photograph of Marie-Claude, together with an advertisement, in a daily paper called *Le Petit Parisien*, asking whether anyone knew the identity and address of this woman, found wandering in the streets, confused and having lost her memory. When they showed the paper to Marie-Claude, she was secretly delighted; she knew it would warn the others that she was under arrest, and that they would then avoid all fixed meeting places and take extra precautions. Dallidet had impressed on all of them to do everything they could to give nothing away for at least twenty-four hours, which would give the others time to cover their tracks.

By now, however, David and his men had become increasingly aware that the men and women they were following – André Pican, 'Moustaches', 'Femmes Trocadéro', 'République', 'Franklin' and the others – had become excessively nervous, constantly changing direction as they moved around Paris, entering and then leaving métro stations, crossing roads only to re-cross them. On 15 February, David, fearing that they might all disappear underground, decided that he should delay no longer. Sixty police officers were dispatched to arrest all those they had been following, if possible in the street rather than at their homes, where they might be able to destroy any evidence and, most important, lists of names and addresses.

The Brigades Spéciales began by staking out Maï and Georges Politzer's flat in the rue de Grenelles. Maï, they had now established, was 'Femme Vincennes' (1.60m, 32, fair hair, glasses . . .). They watched and waited until they observed Jacques Decour press the bell, and then they closed in. Decour had come around to warn his friends that he feared the police were on his trail. On him was found a small photograph of Maï. Under a bag of potatoes in the kitchen were discovered manuscripts intended for the *Lettres Françaises*. Decour, charged with 'aiding the enemy' and endangering the lives of German soldiers with his anti-German propaganda, was taken into 'ultra secret' detention.

David then had the sense to leave two police inspectors in the Politzer flat, and this way he caught Danielle, when she rang the bell later that morning. She was carrying a small sack of coal she was bringing as a present. Danielle was identified as 'Femme No. 1 de Balard', and she was taken to join the Politzers in the Paris Prefecture for questioning.

Next, it was the turn of André and Germaine Pican. Germaine, who had recently been released from prison, had come to join her husband in Paris, leaving their two daughters in Rouen. They stayed at the house of their friends Raoul and Marie-Louise Jourdan – 'Femme No. 34' – who ran a dry-cleaning business in the 18th, which doubled as an occasional safe house for the Resistance. It was here that David's men found all four of them, sitting inside, behind closed shutters. They had no chance to escape.

On seeing the police, André tried to swallow a list of names and addresses, but the inspectors were too quick for him. He was stripped and searched. In his shoes were a false ID in the name of Léon Rochand and another list with names and the date of a forthcoming meeting. One of the names on the list was that of Yvonne Emorine, a dressmaker living at 39 rue Crimée. Two inspectors were sent to arrest her. When they searched her, they discovered 3,000 francs in cash in her bag. Yvonne refused to give them the names of any of her clients and insisted that she had won the money on the National Lottery, though she appeared unable to recall the date the lottery had been drawn. Yvonne's husband, Antoine, was already in custody, having been detained earlier as a prominent member of the Communist Party. David's men then turned their attention to Germaine. In her pocket was a letter from Claudine Guérin: the police set off to arrest her from her *lycée* not far away. Claudine was still only 16.

This first sweep, to the great satisfaction of the Brigades Spéciales, brought in nineteen people, all either leading figures in the Communist Party, or liaison officers for the Resistance. Nine of them were women. Many had large sums of money on them as well as false documents and they were clearly on the verge of disappearing underground. One of the crucial figures turned out to be a draughtsman and trade unionist called Félix Cadras, who had been helping to organise the Resistance in the south. Arrested outside his house, Cadras shouted out a warning to his wife, and when the police forced the door, they found her standing on a radiator in the process of throwing a shopping bag full of documents out of the window. They retrieved it and discovered reports on Resistance activities all over the country. What became known as the first phase, the *phase Pican*, had proved exceptionally fruitful.

Better than the people caught, in fact, were the things that the police found in their houses. Hidden behind water cisterns, under food, inside clothes and shoes and buried away in attics and cellars – all combed through by David's men – were not only tracts, manuscripts and caches of money, but detailed lists and addresses of other members of the Resistance, as well as the fragments of cards and tickets destined to be used as the other halves of passes. Some of them related to operations in Paris. But many led to Rouen, Evreux, Tours, Cherbourg, Nantes and Ruffec. On Danielle were found the names of contacts as far away as the Pyrenees.

And so a second phase, the *phase de Province*, was launched. David had long been certain that Pican was part of an extensive network; but just how extensive he was only just beginning to understand.

In Cherbourg, using half a ticket found on Cadras, policemen, passing themselves off as members of the Resistance, visited a man called Mesnil, who, producing his own half, took them to a meeting of the section heads for Calvados and La Manche. This netted six resisters. Tours yielded nine others; Ruffec another nine; Nantes three; Evreux a further three.

Rouen turned out to be the most important centre of all. One of the *passes* found on André Pican, with an address attached, led to 20 rue Montbret. An Inspector Delarue, posing as a member of the Resistance, and carrying half a pass, was dispatched to investigate. The woman who opened the door was Madeleine Dissoubray, the teacher who had helped with the derailing of the train in October and who had provided Feldman, the young member of the armed wing of the Bataillons de la Jeunesse who carried out the attack, with a safe house in Rouen.

Once Madeleine had established that their passes matched, she told Delarue she was on her way to a meeting of the local heads of the Resistance. They went for a walk together and though she was evasive about all the names, she was very forthcoming about plans, printing presses and the way the Resistance was structured in Normandy. Delarue listened carefully, said little, and appeared convincingly part of the Resistance. When he judged there was nothing more he could learn from her, he showed her his police badge and told her she was under arrest. Madeleine struggled to get away, shouted for help, and threw herself to the ground. But Delarue held on and summoned reinforcements. Dragged to the police station and left alone in a first-floor room, Madeleine tried to escape by climbing down a drainpipe. Interrogated repeatedly for names, she said nothing. Later, waiting for a train to take her to Paris, she tried to escape again by throwing her suitcase against the legs of her guards, but she slipped and fell, badly grazing her legs. The *phase de Province* brought the number of the Pican network now in French police custody to over sixty.

But it was the third police operation, the *phase Dallidet*, that would prove most deadly. As with the arrest of Marie-Claude, it came about almost by accident.

On the evening of 28 February, while Paris still lay under deep snow, Arthur Dallidet, the canny security chief of the FTP, known to the others as 'Emile', was seen talking to a woman in a cafe by the métro station of Reuilly. The police had only picked up his trace that morning. For a long time, Dallidet's intense caution had paid off; but his luck had not lasted. When arrested, Dallidet and his companion shouted for help, but the people in the street near them only stared. Dallidet was taken to La Santé prison, where he was chained and handcuffed. Beaten so badly that later his friends failed to recognise him, Dallidet gave nothing away.

But he did not really need to, for a long list of names and addresses had been found on him.

One of these names was that of his most important liaison officer, Betty, *Ongles Rouges*; she was arrested in her flat in Paris at seven in the morning of 3 March by policemen posing as electricity inspectors. She and her companion, Lucien Dorland, were just on the verge of leaving for the south, where they were due to deliver money and orders to the Bordeaux Resistance. They would have left earlier, but she had slipped on the ice and hurt her knee. Later, she would remember that there were tell-tale signs that she was being followed – an odd-looking woman, hanging about with her shopping, a nonchalant school boy – but she had failed to register them. In the flat was found an important cache of false identity papers, manuscripts and a notebook with names and addresses. Conducted to La Santé, where she was soon referred to as 'dure de dure', the toughest of the tough, Betty was slapped, punched and repeatedly interrogated. Like Dallidet, she revealed nothing. Put into a punishment cell, in total darkness, without a bed or a mattress, she lost all sense of time and place. Later, she told her parents: 'But I emerged as proud as when I went in, somewhat ill, but it soon passed.'

* * *

Charlotte Delbo was in Buenos Aires, sitting on a beach reading the paper, when she saw that her friend André Woog had been guillotined. She hurried to find Jouvet, and told him that she had to go back to France. She could not bear to be safe, she said, while her friends were being killed. She wanted to share their risks. Jouvet did all he could to dissuade her. He pointed out how much easier it was for her husband Georges if his wife was safe in South America. As a soldier, fighting for the Resistance, it was better not to have responsibilities. For a while, Jouvet hid Charlotte's passport, but she was adamant and booked a passage on a Brazilian ship bound for Europe. As she said goodbye to him, Jouvet told her: 'Try not to get caught. You're going into a lions' den.'

Reaching France via Portugal, she met Georges in Pau. They travelled back to Paris separately, crossing the demarcation line from free into occupied France with different *passeurs*. While Georges came and went all over the Left Bank for the *Lettres Françaises*, Charlotte sat in their flat at 95 rue de la Faisanderie, chain-smoking, crouching at her desk wrapped up in a blanket to ward off the intense cold, transcribing and translating the news from Russian and British radio broadcasts, ready for inclusion in the Underground news-sheets. She and Georges had decided that it would be safer if they never went out together, but every time he was late coming home, her stomach knotted up in terror.

Charlotte had taken the name Madame Delepine. By now she and Georges knew that the Politzers, Decour, Danielle and Marie-Claude had all been arrested, but they were confident that not one of them would have given away any names. Just the same, it was impossible not to feel constantly afraid, to see in every stranger a policeman, in every unexpected knock a police raid. And what Charlotte did not know was that, when she left the flat, carrying baskets and bags which she exchanged with others at the cafes where she met her friends, she was followed.

On 2 March she was working at home when Georges returned, bringing with him a friend, a crucial early member of the *résistance intellectuelle*, Pierre Villon. The Alsacian son of a Jewish liberal rabbi – and Marie-Claude's lover – Villon had been asked to take Politzer's place as one of the editors of *Lettres Françaises* now that Politzer was in prison. He arrived in his pyjamas, hidden under an enormous overcoat, and his bedroom slippers – a not unfamiliar sight in a city in which many of the inhabitants had chilblains – having escaped arrest through a window that same morning when David's men came to the house.

The news Villon had to report was bad: not only had his landlady, who had helped translate Russian broadcasts, been arrested but Jacques Solomon had failed to turn up for the last three rendezvous. No one had dared to go in search of Hélène. Georges told Charlotte that he thought he was being watched as well. They discussed how quickly it might be possible to leave Paris. As the three were talking, the bell rang. A voice called up the stairwell to say that it was a man come to read the gas meter.

Suspecting trouble, Charlotte pushed Villon into the bathroom, from where he escaped out of the window onto a roof and from there through the flat of two astonished neighbours. The five inspectors from the Brigades Spéciales who forced their way into the Dudachs' flat were apparently surprised to find Charlotte there as well, but told her that she too was to go with them to the police station. She asked whether she might put on something warmer and went into the bathroom to change. There she caught sight of a bit of paper with a list of names, that had clearly been dropped by Villon as he escaped; she quickly scrunched it up and swallowed it. She and Georges were now taken to the Prefecture. In Villon's overcoat, abandoned as he fled from the Dudachs' flat, was discovered the entire manuscript of a forthcoming edition of *Lettres Françaises*.

After Charlotte and Georges, it was Hélène Solomon's turn to fall. She was picked up while collecting a suitcase with a Remington typewriter from a locker at the Gare Saint-Lazare. On her was found a manuscript with the words 'France must liberate herself!'

By 25 March 1942, the operation that the Brigades Spéciales would call one of the most successful ever mounted against the 'terrorists' was over. One hundred and thirteen people, from all over occupied France, were in custody, thirty-five of them women. Among them were members of the central committee of the Communist Party, liaison officers, regional leaders and enough evidence to link them to Resistance movements all the way from north of Paris to the Pyrenees. As the documents found on them made clear, 'total war' was to have been waged against the French police, who were to be regarded as 'enemy number one'.

What made the police operation so rewarding to David and his men was the fact that, along with the vast haul of documents, names and addresses and false papers was found evidence that the Resistance itself was no longer simply inspired by small groups of communists, but had been put into the hands of the FTP and guerrilla fighters. In their searches, the officers of the Brigades Spéciales had been extremely thorough, digging up gardens, stripping off wallpaper, ransacking outhouses, garages and cellars. Reporting, with some pride, that 'France and Paris could count on them', the Brigades Spéciales announced that they were fully aware of the *grandeur*, the importance of the task with which they had been entrusted.

Most of those captured were taken to the depot under the Prefecture. Here they were interrogated. Most gave vague answers or said nothing at all, at which they were slapped and kicked. They pretended not to know one another. Danielle, who was beaten and badly bruised, managed to smuggle out a letter to her mother. 'My heart is full of sunshine,' she wrote with the determination and optimism that marked all her actions, 'I am calm and resolved.' She sang to her friends and told them that she felt proud to be in prison. Taken one by one into the vast hall of the depot, the women were appalled to see what was happening to their male companions.

Arthur Dallidet was so badly tortured that his whole face was disfigured and he went totally deaf. He was chained in such a way that he had to drink his soup from a dish on the floor, like a dog. Georges Politzer, also kept chained and manacled, developed sores which became infected, and his wrist was broken by the police. It was said later that Pucheu, Vichy's Minister of the Interior, was present when Politzer, the 40-year-old distinguished Hungarian philosopher, was stripped naked and whipped. Maï, who was not tortured, knew precisely what was happening both to her husband Georges and to her lover Decour. Félix Cadras was tortured first by the French, then by the Gestapo; but he gave nothing away.

The women, meanwhile, put up a struggle of their own. Realising that they were fortunate to be together, they protested as a group about the extreme cold, the filth and the fleas and they clamoured for warm blankets. On the night of 11 March, they demanded to be moved from the vast draughty semi-underground hall under the Prefecture, from whose windows they could just see the feet of the soldiers patrolling outside, into the smaller, warmer cells. Guarded by an order of nuns in small blue veils, they gave all possible trouble, loudly imitating the noises of wild animals, until policemen were summoned and they were subdued. The older women among them – Charlotte, Germaine Pican and Marie-Claude – did what they could to comfort the younger. Claudine Guérin was miserable with acute earache. What tormented Charlotte was thirst, and the fact that for many hundreds of people there was only one tap to which each prisoner had to be taken separately, in handcuffs.

On 20 March, seven of these women, and five of the men, were moved to the prison of La Santé. Among them were André and Germaine Pican, Maï and Georges Politzer, Madeleine Dissoubray and Marie-Claude. They had been given an escort of armed police and they travelled in police vans. As he was climbing in, André Pican managed to slip free and run off, pursued by four policemen. Realising that he was not going to be able to get away, he climbed a wall and jumped over the parapet into the Seine, where he swam for 150 metres against the current, struggling with the weight of his heavy coat. Too exhausted to continue, he made for the bank, and before the police reached him, he called out to the gathering crowd: 'Look what French police are doing to Frenchmen!' In the police vans, his wife Germaine, unable to see what was happening but hearing the shouts of the onlookers, began to sing the Marseillaise. Then, all together, at the top of their voices, the prisoners shouted 'Vive la France!'

* * *

La Santé, in the 14th arrondissement, was one of a number of prisons shared by the French and the Germans, each occupying their own section, and staffing it with their own men. Over time, these prisons would become known as the *châteaux de la mort lente*, the castles of slow death. There were separate blocks for men and women, for civilians and political prisoners; and there were punishment cells, to which detainees were sent for the slightest misdemeanour, tight, black holes without mattresses where prisoners could only crouch, in complete darkness. Though in theory the Germans had jurisdiction over only their own section, in practice they poached at will from the French detainees. In La Santé, there was very little food, no heating, and condensation trickled down the stone walls. Fleas and lice were endemic. The chance of release was virtually non-existent. At night, prisoners in the German wing or those awaiting execution could be heard singing revolutionary songs. A man in one of the upper cells, night after night, whistled Mozart's *Eine kleine Nachtmusik*.

Danielle, Maï, Marie-Claude, Charlotte and the other women from the Politzer, Pican and Dallidet groups were put into cells in twos and threes, though a few, such as Madeleine Dissoubray, judged troublemakers, were placed in solitary confinement. Madeleine spent five months on her own, all contact with other prisoners forbidden the entire time; she left her cell only twice, once for a shower and once for exercise. Marie-Claude, Betty and Charlotte also spent many weeks in solitary confinement. Even for independent-minded women, accustomed to spending periods of time on their own, the solitariness of being totally alone, day after day, never knowing what would become of them, was terrifying. Chasing their anxious thoughts round and round in their minds, holding on for the moment when they would hear some sign of human life outside their cells, they lived in a silent, empty world. It took all their reserves of courage not to sink into apathy and despair.

Those deemed less culpable were allowed to receive a parcel of clean clothes and food every two weeks, and, very occasionally, a book. Exceptionally, no more than once a week, they were taken into the small central courtyard for ten minutes' exercise. For the rest of the long, cold, anxious days there was nothing to do but think, talk, plan for a better future. Claudine, once she had recovered from her earache, sang. Not many of this first group of women prisoners had children. But for those who did, like Maï, thinking about their children but never being allowed to see them or know what would become of them, was a form of torture. The absence of the familiar smell and physical presence of the children was like a constant pain.

Charlotte, struggling not to lose all sense of reality when locked away on her own, tried to conjure up characters from Louis Jouvet's productions, but they refused to appear, remaining firmly in 'the shadows'. She spent the solitary hours watching the light form patterns on the walls of her cell. But one day she made contact through the pipes with the woman in the cell below her, and discovered that she had a book, Stendhal's *Chartreuse de Parme*. Weaving a rope from threads pulled out of her blanket, she drew it up into her cell, terrified that at any moment she might be discovered. After that, she said, 'my cell was inhabited'.

From the beginning, as soon as they had settled into La Santé, Danielle took it upon herself to become their leader. Just as she had once masterminded the activities of the young women in the Union des Jeunes Filles de France, so she now tried to keep her friends' spirits buoyant. She soon mastered the prison system of communicating by means of the rusty old pipes that ran up the walls, along which, using a form of Morse or carefully articulated sentences, it was possible to be in touch with other cells and other floors. The women were able to tell each other stories. And they sang. Describing life in La Santé later to her parents, Betty wrote 'We sang every night. If walking past those filthy walls, you heard singing, it was us. By "us" I mean the "dangerous elements".'

Every evening, Danielle put together a news bulletin of information gleaned from the guards or from other prisoners, and it was conveyed from cell to cell by prisoners lying on the floor, near the door, and shouting through the crack at the bottom. For a while, the guards were tolerant. But one day they arrived in the cell Danielle shared with Germaine Pican to find her writing and when she stuffed the bit of paper into her mouth and tried to swallow it, they shook her hard and took her away to the punishment cell. For the next ten days she had no bed, no blanket, no light and was given only bread and water. She emerged pale and emaciated but defiant.

As spring came, and the prison warmed up, she arranged for all the prisoners to break one pane of their windows, and from her own, shouted out news, encouragement and plans. No one could see her, but, standing by their own broken windows, they could hear her words. Again she was punished, by four days without food, but the guards did not bother to replace the window-panes. All over La Santé, the prisoners felt in touch with one another. On Claudine's 17th birthday, the entire prison sang to her through the air vents. 'We didn't feel alone,' Germaine would later say.

*　　*　　*

Commissioner David and the Brigades Spéciales had been right to remark on the content of the documents found in the possession of the now broken Dallidet and Pican networks. The nature of the Resistance was indeed changing. It was no longer a question of small bands of individual resisters, on their own or in little groups, often bound by sectarian beliefs and acting out of a sense of personal outrage and distaste for the occupiers; but of a larger, united, infinitely more powerful and threatening entity. The armed wings of the various parts of the early Resistance, such as the Bataillons de la Jeunesse, had been carrying out joint actions for many months now, but on 3 April 1942, an article appeared in the clandestine edition of *L'Humanité* formally drawing attention to the Francs-Tireurs et Partisans – *francs-tireurs* after Victor Hugo's description of the fighters of 1870, *partisans* from the Soviet use of the word to describe guerrillas.

The FTP, as *L'Humanité* described them, were to be an amalgamated force of armed fighters, whether Communist, Jewish, Italian, Polish or Catholic, waging a common *lutte armée*, armed struggle, against the German occupiers and their Vichy collaborators, under a united political front. Though there was little to encourage the French resisters in the news of the war between the Allies and the Axis – Rommel was advancing across the western desert, Singapore had fallen to the Japanese, and the Americans were stalled in the Philippines – the moment was fast approaching when de Gaulle's *France combattante* would be a rallying call for most of the French Resistance.

The resisters themselves, however, were not alone in seeing the need to unite and regroup. Faced by the incessant round of attacks on their men, the Germans too were rethinking their strategy of repression.

Otto von Stulpnägel, military commander of France, a man described as being at once graceful and like a wooden puppet, both melancholy and maniacal, had never liked the policy of mass execution in reprisal for attacks on German soldiers. He considered the tactic counter-productive, more liable to inflame hostility towards the occupiers than to quell the resisters. Despite the several hundred hostages executed during the autumn and winter of 1941, armed attacks were not just continuing but multiplying, while those shot in reprisal were seen as martyrs, their graves turned into shrines, their photographs passed from hand to hand. Lucien Sampaix, Simone's father, widely known for the courage with which he had confronted the occupiers, had become a hero.

In February 1942, von Stülpnagel went to Berlin to argue for a more subtle response to the Resistance: punishing only those proven guilty and their accomplices, not the entire population, deporting more people, and having longer curfews. Hitler refused to see him. Von Stülpnagel returned to Paris and resigned his post. When it came to mass executions, he said, 'I no longer can – at least for the moment and in the current circumstances – in all conscience accept responsibility before history.' His place was taken by his cousin, Karl Heinrich, a man made of sterner stuff. Before he left Paris, von Stülpnagel spoke of the *tourbillon*, the whirlwind, of hatred unleashed in France by the mass executions.

More significantly perhaps, power in France was shifting away from the Wehrmacht and towards the Gestapo. In the wake of further armed attacks by the French Resistance, Himmler persuaded Hitler that the German army of occupation was not acting toughly enough and, early in May, General Karl Oberg, keen exterminator of the Jews in Poland, was named supreme chief of the SS and the German police in occupied France. He spoke almost no French and knew virtually nothing about France. In a great ceremony held at the Ritz, Oberg was officially installed in his office by Heydrich, just a few days before Heydrich was ambushed by Czech patriots in Prague. Oberg's assistant was Helmut Knochen, the young philosophy graduate and keen anti-Semite who had reached Paris in 1940 as the spearhead of the SS. Knochen was made a full colonel; and now that Otto von Stülpnagel had gone, he was able to unleash his men to act with all the brutality of which they were capable.

Oberg was also to draw on the services of a team of jurists, who were to help him determine who was to appear before a tribunal, who would be deported, and who shot. In practice, however, all semblance of legality and German attention to correctness and bureaucracy was soon abandoned in favour of speed and expediency. Gone were the days when sympathetic French judges could hurry through the cases against members of the Resistance in such a way as to make them incomprehensible to German observers, or maintain that those arrested for listening to the BBC had in fact pushed the wrong button on their radio sets.

Oberg was 45 and wore his fair hair shaved to the skin; he had a pink face, a beer belly and protruding blue-grey eyes. Known to his colleagues as a genial family man, a meticulous and level-headed bureaucrat who carried out his orders with Nazi punctiliousness, Oberg soon became the most hated man in France. As the spring wore on, he announced measures that would not only hit hard the perpetrators of attacks, but their families as well, proposing to send women into forced labour camps and their children into care. In six months, he increased Knochen's forces from six hundred to two thousand. Torture, sanctioned by Heydrich and Göring, was to be used to force people to give away the names of fellow resisters and to confess to their own crimes. In the case of communists, 'terrorists', resisters, 'Polish or Soviet vagbonds', Jehovah's Witnesses and 'antisocial elements', the third degree – bread and water, dark cell, prevention of sleep, exhausting exercises and 'flagellation' – was permissible with no prior authorisation. Some of Oberg's men attended special classes in Germany to study the theory and practice of torture. When suspects refused to talk, torture became frenzied.

Agreeing with Heydrich that the French would be far more zealous in their repression of the Resistance if they were allowed a certain latitude, Oberg favoured 'true collaboration' with the French police, co-operation at every level, with generous funds provided by the Germans and ever more strenuous efforts on the part of the French. This was even more necessary now that so many German troops were needed for the eastern front. The French collaborators were happy to accept, even if, in the months to come, the Germans would pay very little heed to the accords drawn up between them.

Under Oberg and Knochen, and with French connivance, suspects picked up by the French police were handed over to the Germans on demand. They were often passed from interrogator to interrogator. Held manacled in the underground cells of the Gestapo offices in the rue des Saussaies, or in any one of the other elegant eighteenth-century town houses commandeered by the Germans, they waited to be tortured in sadistic and imaginative ways. Politzer, Decour, Dallidet, Cadras and Solomon all passed through the hands of the Gestapo. And when the German interrogators had had enough, or felt that their knowledge of French was not up to the task, or simply wanted their dirty work done for them, they turned to Commissioner David and his French colleagues for help. The Brigades Spéciales became a parallel

Gestapo. A manual was issued, in French, about what forms of torture to use, and for how long. French police assistants became renowned for the money they made out of ransoms and extortions, and for the relish with which they plunged the heads of their prisoners into baths of cold water. Rottée, as head of the office of Renseignements Généraux in charge of the Brigades Spéciales, let it be known that he would make certain that there would be no investigations into brutality once the war was over.

One of the measures advocated by Otto von Stülpnagel had been the deportation of far greater numbers of suspects to Germany. A policy of *Nacht und Nebel*, sending enemies of the Reich into 'night and fog, beyond the frontier . . . totally isolated from the outside world', had already been used to some effect inside Germany itself. The idea was that these 'disappeared' people would have no rights and receive no letters; nothing at all would be known about them, neither their whereabouts nor whether they were even still alive. Such uncertainty, it was argued, would serve to terrorise and deter their families and comrades from further activities. In France, the new measure began with *Schutzhaft*, protective custody, which meant arbitrary arrest and detention without charge or trial: the detainee would be handed over to the Gestapo before being 'disappeared' in the east.

At first opposed by the Wehrmacht, *Schutzhaft* and *Nacht und Nebel* would in the coming months be used against countless French men and women suspected of espionage, treason, aiding the enemies of the Reich or the illegal possession of weapons, all crimes which might otherwise have resulted in the death penalty.

* * *

The winter and early spring of 1941 and 1942 had not been very productive or successful for the Bataillons de la Jeunesse. After their three dramatic attacks in October, in Rouen, Nantes and Bordeaux, a series of sabotages had caused little damage and a number of train derailments had failed altogether. As achievements, they could list only one German soldier killed and two wounded. But they were about to pay a heavy price for their activities.

The first arrests came about because of lack of prudence. It was sometimes as if the young resisters could not quite comprehend their vulnerability, or the fact that so many of the French police had gone over to the occupiers. One young man showed his girlfriend his revolver; she told her father; he informed the police. His comrades were not hard to find, since most were still in their teens and living at home with their parents.

The Gestapo had decided that a series of highly publicised trials might act as a form of deterrence. The first, of seven young resisters, resulted in seven death penalties; Karl Heinrich von Stülpnagel was present at their execution on 9 March. Soon after, a second, larger trial opened in the hall of the Maison de la Chimie, which had been decked out in swastikas. Twenty-five of the twenty-seven in the dock had been tortured and were brought into the room in shackles. One boy of 15 and one of the two girls were given long prison sentences. The rest were condemned to death. The writer Jean Guéhenno, hearing about the sentences, wrote sadly in his diary: 'Hunger, cold, misery, terror. The country is in a state of prostration.'

Appalled by the sentences, but more resolute than ever, the surviving young members of the Bataillons continued to meet, to exchange information, pass on weapons and plan future actions. Having carried out the first real armed attacks on the Germans, they regarded themselves as something of an elite, a first united band of fighters. Ouzoulias, who with Fabien had been the author of the first attacks on the German soldiers, would say proudly that he estimated the active life of one of his young fighters to be no more than six months.

Simone Sampaix's boyfriend André Biver – known as Dédé – had moved into a small room in the rue Rafaelli, but when he got pleurisy and went to the countryside to recuperate, Simone spent much of her time with her friends the Grünenbergers in the rue de la Goutte d'Or, where Isidore's mother-in-law gave her lessons in French and German. Grünenberger, an active member of the Bataillons, was a shy, serious young man who had once worked with Lucien Sampaix at *L'Humanité*. Since Simone's mother worried about her coming home late, Simone sometimes spent the night in the rue de la Goutte d'Or. Two or three times each week, she went to meetings with another Isidore, Isidore Grinberg – 'Robert' – the third member, together with Biver, in her cell of the Resistance. To and from these meetings she transported news-sheets, ammunition and, occasionally, revolvers. Grinberg called her his *petite soeur*, his little sister. For all their bravado, there was something curiously innocent, even childlike, about them all.

On 10 May, Simone received word that she was to meet the others at their usual spot among the cypresses in the cemetery of the Père Lachaise. She waited, but no one showed up. Obedient to orders, she returned twice more, to the same place, at the same time of day. No one came. On the 13th, she decided that she would go to the Grünenbergers'. The door of their house was opened by inspectors from the Brigades Spéciales. Simone told them that she was Lucien Sampaix's daughter, that she was still at school and that she had come to the rue de la Goutte d'Or for her usual French lesson. She was made to accompany the police to her mother's house, so that it could be searched. The police found nothing, but told Simone that they were taking her to their headquarters for further questioning. She whispered to her mother that she would soon be home, 'because they have nothing on me'.

Later, Simone was taken to the depot and interrogated for most of the night; she was threatened, but not tortured. A revolutionary song that she had been learning was found in her bag, and the policeman kept shouting at her to tell them who had given it to her. In the end she gave then the name of her grandmother, who had been dead many years. Shown photographs of a series of young people, all of them members of the Bataillons, she said she had never seen any of them before, except for André Biver, who had been a neighbour, and to whom she said she was now engaged. Another girl, called Simone Eiffes, a seamstress with a six-month-old baby, had also turned up at the rue de la Goutte d'Or, and was brought into custody. Eiffes, an excitable, indiscreet young woman, had been mistrusted by the group. She had come bearing an enormous strawberry tart, to ingratiate herself with her more disciplined companions.

What Simone Sampaix did not know was that one of the young men in their group, Georges Tondelier, picked up on 25 April, had, under torture, given the Brigades Spéciales enough information to lead them to the rue de la Goutte d'Or. Here, one evening when the family was out, the inspectors had found lists of names and addresses, notebooks, maps and manuals about weapons. Grünenberger had managed to flee, but had since been captured on the demarcation line and shot in the foot and shoulder as he tried to escape. Handed over to the Germans, he had tried to take sole responsibility for a number of the acts of sabotage. Nor did Simone know that André Biver had also been caught, in an earlier trap laid at the rue de la Goutte d'Or.

By now, ten young men and women of the Bataillons had been arrested. Two of the men were Moijase Feld and Mordka Feferman, inseparable friends since early childhood; Feferman had studied under Politzer and Decour. They had been caught in an exchange of gunfire with the police, during which Feferman, though wounded, had tried to escape on a bicycle, been cornered against a wall, swallowed a cyanide pill and shot himself in the face. He had since died. Feld was in police custody. Fabien, the member of the International Brigades who had trained the young people in the forests around Paris, had been warned in time and got away. The days of innocence were over.

As she was taken into the big hall of the depot, Simone noticed that at one end there were people lying on the floor. These were the young men who had been tortured. She recognised André Biver among them and for much of the night she lay listening to his groans. She begged to be allowed to go to him, but her jailers refused.

Next morning, her mother managed to deliver some clothes and food, which she shared with the other women. Two days later, she glimpsed André leaving the cell opposite hers, in handcuffs and leaning heavily on the arm of another man. His face was white and swollen and she could barely recognise him; but he saw her, and next day they managed to have a few minutes together.

The food in the depot was terrible and there was very little of it. Despite the efforts of the older women, who did what they could to look after the schoolgirls among them, Simone grew thinner, more depressed and increasingly weak. She was haunted by fears of what might happen to André, whom she had not been allowed to see again. Finally a doctor had her transferred to the prison at Fresnes, on the outskirts of Paris, another jail shared between the French and the Germans. Conditions here were little better, but Fresnes had an infirmary; the nuns gave her a proper bed, sheets and food, and slowly nursed her back to health.

Simone was still in Fresnes when she heard that André had been shot. Moijase Feld was also shot; Isidore Grinberg, referred to by the French as a 'dangerous criminal', was guillotined. Before being led out into the courtyard, he said that the only thing he regretted was not having killed more Germans. Just before dying, Feld wrote to his sister, asking her to break the news gently to their parents. He was 17.

* * *

May 1942, in the words of Aragon, which soon became part of the vocabulary of the French Resistance, was *le mai noir*, the black May. Marie-Claude would later say that it was a time of almost spiritual purity and heroism, when the prisoners in German custody tried to behave with perfect dignity and pride. Several of the women had by now been in solitary confinement for many weeks. One was Yvonne Emorine, who had left her four-year-old daughter with her mother in order to organise the Resistance in the Charente. Yvonne's husband, Antoine, a trade unionist in the mines, had been arrested before her and was also held in La Santé. Antoine was believed to have informed on the others and to have begged 'les Messieurs de la Gestapo' to spare his life; but he now died. The Germans said that he had committed suicide, but a prisoner who saw him carried back from interrogation, lying senseless and badly battered, said that he had been in no condition to hang himself.

The Pican–Politzer–Dallidet women had been joined by the two Alizon sisters from Rennes. Brought separately from other jails, Marie and Poupette were kept in isolation, and did not even know of each other's presence until alerted by the other prisoners through the air vents. Poupette, 17 and extremely lonely, begged the guards to be allowed to see her sister, but the men were immovable. She derived what comfort she could from knowing that Marie was not too far away, but it would be several months before the girls were allowed to meet, and when Marie turned 21 on 9 May, all Poupette could do was send her a message. There was also a schoolteacher from Indre-et-Loire called Germaine Renaud who had helped Raymonde Sergent and the abbé Lacour ferry people across the demarcation line, and who had been so badly beaten that she arrived at La Santé covered in blood. And in another cell on her own was a young woman called Marie-Jeanne Dupont, arrested soon after her 20th birthday, who tried to kill herself by breaking a light bulb and swallowing the shards of glass. 'We are indulgent towards women,' a German captain told one of the detainees. 'Very indulgent.'

But there was worse to come. Since spring, when Oberg had taken command, the SS had increasingly been choosing to bypass all tribunals and to make their own administrative decisions as to the fate of the arrested members of the Resistance. Now that Otto von Stülpnagel had gone, Oberg thought that mass executions should be resumed, in order to inject terror in people apparently disposed to rebel. The SS were given the task of selecting the hostages and arranging the date, place and time for the executions. On 12 April, the French police handed *l'affaire Pican* over to the Gestapo. On 22 May, the women in La Santé learnt that a number of their men were to be shot the following day in reprisal for a series of attacks that had left two Germans dead in an exchange of fire. Those whose husbands were to die were told that they might see them once to say goodbye.

Among the first to be shot were André Pican, husband of Germaine, Georges Politzer, husband of Maï, Jacques Solomon, husband of Hélène, and Charlotte's husband, Georges Dudach. A few days earlier, Politzer had whispered through the air vents that he had finally completed a new book of philosophy in his head, and that if he could only get hold of some paper, he would be able to write it straight out. After seeing him for the last time, Maï wrote to his parents that Politzer had been 'sublime . . . he seemed particularly happy to be dying on French soil'. Politzer, the Hungarian refugee, had always admired the French. When Germaine Pican was taken to see André, she found that his face and much of his body were covered with bruises from torture. André had drawn a car on the wall of his cell. It was full of suitcases. 'Look,' he said to her. 'This is for our holiday in Italy.' Pican was 41 and the eldest of the four to die.

Jacques Solomon, the quantum physicist, had a few minutes

with Hélène; she found that his elbow had been broken and that he had a deep gash in his head.

Just before dawn, a soldier came to Charlotte's cell. 'Get dressed, if you want to see your husband one more time,' he said. She followed him to Dudach's cell. When the moment came to part, she clung to his hand. The soldier took her back to her own cell and there, she wrote later, 'my companions laid me down on my cot. They asked no questions and I told them nothing, nothing of what I said to him who was about to die.'

Germaine, Maï, Hélène and Charlotte were now widows. Charlotte was 28 – the same age as Dudach – and Maï and Hélène were in their thirties. Germaine was 41. Both Maï's son Michel and Germaine's two daughters had lost a father. The worst that could have happened had arrived with extreme suddenness. The other women prisoners in La Santé, with husbands and lovers in custody, began to live in a state of dread.

*   *   *

The popular image of the *fusillade*, the shooting of hostages and resisters, was of a man standing, tied to a post, upright and resolute. The reality was neither as clean nor as clear. Most of the executions in Paris were carried out on the site of a disused barracks on a green hill west of the city, Mont-Valérien, where Napoleon III's adversaries had been held in the 1850s and which had served more recently as a school for military telegraphy. The men about to be shot were kept in the old chapel, guarded by the SS, until led up the hill to the execution ground. Some found time to scratch last-minute messages on the walls. But the path was very steep, and at times of rain or ice extremely slippery, and those who had been badly tortured found the climb difficult. Those unable to stand at the post were shot lying down. A German soldier was once heard to observe that these occasions were *fêtes sportives*, sporting events.

A modest, quiet-spoken, Francophile and fundamentally decent German priest, the abbé Stock, had been appointed military chaplain to the Paris prisons and it was he who accompanied the men on their last walk. The bodies were put into coffins and driven to a number of different cemeteries around Paris, where they were buried in unmarked graves, so that the plots should not become shrines. When the numbers of those shot on any one day were particularly high, some of the bodies were taken to Père Lachaise, where they were cremated and their ashes placed in urns with no names. Privately, after each execution, the abbé Stock noted down in a lesson book all the details, so that families could later find their dead. Most of the two thousand or so men the abbé Stock accompanied to the stake went to their deaths, he wrote later, with exceptional courage, refusing to have their eyes bandaged, silent, 'disdainful and strong'.

Many years later, Georges Dudach's body was exhumed and reinterred next to that of his guillotined friend, André Woog, in the section of Père Lachaise reserved for members of the PCF.

*   *   *

The next group to die, a week later, included Arthur Dallidet, his face so battered and swollen that he could no longer open his eyes; one of his arms was paralysed. Dallidet had become a hero to the other resisters, having informed on no one, despite weeks of appalling torture. He had no wife or girlfriend, but before he was taken to Mont-Valérien, Marie-Claude was allowed to see him. 'Now, my old friend,' Dallidet said to her, 'it's all over with me. But you others, whom I love, you must continue . . .' He was 36.

With Dallidet went Félix Cadras who, forbidden to write a farewell letter to his family, managed to scribble a few words on a handkerchief, which they later found tucked into the lining of his coat when his clothes were returned to them. That day also saw the death of the tall, sporty, scholarly Decour, Maï's lover, who in his final letter to his parents asked them to return to her parents some things of hers that were in his flat: a copy of La Fontaine's *Fables*, recordings of Wagner's *Tristan* and Vivaldi's *Four Seasons*, and two watercolours. He wanted his fountain pen, propelling pencil, wallet and watch to go to Maï's son, Michel. His own death, wrote Decour, was not to be seen as a catastrophe. He had no religious faith, but he now saw himself as a 'bit like a leaf, which falls from the tree and becomes compost'. Within the space of just over a week, Maï had lost both her husband and her lover.

Raymond Losserand, Cécile's friend and mentor, was executed at the shooting range at Issy-les-Moulineaux; he, too, had been badly tortured.

In all, forty-six of the men caught in the Politzer–Pican–Dallidet *affaires* were shot. Only a few of them had done more than print and distribute anti-German material and talk with longing of the day when there would be no more Germans on French soil. Their deaths did nothing to silence the *résistance intellectuelle*: their places were immediately taken by others. *L'Université Libre* continued to appear, *Le Silence de la mer*, briefly held up, was published and swiftly sold 10,000 copies, and the *Lettres Françaises* were soon inspiring others to resist. 'And I know that there are those who say: 'they died for precious little,' wrote Jean Paulhan, one of the men who took over as editor from Politzer and Decour. 'To such people, one must reply: "it's that they were on the side of life".'

When, at dawn or at dusk – Pétain, fearing protests, had asked the Germans to be discreet – the men were collected from their cells to be taken to Mont-Valérien, the prisoners in La Santé began to sing. They sang the Marseillaise, which had become an anthem for the Resistance, sung at moments of despair and fear, and the sound of their voices rose clearly through the silent prison. From one cell could be heard the prayers for the dead, intoned in a high, fervent female voice. Afterwards, the women did what they could to comfort the new widows; for Germaine Pican, alone in her solitary cell, or Louisette Losserand, who had seen the way her husband Raymond had been battered by torture, there was very little comfort to be had.

One day, the women in La Santé learnt that four men arrested for demonstrating against the food restrictions imposed by the Germans were to be guillotined in the courtyard next morning. At dawn, they heard the boots of the soldiers arriving to collect them. Four male voices rose into the silence and the pale light, singing the Marseillaise; then three; then two; the last solitary voice fell silent in the middle of a word. Then, throughout the prison, people picked up the verse and began to sing.

Charlotte, Maï, Hélène and Germaine were all still in La Santé on 14 July, Bastille Day. At three o'clock the prison fell silent, to commemorate the men who had been shot; after which the

Marseillaise, and the two best-known songs from the French revolution, 'La Carmagnole' and 'le Chant du Départ', were sung. The guards were edgy, and the women speculated that there might have been some major Allied breakthrough. All agreed that they were unlikely to be in German hands in a year's time. 'Even the frailest,' noted Marie-Claude, ever prone to be of good cheer, 'felt themselves grow stronger.'

CHAPTER SEVEN

Recognising the unthinkable

By early February 1942, the Germans had begun to prepare for the large-scale deportation of France's Jews. Pétain expressed some unease at first, especially with regard to French Jews; he was less troubled by the fate of the 140,000 who were not French citizens. Even so, rounding up Jews provided René Bousquet, secretary-general to the Vichy police, with the chance to demonstrate his efficiency and commitment to collaboration. The numbers of Jews to deport were rapidly agreed on. The actual deportations were held up for a while because the spring offensive on the Russian front took all the available rolling stock. The first convoy of Jews left France for the extermination camps on 27 March.

Identifying the Jews in France, both citizens and foreign born, was made easier once all Jews over the age of six were required to wear stars, patches of yellow material, about the size of a clenched fist, on which the word *Juif* or *Juive* was written in black. Vichy briefly resisted the stars, which had been worn by Jews in Poland since the end of 1939, and in Germany since the summer of 1941. But, as with the matter of deportations, Pétain soon capitulated. 'Liberate your regions of foreign Jews,' Bousquet urged his prefects, and for the most part they were quick to obey. The yellow star became mandatory in the occupied zone in May. By now there were some two hundred internment camps, holding centres for Jews awaiting deportation, slightly more of them in the free than in the occupied zone. The cover of the catalogue for the exhibition Jews and France, mounted at the Palais Berlitz, showed a Jewish man, in rags and very dirty, his head covered in a prayer shawl, clutching a globe between two talons. Two hundred thousand people visited the exhibition.

All through the spring and early summer of 1942, France as a whole remained unmoved by the fate of its 350,000 Jewish inhabitants. The country that had so fervently embraced the Rights of Man seemed curiously willing to sit by while one decree after another was enacted against the Jews, watching them debarred from professions, forbidden places of entertainment, relegated to the last carriages on the métro, and now herded on to cattle trucks bound for Poland. The Germans had not actually asked for the cattle trucks; this initiative came from the French railways, the SNCF. It was on French trains, driven by French engine drivers, that deportees were conveyed to the border.

Not everyone, however, sat by unprotesting. Once the deportations got under way and trains began to leave regularly, sometimes as often as three times a week, from the central camp for Jews at Drancy on the outskirts of Paris, the general sense of hostility to the Germans, already on the increase, began to rise. The compulsory wearing of the yellow star by Jews saw a flowering of other yellow symbols, worn by non-Jews, patches of material shaped like roses or rosettes and pinned on to clothes. In Paris, the *zazous*, the youthful, flamboyant admirers of jazz, in their quirky clothes and dark glasses, took to adding a yellow star to their outfits. In due course, a group of cardinals and archbishops in the occupied zone wrote an open letter to Pétain, in the name of 'humanity and Christian principles', protesting against the round-up of the Jews. Hélène Beer, a Jewish student, self-consciously walking around Paris in her new yellow star, noted in her diary that strangers often smiled warmly at her as they never had before. But the deportations went on.

In July, the Germans agreed with Vichy that there would be a new round-up of 30,000 Jews. Twenty thousand were to be taken from Paris; the rest from the free zone. Until now the policy had been to take only men. It was Pierre Laval, once again Prime Minister in the Vichy government and constantly negotiating compromises with the Germans, who proposed adding women and children, not least because when the convoys left children behind, the frantic scenes of their desperate parents upset the police. On the 16th and 17th, a great *rafle* took place in Paris. It was conducted by the French and the German police working together, and it netted 3,031 men, 5,802 women and 4,051 children, less than the desired amount but enough to fill many trains.

Around seven thousand were taken to the Vélodrome d'hiver, a cycling stadium in the 15th arrondissement, where, in September 1936, 30,000 people had turned out to hear Dolores Ibárruri, La Pasionaria, call for an international struggle against Fascism. Here, in acute discomfort and extreme apprehension, they awaited events. Some of them, at least, now knew what to expect. Since the spring, Radio London had been putting out broadcasts about the extermination camps in Poland, and on 1 July there had been a report on 700,000 Polish Jews massacred since the invasion of Poland by the Germans. News-sheets describing the gassing of childen and old people had been handed out in Paris.

One of the people caught up in the *chasse aux Juifs*, the hunt for Jews, was a tough-minded, outspoken doctor from Alsace. Dr Adelaïde Hautval was not Jewish herself, but one of seven children of a Protestant pastor. In April 1942 Adelaïde was crossing the demarcation line to visit her sick grandmother in the free zone when she saw a group of German soldiers mistreating a family of Jews in Bourges station. She had spent several years working in neuropsychiatric hospitals in German-speaking Alsace and spoke good German. Adelaïde approached the soldiers and told them to leave the Jewish family alone. 'Don't you see that they're Jewish?' one of the soldiers asked her. 'So what?' replied Adelaïde. 'They are human beings like you and me.' She was arrested and taken to Bourges prison. A few weeks later, she was asked whether she would care to take back her words. She did not choose to. 'In that case,' said the officer in charge, 'you will share their fate.' It was only now that she discovered just what this fate consisted of.

She had been in Pithiviers internment camp, in the Loiret, for less than twenty-four hours when she witnessed the departure of a convoy of lorries full of Jews bound for Drancy. It was organised by French police, helped by French frontier guards.

That evening the camp was empty but for a few others, like herself, whose 'cases were not clear'. The Germans had pinned a yellow star on her chest with the words 'Friend of the Jews'.

In Pithiviers there were two barracks for women and before they left, some managed to tell Adelaïde their stories. One, elderly and blind, could not quite take in what was happening. Another, a young woman nearly deranged with anxiety, told her that when the police came for her she had been made to abandon her six-month-old baby in an empty house and that there was no one who would know that he was alone and who would go to get him. Several of the women were heavily pregnant. 'It's hard for the normal human mind to recognise the unthinkable,' Adelaïde wrote.

Over the next few days, five thousand other Jewish men, women and children arrived at Pithiviers. The camp turned into mud; there was very little water and not much food. Adelaïde was allowed to take over an enormous hangar just outside the gates as an infirmary and here, with the help of a 19-year-old Lithuanian girl, she did her best to look after the sick. A few seemed to have lost their senses. As their names were called, people thrust little packets of money and jewellery into Adelaïde's hands, begging her to find a way of getting them to their relations who were still at home. Outside the camp, the French guards shaved the heads of the men, so that soon the surrounding mud was deep in hair. The Gestapo, carrying buckets, went around seizing anything of any value that they spotted. Suitcases were ransacked, eiderdowns slit open. Duck feathers and goose down floated in the air.

The most sickening departure witnessed by Adelaïde took place on 2 August. A decision had been taken that in this convoy only children aged over 15 would accompany their parents to Drancy and then Poland. Adelaïde watched as babies were wrenched out of their mothers' arms. When the convoy of lorries drew away, rows of small children lined the fence inside the camp, staring or crying; on to the clothes of the smallest were sewn bands giving their names and ages, and Adelaïde wondered how they would ever be found by their parents if the bands came off. Over the next few days, four children went completely mute. It was only when a guard, arriving from Drancy, announced that all the armbands, even those on the babies, were to be removed, that Adelaïde fully understood what was intended for them. By the time Pithiviers was closed, 12,000 Jews had been deported to the east, 1,800 of them children.*

Over the next few weeks, having been moved to the camp of Beaune-la-Rolande, 18 kilometres away, Adelaïde nursed the

---

* In all, between 1942 and 1944, 75,721 Jews were deported from France; 2,500 returned. 13.5 per cent of French Jews were deported; 42 per cent of Jewish non-French citizens.

detainees who had dysentery, spending her nights emptying the overflowing pails with a jam jar. She wrote to her sister that she was covered in fleas, that she had caught diphtheria, and that she was also trying to help look after a three-year-old boy who had been brought in on his own. This child had been found and cared for by friends after his parents had been arrested and taken away and he was spotted wandering the streets. But the police tracked him down and brought him to Beaune. A few days later he caught diphtheria and died. Adelaïde herself was eventually moved to a prison in Orléans, after an order was issued that there were to be no more Aryans in camps for Jews. There was a moment when she might have escaped, passing herself off as a Red Cross worker, but a German soldier suddenly appeared and the moment was lost. She was a prisoner, and there were no more offers of release.

*　　*　　*

Adelaïde was not alone in finding the behaviour of the French towards the Jews repugnant. After witnessing heart-rending scenes during the round-ups of Jews in Paris, a young lorry driver called Pierrot, whose father ran a cafe in the rue des Amandiers near the Père Lachaise cemetery, decided to organise an escape route of his own. His fiancée, Madeleine Morin, ran a hairdressing salon with her widowed mother in the same street, and the salon proved the perfect cover for setting up and running the network.

At first, Pierrot hid families of Jews in crates in his lorry and took them to the demarcation line. Later, realising that he was not getting enough people out, he joined forces with friends and together they printed false identity cards and train tickets and set up a chain leading from Paris to the free zone. Madeleine's salon became the place where the papers were collected and given out. But one morning a group of clandestine travellers was stopped by the police and when their papers were found not to match those registered with the police, they were arrested. Following the chain back to its source led the Gestapo to Madeleine's salon in the rue des Amandiers. She and her mother were arrested, taken to the rue des Saussaies and badly beaten. Unexpectedly released, they insisted on returning to the salon, in spite of warnings, and were soon picked up again, this time for good. They were joined by Olga Melin, another woman in the chain, whose husband was a prisoner of war and who had a 13-year-old son, disabled by polio. Olga and her husband were on the point of divorcing when war broke out.

Some time in 1941 Jacques Solomon and Georges Politzer had asked Marie-Elisa Nordmann, their Jewish scientist friend, whether she would help them to distribute anti-German material throughout the Sorbonne. As a prominent research chemist, Marie-Elisa was closely in touch with both students and faculty. She joined the editors of *L'Université Libre*, wrote and prepared articles and, in the evenings, helped by her widowed mother, put the news-sheets into envelopes and posted them through people's doors. She also continued to provide her friend France Bloch with chemical ingredients for the explosives that France was making for the new united Francs-Tireurs et Partisans in her secret laboratory in the rue du Danube.

However, in the late spring of 1942, the Brigades Spéciales arrested three young men working for the armed Resistance, and, after carrying out what their reports referred to as 'une intérrogatoire énergique', they heard that a young chemist known as 'Claudia' was producing gunpowder, medicines and vaccines for the Resistance. They soon extracted enough information to lead them to the rue du Danube, where they spotted a young woman, '1m58, pretty face, frizzy brown hair, of "bohemian appearance", glasses' and a particular way of walking, her feet splayed outwards. 'Claudia' was observed handing a bottle to a man in the street. 'Claudia' was France Bloch. She was placed under observation.

Towards the middle of May 1942, the Underground learnt that Frédo Sérazin, France's husband, interned in a camp at Voves for communist activities, was about to be shot. Plans, in which France and Marie-Elisa were included, were made to free him. France went home to collect some clothes and found the police waiting for her.

When arrested, France would say only that she had a two-year-old son, that she was the daughter of the historian Jean-Richard Bloch, now in Russia, and that she had indeed given a bottle of sulphuric acid to a man in the street, but who he was and what it was for she had no idea. From France's laboratory, the police took away ammunition, batteries, cordite, metal tubes, false identity papers and chemicals of every kind.

Marie-Elisa Nordmann and her friend France Bloch,
makers of explosives, with Francis

It was not long before David's inspectors tracked down Marie-Elisa Nordmann, having identified her as one of France's close friends. Marie-Elisa was taken to the depot of the Prefecture to be questioned, first by the French police, later by the Germans, before joining France in La Santé. What the Brigades Spéciales did not know was that the two women were Jewish. After Marie-Elisa, many others from this same *réseau* were picked up, men and women who, after more *intérrogatoires énergiques*, admitted using false identity cards, taking in other resisters, and helping to plan and carry out acts of sabotage against the Germans. Under questioning, Marie-Elisa agreed that she had known France for eight years, but maintained that they had never discussed politics. What she did not learn until later – when a friend smuggled in to her a note concealed in a cigarette packet – was that her widowed mother, who was in her sixties and had been helping to look after her son Francis, had also been arrested, and after being beaten, had admitted that she was Jewish. Frantic with worry about her mother, and not knowing where Francis might be, Marie-Elisa could only wait. On 24 June, news reached the two women that France's husband Frédo had been shot. As Jews, Marie-Elisa and France had the added terror of being sent at any moment to Drancy for deportation to the east; as resisters, neither they nor any of the other women had any idea of what might happen to them.

What the Brigades Spéciales referred to as *l'affaire Sérazin* brought into captivity five more women.

*   *   *

There were two more early networks in the Resistance in which women played a crucial part. Their downfall was once again a mixture of painstaking work on the part of the French police, and bad luck. As with *l'affaire Pican*, the ball of wool, once it started to unravel, led far and wide.

From his repeated and brutal questioning of the Pican–Dallidet–Cadras prisoners, Commissioner David had discovered that, alongside the network of editors, journalists and publishers, there existed a second network, an *équipe de militants techniques*, a team of printers and typesetters who actually produced the clandestine papers, along with forged identity cards and military passes. The Germans continued to find the Underground press extremely threatening, and though the earlier arrests had resulted in a momentary drop in publications, numbers picked up again, as other editors and journalists took over from their imprisoned colleagues. But it was not until late March 1942 that David's inspectors began to remark on a young man to be seen frequently in the rue Saint-Ambroise, in the 11th arrondissement, exchanging packets and baskets with a series of companions. They nicknamed him *Ambroise 1* and set about following him.

Ambroise 1 turned out to be a 29-year-old machine fitter called Arthur Tintelin, who had been an active member of the Jeunesse Communiste before the war. Tintelin was seen to visit a number of printing shops, carrying a bag. Sometimes he travelled by métro, sometimes he walked, hurrying along the street, constantly looking over his shoulder. On 7 April he was spotted talking to a young woman in brightly coloured clothes which made her stand out against the drab greyness that had settled over the city with the second year of occupation. This was the short-sighted stenographer, Jacqueline Quatremaire, who had lost her job with the Labour Exchange and become a liaison officer for the printers.

Femme Saint-Maur – David's men continued to use nicknames taken from the names of Parisian streets and métro stations – whom Tintelin met next, was Danielle's 21-year-old protégée

Mado, with whom, to dispel the loneliness, Jacqueline sometimes spent her evenings. A third young woman with whom Tintelin was evidently closely in contact was Lulu, who with her sister Carmen was busy transporting stocks of paper on a wheelbarrow from one printing press to the next.

All of Tintelin's contacts, the inspectors reported, appeared highly nervous. On the night of 17 June, David decided that the time had come to strike. Mado was one of the first to fall. As she was being arrested at her parents' house in Ivry, her father said to the police: 'I have taken a picture of you. If you harm my daughter, I will find you.'

That same day, Lulu had gone to visit her small son Paul, who was living in the country with her parents-in-law. Returning to Paris, she went straight to a friend's house, bearing a litre of milk for his sick wife. The door was opened by inspectors from the Brigades Spéciales. Seeing the men, Lulu turned round and ran down the street, broke the bottle of milk and, with a piece of glass in her hand, struck out at the policemen following her. She was cornered, pinned down, handcuffed and dragged along the pavement to a waiting van. As she struggled, she shouted out to the people walking by: 'They're arresting me because I am a French patriot!' I won't come back alive. Tell everyone that they have arrested Lucienne Serre, a mother who will never see her child again.' In their report, the inspectors called her *la tigresse*. Though the crowd watched in silence, news of her arrest was given to the concierge of her building, who in turn, via the Underground, got it to her mother in Marseilles. Her sister Carmen, arrested in the same sweep, gave a false name. It was as Renée Lymber that she would be registered, and for a long time no one discovered that she and Lulu were sisters. Sensing that it was better this way, they feigned no knowledge of each other.

In the basement of the Prefecture, the two young women plotted their escape. They discovered a poorly secured window and persuaded some of the other women held with them to cover their departure. But as darkness fell, and Lulu and Carmen prepared to unscrew the window, a police lorry suddenly turned up full of prostitutes who had been arrested, and the whole place was flooded with light. The two sisters did not get a second chance.

Over the next twenty-four hours David arrested thirty-seven printers, typesetters, distributors and their liaison officers, discovered two large illegal presses, six depots of clandestine material, and two secret photographic studios. As with his earlier *filatures*, his tailing and shadowing of suspects, each detainee filled in yet one more piece in the jigsaw, every name, every address, leading to more arrests. Before he was done, *l'affaire Tintelin* had drawn in a hundred suspects. One of David's most important catches was Henri Daubeuf, a somewhat truculent printer who claimed that he had been coerced and blackmailed into working for the Underground. His wife Viva, the Italian Socialist leader Nenni's daughter, could have got away. All her friends begged her to flee. Instead she chose to visit her husband every day in detention, to bring him clothes and food and cigarettes; eventually, the police decided to arrest her as well. As she prepared to leave the prison after a visit, they informed her that she was no longer free to go.

And, as in all the other police sweeps, there were people who fell into the net by accident. Madeleine Dechavassine was a chemical engineer who had already spent some time in prison for distributing clandestine copies of *L'Humanité*. Having escaped once, she had since managed to elude capture for her activities as a chemist preparing explosives for the FTP when the rest of her group was caught. Now, she happened to be with Jacqueline, whom she had known before the war, when David's men came to the house. The police were delighted with their additional prisoner.

* * *

Crucial to the network of printers was Cécile Charua, known to the police only as the *Cygne d'Enghien*. Cécile had been spotted on 1 June in a cafe in the rue d'Amsterdam, talking to *Nancy*, a man called Grandcoing whom the police had been tailing for some time. On 8 June an inspector spotted her again with Grandcoing outside a tobacconist's in the rue Lafayette; they strolled for a while together along the boulevards then sat on a bench in the sunshine. In all, she was seen and followed on eight occasions. But Cécile managed to avoid the round-up on 17 June.

Sitting on a bus on her way to a meeting with a printer, she noticed that the man in front of her was wearing a jacket with a very shiny lapel; and shiny lapels were a sure sign of the police, since they were worn smooth by being flicked back to reveal the police badge. As she got off the bus, Cécile managed to whisper out of the side of her mouth to the member of the Resistance waiting for her at the bus stop that she was being followed; she aborted her visit to the printer, and when she failed to turn up, he hid all evidence of his clandestine work.

Hearing of the arrests of her colleagues, Cécile moved house and lay low for a while, then joined a new network. One day, returning to her small flat, where she was hiding two Lithuanian Jews, she was told by her sympathetic concierge that two policemen had come to the house while they were all out, and left a very clear and insistent message that she and her two Jewish lodgers should 'certainly be at home' that afternoon. As Cécile would later say, the French police could occasionally behave decently. She took heed, and they all moved to live elsewhere.

Her luck, however, did not last. On 5 August, shopping in the Place Monge in the 5th, she was spotted by a policeman who had once tailed her to a meeting with Tintelin. He and his colleague arrested her, found that she was carrying false papers and ration cards concealed inside the pages of a newspaper, and a key, and took her to the Prefecture for questioning. Cécile told the police that she was an out of work furrier, that she had a child being cared for by a foster family, and that she had joined the Communist Party in 1937. She admitted that she had indeed worked as a liaison officer for the French Communist Party and been paid a small salary. However, as to the identity of the men she had been seen meeting, she had no idea at all. She also refused to say what door the key opened. In fact she claimed she had no idea how it had got into her bag.

Tracking down a certain Goliardo Consani, whom the police established to be Cécile's lover, they found in his flat a series of her notebooks, with pages of coded names and amounts of money to be paid. But who the codes referred to and what it was all about, Cécile declined to say. Consani told the police that he had met Cécile in a restaurant, that she had been his mistress for a year, but that he knew nothing at all about her activities. They never talked about politics. Confronted later with the leaders of the Tintelin group, the men who had given her the sums of money to be passed on to the printers, Cécile declared that they were all complete strangers to her. The men said they had never set eyes on her. To her immense relief, though the police refused to release her, she was only briefly interrogated: they assumed her to be the missing 101st person on their Tintelin list, and had not realised that she had since worked with another group. She was taken to join the other women in custody, among whom she found her friends Lulu and Carmen.

Seventeen of the *équipe technique* arrested by David's men were women. Ten were in their twenties, and several had young children. Paul, Lulu's son, was not quite two.

The men in the Tintelin group, appallingly tortured by David's inspectors, were turned over, half dead, to the Gestapo. On the morning of 11 August, before it was light, the women woke to the sounds of the Marseillaise. It was only then that they learnt that their husbands were already on their way to Mont-Valérien, to be shot as part of a group of one hundred hostages, executed in reprisal for a grenade thrown at members of the Luftwaffe training in a Paris stadium, and for the death of a number of others in the preceding weeks. Of the one hundred, only four had actually been condemned to death by a German tribunal, though several had been 'especially marked out for execution' as dangerous terrorists; the rest were hostages. Viva was not permitted to see her husband to say goodbye.

CHAPTER EIGHT

'We have other plans for them'

Bordeaux and its surroundings were crucial to the Resistance, the long beaches between La Rochelle and Bordeaux perfect for escape routes. The Charente, Charente-Maritime, Gironde, Landes and Basses-Pyrénées, traditionally strong in trade unionists and communists, had from the beginning of the war been building up Resistance networks of their own. They had been able to draw on the help of those men who, in the late 1930s, had crossed the border into Spain to serve with the International Brigades, and returned more militant and better trained, and on the Spaniards who had come to south-west France as refugees from Franco.

But the long stretch of sandy coast running north from the Pyrenees up to Brittany was no less crucial for the Germans. From the port of Bordeaux, a natural safe harbour for minesweepers, torpedo boats and submarines, cargo boats left for Indonesia and Japan to collect rubber and rare metals for the war industry. Not far away was the airport of Mérignac, soon transformed into an important German military base. The mayor of Bordeaux who had welcomed General Kleinst's army of occupation as the Germans entered the city towards the end of June 1940, was a dentist called Adrien Marquet, well known for his admiration for Mussolini; Marquet was a good friend of the German ambassador, Otto Abetz. Then there was the Prefect of the Gironde, François Pierre-Alype, a devoted Pétainist, and Georges Reige, a zealous, passionately pro-German senior civil servant who worked in Pierre-Alype's office. All three were keen to do the Germans' bidding.

In the wake of the occupying troops had arrived the new commandant of *Gross-Bordeaux*, General Moritz von Faber du Faur, a man whose courteous and distinguished appearance belied a cold heart. Within hours, the swastika was flying from every public building, *lycées* had been converted into German offices, a German military tribunal was established and the military camp at Souge, 25 kilometres south-west of Bordeaux, was turned into a barracks. In the middle, a clearing was left for executions. As in Paris, the German troops had been ordered to behave correctly; as in the capital, the people of Bordeaux were wooed with military bands playing Beethoven. And, for a while, like the Parisians, the Bordelais remained quiescent and watchful, though they complained bitterly about the shortage of fish, scared from the coastline by the artillery or commandeered to feed the occupiers.

Long before Hans Gottfried Reimers of the Wehrmacht was shot dead by the armed wing of the Paris Resistance on the corner of the Boulevard George V with two bullets to his spine in October 1941, however, the Germans had taken the Resistance in Bordeaux and its surrounding departments seriously. All infractions – tracts, posters, messages scribbled on walls – had been put down swiftly and harshly. By the autumn of 1941, the area was being rigorously patrolled by members of the Feldgendarmerie, the Geheime Feldpolizei, the Abwehr and several dozen Gestapo agents, under an anti-Semitic SS colonel called Herbert Hagen, who took all those suspected of Resistance activities to the old medieval Fort du Hâ or to the barracks in the rue de Persac. For a while Hagen, a colleague of Eichmann's, lived on the yacht belonging to the King of Belgium, which had been abandoned at the outbreak of war in the port of Bordeaux.

It was not only the Germans, nor indeed principally the Germans, however, who had embarked on a determined *chasse aux résistants*, but the French police themselves, under a chubby, smooth-faced, black-haired commissioner called Pierre Napoleon Poinsot. When it came to brutality, Poinsot was inventive and thorough.

Born in 1907, Poinsot was a former seminarian, who had joined the French air force in Casablanca before entering the police force. There, thanks to his immense ambition and above average intelligence, he rose rapidly through the ranks, despite clumsy attempts to bypass his superiors. By 1936 he was known for his hatred of the Front Populaire and the Communists. With the arrival of the Germans in 1940, Poinsot's career took a promising leap when both the Prefect and his assistant quickly perceived how useful a fanatical anti-communist could be to them. In January 1941, in a police report,

Pierre-Alype gave Poinsot a mark of 20/20 for 'professional qualities'.

What Poinsot instinctively grasped was that he would need a team of loyal supporters, men who obeyed his orders without question because they too were ambitious and brutal. Two inspectors, Laffargue and Langlade, joined him, followed by two of his own brothers, Jean and Henri. Carrying out widespread house to house searches, following up every lead, threatening and bullying everyone they stopped, Poinsot and his men soon built up a dossier of suspects, recruited a large band of informers and set about turning resisters held in custody.

The shooting of Reimers in October 1941 proved very helpful to Poinsot, who was one of the French officials who made certain that the requisite number of hostages was handed over to the Germans to be shot at Souge.* His willing collaboration over these killings enabled him to position himself ever closer to the Gestapo in Bordeaux, now under the leadership of a tall, meticulous, blue-eyed disciplinarian, Hans Luther; though, as Poinsot soon discovered, the real power lay with the 29-year-old son of a professor of French in Hamburg, Friedrich Dohse, a protégé of Knochen in Paris. Dohse and Poinsot made a formidable partnership.

In his offices in the Prefecture of Police, Poinsot conducted his interrogations. He backed them up with torture. Men were hung from their thumbs, burnt with cigarettes and had their heads plunged into baths of water; women were stripped naked, made to kneel, and forced to listen to the screams of their husbands, being tortured in the next room. Those who refused to speak, to give names and betray colleagues, were held and tortured until they did so; or they died. Poinsot's team was soon known as the *brigade des tueurs*, the brigade of killers, and his *interrogatoire prolongé* became an experience known and dreaded by the Underground. Poinsot, said a Bordeaux policeman, 'massacred' suspects.

The Gestapo – who gave him his own number, 192, in their ranks – took to warning recalcitrant prisoners that unless they co-operated they would be turned over to Poinsot and his men.

---

* Poinsot would later say that of the forty-seven men executed, twelve should not have been on the list at all, for they really posed no kind of danger.

Along with torture, the French inspectors went in for looting and extortion. Bordeaux, after Paris, was the place in which repression would become the most brutal in the whole of France, and the city itself, as Ouzoulias of the Bataillons de la Jeunesse would later say, turned into 'a cemetery of the finest fighters'.

*　　*　　*

In the late summer of 1941 a friend of Danielle Casanova's, Charles Tillon, arrived in Bordeaux to co-ordinate Resistance activities in the south-west. Tillon was one of the founders of the armed wing of the Front National. Calling himself Covelet and posing as an amateur artist in the Gironde on a painting holiday, he visited old friends and contacts, set up a Resistance structure of three-person cells, impressed on everyone the need for caution, and set out to find recruits. Many of them were young women, soon to become as skilled and intrepid as Betty and Cécile.

With Tillon's help, and an ever closer co-operation between the various groups and networks, the battle in the south-west between occupiers and occupied, Germans and resisters, was about to move into a new, more lethal phase.

Tillon had a friend called André Souques, who ran a laundry and hid Resistance newspapers under the piles of dirty washing collected from Bordeaux's hotels; together, they set up a printer in Bastide. Two sisters, Gilberte and Andrée Tamisé, offered to recruit Bordeaux students and young people from the youth hostels, and Gilberte, the elder by ten years, agreed to act as a liaison officer between Tillon and Bordeaux, Bayonne and Tarbes. She was a highly competent young woman in her late twenties, who had looked after her father and the household since her mother's death when Andrée was just seven months old. Gilberte felt very protective towards her younger sister, who had just turned 18.

Nearby Bègles, long a bastion of trade union activities, soon provided Tillon with new volunteers. Souques's friends included Bonnafon, who ran a furniture shop in the rue des Anguillons, and the two men exchanged information on Mondays, when Souques did his laundry rounds, his wife Jeanne concealing the false papers and a printing machine under the dirty sheets. Bonnafon's daughter Germaine proved naturally talented at the

Underground life. One day she boldly asked a locksmith to open an apartment where there was rumoured to be a case of weapons. She told him that it was hers, and that she had lost her keys. Suspecting nothing, the locksmith picked the lock, and Germaine came away with a valuable hoard of guns.

Guns, by the late autumn of 1941, had become more important than tracts. Tillon and his contacts decided that a special group in Charente and the Gironde would be responsible for acquiring and hiding weapons. There was an old quarry called Heurtebise in Jonzac, a series of deep underground caves once used to grow mushrooms, and here the Germans had set up a weapons depot – the second largest in France – to supply the Normandy front and the Atlantic coast. The depot had been successfully infiltrated by the local Resistance, which had around two hundred young men working with the Germans, and a steady supply of weapons and ammunition was being smuggled out of Jonzac each week. The question was where to hide them.

Aminthe and Prosper Guillon kept a small farm in the hamlet of Sainte-Sévère, which lay near Cognac, about 40 kilometres from Jonzac. It was known as Les Violettes for its tranquil, wooded position; the countryside around was sparsely inhabited, flat and often flooded in the winter, and the farm was hidden from the road by fields and hedgerows. Aminthe had inherited Les Violettes from her father. She and Prosper had a single horse, a few vines and five hectares of land, put to pasture and wheat. In exchange for flour, the local baker provided them with bread.

Their younger son, Pierre, was a prisoner of war, but the elder, Jean, and his new wife Yvette, a neighbour's daughter, had taken over one of the outbuildings and the two families farmed the land together. They were poor, but not destitute. Before the war, Prosper had supported the Communist Party. The family were well liked locally, though neighbours worried about Aminthe's loose tongue, and the way that she kept telling anyone who would listen how she loathed and despised Pétain and the German occupiers. Aminthe was a strong-natured woman, not easily cowed; she was 56 and had already lived through one war with the Germans.

To the Guillons' modest farm often came their friends Marguerite and Lucien Valina: Lucien was a Spaniard who had come to France at the age of 15, gone back to serve as a pilot for the

Aminthe Guillon, the outspoken farmer's wife from Sainte-Sévère

Yvette, newly married to Aminthe's son Jean

republicans in the civil war and returned to the area to work as a truck driver. Marguerite sheltered resisters, scouted out safe houses for saboteurs and transmitted instructions. The Valinas had a teenage boy and girl, and a six-year-old son.

It was Lucien Valina who suggested to the others that they help get hold of weapons for the Resistance by collecting those stolen from Jonzac, and by asking their neighbours for any hunting rifles and ammunition not handed in to the Germans. The Guillons, for their part, agreed to hide the guns under the hay in their derelict outbuildings, to be collected periodically by Tillon's men. All around Jonzac, other farmers agreed to do the same, and there was a constant traffic of weapons along the lanes and across the fields of Charente and Charente-Maritime, often transported by night in horse-drawn carts or in the saddlebags of bicycles. It was not unusual for one of the farmers to do the 40-kilometre journey to Jonzac on foot, carrying the weapons in a backpack.

The farmers and the Resistance across this vast area needed points of contact and above all liaison officers, and one of these was 16-year-old Hélène Bolleau, whose father ran the local post office. Even before the arrival of the Germans, Roger Bolleau had been stockpiling weapons, while his Underground news-sheet, *La Voix des Charentes*, printed on a mimeograph with the help of his wife Emma, had been given out surreptitiously from under the counter of the post office. Emma had established a local branch of Danielle Casanova's Union des Femmes Françaises, and she took Hélène with her when she went to help out at a camp for Spanish refugee children nearby. At home, the talk was all of politics, injustice and the eventual defeat of the Germans. One of Hélène's clearest memories was of seeing a film about the Ku Klux Klan in a travelling cinema that came to their home town, Royan.

Hélène was an only child, quick, bold and apparently fearless, and she was studying for a commercial certificate at school when the Germans reached the area in the summer of 1940. Soon she took over the typing of texts for the Resistance, on a machine hidden in her grandmother's house; when that was judged too risky, she moved it from hiding place to hiding place. One of her first jobs was to conceal herself in a haystack on a farm near Bordeaux, watching and noting down German movements in a nearby airfield.

Once the theft of weapons from Jonzac got under way, the Resistance needed messengers. A transport group was set up, and Hélène, as she would later say, 'drifted' into it. Ferrying orders and information around the countryside on her bicycle, she also collected ink and paper. 'It happened,' she explained. 'We did it because we had to.' At home, the Bolleaus took in resisters on the run from the Germans, and Jews trying to make their way south.

Hélène Bolleau, the school girl from Royan

Her mother, Emma, who took over her husband's
resistance work after his arrest

In the early spring of 1942 the police were tipped off by
informers, and Hélène and her father were arrested. To her great
surprise, Hélène was released five days later, but Roger was taken
to the prison in Royan and so badly beaten that his throat was
crushed. It was many days before he could eat again. When Emma
went to collect her husband's laundry, she found his clothes caked
in blood. Like Aminthe Guillon, Emma was not easily silenced:
she went around loudly denouncing the brutality of the Germans
and the collaborating French.

Hélène had no intention of giving up her Resistance activities
– indeed, her father's arrest and treatment had made her all the
more determined – but it was not easy. Royan was patrolled night
and day by mounted police, and after a German guard was killed
a curfew was set at 5 p.m. But she continued to liaise with the
farmers hiding weapons, kept in touch with the Valinas, and when

the Germans stopped her as she bicycled around the countryside, she said that she was out collecting food for her rabbits. She looked too young and too innocent to be capable of subterfuge. At times the roads were simply too dangerous; then she pushed her bicycle across the fields. She also took the little train along the coast to Saintes to meet her contact, with whom she exchanged her half of a picture of a statue and the password: 'Do you know the Place Louis XVI?' To which the correct answer was: 'You mean the Place Louis XIV?'

* * *

Not far away, in her cafe in La Rochelle, opened after the Germans curtailed the movements of French trawlers and her fisherman husband lost his job, Annette Epaud acted as another point of contact for the Resistance. Annette was an old friend of the Valinas, a vigorous, energetic woman who came from a large family of metalworkers and seamen. She had one child, Claude, who was 12, and to whom she was very close. Annette called her cafe L'Ancre Coloniale, and served German soldiers in the front rooms while hiding resisters at the back, along with weapons. In the cellar, she kept a printing press and roneo machine. Annette was the kind of woman who could never say no to anyone; she needed to help people. Everyone loved her, even the Germans who came to drink in L'Ancre Coloniale. One of Claude's earliest memories was of standing in the damp cellar

Annette Epaud, proprietor of a cafe in La Rochelle, who sheltered resisters

while his mother showed him how to use the roneo machine. After her husband was picked up and interned in the camp at Mérignac, Annette also liaised with the Underground printers, collecting and distributing tracts around La Rochelle.

The great exodus from the north at the time of the German advance had brought other young men and women resisters to the south, to Charente and the Gironde. These were families who in the 1930s had supported Léon Blum and the Front Populaire, and who now carried their own seeds of resistance with them to their enforced exile. Forbidden to return to their homes, now occupied by the Germans, they set about planning their own acts of resistance in the south and south-west.

Germaine Renaudin, with her three children

One of these was a determined young woman with exceptionally blue eyes, called Germaine Renaudin. Germaine was a practising Catholic. Evacuated, together with her whole village, from her home on the Maginot line and resettled in L'Espar, not far from Bordeaux, she was outraged by the way the evacuees were treated. She went to see the mayor to demand better conditions. She then turned her attention to Resistance work, taking in people who needed a safe house. Fearing for the safety of her three children, she sent her two daughters to live with a childhood friend near Libourne; Tony, her only son, she kept at home and all his life he would remember the day the police came to search the house, looking for weapons. The guns were hidden in the fireplace and were not found. But Germaine had the pockets of her apron stuffed with Resistance tracts. Calmly taking it off, she handed it to a neighbour, saying, 'I'm so sorry, I forgot to give you back your apron'. This time, Germaine was left alone; but in the report they filed to headquarters, the police noted that she should be watched for there was no doubt at all that Mme Renaudin was a 'militant and convinced propagandist for the communist party'.

Madeleine Zani, with her son Pierrot

And there was another refugee from the north, Madeleine Zani, one of the first to be evacuated from her house near Metz as the Germans approached, since she was the mother of a new baby,

Pierrot. Her husband, like Germaine's, was a prisoner of war in Germany. The house they abandoned was looted and stripped bare by the soldiers. Madeleine and Pierrot settled for a while in Libourne, but then moved into Bordeaux, where she was soon hiding members of the Resistance, to the fury of her sisters, who had been evacuated south with her and were terrified that she would put them all in prison. Madeleine was not particularly interested in politics but she was bold and she hated the Germans. She had always disdained conventions. As a young bride, to the immense disapproval of her neighbours, Madeleine had often gone swimming in the river near her house, at a time when few young women did such things.

Two of her friends from the Moselle, Yolande and Aurore Pica, were sent south at much the same time, and in their exile in Bordeaux the three young women continued to meet. Yolande had a baby a bit younger than Pierrot. Like Madeleine, the Pica sisters had Italian immigrant grandparents. At 19, Aurore looked like a Fra Angelico madonna. She joined the Resistance and got herself hired as a cook by the Germans; she was then able to provide the partisans not only with food and information about caches of weapons and movements of troops, but later, by having herself transferred to an office, with stamped passes to enable resisters to cross unchallenged between the occupied and free zones of France.

Some time after her arrival in Bordeaux, Madeleine was befriended by a young man who called himself Armand. Barely more than a boy, Armand was a liaison officer between the Communist Party in Paris and a number of towns in the south-west. What neither Madeleine and her friends, nor Armand himself, knew was that he had already been spotted in conversation with known communists in the area, and been marked down for surveillance. Poinsot and his men, assembling an album of photographs of suspicious people, had circulated a detailed description of the appearance of this stocky 20-year-old 'with a long face and light brown hair, parted to the side and badly cut'. He was to be watched; not apprehended. Had the Valinas and the Guillons, Germaine Renaudin and the young women from the Moselle had any notion of the sophistication and tenacity of the police operation building up in and around Bordeaux, they would indeed have been acutely anxious.

* * *

In April 1942, Pierre Laval decided to purge those of France's préfectures and sous-préfectures he considered too lax towards the communists and the Resistance. Bordeaux and the Gironde were among the first places to be cleansed. The incoming civil servants, the 'able and zealous' Maurice Papon, general secretary of the Préfecture of Bordeaux and in charge of Jewish Affairs, and Maurice Sabatier, Prefect of Aquitaine, agreed that strong measures would be taken to 'dismantle terrorism' in the area. Though Hagen, promoted major, had gone off to join Oberg in Paris, one of the twelve new regional merged security services in charge of the security of German personnel and the repression of all anti-German acts, was set up in Bordeaux. The brutal and ambitious Poinsot, now head of the Section des Affaires Politiques (SAP), was eager to demonstrate his own zeal and ability in flushing out resisters.

Poinsot was thorough and tenacious. By carrying out meticulous house-to-house searches, drawing on an invaluable set of pre-war dossiers on known communists, anarchists and members of the International Brigades, and coercing and bullying all those he questioned, he was soon able to put together a map of Resistance activities in the south-west of France. The Bordelais helped. Neighbours reported confidentially on one another. People were denounced for anti-German sentiments and for listening to foreign news broadcasts. However, until the late spring of 1942, the map remained frustratingly indistinct. It was only with the help of two turned former members of the Resistance, a schoolmaster called Pierre-Louis Giret, whose *nom de guerre* was Albert, and Ferdinand Vincent, known as Georges, that matters took on a clearer light. The story of the collapse of the early networks in the Gironde, Landes and Charente is one of betrayal.

Ferdinand Vincent, the former head of a shipyard, had once studied public works in the Vendée. He was invaluable to Poinsot because, having served in Spain with the International Brigades he was known and trusted by the Bordeaux Resistance. At the beginning of the war, Vincent had been friendly towards the communists, though reluctant to be drawn into any of the networks. But after his brother-in-law was arrested by the Germans, Vincent left his job and was recruited into the Resistance. His first mission was to liaise with a number of old comrades from the International Brigades in order to prepare for a parachute drop of weapons. Soon after this, he fell into a trap set by Poinsot. This time he escaped, lay low and grew a thick moustache. However, he was soon tracked down by Poinsot and arrested, though this was not known by the Resistance. Poinsot offered him a deal: he could collaborate, betray members of the Resistance, or be deported, as would be his wife and children. Should he try to escape, the whole family would be shot. Vincent accepted the deal.

Giret was recruited soon after. Picked up for 'communist attitudes' while working in a youth camp, his name having been found on a prisoner, both he and his wife ranked high in the Resistance in the south-west. In their house were discovered two typewriters and a revolver. Giret was tortured; he agreed to work for Poinsot. A few days later, a woman who had once given the couple a safe house was arrested. Soon after, André Souques, the laundry owner and one of the organisers for the Gironde, was arrested and appallingly tortured; names found on him led back to a man known as 'Raoul'. A trap was laid. One of the first to fall into it was Germaine Renaudin, the Catholic, communist mother of three who had been rehoused in the south-west after the fall of France and who had, despite warnings, stubbornly refused to give up her Resistance activities.

Germaine's son, Tony, was working in the woods when police came to get his mother. Finding the house empty that evening, he learnt that she had been taken to Bordeaux's notorious Fort du Hâ, a medieval fortress that had changed little since the days when it had housed the enemies of the *Ancien Régime*. When he got there, a policeman at the gate said to him, 'Push off, lad. Or we'll take you too.' Tony was 15. His father was in a prisoner of war camp, his sisters living with friends. He was placed, by an uncle unsympathetic to his sister's Resistance activities, on a farm in the Marne.

No one knew that Giret had been turned. He told his comrades that he had escaped from the Brigades Spéciales and that he was on the run. With his wife held hostage, Giret set about infiltrating the networks of the south-west, posing either as an escaped member of the Resistance or as an insurance salesman; he sent daily reports back to Poinsot and the KDS. Seeing the excellence of his information, the KDS appointed him agent 155 and gave him 5,000 francs a month, plus travel expenses. Poinsot issued careful instructions to the police throughout the region that, should he be spotted, he was on no account to be stopped.

Vincent, meanwhile, was doing the rounds of the resisters, posing as someone in search of a safe house. From the Landes to Charente and Charente-Maritime, people were happy to take him in. Staying with Annette Epaud in her cafe in La Rochelle, he spent hours playing with her son Claude. And it was Vincent who led Poinsot and the Germans to the farmers in and around Cognac, who had been storing the weapons stolen from the German depot at Jonzac.

Late in the afternoon of 24 July 1942, two men, saying that they were pork butchers in search of animals to buy, arrived in Sainte-Sévère, asking for directions to Les Violettes, the farm belonging to the Guillon family. Having located the property, the two men, joined by some others, hid out behind a tall hedge 200 metres from the farmhouse, and watched. Not long after four o'clock next morning, a farmer, rising early to milk his cows, saw a convoy of lorries drive through the village before taking the road leading to Les Violettes. He had no time to warn the Guillons.

The farm was surrounded. Inside, the police found not only Prosper and Aminthe, as well as their son Jean and his wife Yvette, but Albert and Elisabeth Dupeyron, who had arrived the night before to collect a consignment of weapons. Dupeyron was an important figure in the local Resistance. All six were put on to the lorries; the men were taken directly to the Fort du Hâ, the women to the small prison in Cognac. They were soon joined by the Guillons' neighbours and friends, the Valinas, and their three children, Jean, Lucienne, and Serge who was just seven.

In the lorry taking them to prison, Mme Valina hugged 13-year-old Lucienne close to her, as if to reassure her. At the same time, she whispered in her ear that she should divulge nothing whatsoever to the police, and particularly not the names of anyone who had visited the family. When they got to Cognac, the police took Lucienne to one side to question her. The girl refused to answer. After a while, one of the policemen lost his temper and began to threaten her: 'Your mother has already told us everything. Do you want us to kill her?' Lucienne still said nothing. Later, she and Serge were released and allowed to go to their grandparents. Sixteen-year-old Jean was held, so that he could watch while Poinsot's men burnt his father's feet with a candle. The police were remarkably knowledgeable about names, but they lacked some addresses.

The day after the Guillons' arrest, Pierre, their younger son, arrived in the neighbourhood, having escaped from a prisoner-of-war camp in the Sudetenland. Neighbours warned him that the house was still being watched by the Germans; he left the area and went into hiding in Provence. No one dared go near Les Violettes. Finally the mayor of Sainte-Sévère persuaded a nearby farmer to tend to the animals. From the Fort du Hâ, Jean wrote to his married sister, who lived not far away, asking her to look after the farm until his mother and wife were released; they were confident that it would not be long.

But the arrest of the Cognac farmers was only the beginning. With information provided by Giret and Vincent, Poinsot was able to arrest, over the next few weeks, 138 people, from all over the Gironde, Landes and Charente. Some were farmers, but there were also factory workers, postmen, train drivers and shop assistants; one was a piano teacher. In their houses were found anti-German tracts, ammunition, explosives, small printing presses and revolvers. In some people's houses was found nothing at all, but they were arrested anyway.

One of these was Annette Epaud, in whose hotel, L'Ancre Coloniale, Vincent had often stayed. Her son Claude was away staying with Mme Valina's sister at the time, and like Tony Renaudin, he came home to find the house empty, his mother gone and the dog barking inside. Just days before, he had seen his mother throw a revolver into the river. Not knowing what to do, Claude went in search of her in the Fort du Hâ. There the guards turned him away. Visiting his father in detention in the internment camp at Mérignac, he found him extremely depressed because his friend, who was Jewish, had just committed suicide, having been told that he was about to be deported to Poland. Claude's family was large and affectionate; he was taken in by aunts, who treated him as their own.

Into this sweep fell Madeleine Zani, the ebullient, unconventional young woman from the Moselle, who just had time to hand her small son Pierrot, who was not quite three, to her parents; her two friends Aurore and Yolande Pica; and the two Tamisé sisters, Gilberte and Andrée, who had been alerted and should have fled, but worried that there would be no one to take food and clean clothes to their father, who was in an internment camp.

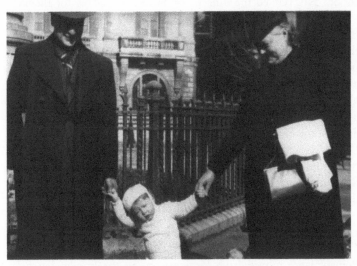

Pierrot Zani with his grandparents,
immediately after his mother's arrest

One of the last women to be caught – almost by accident, for she had only returned to her home in Royan to pick up some clothes – was 18-year-old Hélène Bolleau, the young liaison officer who had assumed some of her father's responsibilities after his arrest in March.

At six o'clock on the morning of 7 August, the Brigades Spéciales came to her house, having found her name on Giret's and Vincent's lists. Hélène was taken to the old lunatic asylum at La Rochelle; now the town prison, it was filthy and full of fleas. As often as she could, her mother Emma came to visit her. But one day, another prisoner, under interrogation, gave away Emma's name as that of someone who had worked for the Resistance, and, on 15 September, arriving at the prison, Emma was arrested. To the relief and pleasure of mother and daughter, they were put into the same cell. Moved a few days later to Angoulême prison, accompanied by German guards, the two women were jeered at for being prostitutes and collaborators, until they held their hands up above their heads, to show their handcuffs. In Angoulême prison, a German soldier was overheard to ask a superior: 'Do they shoot women? Because there are two here we would like to shoot.' No, replied the officer, 'we have other plans for them'.

By the end of October, Poinsot and the Brigades Spéciales in Bordeaux were able to report, with considerable satisfaction, that the 'terrorist' groups of south-west France were totally 'disorganised' and unlikely to rally. In the wake of their success, the museum attached to the Mairie of Bordeaux put on an exhibition that had already proved popular in Lille and Paris. Called Bolshevism against Europe and showing scenes of the destructiveness of the Soviets, the exhibition was, noted the editor of the local *La Petite Gironde*, extremely timely, for it was essential that the 'plague' of communism be known and understood by all, the better to fight it. So many visitors turned up that the exhibition's closing date had to be postponed several times.

Efforts were made to free Elisabeth Dupeyron, whose children were aged eight and four; but they failed. Over the summer of 1942, in groups or on their own, most of the women arrested by Poinsot were moved from local prisons to the Boudet barracks in Bordeaux or to join the men in the Fort du Hâ. It was from here that, in October, they would be sent to the military fort of Romainville on the northern outskirts of Paris, to join the other women being collected from all over occupied France for possible deportation to the east.

CHAPTER 9

Frontstalag 122

The fort at Romainville was a heavy, grey stone building originally put up as part of the ring of fortifications ordered by Adolphe Thiers in the 1830s to protect Paris. Its outer walls were 10 metres high, its buttresses 17 metres wide. Constructed in the shape of a giant star, with a courtyard in the middle, its walls made it look a little like the forts built for the Foreign Legion in France's nineteenth-century outposts.

Romainville was first occupied by the Wehrmacht in June 1940 but it soon become a place of detention for the 'enemies of the Reich'; by the summer of 1942, it was the main holding depot for hostages from the Paris area. By now, the word *Sühnepersonen*, expiatory victims, had largely replaced *Geisel*, hostage, in the vocabulary of repression, and *Sühnepersonen* were seen as collectively responsible for acts committed against the occupying army. 'Mortal enemies' and 'Judaeo-Bolsheviks' held in Romainville's cells could be shot at any moment, whenever an attack on German soldiers demanded reprisals. The Germans did not shoot women, or at least not as hostages, and Romainville had also become a prison for women in the Resistance, the severity of whose crimes made harsh punishment necessary; though just what that might involve was not yet entirely clear. In four years of occupation, almost four thousand women would pass through Romainville. The second in command, Untersturmführer Trappe, ran a regime of callousness and fear. Romainville was known as Frontstalag 122.

The first of the 230 Resistance women who would eventually set out for German-occupied Poland arrived in Romainville on 1 August 1942. She was a 32-year-old Spanish nurse called Maria Alonso, known to her friends as Josée, and she had looked after injured and sick members of the Resistance and assisted a woman doctor in a hospital to perform small operations in secret. Arrested for providing a network of post office workers with a mimeograph that had belonged to her brother, and given away by another member of the Resistance who had been severely tortured, Josée was acquitted at a trial that saw the men in her group sentenced to death. She could have fled, but that was not in her nature and in any case she had two small sons who lived with her since she was separated from her husband. She was a cheerful, good-hearted woman and was soon made head of the women's section of the fort, which was separated from the men's quarters by a fence of barbed wire running down the middle of the courtyard. Josée possessed great natural dignity and it was said that when she did her rounds, distributing parcels and letters and transmitting orders from Trappe, the German soldier who accompanied her appeared as if under her command.

On 10 August Josée was joined by the group of seventeen women printers and *techniciennes* of the Tintelin *affaire*; this brought to Romainville the young Mado, her friend Jacqueline, Lulu and her sister Carmen, and Viva Nenni. Viva could still have escaped. Summoned to Trappe's office, she was told that if she was prepared to renounce her French citizenship, acquired when she married her French husband Henri, she would be sent to Italy to serve out the war, like her father, in an Italian jail. She did not hesitate. Just as she had once convinced Henri to take on printing for the Resistance, on the grounds that her father would have done so, now she turned down the German offer, saying it was not something her father would have accepted. Viva was sent back to join the others.

Soon after came Cécile, the *Cygne d'Enghien*. Then, on 24 August, thirty-seven members of the Politzer–Pican–Dallidet *affaire* arrived at the fort, with Madeleine Dissoubray, Marie-Claude, Danielle Casanova, Charlotte Delbo and Betty, *Ongles Rouges*. Rosa Floch, the 16-year-old schoolgirl who had written *Vive les Anglais* on her *lycée* walls came a little later. She was put into Josée's room and shown the barred windows at the far end of the courtyard, from where the men were taken out to be shot. Once emptied for a mass execution, the holding cells would be filled by those brought from other prisons around Paris to await a call for new hostages. Rosa seemed like a little girl. At night she woke up sobbing, calling for her mother, and in nightmares she saw her father chased by the Germans. Josée used her influence to have her moved into a room with Simone Sampaix, who was just nine months older than Rosa. The two girls clung together, both missing their mothers. Simone was still almost speechless with horror and sadness at the death of her boyfriend André and her other young companions.

The women settled into a routine. After months of living in small, dark cells in La Santé, with very little exercise and nothing to do, the light and companionship of Romainville seemed to some of them almost like freedom. For those who had spent many months in solitary confinement the sense of relief was overwhelming. The women were divided up into dormitories of either eight or twenty-four bunks on the second floor of the main building; the men were housed on the first floor. The blockhouses used for the pool of men held as hostages also served as punishment cells. Exercise was taken in the large central courtyard, and although for much of the time the women were confined to their dormitories, they were able to meet their friends and exchange news in the corridors and on the stairs. Each room had a long central table, with benches and a stove. The *non-isolées*, those not in solitary confinement, which included most of the newcomers, were allowed to wear and wash their own clothes, and to receive parcels left by families at the fort on Mondays and Thursdays.

No visits were permitted, but friends and families discovered that from a hill by the fort it was just possible to glimpse the prisoners at their windows. Many families came to stand on the hill and wave, hoping for an answering sign. One day, the parents of a woman who had given birth in another prison not long before, and had then been transferred to Romainville without her baby, brought the child and held him up for his mother to see.

Marie-Elisa Nordmann, arriving at the end of August with the others from the Pican *affaire*, discovered that her mother had been in Romainville not long before, but had since been transferred, as a Jew, to Drancy. She had missed her by just a few weeks. Where she was now, it was impossible to discover. Nor could Marie-Elisa learn what the Gestapo had done with France

Bloch, her good friend and companion explosives-maker. The Germans had not found out that she was Jewish and her friends took care that they should not do so.

Food at Romainville was better and slightly more plentiful than at La Santé, but even so, the women were hungry. There was only one meal each day, consisting of a great vat of soup collected at lunchtime from the Breton cooks in the kitchens and brought back to be shared out in the dormitories. As the days passed, and more women arrived at the fort, the amount of meat in the soup diminished. More than once, a mouse was found floating on the top. Families sent in whatever they could spare, and the American Red Cross managed to deliver an occasional parcel, but much of it was pilfered by the guards. The women soon decided that all food packets would be pooled in order to make an extra morning soup, brewed on the stoves in the dormitories in large saucepans. Sharing quickly became central to their lives.

For the most part, it was a generous and fair system, with each woman allocated a slightly larger portion of her own contribution, and an extra amount ladled into the bowls of the new arrivals from La Santé, who were often so weak they had trouble climbing down off their bunks. Cécile, whose mother was very poor, was seldom able to provide more than a few carrots or potatoes, but Viva, whose well-connected sister continued to make frenzied efforts to get her released, often received whole chickens. Many years later, Cécile would remember how ungenerous Viva had been with her chickens, minutely picking the carcasses for every last shred of good meat, before handing over the bones for the pot.

However much was delivered – and there were weeks when nothing at all arrived from the women's families – food became, and remained, an obsession. Some women had stomach cramps from hunger and few had much energy. One day Marie-Claude fainted from hunger. Betty took to speaking of a 'community of corpses'. So bad did the hunger become that Danielle, who had once again appointed herself the leader of the women, arranged for all the prisoners whose windows gave on to the street to throw them open at the same time and to shout out together: 'J'ai faim! J'ai faim! J'ai faim!' Outside the fort, passers-by paused and listened. After this, though Danielle and Germaine Pican, perceived as the two ringleaders of the group, spent several days without food in one of the damp, dark punishment cells, Trappe agreed to put a ladle in the watery gruel and taste it, and as a result the soup became a little richer. 'It taught us an important lesson' Germaine would later say. 'It made us understand that we were not completely powerless.'

To her family, Marie-Claude wrote – on scraps of paper, the writing so small that it could barely be read without a magnifying glass, the letter smuggled out of Romainville by the Breton cooks in exchange for money – that the women's teeth were rotting from lack of calcium. 'There are among us friends who are visibly shrinking,' she added, saying that she dreaded the thought of the approaching winter on one bowl of soup a day. 'I dream about beans, lentils, noodles, potatoes and cream puddings.'

Danielle, who kept all discouragement at bay with her constant good humour and determination, told her mother, in another smuggled letter, that she had never looked more elegant, having shed some more of her pre-war extra kilos. Her old friends, she wrote, would never recognise her now, so slender had she become. Cécile would later say that it was not nearly as hard for her as for the other women, because she had so often been hungry as a child. When a photographer came to Romainville on the orders of the Gestapo to take the women's photographs, 17-year-old Simone was the only one who looked healthy and well fed, though in some of the pictures the women could be seen smiling, their friends having pulled faces and giggled as the photographs were being taken.

Simone Sampaix

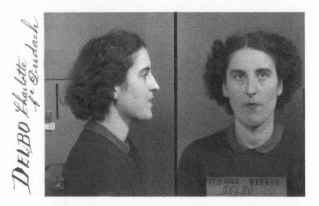

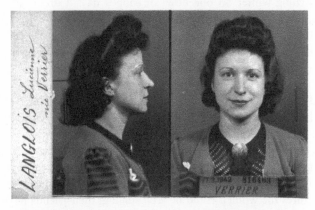

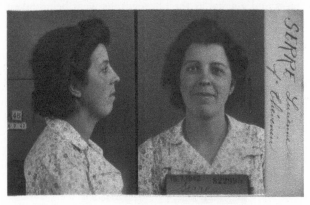

Photographs of Charlotte, Betty and Lulu taken in Romainville

When she found a way to get a letter out of the fort, Annette Epaud, proprietor of L'Ancre Coloniale in La Rochelle, wrote to her family that she was suffering from spells of terrible depression. 'It's very hard to be separated from those you love. I hope this ends quickly . . . I miss my Claude so much.' She added that those women who had no news at all of their families felt very miserable and isolated, particularly those who, like Maï and Lulu, had left small children behind. Annette suggested that her sister bake a cake and send it to her with a letter hidden in the middle, and if possible also a pair of shoes. To Claude she wrote: 'Little Claude, always be good and nice. And always love your mother'.

Under the firm hand of the older women, the female section was soon very busy. Maï, who had been a midwife, organised gymnastics and cold showers every morning, saying that the women needed to be fit to face whatever awaited them. Families were asked to send in wool, sewing materials and old clothes, which the women unpicked and turned into sweaters and bags.

As in La Santé, a news bulletin – the information gleaned from listening to the guards, to the Breton cooks and to any news brought in by new arrivals – was put together in the dormitory occupied by Danielle, Charlotte and several of the other women who had once been part of the *résistance intellectuelle*. Marie-Claude spoke good German, which helped. Written in blue methylene stolen from the infirmary on the brown wrapping paper of the Red Cross parcels, the *Patriote de Romainville* was copied out and handed around the dormitories, to be destroyed at the end of each day when it had been read by everyone. Its tone was upbeat. The news was good: the Germans were under assault in the east, and the Allies were advancing in North Africa. There was every reason to hope that the war would soon be over. The *Patriote* also listed complaints about the meagre ration of soup, the lack of fat and sugar, the prohibition on letters. It was a measure of Danielle's ferocious will, and of Josée's and Marie-Claude's organisational skills, that no one was allowed to sink into a state of depression and apathy. The two women instilled in the others a sense of pride, a resolve not to be beaten, which spread round the dormitories and held them together.

*   *   *

Day by day, the friendships between the women deepened. Cécile arrived in Romainville distinctly wary of those who, like Danielle and Marie-Claude, seemed so assured and knowing. As she saw it, her communist credentials were no less good than theirs, but their education and their class seemed impossibly superior to her own. She felt nervous, ill at ease. Meeting Charlotte on the stairs every day, wrapped in a voluminous cloak and fur hat given to her by Louis Jouvet and holding herself tall and upright, her face made up, having brought with her powder and lipstick, Cécile thought her arrogant and unfeeling. Each morning, with heavy irony, she gave a little bow and said: 'Bonjour, madame.' Charlotte did not reply. But then the day came when the two women began to laugh; and from then on they were inseparable. Charlotte's laugh, said her friends, was particularly attractive.

All across the women's section, in the dormitories, on the staircase, in the courtyard, other friendships were born and grew, women separated by age, schooling, class and profession drawn into patterns of affection and understanding by shared stories and similar losses. Grieving for their executed husbands, missing their children, fearful for their families, they talked, for there was not much else to do; and, as they talked, they felt stronger and better able to cope. Already they were conscious that the nature of women's close friendships would shield them in the weeks to come, and that the men, on the other side of the fort, were often not bound to each other by similar ties. 'We did not need to "make friends,"' Madeleine would say, 'we were solidly together already.' 'We were,' Betty said, 'a team.'

Those women who had husbands and lovers in the Resistance and still free were terrified that they might be caught; those whose men were already in the hands of the Gestapo, some of them in the hostage cells across the courtyard in Romainville, lived in a state of constant anguish: how soon might they be taken and shot as hostages for an attack on the Germans? Madeleine Normand, the farmer's wife who had sold her animals to raise money for her clandestine life, one day caught sight of her husband in the courtyard: he could barely see her, because he had been almost blinded by torture.

Bonds of mutual fear and sorrow linked the women, from dormitory to dormitory. The two sisters, Lulu and Jeanne who

top: Suzanne Maillard, Maï Politzer, Marie-Elisa Nordmann
middle: Olga Melin, Yvonne Noutari, Annette Epaud
bottom: Yvette Guillon, Pauline Pomies, Raymonde Georges

had known Cécile in the Resistance, now grew closer to her; Charlotte became attached to Viva; Germaine grew fond of Danielle. Bit by bit, affection found expression in mutual help, in the remembering of birthdays, in anticipating needs and countering the bleakness with warmth. Many of the women were witty and they made each other laugh. A Spanish woman, Luz Martos, who had come to France after the defeat of the republicans, entertained the others by jumping up on to the table to demonstrate Spanish dances. At night, when it was very cold, the women slept close together, sharing blankets. Anniversaries of every kind were marked and celebrated in dozens of small ways. On 11 November, at midday, every woman stopped what she was doing and sang the Marseillaise in memory of the armistice of the First World War.

At first, there was also a not altogether comfortable political hierarchy. About half the women were communists, and it was the communists who felt that it had been they who had led the most effective life in the Underground. Whether as liaison officers such as Cécile and Betty, or writers and editors such as Maï and Hélène Solomon, or organisers such as Danielle, they remained highly conscious of the cause for which they had fought. 'We don't forget, even in prison, that we are communists,' wrote Betty somewhat primly in a letter smuggled out soon after she reached Romainville. 'Do you see,' wrote Danielle, 'they can kill us, but while we live they will never extinguish the flame that warms our hearts . . . It won't be long before our country is again free, and the USSR wins.' The early Resistance, as they saw it, had been directed largely by them, and they felt not only a sense of personal entitlement but a certain wariness towards those drawn in, either out of loyalty to a relation or simply out of distaste for the occupiers. Such women, they made it felt, lacked conviction.

One result of this political consciousness was that in the early days of Romainville a slight breeze of political purity wafted through the women's section, intimidating to outsiders, who knew that they were being discreetly vetted before being drawn into the fold. Newcomers, without the same political commitment and often more easy-going and less well educated, found the inventive and unflagging determination of the communists daunting.

But that was in the early days. As the weeks passed, and the fort grew colder, the women pushed their bunks together and slept head to toe, sharing their blankets, their political differences forgotten. The confrontational debates softened and a sense of real solidarity took shape among them. It was forged at least in part by the fact that most of the women had known and recognised the risks they had been running in the Resistance, and that shared knowledge, with all its attendant misfortunes, provided a bond that proved far stronger than political allegiances. 'We weren't victims,' Madeleine Dissoubray would later say. 'It wasn't like the Jews or the gypsies. We saw the German posters, we read about the penalties, we heard about torture. We knew what we were doing. It was our choice, and this gave us a strong emotional link.' By the time Dr Adelaïde Hautval joined the other women, a few weeks later, she found a truly 'generous and sisterly community'. Of no strong political convictions herself, she did not feel an outsider.

Nor did the most aristocratic of all the women in the group, Francine Rondeaux de Montbray, though in background, education and money she could hardly have been more different. Francine was a tall, outspoken, confident woman in her early forties, whose first cousin was André Gide. She had grown up, surrounded by nannies and tutors, in a château in Normandy. She was divorced, and had a young daughter, and was one of the very few practising Catholics among the women. After the defeat of the French army and the arrival of the German occupiers, Francine had transformed the ground floor of her house in Paris into a secret hospital for wounded Allied airmen, whom, once they recovered, she helped to escape across the demarcation line, along with Jewish families. Patrician contempt for the occupiers had proved her undoing. Regularly she drove to Normandy to collect food for her patients and one day crashed her car into a Wehrmacht vehicle. Arrested and taken to a police station, she might easily have been released, had she not slapped a sergeant who jostled her.

However, there were in Romainville three women who did feel themselves to be outcasts, and with some reason. These were the *délatrices*, informers, suspected by the others of having caused the arrest of considerable numbers of resisters. Antoine Bibault was reported to have turned people over to the Gestapo in exchange for a reward; instead of paying it, the Germans arrested her. Jeanne Hervé was a disgruntled, sharp-tongued woman who had denounced not only Jews but her neighbours, and would have denounced one of the women in her cell in Romainville had it not been for the intervention of Josée. Twenty-year-old Lucienne Ferre was said by the women from Bordeaux to have been in league with Poinsot's men. All three were cold-shouldered by the others.

Perhaps most important for the cohesion of the women, a desire to learn, and to teach, spread around the dormitories. To fill the long days, to keep at bay memories of what had happened and fears for the future of children, an informal series of classes started up, each woman contributing her own experiences and skills. Viva Nenni gave Italian lessons; Marie-Claude took political history; Maï, remembering the long conversations with Georges, discussed aspects of philosophy. Danielle gave briefings on the daily news. Charlotte, whose excellent memory and long years with Louis Jouvet had filled her mind with entire scenes from plays as well as with Jouvet's meticulous and obsessive stage directions, recreated evenings at the theatre.

Seventeen-year-old Poupette Alizon, whose own education by the nuns had been limited and in any case truncated by the war, arrived at Romainville from almost eight months' solitary confinement in La Santé and Fresnes, in a cell five paces wide and eight paces long, to discover a whole new world of learning and friendship. It was, she thought, like going to university; each day, she learnt something new, each day opened worlds she had never dreamt of. As she would say later: 'Usually people learn about life through their own personal experiences: I learnt it through the stories of others.' In her long and lonely months in La Santé, Poupette had only caught a glimpse of Marie. Now she was overwhelmingly relieved and happy to be reunited with her sister, and they spent hours talking to each other. Once again, Marie fell into the role of older sister, protecting Poupette. In Romainville there was now a group of very young girls, some of whom had never been away from home and were little older than children. They missed their mothers, and the older women did their best to care for them.

A few of the women had managed to bring books with them – Simone had a book of geography her father had been reading before he was executed – and these they shared around. Others they borrowed from a small library put together by one of the prisoners, Julien Cain, former administrator at the Bibliothèque Nationale, arrested in 1941 with the resisters of the Musée de l'Homme. Caen had a little trolley, and wheeled his books along the corridors.

Charlotte had never directed a play herself, but having sat in the wings watching Jouvet, she knew exactly what to do. She soon discovered, among the other women, some with acting talents, others who could sing, others again who could make costumes. Jacqueline had a particularly sweet voice. Together, the women began to put on plays. Charlotte, who was able to draw on the many hours spent with Jouvet, memorising and recording his notes and stage directions, could recall many of the lines of the classics, while others improvised scenes that were missing. Cécile, a skilled seamstress from her days sewing furs, did the costumes. For *Le Malade imaginaire*, she had her mother bring in an enormous old blanket, which she cut up and made into an invalid's costume. What they called 'les après-midis artistiques', the theatrical afternoons, took place on Sundays after lunch, in the courtyard, and they were attended not only by the prisoners but by the German guards. For a while, having been told that the male prisoners could not be present, the women announced that they would suspend their performances; but then Trappe relented and the whole prison turned out to watch.

On Sunday 13 September, a series of *tableaux vivants* of historical incidents across the centuries was staged; the twentieth century came in chains. 'I am absolutely not to be pitied,' wrote Raymonde Sergent to her daughter Gisèle. Though there was no work to be done, there was any amount of 'culture, physical activities, dance, theatre, singing . . . There are not enough hours in the day to do all the things we want to do.'

*   *   *

On Trappe's orders, no contact of any kind was permitted between the men and women held prisoner in Romainville. But ways were found to hide notes in the cracks in the brickwork in the exercise yard, and to pass letters via a priest, who was allowed to visit the fort from time to time, or the prisoner who acted as doctor in the infirmary. By offering to do the men's laundry, it was very occasionally possible for the women to exchange a brief word or a note of encouragement, slipped among the clean clothes. The women were sometimes able to watch as the men exercised; on these days and on the theatrical Sunday afternoons they saw their faces and noted how they looked. Fourteen of the women had men in the hostage pool, and they lived in a state of dread. One of these was Betty, whose companion Lucien Dorland had been described in his Brigade Spéciale report as an extremely dangerous 'fanatical communist', from whom it had been impossible, under interrogation, to extract any information whatsoever. To her mother, Betty wrote that her main 'consolation and joy is to see him sometimes from my window'. Lucien, like the other men, had been tortured.

On the evening of 20 September, Betty and a number of other women were told that they might have a few minutes with their men. They were not particularly worried, for there had been no news of any armed attacks by the Resistance on the Germans. Betty was taken to Lucien's cell carrying with her a pair of woollen socks she had knitted for him. When the German guard who accompanied her remarked, 'Where he's going, he won't need them', she and Lucien agreed that what he probably meant was that the forty-six men in Romainville who had been told to prepare themselves for departure were going to be deported to a factory somewhere in Germany, where they would be provided with all the clothes they needed. '*Au revoir*, my beloved little wife,' Lucien wrote to Betty after she was taken back to her dormitory. 'I think it will be Compiègne and then deportation . . . We mustn't give up hope . . . events are moving at a giant stride.'

None of the women knew that on the evening of 17 September, just before ten o'clock, two bombs had gone off in central Paris by the Rex cinema, which had been requisitioned in 1940 by the Wehrmacht. Ten Germans had been killed and nineteen wounded. Oberg had immediately issued orders that 116 hostages were to be shot. They should all have come from Romainville, but the fort was low on hostages, having provided 88 for a mass execution in August, after which their places had not been filled. To the 46 available would be added 70 from the Fort du Hâ in Bordeaux. What this effectively meant was that men would be executed who had not only been in prison 600 kilometres away at the time of the attack, but who knew nothing at all about it.

Those chosen in Bordeaux included the farmers from around Cognac who had been arrested in July by Poinsot's men. Aminthe Guillon's husband and son, Prosper and Jean, were among them, as were Elisabeth Dupeyron's husband, arrested with the Guillons at Les Violettes, and Marguerite Valina's husband Lucien, with whom she had sheltered resisters from Poinsot's men. Lulu and Carmen's 19-year-old younger brother, arrested not long before and brought to Romainville, would have been among them, but he was in the infirmary with impetigo.

On Monday 21 September, at seven o'clock in the morning, the women in Romainville heard the sounds of marching boots and of men's voices singing the Marseillaise. Lorries with darkened windows were seen in the street outside the fort. Still wanting to believe that the men were on their way to the station at Compiègne, ready for deportation to Germany, the women were not unduly frightened. Six hundred kilometres away, the same performance was being enacted in the Fort du Hâ.

For several days, Romainville was full of rumours. The men's luggage was spotted still piled up outside the bunkers, but the women kept telling each other that it was probably waiting to travel on separately by another train. But then one of Lucien's friends was moved into the cell in which the forty-six men had spent the night of the 20th, and there on the walls he found, scratched in pencil, a single sentence: 'We are 46 men awaiting death, without regret, with pride and courage.' Asking a guard where the men had gone, he was told, 'You don't want to know . . . I'm sure you understand me.'

It was now that the woman learnt that the forty-six men had been taken in groups of five up the steep slope to the firing range at Mont-Valérien. Not one had agreed to have his eyes bandaged. After it was over, twelve bottles of cognac had been distributed among the members of the firing squad. The bodies had been cremated in Père Lachaise cemetery, with orders that the families were not to be informed. It was from a note hidden in a tube of aspirin and smuggled into the fort that the women discovered where the ashes were. 'They were so remarkable, those who fell,' wrote Marie-Claude in a letter smuggled out of the fort, 'that one has the impression that a whole lifetime would not suffice to be worthy of them or to avenge their deaths.' Only one of the

116 men executed in Paris and Bordeaux had actually been tried and convicted by a German tribunal for having carried out an attack on German soldiers. 'Some days,' wrote Danielle, 'I think that I have reached the limits of horror.'

For her part, Betty, usually so resilient and robust, was silenced by grief and horror. She found out from Lucien's friends that there had been another message written on the wall of the bunker by Lucien and addressed to her. 'Courage,' it said, 'dearest friend, this is a painful moment you must get through.' To her parents, she wrote short, despairing notes. 'He was so good; my heart is breaking. I loved him so much . . . We are all widows now . . . These executioners must really hate the young French, and especially the intellectuals. They are barbarians.' What she minded most was that she and Lucien had never had a child. She kept herself going by thinking of the moment when the war would be over and she would return to the house they had shared in Paris, and sit at the desk at which they had so often worked together. 'It was so good living with him, with his bohemian temperament and all our books . . . I think of only one thing, and that is getting out to avenge his death.'

There were now fourteen new widows in Romainville. Their friends did all they could. There was not much to say, but they held them close, hoping that the warmth and physical contact might lessen the pain. 'There are only widows here,' Betty wrote sadly to her parents. Many years later, one of the women described her last moments with her husband. 'When I was called that morning, something in me stopped, and nothing can set it off again, like the watch that stops when the wearer stops living.' But though she wanted to die, she chose to live, to defy the Germans, and not to yield to anyone. 'I had to hold fast to the end, and die of living.'

On 14 October, a new group of widows arrived to join them. Among the thirty women sent to Paris from Bordeaux were Marguerite Valina, Elisabeth Dupeyron and Yvette and Aminthe Guillon, whose husbands had been shot together at the Souge barracks on 21 September. With them came Madeleine Zani, the two sisters, Yolande and Aurore, and Annette Epaud, mother of Claude. None of the women had been permitted to see their small children before leaving.

A few hours before being taken out to be shot, Prosper and Jean Guillon had been given paper and pencils with which to write farewell notes to their wives. The pencils were blunt and the messages were scrawled unevenly on the rough sheets of paper. 'You, my dearest wife, you must try to forget and to remake your life,' Jean had written to Yvette. 'Forgive me if I have ever caused you pain . . . Goodbye for ever. I am going to die bravely and for the cause for which I fought.' Prosper's letter was shorter. 'I am going to die bravely,' he wrote to Aminthe, 'in spite of every-thing. Try to end your days as well as you can. My last thoughts are for you.' What neither man had known was that their wives were not safely back at the farm but in prison; nor did each of them know that the other was to die at the same time.

Oberg had counted on the fact that the savagery of the reprisals would deter further attacks. He was soon proved wrong. Within a couple of weeks, sixty-four more Germans were dead and prefects were reporting from around France that 'anti-German feelings are growing more and more violent'. Orders went out for another mass execution. But the *politique des otages* was clearly not working and the shootings were postponed while a new policy, that of deportation into *Nacht und Nebel*, was discussed.

Betty was living in the same dormitory as Madeleine Dissoubray and, as they did their morning exercises, they discussed plans to escape from the fort. Exploring the courtyard during their exercise periods, they decided that the only possible way would be to follow the drains into the sewers, hoping to emerge well beyond the fort's outer walls. The first part of the plan went well: they escaped below unnoticed. But before long they reached an iron grille barring the way out, and no amount of heaving or pushing would move it. Extremely downcast, they were forced to crawl back the way they had come. No one had noticed their absence. Keeping alive a spirit of resistance, even in the face of impossible odds, seemed to them essential. On the anniversary of the October revolution, they helped some of the men prisoners in the courtyard make a hammer and sickle, fashioned out of boxes and paper and stones; they considered the thirty days' punishment in the humid and dark cellars, without a mattress or blanket, well worth it.

Christmas was approaching. Charlotte and the women involved

in the theatrical afternoons, thinking it important to divert and involve those grieving for their husbands, redoubled their activities. Plans were made to put on a sketch about Joan of Arc, with Danielle as Joan and Marie-Claude as a German sentinel. Cécile began scrounging material for costumes; she could never act, she would later say, because sooner or later she always started to laugh. Poupette was learning her lines; she was not unhappy, listening to the older women as they talked about literature and politics. Once the older communist women realised that neither she nor her sister Marie had much interest in politics, despite their work for the Gaullist Johnny network, they made much fuss of them. Political differences no longer divided the women, for whom friendship and solidarity had become a way of warding off fear and hunger. There was talk about pooling food for a special Christmas lunch and getting hold of nuts, apples and *pain d'épice* (gingerbread) to celebrate the New Year. The women were busy knitting and making little presents for each other. But it was getting cold, and the mood in Romainville was sombre.

It was not much lighter in France as a whole. At 7a.m. on 11 November, in spite of Laval's frantic diplomatic attempts to prevent them, the Germans crossed the demarcation line and occupied the whole of France. Oberg and Knochen's men followed closely behind and soon the Gestapo were at work throughout the entire country. Vichy lost its zone of independence, its army, its fleet and its empire, though Pétain remained head of state. An earlier call for volunteers to go to work in German factories – with the promise that for every one volunteer, three prisoners of war would be released – had met with such little enthusiasm that a compulsory work scheme was being set up. Any Frenchman between the ages of 18 and 50 not in a job essential to the state would now become liable for the draft. All over France, resisters began to put up posters: 'Do not go to Germany!' Among the young men who had become rootless during the years of occupation, and to whom Vichy's views on collaboration and anti-Semitism seemed attractive, a militia was, however, taking shape. It would soon prove efficient in the capture and torture of resisters.

The one note of hope was to be found in a surge of young men, drawn into the Underground by the prospect of compulsory labour in Germany, who began to make their way into the forests and hills of rural France, to join the Maquis, which took its name from the Corsican for scrubland. All over the now wholly occupied regions of France, many of the small networks and larger Resistance movements were joining forces, brought together by shared political victimisation, by the persecution of the Jews and by such figures as Jean Moulin, bringing supplies, weapons and money from the Allies.

Although some of these networks were mistrustful of the Gaullists and communists alike, and the Resistance movements had periods when they were riven by animosities and rivalries, most subscribed to the idea of a vast assembly of resisters from which no faction should be excluded, and most professed at least a measure of confidence in de Gaulle's leadership. Another small act of progress was a new law, passed by Vichy in September, rescinding the 'incapacity' of women, which they had once shared with minors, the insane and convicted felons, a measure made necessary by the fact that there were now 800,000 women in France, most of them wives of prisoners of war, running their own households.

Now, perhaps more than ever before, the full meaning of occupation was impossible to ignore: 42,500 Jews already deported to the death camps (and not one of the trains bearing them there derailed by the Resistance), the whole of the country in the hands of the German military, the people hungry and miserable, facing their third winter without fuel, and many thousands of resisters either dead, in prison, or on their way to factories in Germany. In his monthly report, the Prefect of Eure-et-Loir noted that the people in his area had become apathetic and wretched: 'The spirit of Verdun has vanished, and a mood of terrifying individual egotism has taken hold.' Paris, in the grip of another cold winter, was grim.

* * *

Not long before Christmas 1942, one last group of women destined to join the others in exile arrived at Romainville. They were Polish, and not all of them spoke French. Drawn to France in the 1920s and 1930s by the pull of jobs in the north, they had planned to go home when circumstances allowed. They had been a tight-knit community, highly nationalistic, cooking Polish meals of sausage and red cabbage; and, on warm summer evenings, the men played polkas on their harmonicas. But the war and the Nazi persecution at home had trapped the Poles in France and with the armistice had come a Polish Resistance movement called POWN, under the former Polish Consul-General, Aleksander Kawalkowski, who went by the *nom de guerre* of Justyn. In the summer of 1942, the name Angelika, later changed to Monika, was given to a plan to help paralyse German troop movements in the event of an Allied landing; in the meantime, members helped with sabotage, the gathering of information and the smuggling of Jews out of France.

Into the net of David and his Brigades Spéciales, during the early autumn of 1942, had fallen a number of women working for Monika. Some were teachers, come to teach Polish in the mining communities; others worked in shops in Paris, helping repair radio transmitters for the Resistance, or using their homes to shelter Jews. And some were Frenchwomen, who happened to be married to Polish Jews and who had been caught up in the *rafles* of Parisian Jews.

The entire Brabander family – François, his wife Sophie, their daughter Hélène and younger son Romuald – arrived in Romainville together. François had fought with the French in the First World War, and after the armistice had joined the campaign to liberate Poland before finishing his medical studies and opening a surgery for the families of Polish miners living in France. After the fall of France, he tried to reach England with his wife and children via Spain but was turned back at the Spanish border. Resigned to remaining in France, he and Sophie joined the Monika network, until they were finally picked up by the Gestapo. For twenty-four hours, 19-year-old Hélène, who had been staying with a friend, avoided capture; but then she too was caught. In Romainville, François and Romuald spent a terrifying day in the bunker where the hostages about to be executed were kept, and were then transferred to the camp of Compiègne. Sophie and Hélène were put to share the dormitories with the Pican and Tintelin resisters.

Then there was Anne-Marie Ostrowska, who, though not Jewish herself, was married to a Polish Jew called Salomon, with whom she had set up a small leather workshop on the rue Oberkampf in Paris. As the racial laws had become ever more restrictive, so Salomon and their 19-year-old son Alfred tried to cross the demarcation line to safety in the south; but they were arrested and interned. Anne-Marie could think only of trying to find and save her husband and son. As a 'non-Jew', she was theoretically allowed to move around freely, but she and her 17-year-old daughter were picked up at Vierzon by the Gestapo. Since Anne-Marie was not Jewish, she was sent to Romainville; to her terror and misery, her daughter, considered a half-Jew, had been taken to the camp at Pithiviers and was now awaiting transfer to Drancy.

Just before Christmas, two other young Polish girls arrived at the fort. Their names were Karolina Konefal and Anna Nizinska and they were dressed like peasant girls, with enormous brightly coloured shawls. Their only possession was an alarm clock. They spoke no French. They seemed uncertain as to why they were in France at all, beyond the fact that they had been given the name of a man who worked with the Monika network.

Alice Viterbo, an Italian singer in her late forties, born in Alexandria in Egypt and who had sung at the Paris Opéra, reached Romainville on 15 December. Not long before the war, Alice had lost a leg in a car accident. No one could discover just what she had done in the Resistance but it was thought that she had helped a Gaullist network. She was a sunny presence, uncomplaining about her wooden leg, and she could often be heard singing in her dormitory. Alice was followed by 31-year-old Charlotte Decock, a metalworker from Nogent arrested after her resister husband escaped from prison, and held hostage in his place. Charlotte had been given leave to attend a christening, and could have used the occasion to escape, but voluntarily returned to prison. Her husband was persuaded by the family not to turn himself in. No one believed the Gestapo would really hold an innocent woman, mother of a 10-year-old boy and seven-year-old girl, for long. Charlotte was immediately popular; like Alice, she was certain that nothing bad would befall them, and that they would soon be on their way home. In her wake came Mitzy Ferry, a 24-year-old waitress who had been helping Jews across the demarcation line. Mitzy had spent three months in solitary confinement, manacled to the wall, and had been repeatedly tortured. The other women closed in round her and did what they could to comfort her. One of the last to join them was Georgette Rostaing, who had teetered so cheerfully around Ivry on her high heels.

Later, Pierrette would remember clinging to her hands and crying.

Even with the huge efforts made to keep up their spirits, many of the women gathered at Romainville were in mourning, whether for their lost husbands or for their children, scattered among grandparents and relations and not seen now for many months. Annette Epaud had managed to smuggle into the fort with her a photograph of her son Claude, in his beret. One of the men prisoners she met in the courtyard was an artist, and he offered to make a drawing from the photograph. It was an excellent likeness and she was very pleased that she now had two pictures of her son to look at. Those who had left babies behind, however, like Lulu and Madeleine Zani, were painfully conscious that they were missing all the stages of their infancy, as they learnt to talk and to walk; and that, already, the children would not know them. It was a bitter punishment that none had imagined.

*   *   *

The 9th of January 1943 was Danielle's 34th birthday. The women in her dormitory managed to have a bunch of flowers smuggled into the fort; all day, as she walked along the corridors and in the exercise yard the women she met presented her with little gifts, sewn from scraps of material, or cards, drawn and decorated on paper saved from the Red Cross parcels. 'You cannot imagine how fond we are of each other,' Danielle wrote to her parents, 'nor just how important each of us is to the others.' Friends had sent in a present of a pot of veal and carrots.

It was mid-January when Trappe suddenly announced that the women in Romainville would be allowed to receive and send letters. 'A wind of departure is blowing,' noted Marie-Claude, though she, like the others, thought it would be some months before they were actually freed. 'But I have in me a wealth of patience, so sure are we that the end is coming.' There were rumours that the Allies were about to take Tripoli, and that the Germans were facing defeat at Stalingrad. Poupette and Marie had just learnt that their mother had died of stomach cancer. When she heard the news, Marie fainted.

In July 1942, a first contingent of 1,170 *Nacht und Nebel* prisoners had left the nearby camp of Compiègne for an 'unknown destination'. They were all men. On board were metalworkers, plumbers, electricians, railwaymen, dockers, tailors, postmen and farmers. Ninety per cent were communists and all had been arrested for Resistance activities. One was Betty's uncle, Charles Passot. In Compiègne they had kept up their political studies, exercised and shared their food. Where they had gone, no one had any idea. With the realisation that mass executions had failed to deter resisters, and that deportation, especially cloaked in secrecy, might prove more effective, the Germans decided to send off a second train into the unknown, thereby disposing of the troublemaking women in Romainville.

On the evening of 22 January, just as they were going to bed in their dormitories, the women were called together and the names of 222 of them read out. They were instructed to keep just one small case, which they could carry themselves, with warm clothes. 'What fate awaits us?' Danielle wrote quickly to her parents. 'But never feel downhearted when you think about me . . . I feel I have energetic and youthful blood flowing in my veins.' Her companions, she said, were 'ready for anything'. She had just been informed that her brother, who was attached to the civil governor of Morocco, had arranged for her to be transferred to a prison in the south; but she had refused to go, saying that she needed to stay with the others. Her resolve was both a measure of how she perceived herself as their leader, and the fact that no one yet realised what danger they were in.

Marie-Claude Vaillant-Couturier's last letter from Romainville, written on 21 January 1943

To her mother, Marie-Claude wrote that she was taking with her a small volume of Rimbaud's poems, and that she was in very good physical shape, except that she seemed to have had an early menopause, 'but since this is more practical when travelling, I am not complaining'. Betty's letter to her parents was equally cheerful. Observing that she had already spent five months in La Santé and five in Romainville, she said that she thought she would be home before another five months were up.

Rumours filled the fort. Betty remembered that, during her many interrogations, she had been told that she was not very likely to be shot, but that what lay in store for her would probably be worse than death. Hélène Bolleau reminded the others of the remark she had overheard in Angoulême prison, when an officer told one of the guards that the Germans had 'other plans' for the women. But for the most part the women were excited: even labour in a German factory could not be worse than enforced idleness, uncertainty and too little food in the hands of the Gestapo. Marie-Elisa Nordmann urged Simone Sampaix, whom she had taken under her wing, to dress as warmly as possible for the journey, wearing the sweater and wool jacket that her mother had made for her, as well as an almost new overcoat given to her by one of the other prisoners; and to put on two pairs of woollen socks. They should wear as many layers as possible, the women agreed, in case they were going somewhere very cold. Poupette and Marie Alizon decided to take the fur scarves that they had brought with them from Rennes and clung on to during all the months of captivity.

No one slept much. Last-minute notes were written to families; bags were packed and unpacked. Guards came round bringing a loaf of bread and a 10-centimetre piece of sausage for each of the women, saying that they should make them last because the journey might take several days. On the 23rd, the women were driven to the camp at Compiègne, near the railway station, where eight other women, recently arrested or brought from other prisons, arrived to join them. They spent the night in bunks, in a vast hall.

One of these new eight women was Georgette, Danielle's organiser in Ivry. She had finally been caught by the Gestapo on 3 January, after a tip-off to the police by her concierge. From Compiègne, Georgette managed to smuggle out a letter to her family. She was, she said, 'sans linge, vivres et argent', without clean underclothes, food or money, everything having been taken from her. 'I leave to your care my Pépée . . . my little Pierrette . . . I kiss you with all my heart, our morale is very good . . . I'll be back soon'.

The morning of 24 January 1943 was damp and very cold. There were wisps of fog and low clouds. It was a Sunday. Just as it was getting light, the 230 women were taken to the station in lorries, escorted by German soldiers and French policemen, and led across to a siding known as the 'platform of the deportees'; there they were put on to four empty cattle trucks. On the way to the station they had shouted out to the few people already about; but these had looked away and hurried past. The front carriages of the train, already closed, contained 1,446 men, put on board the night before; among them was Georges Grünenberger, Simone's friend from the Bataillons de la Jeunesse. Between sixty and seventy women were directed to each of the first three cattle trucks; that left twenty-seven for the fourth, into which Charlotte, Danielle, Marie-Claude, Betty, Simone and Cécile climbed. Each contained half a bale of straw, which reminded Charlotte of a barn that needed sweeping. There was a barrel to serve as lavatory. What Madeleine Normand did not know – and would never learn – was that just as they were leaving Compiègne, her mother, sick with anxiety about her daughter, was dying.

The doors were closed and bolted. In the fuller carriages it was impossible for all the women to stretch out at the same time, so a rota was established, with half of them lying and half sitting, at any one time. Suitcases were piled up around the barrels, to stop them tipping over when the train began to move. In Charlotte's carriage, Jakoba van der Lee, a Dutch woman in her early fifties, who had once been married to an Arab sheikh, placed her black hat on top of her suitcase, unfolded her blanket and wrapped her magnificent otter coat around her legs. Of all the women on the train, the reason for her presence was perhaps the most absurd: she had written a letter to her brother in Holland, wistfully predicting Hitler's defeat. It had been intercepted by the Germans.

Before leaving, urged on by Marie-Elisa, who thought it important to record and remember the identity of each and every woman on the train, efforts had been made to establish names, ages, number of children and any small important facts about each one's story.

Of the 230, 119 were communists. Nine were not French. The majority came from every part and region of France, from Paris, Bordeaux, Brittany, Normandy, Aquitaine and along the banks of the Loire. They had sheltered resisters, written and copied out anti-German pamphlets, hidden weapons in shopping bags, helped carry out acts of sabotage. Twelve, of whom Raymonde Sergent was one, had been *passeurs*, guiding people across the demarcation line. Thirty-seven came from the Pican–Dallidet–Politzer *affaire*, seventeen from Tintelin's printers and technicians; forty had been active in and around Charente, Charente-Maritime and the Gironde. Some two dozen of the women on board – like Mme van der Lee – had had almost nothing to do with the Resistance, beyond making ill-judged remarks about the occupiers or having connections to resisters. There were the three *délatrices*, informers, their presence on board all the more peculiar in that they had supported, rather than opposed, the occupiers.

There was one doctor on the train, Adelaïde Hautval, one dentist, Danielle, and a midwife, Maï, and four chemists, of whom Marie-Elisa was one. There were farmers, shopkeepers, women who had worked in factories and in the post office, teachers, and secretaries. Twenty-one were dressmakers or seamstresses. A handful were students. One was a singer. Forty-two described themselves as housewives. Just over half were married and fifty-one had had their husband or lover shot by the Germans. Ninety-nine had between them 167 children, of whom the youngest was a baby of a few months. Marguerite Richier, a widow in her sixties, had given birth to seven children; two of her daughters, Odette and Armande, were on the train with her.

Of great importance, for what was about to happen to the women, was the fact that there were fifty-four who were aged 44 and over, though most were in their late twenties and early thirties. The youngest girl on the train was Rosa Floch, who had just celebrated her 17th birthday. The eldest was a 67-year-old widow from Chalon-sur-Saône, Marie Chaux, denounced for keeping her son's revolver, a memento of the First World War, in her kitchen drawer; though it was later discovered that she had also provided a safe house for resisters.

On board were also a number of families. Lulu and Carmen, Yolande and Aurore, were only two of several pairs of sisters; and there were six mothers and daughters, among them Emma and Hélène Bolleau, who had desperately tried but failed to be allowed to travel together in the same cattle truck. The entire Brabander family were on the train, the men in the front carriages, Hélène and Sophie at the back. The previous day, Dr Brabander, catching sight of his wife and daughter at Compiègne, had begged to be allowed to speak to them. Permission was refused. And there was Aimée Doridat and her sister-in-law Olga Godefroy, members of an extended family of communists from Nancy. Aimée was another woman who might have escaped, having been warned by a railway worker, using her eight-year-old son as messenger, that she would do well to go into hiding; but she did not want to leave her six brothers, all of whom had also been detained.

But most important of all was the fact that the women, despite differences of age, background, education and wealth, were friends. They had spent the months in Romainville very close together and it was as a train full of friends, who knew each other's strengths and frailties, who had kept each other company at moments of terrible anguish, and who had fallen into a pattern of looking after each other, that they set out for the unknown. Adelaïde, assuming that they were bound for a German factory, wondered how they would all manage, working together, mindful of one another.

One of the notes slipped through on to the tracks as the train crossed France

As the train pulled out of Compiègne, the women took pencils and scraps of paper out of their bags and began to write notes. Viva ended hers 'I will return', underlining the words. On one side they gave the names and addresses of their families and wrote that they were on a train, bound for some distant place, which they suspected would be Germany. Using nail files to gouge out knots in the wood of the carriage walls, they waited for the train to pause at a station before pushing the notes out, with a little money and a request that anyone who found them should send them on to their families. 'Look after Claude,' wrote Annette

Annette Epaud with her husband and son Claude

The drawing of Claude done in Romainville which
Annette kept always by her

Epaud to her family. And to her son: 'Maman t'embrasse, mon cher fils.' She had packed among her few things Claude's photograph and the little portrait of him done in Romainville. There was some talk of trying to escape from the train, but the doors were bolted on the outside.

As the first day wore on, the women took it in turns to keep watch at the holes, trying to make out the names of the places they passed through. At Chalôns-sur-Marne, where the train stopped, a railway worker walked along the side of the carriages, whispering, 'They're being defeated. They're losing Stalingrad. You'll be back soon. Be strong, girls.' At Metz, the French train driver was replaced by a German; it was the Gestapo who were now in charge. When a few of the women were allowed out to collect water for the others, a station guard told them, 'Make the most of it. You're going to a camp from which you'll never return.' His ominous words meant nothing to them. The women sang, songs remembered from their childhood, to keep cheerful.

It grew colder and in the dim light of the windowless cattle trucks the women huddled together, rubbing each other's backs. One of the women took Simone, whose teeth were chattering, into her arms. The buckets were soon full to the brim with urine, and it splashed out, but then it froze, which made it better. Though the bread and sausage were soon eaten, thirst was more tormenting than hunger and whenever the train paused in a station, the women begged for water; Marie-Claude kept shouting at the top of her voice: 'Give us something to drink, we're thirsty.' Nothing was given to them. Soon, they fell silent, trying to conserve their saliva. The second night, the train stopped at Halle so that the cars containing the men could be uncoupled; their destination, it turned out, was the concentration camp of Sachsenhausen, though at the time no one knew. The Brabander family, though they had yet to discover this, were now split up.

On Tuesday morning, 26 January 1943, the train stopped at Breslau, where the women were given tepid water to drink. It had become much colder and what little stubs of bread remained were frozen solid. They could hear Polish voices. When they moved off again, the women posted at the holes in the planks stared out at a vast white snowy landscape, deserted, flat and frozen. That night, the train stopped and did not move again.

Part Two

CHAPTER TEN

Le Convoi des 31000

It was not the cold that hit the women as the cattle truck doors were pulled back in the pale light of a Silesian dawn: they were cold already, so cold that almost all feeling had left their bodies. It was the noise. The first sounds were shouts, orders rattled out, fierce and rapid, the German words incomprehensible but the meaning – to hurry, to move, to climb down, to get into line, to leave the heavier suitcases – was plain. More frightening were the sounds made by the dogs, snarling, growling, barking as they pulled on their leads to get at the women.

One by one, helping each other, putting out a steadying hand, clutching one another's shoulders, trying not to fall or to panic, the 230 women climbed down on to rough ground, fearful and confused. They felt weak from lack of food and their mouths were parched from thirst. All around them stretched an enormous frozen plain, with trees in the distance. Deep snow, that looked as grey as the immense grey sky above, lay as far as the eye could see. Stiff and shocked, huddling close together, they shuffled into ragged lines of five, one behind the other, as ordered by the shouting soldiers. Among the SS men with guns were a number of women, in long black capes, their hoods high above military caps, and tall black leather boots. They reminded Poupette of crows. The SS had truncheons and whips. The platform, with its single line, stood out in the countryside on its own; there were no buildings, no station.

The order was given to march. Marie-Claude, who spoke good German, translated, and her words were repeated back down the line. As they moved off across the icy, slippery, uneven ground in their thin shoes, they saw approaching in the half-light a group of women who seemed to belong to another world, emaciated, stumbling, their heads shaven and wearing a grotesque assortment of ill-fitting clothes, most of them striped. The smell the women gave off was repugnant, unidentifiable. 'How filthy they are,' Lulu said to her neighbours. 'They could at least wash.' Simone noticed that the women's faces were almost purple with cold. In the distance they could now see lights, hung at regular distances across a vast area.

A little further on they encountered a party of thin, ragged men, wearing the same striped clothes. None replied to their calls. As they walked, Jacqueline, the young secretary with the very sweet voice, began to sing the Marseillaise, soon picked up by a 23-year-old locksmith's daughter called Raymonde Salez, who had taken part in an attack on the German bookshop in Paris, and then, in ones and twos by the others. The women straightened their shoulders and tried to stand taller. So it was that singing loudly the 230 women approached the double rows of barbed wire and the watchtowers and passed under the sign that said *Arbeit Macht Frei* and into the camp, where other women, amazed to hear such sounds, opened the windows of their huts to listen. The Frenchwomen had no idea where they were, though Marie-Claude had translated a sign nailed to a post spotted along the way: *Vernichtungslager*. '*Nichts*,' she said, 'nothing, nothingness, toward nothing.' Had they heard the words Auschwitz or Birkenau, they would have meant nothing to them.

*   *   *

In the summer of 1941, Heinrich Himmler, supreme head of the SS and chief of the German police, appointed a former sergeant in the German army, a man called Rudolf Hoess who had been sentenced to ten years in prison for murdering a teacher suspected of treachery, as commandant of the new camp of Auschwitz in Silesia. This camp, he told him, was to be different from the several hundred concentration, slave and prisoner-of-war camps already scattered around Germany and occupied Europe. It was going to be an extermination camp, 'the largest such centre of all times', and Hoess was to come up with ideas as to how it could function most effectively.

Hoess was not a sadist in the way of Eichmann, but he was obsessed with order, duty, obedience and efficiency. He had a model for how a concentration camp should be run, based on Theodor Eicke's camp at Dachau, opened in 1933 to take the 'dangerous enemies of the state': political opponents, clergymen, Jews, Jehovah's Witnesses, beggars, the mentally ill. Here the SS had been trained to humiliate and torture their prisoners, and were themselves subject to collective punishments designed to destroy all sense of self-worth and to pit one against another. The camps, as Eicke created them, were closed worlds, where inhumanity was routine, barbarity the norm, and the inmates reduced to filthy, diseased animals, whose deaths from hunger, sickness and brutality were all part of the system. But what Hoess was now ordered to come up with was a killing machine, a means of getting rid of people efficiently and rapidly, particularly in view of the Final Solution currently being discussed: the extermination of the Jews of Europe, and in their wake others the Reich might wish to discard and eliminate. As he would later say, by the time the war was coming to an end, he was commandant of the greatest facility for mass murder in the history of man.

The first camp, Auschwitz proper, had opened on the edge of a small Polish district town called Oswiecim, 30 kilometres from Katowice, the industrial heart of Silesia, which had been annexed by the Reich in 1939. Here had been sent three hundred Jews from Oswiecim to tear down an old Polish cavalry barracks and evict twelve hundred people living in nearby shacks and cabins. They were soon followed by Soviet prisoners of war who continued to level the ground and work on the new camp, but who died in tens of thousands from lack of food and water, disease and the savagery of the guards set to watch over them. The marshes around the confluence of the Vistula and the Sola were extremely unhealthy, and in winter an icy wind blew from the east; in the spring, when the melting snows left a thick gluey mud, little grew.

Part of this foggy, humid valley of swamps was Birkenau, whose name in German meant birch grove. When Himmler visited the area in March 1941 plans were discussed to build a second camp here for 100,000 prisoners of war as well as for slave workers for a new industrial IG Farben plant, whose synthetic chemistry was crucial to the German war effort. The site, surrounded by mines, quarries and lime pits, with plentiful water, was also well provided with railway links. It was not long after work began on Birkenau that Himmler informed Hoess that the Final Solution was to be implemented and that the extermination of Europe's Jews was now official policy, with Birkenau as a main killing centre. The question was: how to kill great numbers of people without a blood bath, which upset the executioners? And how to dispose of their bodies? Mass machine-gunning and toxic injections to the heart by phenol were messy and unreliable. Something aseptic and impersonal was needed.

The barracks at Birkenau

Collective gassing using motors had already been tried out, but proved too limited. Hoess's deputy, Karl Fritzch, suggested experimenting with Zyklon B, a poison used on rats and cockroaches and produced by a subsidiary of IG Farben, Degesch. It came in the form of pellets the size of haricot beans, which, soaked in prussic acid, turned into gas in enclosed and packed spaces. Zyklon B rendered people unconscious in just a few minutes. A first trial was carried out on six hundred Soviet prisoners of war and two hundred sick men and Hoess was delighted with the result: there was no blood and no distress to the executioners. The first purpose-built gas chamber, in an isolated farmhouse, was ready for use in

January 1942, a year before the French women reached Birkenau; a second, in another farmhouse, opened in June. Between them, they could gas to death two thousand people a day. The bodies were at first buried in vast pits, but later, for greater efficiency, they were drenched with oil and wood alcohol and burnt.

But the camps at Auschwitz and Birkenau had a second purpose, which by the end of 1942 was becoming essential to the Germans. With more and more soldiers tied up on the eastern front, and a growing shortage of armaments and supplies for the army, the camps were turning into important centres of slave labour: the strong and the fit were picked out and sent to one of the many industrial enterprises springing up around the camps, the weak and the infirm 'selected' on arrival and sent straight to the gas chambers. Destruction by punishing, backbreaking, brutal work would serve the ultimate goal of extermination as effectively as instant killing, with the added advantage of providing for the German war effort in the meantime. As an SS officer was heard to say: 'You are all condemned to die but the execution of your sentence will take a little time.'

By early 1943, IG Farben's presence, along with that of other major industrial concerns, was already contributing to the camp's expansion and eventual evolution into the Nazis' main industrialised killing centre. Under pressure to increase the supply of synthetic fuel, IG Farben's men were proving as brutal as the SS guards, meeting the trains as they arrived to select welders, chemists and electricians. There was no mercy for the frail. The quarries, mines, factories and marshes were already death traps for emaciated, sick, underfed men and women, without protective clothing, harried by dogs, permanently terrified.

By the time the French women arrived in Birkenau, the camp's dual activities were just reaching their full potential. Every new train, for the most part filled with Jews from the ghettos of Holland, France, Belgium, Greece, Germany, Yugoslavia, Czechoslovakia and Poland, brought a small number – perhaps 10 to 15 per cent of the total – of people judged fit enough to be worked to death. The rest – the elderly, the infirm, the children, the women with babies or who were pregnant – were sent straight from the railway siding to the gas chambers.

Four new crematoria, built by Topf and Sons, were almost

completed, together with underground undressing rooms, which would not only vastly speed up the process of extermination – in theory 4,416 people would be 'processed' every twenty-four hours – but remove the smell of burning flesh that hung over the surrounding countryside. Under the new streamlined system, teams of *Sonderkommando* prisoners* loaded the ovens, having extracted gold from teeth for shipment back to the Reichsbank in ingots, shorn the hair for later use as felt and thread, removed the ashes from the grates and taken the crushed residue by lorry to the river Vistula. The forty-fourth transport of French Jews from Drancy reached Birkenau shortly before the arrival of the French women. All but a very few of the people on board had been gassed. Plans were now pushing ahead to receive the gypsy populations of occupied Europe.

Alongside its function as a death and labour camp, Birkenau had, since the late spring of 1942, been the main women's camp in the Auschwitz complex. Here, in January 1943, were living some 15,000 women from every corner of Europe, in conditions worse than those in all other parts of the camp. There was appalling overcrowding, a chronic lack of water, and latrines which were no more than open concrete sewers deep in mud and excrement. Together with endemic typhus, dysentery, tuberculosis, scabies and impetigo, the women suffered from abscesses that seemed never to heal. Already severely malnourished, they were dying at the rate of about a fifth of their number every month. Debilitated, covered in sores, their limbs bloated, they inhabited a world in which all normal patterns of behaviour had broken down, in which men and women of the SS, free of constraints, exercised a reign of violence, corruption and depersonalisation, in which not to steal or to lie would most likely result in death, and in which the worst traits to be found in human beings, not their best ones, were rewarded. And over them presided a hierarchy of female *kapos*, inmate supervisors and *Blockältesten*, 'block elders', for the most part German criminal prisoners who effectively collaborated with the SS, whose own survival depended on brutality and whose viciousness and vindictiveness was said far

---

* The name given to teams of men prisoners, kept separate and alive to work the crematoria, before themselves being gassed and incinerated.

to surpass that of their male counterparts.* Later, Rudolf Höss would write of the women of Birkenau that they 'stumbled about like ghosts, without any will of their own . . . These stumbling corpses were a terrible sight.'

It was in this version of hell that the 230 French women, some of them in their late fifties or early sixties, others still schoolgirls, accustomed to having enough to eat, warm beds to sleep in, clean clothes and the civility and decency of strangers, now found themselves.

*   *   *

Marching raggedly in their rows of five, keeping pace as best they could, clinging on to their few possessions, Charlotte in the fur hat given to her by Louis Jouvet, Mme van der Lee in her otter coat, the women were directed towards a building just inside the perimeter of the camp. What they saw, stretching in orderly lines over an immense white snowy field, were barracks, single-storey structures made of wood or stone, somewhat like stables with small windows. There was a corpse lying in their path. Too shocked to take much in, they jostled against each other and stepped over it.

There was no heat in the barracks into which they were led, but, after their agonisingly cold, faltering, slithering walk, they were pleased to sit down, even if all they could find to sit on were the edges of stone and wooden slatted bunks that rose in tiers to the ceiling. At midday, two prisoners in striped clothes arrived with a cauldron of hot liquid, a thin gruel-like soup made of grasses, and red enamel bowls were handed out. Not everyone drank the soup, saying that the bowls had a fetid, sickening smell, and that they would prefer to wait for the bread. There was no bread, they were told, and they would do better to eat whatever came their way. It was only later that they learnt that the smell that stuck to the bowls came from the fact that the women in the barracks, suffering from dysentery, could not always reach the latrines in the night and used

---

* The SS chose the prisoners most willing to do their bidding, gave them some privileges and special armbands and set them, with almost unlimited power, over the others: *kapos* to oversee work commandos, *Blockältesten* to maintain order, *Lagerältesten* who reported directly to the camp commandant.

the bowls instead. As the French women hesitated, the Germans and the Poles who were already in the barracks when they arrived pressed forwards, fighting each other to get at the soup.

Inside one of the women's barracks

After this, the doors to the barracks opened and a group of SS men entered. One stepped forward and asked whether there was a dentist among the French women, the camp dentist having recently died. Danielle put her hand up and was led out.

Now began the process of induction into the life of Birkenau. The women's names were called out, with Marie-Claude acting as interpreter. They were told to undress, put their clothes and all their other belongings, including any photographs of their families, into their cases and mark these with their names. By some sleight of hand, Charlotte managed to hold on to her watch. Forced to hand over her photograph of Claude, Annette Epaud found a way of hiding the little drawing of him.

They were led into a room where other prisoners were waiting with scissors to cut their hair, getting as close to the scalp as possible. Their pubic hair was also clipped while another woman wiped the shorn and bald parts with a rag dipped in petrol as a disinfectant. 'Look,' said Josée Alonso, who went first and whose good humour had done so much to cheer them up in Romainville, 'you will all be able to look just as elegant as me.' When it came to the turn of 18-year-old Hélène Brabander, whose doctor father François and brother Romuald had been unloaded from the train at Sachsenhausen, her mother Sophie took the scissors and cut her daughter's hair herself. Janine Herschel, one of the very few Jews on the train – though, having used a false certificate of baptism, no one knew that she was Jewish – offered an SS guard her gold watch, studded with diamonds, in return for sparing her bleached, blond hair. The SS man took the watch and Janine's hair was chopped off anyway.

As there was not enough water for a shower, they were next led, naked, into a room full of steam. Some of the women had never taken their clothes off in front of strangers before. They shrank back as SS guards, men and women, came in and laughed at their naked bodies. Simone, looking around desperately for a face she recognised among the bald heads, heard Cécile call out: 'Come here, come and sit with us.

Women prisoners in Birkenau, soon after arrival

After this came the tattoo, a series of pricks, each woman's number taken from the transport on which she reached the camp – theirs was the transport of the 31000 – traced on the inside of their lower left arm by a French Jewish prisoner, who assured them that it would not hurt. They felt that they were being branded, like cattle. Charlotte became number 31,661, Cécile 31,650, Betty 31,668. The 230 women, for ever after, would be known as *Le Convoi des 31000*.

Next, still naked, they were led into yet another room, this one full of what looked like rags piled up on the floor, where other prisoners were waiting to issue each woman with a sleeveless vest, a pair of grey knickers reaching to the knees, a scarf, a dress, a jacket and rough grey socks and stockings without elastic. The outer garments were all made of the same striped material. They took what they were given, regardless of size, the large women crammed into small dresses, the small enveloped in sacklike jackets. Worse, the clothes were filthy, spotted with blood and pus and faeces, and damp from some rudimentary attempts at disinfection. When Simone's turn came to get shoes, all that were left were clogs, with a band of material roughly nailed over the top, which meant that her toes and heels were bare. It made walking hard. Mado got slippers of torn felt.

Their last task was to sew on to each jacket and dress their personal numbers, as well as an F, for French, and a red triangle. Asking what this meant, they were told that it denoted their status as political prisoners, those held for 'anti-German activities', and that they would do well to learn the meaning of the other symbols: green for the criminal prisoners, purple for the Jehovah's Witnesses, black for the 'asocials', pink for homosexuals, a six-pointed Star of David for the Jews. Some prisoners wore a combination of symbols – as Jews, 'race defilers', recidivists and criminals.

The women discovered that they were regarded as 'dangerous', and that the other prisoners had been ordered to turn their backs as they passed by. A Dutch woman in the sewing room asked: 'How many are you?' Told that there were 230 of them, she said: 'In a month, there will only be thirty of you.' She herself, she added, had been one of a thousand women arriving on a train from Holland in October: now she was the only one left alive. Had the others

Simone, Charlotte, Betty and Emma, taken soon after arriving
in Birkenau

been executed? No, she replied, they died after the roll calls, hours and hours standing still in the snow and ice. It was easier, more comforting, not to believe her. When the French women left to return to the barracks, the icy cold froze their damp clothes stiff.

Block 14, where the women were taken, to their immense relief all together, was a quarantine block; it was here that they were to spend the first fortnight in Birkenau, though one morning they were marched off to the men's camp, to be photographed and measured. Spared the work details that would later take them to the factories, brickyards and marshes, they were not let off the roll calls; all too soon, they understood the Dutch woman's warning. At 3.30 in the morning, long before it grew light, every woman in the camp was harried out of her bunk and barracks by *kapos* with whips, to stand in the gluey mud and snow to await the arrival of the SS to count them.

From the first, the French women clung together, in groups, each slipping her hands under the arms of the woman in front, the rows constantly changing place so that no one spent too long on the outside. 'We held on to each other,' Madeleine Dissoubray would later say. 'If someone was particularly cold, we just kept them in the middle.' Using Charlotte's watch, they decided that they would swap places every fifteen minutes. To deal with the extreme cold, Charlotte tried to pretend she was somewhere else, to recite poems to herself in order 'to remain me', but the reality of the cold and exhaustion was too overwhelming. One of the women was having trouble standing up, and a guard hit her. Adelaïde went over to help her and was hit herself. The French women felt terrified and confused.

With the dawn, the count began. When the numbers did not tally, the counting started again. The rows had to be neat, the squares of women perfectly formed up. The guards shouted, shoved, dealt out blows; the dogs growled and snapped. Roll calls could last several hours; they were repeated at the end of each day. It was impossible to clean off the mud and excrement that clung to the women's feet, and mud haunted their dreams. Lulu kept thinking of the mud and trenches of the First World War, and of her father at Verdun. To fall during roll call could mean death, for there was no way to clean or change and the wet muddy clothes froze on their backs. To lose shoes could also bring death, for there were no others. Women spotted barefoot were often sent straight to the gas chambers, women being easier to replace than shoes. Every dawn, Charlotte wondered whether she would survive another day. One morning she fainted, but was caught and slapped by Viva to bring her round.

*   *   *

Even as the French women reached Birkenau, it was clear that not all would, or could, or would choose, to survive. A look of death became imprinted on some of their faces. There was something too degrading, too shocking for some of the women to bear. Using the latrines meant wading through excrement and crouching over a long open sewer, trying not to fall in. Accustomed to order and predictability, they had neither the strength nor the desire to adjust to a world whose rules seemed so arbitrary and so barbaric.

The first to die were the older women, but precisely what they died of would be hard to say, other than of shock. Marie Gabb, who was 53 and had belonged to the Resistance networks around Tours, died on the first day in Birkenau, even before the roll call. Soon after, at the second roll call, Léona Bouillard slipped to the ground; when her neighbours tried to lift her up, they found that she was dead. Léona was 57 and came from the Ardennes and she had become popular among the younger women for her kind ways; they thought of her as their grandmother and called her Nanna Bouillard. Four of the others carried her body back to the barracks.

After her came 50-year-old Léa Lambert, who had sheltered prisoners escaping from Germany. Then Suzanne Costentin, a schoolteacher friend of Madeleine's and Germaine's, arrested for writing a tract about the men shot as hostages, who was beaten by a guard so badly that her body was bruised all over. Suzanne died when her fingers and toes became so frozen with frostbite and gangrene that she could no longer climb on to her bunk. Yvonne Cavé, whose parents ran a mushroom farm and whose only crime seems to have been that she had cursed a young Frenchman, preening in his new uniform as a German volunteer, died because her shoes were stolen in the night. Forced to go barefoot to the morning roll call, which was particularly long that day, she got frostbite in her feet. All day her legs became more and more swollen; she died, as dusk was falling.

Neither Antoine Bibault, nor Jeanne Hervé, nor Lucienne Ferre – the three suspected *délatrices*, believed to have informed on the Resistance – survived for long. Ostracised by the group, they rapidly became defenceless. Many years later, asked why they died so quickly, Cécile would only say: 'They died. That's all.' Knowing that she did not have long to live, Lucienne said to Hélène Bolleau: 'Well, I only got what I deserved.' She was 21.

When the women had been in Birkenau about a week, the roll call one morning took a slightly different form. An SS doctor asked, in a surprisingly mild voice, whether there were any women among them who felt too fragile for these long roll calls and would rather skip them altogether? Magda, the Czech *kapo* of Block 14, a woman the others were coming to like, nudged Marie-Claude who, without pausing in her translation, added the words: 'but it is better not to admit to it'. Several of the women, whose hands were already raised, put them down, but not Marie Chaux, the widow from Chalon-sur-Saône, who had sheltered resisters in her boarding house. Mme Chaux was a very short woman, and she was standing at the back. Rising on to her tiptoes, she called out: 'Me. I'm 67.' And then Marie Dubois, whose cafe in Saint-Denis had been a meeting place and mail drop for the Resistance, put up her hand too, though Marie-Elisa Nordmann, standing next to her, begged her not to. 'Stay with us. You don't know where they will take you.' But Mme Dubois kept her hand up anyway. '*Komm*,' said the SS doctor and led the two women away, but where they were taken no one knew. When Cécile asked a Jewish girl in the barracks what had happened to her parents, and was told that they had 'gone up in smoke', she still didn't understand what this meant.

What was clear to the younger, stronger women, particularly those who like Cécile were used to hard lives and the discipline of the Communist Party, was that in order to survive the women would have to take some kind of control over what was happening to them. They could not, they told each other, become victims, vulnerable to every twist of chance. They needed to organise themselves, to try to understand their surroundings, so that they could navigate the dangers and respond quickly enough to the orders shouted at them in the camp jargon, with its mixture of Polish, Yiddish, Silesian and German.

On the third morning, returning from the roll call stiff, cold and hungry, Maï, Viva and Charlotte suggested that the women all do gymnastics together. It would make them strong, they said, give them energy and hope. Forcing their companions outside, to jump and stretch, they were seen by a group of other women, themselves on their way to a work detail. 'You must be mad,' one of them called out. 'Don't use up your energy. You are going to need it.' Maï tried to start folk dances. The women knew that they looked absurd, as Adelaïde later wrote, shuffling awkwardly around in their ill-fitting striped clothes, 'but it gave us a feeling of being ourselves'. The full horror of Birkenau was still to hit them.

It was not long in coming. On 10 February, when they had been in the camp a fortnight, the entire contingent of 15,000 women was roused at 3 a.m. for roll call. Only this time, no order came for them to return to their barracks. Dawn came and went. A bitter wind blew from the Carpathian mountains and their breath seemed to freeze inside their heads. It was a blue, clear, sparkling day and the sun on the snow was hard and blinding. The women stood, inert, glacially cold. The SS guards, in their heavy capes and great-coats, circled with dogs, also wrapped up in warm coats. An SS officer on horseback came to look, then rode away. 'Stay still,' called out Marie-Claude, 'stay calm.' Charlotte noted that there were no birds other than crows in the vast frozen plain that surrounded them.

Here and there, in ones and twos, breaking the neat pattern of the rows, women began to fall and to lie still in the snow. The hours passed. The living tried to rub one another's backs, to talk to one another. When they stamped their feet, it made no sound in the snow. Madeleine said to Simone, who was standing next to her, 'Move your feet inside your socks.' 'I can't,' Simone replied, 'I don't have my socks, I lost them.' Her neighbours now crowded more closely round her and forced her to move her feet.

Towards the end of the morning, the sound of lorries was heard. Turning their heads to watch, the women saw that they were full of bodies, naked corpses piled one on top of another, arms and legs jutting out at different angles. A whisper passed down the lines: 'They are emptying Block 25.' Block 25, as they now knew, was the antechamber of death, the barracks to which the frail and sick were taken to die. What was so terrifying was that not all the bodies were still, and as the lorries passed, among the shorn, boy-like, narrow heads could be seen living faces calling out for help. On one lorry, standing upright in a posture that conveyed both dignity and hatred, stood a very young woman, her head newly shaved. 'As for us,' Charlotte would later write, 'we were walled in the ice, the light, the silence.'

It was getting dark when the order was finally given to move. The landscape had grown hazy in the dusk and the edges of the trees were blurred. Even then, the ordeal was not over. Stumbling, taking what Charlotte described as 'shrunken' steps, leaning on one another, walking as if automatically on legs so cold that they had no feeling of any kind, the women set out slowly and silently for the barracks. All around lay the bodies of those who had fallen during the day. It made Marie-Claude think of a battlefield strewn with corpses. The snow, as far as the eye could see, was spotted with diarrhoea. Simone's bare feet refused to move and Madeleine took hold of her and pulled her forward. Later, Simone would remember that, unable to speak, her body paralysed, she had kept repeating to herself: 'I will get through this. I will.'

As they neared the gates, Josée, who was walking at the front, sent back an urgent message down the lines: 'When you get near, run.' It was now that the women perceived that two rows of SS guards, men and women, and *kapos* as well, had formed, each holding a truncheon, whip or belt, leaving a corridor down which the women were to pass, shouting 'Schnell! Schnell!' Scrambling, jostling, holding their frozen arms above their heads to ward off the blows, the women began to run. Hélène Bolleau, standing near her mother Emma, took her arm to help her. As they ran, the stragglers were hooked out of the line by the guards and thrown to one side. Hélène Solomon was helping Alice Viterbo, whose wooden leg made running in the snow all but impossible. She told her to cling hard to her coat. But then Alice fell, and Hélène found herself alone. Looking back, she saw that Alice had been caught and pulled out of the line. She ran on.

In the barracks, there was a desperate count. 'Who is back? Where is Viva? Is Charlotte here?' They counted again and again: fourteen were missing. The other women, in silence, waited; no one else arrived.

The *kapo* Magda appeared and called for volunteers to collect the bodies of those who had fallen. She wanted to take Simone, but Simone, shocked and frozen, was in no shape to move. Cécile volunteered to take her place. She wanted, she said, to see what had happened to everyone. When she came back, she was crying. Collecting the bodies, in a long line of women with stretchers bearing away the dead, she had come across a woman who was still alive and who had clutched desperately at her ankle, begging to be saved. But then a guard saw her and cracked her head with his truncheon. As Cécile talked, her teeth chattering and tears running down her cheeks, the other women crowded around her, rubbing her back, to comfort and warm her.

That day, 10 February 1943, a thousand women died in Birkenau. It was later claimed that the *course*, the race, was an act of revenge on the part of the SS. On 2 February, Stalingrad had finally fallen to the Russians; 100,000 German soldiers and twenty-five generals had been taken prisoner.

Among the fourteen French women who died were Mme van der Lee, whose otter coat had long since gone to warm the guards, and who was said by those close to her to have lost her mind, standing all those hours in the cold; and Sophie Brabander, whose daughter Hélène could do nothing to help her; and Yvonne B., whose surname was never spelt out to protect her identity, and who was a farmer's wife from Indre-et-Loire, aged only 24 and pregnant. Had Yvonne told the guards at Romainville that she was pregnant, instead of being too embarrassed to come forward, she might never have been sent to Birkenau at all; but Yvonne's husband had been a prisoner of war in Germany since 1940, and she felt ashamed.

Forty-five-year-old Sophie Gigand died too, but how much she minded no one was sure because her daughter Andrée, who was 21, had died soon after arriving at the camp, almost unnoticed in the crowd of dazed women. Aminthe Guillon was dead, though Yvette, her daughter-in-law, had struggled back to safety. The causes of these deaths, recorded in the camp register, were assigned randomly; some days, all deaths were noted as being due to pneumonia, others all to heart failure. Aminthe was said to have died from a blocked heart valve. The deaths filled the survivors with dread. If all these women could die, so suddenly, so arbitrarily, how could they hope to live? Later, looking at all the bodies piled up outside Block 25, trying to find their friends, the women saw rats, the size of cats, digging among the frozen corpses. For a while, Alice Viterbo, taken to Block 25 after falling in the snow with her wooden leg, stayed alive. From their barracks the other women could see her at the window. Alice kept calling out, begging them to get Danielle to bring her some poison. Then one morning Simone caught sight of something lying in the snow. When she went over, she discovered that it was Alice's wooden leg. She called the others, and they went to look. For several weeks it lay there, and then one day it was gone.

Twenty-seven of the French women were now dead. They had died still not knowing where they were. Two days later, the survivors were moved from Block 14 to Block 26. It was now, Poupette would later write, that they discovered the true meaning of hell.

* * *

Terrible as the roll calls were, their stay in quarantine had allowed the French women to spend the hours in between in relative shelter and safety. Moved to Block 26, they found themselves sharing the space with a number of Polish women, eight to a bunk in something that looked rather like an open rabbit hutch. The bottom bunk was on the earth, permanently damp from melted snow and urine. They lay head to toe, twenty-four to a hutch, eight to a bunk, sharing their thin cotton blankets. Next morning the assignment to work tasks began. It was seventeen days since the women had washed or changed their clothes, and many more since they had last eaten a proper meal. They were weak, hungry and exhausted. After a bowl of watery ersatz coffee and the interminable morning roll call, they were now marched out of the camp, through squalls of snow and wind that felt as if it were a solid wall.

In the spring of 1943 work was continuing on the expansion of Birkenau: there were still buildings to be knocked down and cleared and the marshes were being drained for agricultural projects or to be made into fish ponds. On the first morning, the women were walked, for almost two hours, in their lines of five, the guards shouting 'Links! Zwei! Drei!', holding one another's arms so as not to slip on the ice in their ill-fitting shoes. To keep up their spirits, they sang. It was so foggy that Charlotte Delbo kept worrying that they would become separated. Those whose swollen legs made walking hard were supported by the others. When they reached a swampy field, they were given shovels and hods, wheelbarrows without wheels, which had to be loaded with mud and stones and carried to a ditch to be emptied. All day, except for a pause in the late morning when a tepid, thin soup of swedes and cabbage arrived, they dug through the ice, lifted and shovelled, staggering and falling under the weight. With the temperature far below zero, the metal stuck to their hands.

When a pale sun rose and the ice began to melt, their feet sank ever deeper into the mud so that they were soon standing ankle deep in freezing mud and water. Women unaccustomed to physical work, whose lives had been spent in offices or schoolrooms, found the work acutely painful. Their backs, arms and legs ached. The SS guards, well fed and warmly dressed, lit fires, around which they crouched, and if the women paused in their work, sent the

dogs over to snap at their heels, or came themselves to deal out blows. From all over the misty field could be heard shouts and cries of pain. Charlotte, watching the rows of women at work, thought that they looked like ants, 'a frieze of shadows against the light'. Viva and Lulu, strong and cheerful by temperament, did their best to keep the spirits of the others up. The shovels grew heavier and heavier. The women felt feverish. At dusk, when the whistle blew to stop work, it was found that every French woman had survived the day. Not all the Poles had, and they had to wait for the bodies of the dead to be collected. Then came the two-hour walk back to camp and the evening roll call. It was dark by the time they got back to their barracks.

When the women had been in Birkenau for about three weeks, a transport arrived from Paris, bringing more Jews from Drancy. On it was Gisèle Kotlerewsky, whose mother Marguerite – who was not Jewish – was with the French women in Block 26. Gisèle, who was 19, was not selected with most of the others at the ramp, but directed to join the workers' camp. That night she came to find her mother. They clung to each other and wept. Then Gisèle suddenly turned on her mother and cried out: 'Why am I Jewish? Why is this happening to me? You see what you've done! Look at me!' Marguerite was mortified and wretched. Soon after, coming to see her mother again, Gisèle was beaten by one of the SS guards, who crushed her nose and badly injured one eye. Marguerite managed to get hold of some water and bathed her daughter's face; but a few days later Gisèle died. Marguerite stopped eating; then she, too, died. Hélène Bolleau saw her body lying in a pile outside Block 25.

Half a litre of black coffee in the morning, watery soup at midday, 300 grams of bread with either – if they were lucky – a scrape of margarine, a bit of sausage, cheese or jam at night, was not enough to stop the women's bodies shrinking and feeding on themselves, the fat disappearing first and then the muscles. The food never varied. It left the prisoners famished, bloated and constantly needing to urinate, their stomachs swollen as if pregnant. Cécile continued to say that it was not as bad for her, since she had spent most of her childhood hungry, but Marie Alizon, who had arrived in Birkenau a healthy, energetic young woman, was tormented by cravings for food.

One night, Simone dreamt that a horse bent over her and she was so hungry that she took a knife and cut a piece of its flesh, but then the horse began to cry and she cried too. They were all growing scrawny, angular, their bones beginning to protrude. Their shaven heads, where the hair had grown back in tufts and clumps, made Simone think of porcupines; their faces were pinched and sallow and seemed longer and more lined. Their breasts had disappeared, or fell in loose folds. Plagued by lice and fleas, so numerous that in the sunlight they looked like ants, the women scratched continuously. Many had sores that festered and suppurated and would not heal. When they walked to the marshes, they had the gait of long-term prisoners, their heads and necks stuck forward, as if pulling the weight of their reluctant bodies behind them, their legs shapeless and swollen, their lips black from cold or red from bleeding gums. Jacqueline, whose musical voice had given them hope, developed an abscess on her shoulder, which quickly spread. As she lay dying, her body was covered in lice.

But it was the thirst rather than hunger that haunted Charlotte, agonising, unceasing thirst that made her jaws lock together and her teeth feel as if they were glued to her cheeks. The women's camp had just one tap for 12,000 prisoners, and it was fiercely guarded by the green triangles, the German criminal prisoners.

Charlotte became increasingly obsessed. To the horror and fear of the others, walking one morning towards the marshes, she left the line and went over to a brook to lick the ice. The guards did not see her. Later, she drank the muddy water of the marshes. At night, back in the barracks, she exchanged her small portion of bread for a mug of tea. She dreamt of oranges, their juice flowing down her throat.

Then came the day when, assigned to a tree planting detail with Viva and Lulu, her desperation was such that she feared she was going mad. That night, her friends pooled all their bread for an entire bucket of water. When they gave it to her, Charlotte plunged her head in, rather like a horse, and drank until she reached the bottom. Her stomach swelled alarmingly. But in some miraculous way, she was cured. The obsession lifted. She would later say that if she thought of suicide, she rejected it. In a place of such constant death, the immediate aim became not to die but to live, to get enough to eat and drink, to keep warm. That was all she thought about.

By now the French women were no longer under any illusion about the smoke that rose from the chimneys at the far end of the camp and that filled their mouths, throats and lungs with a cloying, nauseating taste. They could see for themselves the way the chimneys belched out flames about three-quarters of an hour after the arrival of a Jewish transport. What haunted Marie-Elisa Nordmann was the thought that her mother might be on one of the trains. When, now, they saw the lorries carrying the dead and the dying from Block 25, they knew that those still alive would also be thrown straight into the flames along with the dead. 'It was a ceaseless battle,' Madeleine would say, 'with ourselves, not to give up.'

Walking back from long days in the marshes, Cécile felt guilty that, when she could smell the acrid smoke she was relieved, knowing that they no longer had far to walk. At night, she dreamt of the smell, which made her think of the boiled-down carcasses of animals. Looking around at her emaciated and sickly companions, knowing that most would soon be dead, she kept seeing herself in the mound of corpses. 'I don't know if anyone else felt hope,' she said later. 'But I never did.' She rarely wept, she would say, because she was in such a permanent state of horror that no tears came. But when Josée, who fought back when the *kapos* beat her, was herself beaten so savagely that she died, then Cécile cried. If Josée, so strong, so courageous, had not survived, how would she?

* * *

One Sunday, the whistle for roll call blew earlier than usual. Because Simone was still weak from the day of the *course*, she took longer than usual to get her shoes on and so found herself separated from the others. She was standing in a line of Polish women when a lorry with SS men stopped close by. One leant out and indicated that a number of the women were to fall out. One of these was a mother with twin girls of about eight or nine. She clung to them, but was yanked away and pushed on to the lorry, which then drove off. The little girls, left standing on their own, were crying. Simone took one by each hand and when the whistle blew to return to the barracks, she began to lead them away, singing to them. But then two SS women appeared, unleashed their dogs and gave an order in German. The dogs leapt on the girls and seized them by the throat. Simone stood paralysed. When the dogs were ordered to let go, the girls were dead, their faces savaged beyond recognition. Simone continued to cling to their hands, the children's bodies hanging limply by her side. Cécile and Charlotte, seeing what had happened, ran over, dragged Simone away and then carried her back to the barracks. For several days, she did not say a single word.

Such scenes were constant now. Berthe Lapeyrade, arrested by Poinsot's men in the Bordeaux round-ups, collapsed one day in the marshes and refused to get up. An SS guard picked up a spade and beat her to a pulp. That evening, Lulu, Viva, Charlotte and Cécile carried her body back to the camp, because no one could be left in the marshes or the numbers would not tally at roll call. They had to keep stopping to fold Berthe's hands over her chest and prevent them trailing in the mud. As they staggered along, they felt torn between relief for her, that she was now out of this misery, and despair at having to carry her heavy body back to the camp. It was not long after this that Alice Varailhon found the body of a little girl lying by a well with a doll in her arms.

Picking the doll up and brandishing it furiously in the direction of the SS guards, Alice shouted out: 'Assassins!' One of the men calmly took out his revolver and shot her. That night, Hélène Bolleau and the others helped her back to camp; she died soon after roll call.

One day, the women returning from the marshes passed a group of especially emaciated men, so reduced by starvation that they appeared barely human. Having a little bread left over, they threw it in their direction. In an instant the men were fighting, tearing the bread out of each other's hands. Their eyes made Charlotte think of wolves. The SS guards set their dogs on them.

There were few days, now, when the women did not witness killings and deaths, women driven insane by hunger and misery, set on by dogs and mauled, or clubbed by guards. On 20 February, Annette Epaud, whose cafe in La Rochelle had sheltered so many resisters, and whose 15-year-old son Claude had watched her throw revolvers into the river, took some water to a woman who had been crying piteously for a drink for several hours. 'Wasser, Wasser, Wasser.' Annette carried it across in a cup and passed it through the bars. But she was spotted by an SS guard called Hasse, who was walking past with her Alsatian dog. Hasse ran over, seized her by the neck and threw her into Block 25. Annette was just able to give the drawing of Claude, miraculously held on to through all this time, to Félicienne Bierge, who promised to look after it.

A few days later, while they were at roll call, her friends caught sight of Annette, standing on the lorry carrying the sick and the dead to the crematoria. Seeing them, she called out, 'Danielle, take care of my son!' Fear consumed them all now, fear of getting colder, of being bitten by the dogs, of being beaten by the *kapos*, of falling, and, as bad as anything, of being separated from their friends.

As the days passed, so the women learnt which guards to dread the most. All, the men as well as the women, had been trained according to a strict Prussian drill and told that if they showed signs of 'softness' they would be stripped of their rank and humiliated before their colleagues. There was the brutal Aufseherin Margot Drechsler, a woman in her early thirties who had come to Birkenau in October 1942 and who set her Alsatian dog on the women at every minor infringement of the rules, and was present at many of the selections. Drechsler had large protruding teeth like a horse and was known to the women as *Kostucha*, the reaper. When the trucks left from Block 25, carrying the dead and the just living, Drechsler laughed and waved. Everyone feared her. She often stood at the door of the barracks with her hooked stick, yanking people out for the gas chamber. On a piece of land, in full view of the barracks, Drechsler and the others trained their dogs, using stuffed dolls in striped clothes as dummies, urging them on to bite and tear. One of her helpers was a very pretty Polish girl, Stenia, who had been made block elder. She delighted in kicking over the buckets of precious water just as the women brought them into the barracks, and shouted obscenities at them if they fell over.

The guards in Auschwitz

Then there was Rapportführer Adolf Taube, a big heavy man who reminded the women of a bull; Taube took particular pleasure in hunting down the weaker women. At roll calls, he enjoyed making the Jewish women kneel, their hands above their heads, in the icy mud. As Marie-Elisa would later say, if it was terrible for the French women, it was far worse for the Jewish ones, on whom the guards vented their sadism, and who seemed especially defenceless against the endless degradation, public nakedness and verbal abuse. Taube was 'their worst tormentor'. When Suzanne Roze, a strong, well-built woman, robust from years of transporting heavy typewriters and mimeograph machines for the Resistance, fell ill and was hidden by the others behind the bunks, she was discovered by Taube and beaten to death. She had helped Madeleine Dissoubray run the networks in Rouen.

And it was not only the SS and the *kapos* who were so lethal. Some of the women prisoners were no less vicious. Léa Kerisit was a nurse from Tours, where she had belonged to a network of *passeurs*. Sent to work in an infirmary for German criminal prisoners – because these were German women, there were better conditions – she was repeatedly beaten for rejecting lesbian advances. When she fell sick with typhus, her tormentors bludgeoned her to death.

February and March brought trains full of Jewish women from Salonica, train after train of healthy looking Greek women, some in Soviet paratrooper uniforms seized by the Germans on the Russian front, others in brightly coloured dresses and shawls, bringing with them olives, which Simone had never tasted before. Poupette thought how beautiful the women looked, and how wonderful their clothes were against the drab greyness of Birkenau. But the Greek women were thought to be carriers of typhus and within a few days all but a handful had been sent to the gas chambers.

The early spring also brought gypsies, train after train of Roma and Sinti families, with many children, from all over occupied Europe. They were put into a special gypsy family camp, where there was no water and no electricity and where their rations were less than those of the rest of Birkenau. Over the next few months, 363 babies were born to gypsy mothers. Many were put to death immediately. All her life, Lulu would be haunted by the memory of SS guards murdering gypsy babies by battering their heads against a wall. The others died slowly of starvation. At roll call one morning, Charlotte saw a gypsy woman cradling a baby who was clearly dead; its face was bluish-black and its head lolled to one side. Later she saw it lying on a garbage heap by the kitchens and heard that the mother had fought frantically to prevent the SS from taking it from her, and had herself been clubbed to death. 'How do you know it's a gypsy,' she wrote later, 'when all that is left of it is a skeleton?' Walking back to the barracks through a sudden flurry of snow, she passed an isolated house and saw a single pink tulip in a vase in the window.

What all the women feared most was the *Revier*, the so-called infirmary. When orders came from Berlin early in 1943 to make Auschwitz more productive for the war effort, some small attempts were made at keeping the stronger prisoners alive. One of these was to appoint from among the prisoners a number of doctors and nurses to care for the sick in special infirmary barracks, where in theory they might be nursed back to health. In practice, however, these infirmaries were, like Block 25, antechambers of death. There were virtually no drugs and no dressings, only scraps of paper. Wedged in together, those with tuberculosis in the same bunk as those with dysentery, the patients gave off an appalling stench; rats mauled the living as well as the dead.

For the women sent because of illness to the *Revier*, the few days' reprieve from the marshes might at any moment be broken by a selection, when an SS doctor, accompanied by Taube, Drechsler or one of the other guards, would suddenly appear, demand that all the patients stand, naked, by the bunks for inspection, and then dispatch those judged unlikely to recover to Block 25. Some were murdered directly with lethal injections. The spectre that hung over all of them was that they might become *musulmans*, the walking dead, those so exhausted and apathetic that they drew on to their heads endless punishments, and who burnt themselves on the stoves because they no longer noticed pain.*

Because the windows of Block 26 gave directly on to the courtyard of Block 25, the spectacle of dead and dying women was always present before the French women. Sitting on their bunks, with their tin bowls of gruel, they could see, lying in the yard outside, the naked bodies awaiting collection, their heads shaved, their pubic hair in stiff tufts, their bluish-white bodies frozen in grotesque positions, their toenails brown. They reminded Charlotte

---

* No one was sure where the word came from. Some said that it was derived from the image of Arabs praying, others from a popular German song in which a *musulman* is a Turk weakened and made pale by drinking too much coffee.

of tailor's dummies, which she had once seen outside a shop as a child, when she had been embarrassed by their nakedness. She thought of them as 'yesterday's companions', women who, like herself, had eaten, scratched, gulped down murky gruel, felt hunger and been beaten, and whose lives had been brought to a sudden end because they had not run fast enough or because their faces had looked ashen during a selection. Seeing her staring in horror at the bodies, having caught sight of one that was still moving, Cécile said to her: 'Eat your soup. These women no longer need anything.'

CHAPTER ELEVEN

The meaning of friendship

The French women were not, however, entirely without resources. Marching into Birkenau singing the Marseillaise, they had been overheard by the surviving members of the convoy of French Resistance men, *le Convoi des 45000*, which had preceded them to Birkenau in July 1942. Marie-Claude, since she spoke good German, had been appointed to work as secretary in one of the German infirmaries, and she had been able to make contact with the French men, who told her that of the 1,175 who had set out from France eight months before, only just over a hundred were still alive. But simply finding friends, hearing news, brought the women some kind of hope. The Frenchmen, who had, with the help of their communist comrades, been able to place a few men in the garage and gardening details, had found ways of smuggling information inside empty acetylene bottles.

More important, Danielle Casanova, working and sleeping in relative ease as a dentist for the SS guards and privileged prisoners, was able to get hold of extra bits of clothing and even medicine from 'Canada', the name given to the barracks overflowing with the possessions of the Jews, taken from them when the trains arrived. 'Canada' had acquired its name because of the country's image of a land of unimaginable plenty. The men too had found ways to barter for warm clothes and even medicines in 'Canada' and when Hélène Bolleau developed an abscess that would not heal, they brought her ointment. Having got hold of some precious item – a towel, a toothbrush – the overwhelming problem was how not to lose it. 'Foreign hands grazed our faces at night,' wrote Adelaïde later, 'trying to steal anything we had.'

In the evenings, after the roll call, Danielle came to find the others and, as in Romainville, she brought encouragement and comfort. Because she was in constant physical touch with the SS, who were terrified of the epidemics in the camp, she had been allowed to keep clean and to wear decent clothes. Her energetic, cheerful, determined presence and her healthy appearance became a source of strength to the others, who told each other that, whatever happened to the rest of them, Danielle was bound to survive and bear witness to what had happened to them.

Danielle managed to find a place in an infirmary for Maï Politzer, who, as a midwife, had medical skills, and places for several others in a sewing commando. She had also been able to place Betty in the infirmary, where her job was to scare the rats away from the living and carry the dead outside. When Hélène Solomon got an open sore on her foot, which became infected and turned black, Danielle invented a job as a nurse for her as well, and in the greater cleanliness of an infirmary barracks the infection cleared up. Sometimes, when Danielle came to visit the others in the evenings, her face was wet with tears; so many of the friends were dying and she felt responsible for not keeping them alive. So certain were the others that Danielle would live to see the end of the war that when they felt themselves near death they gave her their wedding rings to return to their husbands. For most of the women, these rings were the only personal possession they had managed to hold on to.

Friendship between the French women had, if possible, grown stronger. They took pride in their closeness and the fact that, unlike the Polish and German women who shared their barracks, they were as kind, helpful and polite towards one another as they would have been back at home. In the evenings, as they crouched in their dark damp bunks, Georgette Rostaing would sing to them, her strong voice rising in the silent barracks, and for a while they forgot and felt better. From the days working in the marshes, Marie-Jeanne Pennec, a countrywoman with a keen sense of what could be eaten, returned with snails, dandelions and grasses for the common pot.

Each of them, as Madeleine Dissoubray would later say, had come to regard her own survival as of no greater or lesser importance than the survival of any one of the others. The women kept back rations of their own bread for those among them who seemed especially weak, protected them at roll calls, and watched out for them when Taube and Drechsler were around. Knowing that the fate of each depended on the others, Poupette would say that all individual egotism seemed to vanish and that, stripped back to the bare edge of survival, each rose to behaviour few would have believed themselves capable of. 'We didn't stop to ask ourselves whom we liked and whom we didn't,' Cécile would later say. 'It wasn't so much friendship as solidarity. We just made certain we didn't leave anyone alone.'

When Charlotte came down with typhus and for a few days was almost blind, the others held on to her all the time, leading her to work, putting the shovel in her hand, and telling her when and where to dig when the SS were close by. Few of Birkenau's other women prisoners had the same closeness. Marie-Elisa was filled with pity for the Jewish women who, separated from their friends and families, mourning those who had gone straight to the gas chambers, struggled on their own, isolated in a fog of terror, exhaustion and grief. 'We watched them, we knew how terrible it was for them,' Marie-Elisa would say, 'but we couldn't help them.'

On the dreaded Sundays when the camp was suddenly disinfected, and all the inmates were driven out naked to stand about in the open while the barracks were cleaned out, the French women would look at one another with concern and affection, noting the bruises and the sores, teasing one another about their spiky tufts of hair. Even now, they could laugh and vanity had not altogether died. It was at these times, when the women had no clothes on, that the SS in search of maids came to choose ones they liked the look of.

The two sisters, Lulu and Carmen, together with Charlotte, Viva, Maï and Cécile were a particularly devoted group and they did what they could to look after Poupette and the other younger girls. During pauses in the work in the marshes, the women talked about going home, about literature and politics, about how they would remain friends for ever, and about what they would do once the war was over. But they were careful never to say too much about the children they had left behind, because the topic was too painful to bear. Poupette would later say that, like a sponge, she tried to absorb all they said.

Poupette was now one of the few left who still had a sister alive. Marie, however, had been particularly broken by Birkenau. She had been an optimistic, happy young woman, but now her eyes seemed permanently clouded over by disgust and disbelief. Haunted by their mother's death, brooding over her fiancé's treatment at the hands of the Gestapo, she kept wondering and worrying about who had given them away. But she and Poupette felt as if they were one, indissolubly linked, watching over each other.

Hélène's mother Emma, who was still only 42, found the horror of Auschwitz doubly hard to bear. She feared and suffered for herself, but this was nothing to what she suffered for her daughter, dreading at every moment that Hélène would fall ill and feeling desolate that she could do nothing to protect or feed her only child. Increasingly, she came to feel a burden on Hélène. Then, in February, she came down with dysentery. Unlike many of the women, however, she clung on for a while, but she was growing weaker and more emaciated all the time. One morning, in the fields, Hélène watched her mother crawl over to some ruts left by horses' hooves and drink the muddy water collected in them. On the 52nd day, so dehydrated that she could no longer drink, Emma died. She had become a skeleton. Hélène now clung to Poupette and Simone for survival.

Not one of the women believed that she would survive alone. It was only when they were together, Charlotte thought, that it was possible to ward off desperation. All her life, characters in plays and novels had lived with her inside her head. Since reaching Birkenau, they had fallen silent. 'Where human beings are suffering and dying,' she would later write, 'there characters from the theatre cannot live.' There was, she said, no place for theatre without a society, and in Auschwitz people so 'diminished, so demeaned, so without their own selves, do not make a society'.

There were occasional moments of comradeship with outsiders. One day, walking back to the barracks, Simone crossed the path of a male prisoner who, pretending to stumble, dropped something at her feet. It turned out to be a present of woollen stockings, though she never discovered who the man was. And Charlotte was mysteriously befriended by a young Belorussian woman called Esther, who worked as a block elder in a barracks of German women and was clean and decently dressed. Every day, for a few weeks, Esther brought her a small present, a toothbrush one day, a sweater another. Then one day she vanished.

More remarkable, perhaps, was the story of how Aimée Doridat, who had helped her communist brother hide tracts at the beginning of the German occupation, was saved.

Working as a cleaner in the *Revier*, Aimée fell from a stepladder and broke her leg. Gangrene set in. Then Erna, the Czech head of the *Revier*, arranged to have her transferred to the men's camp, where a Polish surgeon told her that he would have to amputate. Aimée said that she would rather die. 'But don't you have young children?' the surgeon asked. 'They will need you.' Aimée had two children and the younger was just nine. The operation went ahead. While Aimée was recovering, an SS doctor, one of the very few humane men among them, said to her that he so admired her courage that she could ask for something she wanted. 'A French friend I can talk to,' Aimée replied. Betty was brought over by Danielle to look after her. A pair of crutches was 'organised' from Canada, and she rejoined the others, who now never abandoned her for a moment, to ensure that she would not be left defenceless. Marie-Claude, working in the administrative offices, was able to get advance notice of special selections for the gas chambers, and on those days, Aimée was hidden. So cohesive had the women become, so attuned to each other's frailties, so watchful and protective, that planning how to keep the group alive had become a way of life.

*   *   *

March brought rains. The snow melted and the marshes turned into a sea of mud. Those responsible for collecting the vast cauldrons of soup sank in the mud up to their thighs. Sixty-seven days after reaching Birkenau, the women removed their stockings for the first time, and were permitted to wash their feet in the water now flowing in the ditches. They discovered that, except for their big toes, all their other nails had gone. Looking at her friends sitting caked in mud reminded Charlotte of a 'miserable swarm that made one think of flies on a dung heap'. She dreamt of having three baths, one after the other, in warm, soft, soapy water. During the interminable roll calls, the women had taken to playing a game. One would ask another: 'If you could choose between a big bowl of boiling hot, foamy chocolate, or a bath with lavender soap, or a warm cosy bed, which would you choose?' Nearly always the answer was the same: the hot bath or the warm bed.

But the number of survivors was dwindling. Dysentery set in and the women aged before the eyes of their friends. Typhus, brought to Auschwitz in April 1941 by prisoners transferred from a jail in Lublin, was ravaging the camp. One by one the French women, who had survived the hunger, the back-breaking work, the intense cold and the endless skin infections, began to fall ill. At roll calls, they pinched their ashen cheeks to appear healthier. All night, death rattles could be heard rising from the bunks. Women woke to find that their faces had swollen during the night and that they were too ill to move. They were now dying at the same rate as the Jewish women, who were more brutally treated by the guards. On one single night, nine of the remaining French women died. André Montagne, a 19-year-old survivor from the *Convoi des 45000*, sent to work in Birkenau one day, happened to look into the French women's barracks. He would never forget the horror of what he saw, the appalling dirt and overcrowding and the groans of the sick.

In March, Raymonde Sergent, who had promised her daughter Gisèle that she would soon be home, began to feel ill. Raymonde had been very strong for the first few weeks, making plans with all the women from the Tours region that once they were released they would come to her cafe in Saint-Martin-le-Beau to share some good bottles of wine that she had hidden away for the end of the war. But as the days passed she seemed to give up hope. One day, one of the other women asked her if she really thought that they would ever return to drink the wine? Raymonde replied: 'No, neither you nor I will ever drink it.' She entered the *Revier* with her legs swollen and bleeding from oedema, and died there. To Hélène Fournier, who was the last of the seventeen women from the Tours area still alive, she said, 'Tell my husband and Gisèle that I never forgot them, and that I tried to hold on.'

Then one morning, Maï, who as a nurse working with Danielle was living in the comparative comfort of a *Revier*, woke with a boil on her upper lip. It grew larger and spread: she was diagnosed with typhus. Her temperature rose and she fell unconscious. A few days later she was dead. Rosa, the youngest girl in the group, who had cried so bitterly for her mother in Romainville, also caught typhus. Ill and weak, she became childlike again and kept begging for her mother. Then she too died. These deaths were terrible to the survivors. Maï had been a constant and encouraging presence; Rosa, a child, they counted on saving.

What was becoming clear to all of them was that the younger girls did not appear to possess the resilience of the older women. Even when physically strong and capable, they seemed to be mentally more fragile, and thus more vulnerable. Twenty-year-old Andrée Tamisé was already weakened by dysentery when she picked up a chest infection. Desperate not to be parted from her sister Gilberte, she dragged herself, with Gilberte's help, to the marshes. Each day, she found breathing a little harder. Finally one morning, she said to Gilberte, 'I can't follow you any more.' When the others left for work, she tried to join the line of women queueing by the *Revier*, but a guard pushed her away. Andrée crept back into her bunk and hid. But a *kapo* spotted her, dragged her outside and beat her. That night Gilberte returned to find her sister covered in mud, bruised and semi-conscious. During the night, Andrée died. Rising before dawn next morning, Gilberte carried her body outside and laid it tenderly by a wall.

One of the next to go was Claudine Guérin, Germaine Pican's young friend from Rouen. In Birkenau, Claudine had managed to remain cheerful and uncomplaining, trying to make the others laugh. One day she came over to Germaine, to whom she was very close, looking so white that Germaine hardly recognised her. She was wearing, under her striped jacket, a crêpe de Chine dress that someone had given her from 'Canada'. She said to Germaine: 'Hug me'. It was a Sunday, and Germaine urged her to go outside to sit in the fresh air and sunshine. A few days later, Claudine found a frog in the fields and insisted on sharing it with Germaine.

Then came a disinfectant day, and the women were driven out of the barracks to stand around naked while the mattresses were shaken out. Claudine was separated from the others when they went back inside. They heard her saying softly, over and over again, 'Maman, maman'. She died a few days before her 18th birthday.

But perhaps the most demoralising and upsetting blow to the group as a whole was when Danielle Casanova caught typhus. The SS, appreciating her usefulness as a dentist, vaccinated her, and gave her tea and lemon to drink. But it was too late, and Danielle died. When Charlotte went to see her, she found that one of the gardening detail had put a bunch of lilac in a glass by her bed, and some branches, with leaves, between her hands. Her corpse was said to be the only healthy body anyone had seen for a long time, and beautiful in death. They mourned her bitterly. The wedding rings that she had looked after so carefully disappeared. Marie-Claude, to whom she had been so close, was overwhelmed with sadness.

Two and a half months after reaching Birkenau, the French women were down to eighty. A hundred and fifty of them had died, from typhus, pneumonia, dysentery, from dog bites and beatings and gangrenous frostbite, from not being able to eat or sleep, or from being gassed. In the filth and cold and danger of Birkenau, almost anything was fatal. The ones still alive were the stronger women, those neither too old nor too young, those sustained by belief in a new world order; or, quite simply, because they had been lucky. Without the help of the others, they knew that many more of them would already be dead. One Sunday, when the sky was blue and the women were allowed to rest, Charlotte remembered other spring Sundays, walking by the Seine under the chestnut trees. 'None of us,' she thought, 'none of us will return.'

CHAPTER TWELVE

Keeping alive, remaining me

By the late spring of 1943, when the snows began to melt and the meadows beyond the barbed-wire fence turned green with yellow buttercups, and the blackthorn was covered in white down, Auschwitz was well into its phase of maximum activity. There were trains arriving almost daily from the ghettos of Pruzana, Theresienstadt and Zamosc, from Holland, Germany and France. About one in ten of all new arrivals was being picked out to work, the rest 'lodged separately', that is to say gassed. Every one of the 1,750 children from Poland, all of them under 10, who arrived over a two-day period before the snows had melted, was gassed on arrival. The new crematoria were working night and day, and the flames could be seen rising brightly against the sky. A high-ranking party of SS officials from Berlin and inspectors from J.A. Topf and Sons came to Birkenau on an official visit and pronounced the ovens to be efficient.

Thirty barracks, vast empty hangars, were filled to overflowing with the possessions of Europe's Jews, who had been encouraged to bring with them all that they would need for their new lives in the east, not only gold and jewellery, but professional equipment, medicines, fur coats, extra clothes, vitamins and prams. The trains that brought people to Auschwitz returned to Germany packed with loot, to be funnelled into elaborate networks that permeated the whole of the Third Reich.

Auschwitz itself, now the Reich's largest concentration and extermination camp, had become a vast complex of offices, storerooms, workshops, canteens and houses for the three thousand or so SS present at any one time, while some thirty-nine separate satellite camps were turning out spare parts for tanks, lorries, planes, anti-aircraft guns, as well as synthetic rubber, ammunition, cement and uniforms. For every worker leased out to IG Farben or Siemens, the SS charged three marks a day; for a specialist, a skilled electrician or welder, five marks. Those unable to function productively on the 1,200 or less calories allotted to them were returned to the gas chambers at Birkenau. Employers sometimes complained that they were being sent skeletons, not men and women.

What was now absolutely plain to the eighty surviving French women, many of whom were extremely frail, was that their continuing survival would depend on great luck and on their continuing ability to adapt and organise themselves. They had taken care to master enough German and the bastardised language of the camps to avoid blows by reacting too slowly to orders. They had learnt to hang back, when the cauldrons of soup arrived, in order to get the bottom layers, where shreds of meat or vegetables gathered. They knew to cultivate friends in 'Canada', who, in return for extra portions of bread, might take the risk of stealing a pair of woollen stockings or some decent shoes. They had discovered how important it was to stay together, not get separated, so each could watch the others' backs.

Their own particular skills as women, caring for others and being practical, made them, they told themselves, less vulnerable than men to harsh conditions and despair. Adaptibility was crucial, resignation fatal. The inability to undo a vision of life as it should be and not cope with what it was, led, as they had observed, to apathy and the condition of *musulmans*, those more dead than alive. They did their best to stay clean, to wash their faces in the snow or icy brooks, believing that it made them both healthier and more dignified. And they wanted, passionately, to live, to survive the war, and to describe to the world exactly what they had been through and what they had witnessed.

When Germaine Pican found a dead crow in the marshes, even the mouthful she shared with the others gave them a sense of achievement. Charlotte, for her part, fought the cold and exhaustion by pretending that she was somewhere else, reciting to herself poems and plays. Her refrain was 'to keep alive, to remain me'. It did not nullify what was going on around her, but it made her feel some kind of 'victory over horror'.

Even so, by now most of the women had ceased in their hearts to believe that they would live to see the end of the war. Conditions in the women's camp at Birkenau, worse than elsewhere in Auschwitz, with more overcrowding and less water, were getting harsher, and few felt confident that they could for much longer escape the sudden and arbitrary brutality of the SS and the *kapos*. Their bodies were covered in soft, fat, white lice. They were exhausted. Walking back at the end of a long day in the marshes, Cécile, so strong and positive by nature, could only think how close she felt to the end, how without hope of any kind.

But then, something completely unexpected happened. Their luck, the ultimate arbiter of life and death in Auschwitz, changed.

* * *

In Ukraine and Belorussia, the Germans had seen fields of kok-saghyz, a dandelion from central Asia whose root and juice contained latex, and from which the Russians derived rubber. In desperate need of rubber themselves, the Germans thought they could cultivate kok-saghyz on the swampy plains of Auschwitz and, under the auspices of IG Farben, appointed an SS Obersturmbannführer with a PhD in agricultural sciences, Joachim Caesar, to run the laboratory.

The first recruits chosen to work under him were Polish women from Birkenau, but in March word reached Marie-Claude, whose position in the camp administration meant she was aware of any new developments, that Caesar was looking for biologists. Marie-Elisa Nordmann and Madeleine Dechavassine, both chemists before the war, applied. Marie-Elisa was actually in the infirmary with pneumonia and such a high temperature that she could not stand up, but a nurse showed her how to bring the fever down with an instant remedy of 90 per cent alcohol and a bit of coffee, and she pulled round before the medical inspection. And in the wake of Marie-Elisa and Madeleine, claiming scientific expertise that few had any notion of, fifteen more French women set off for the experimental station at Raisko. Among them were Cécile, Charlotte, Germaine Pican, Lulu and her sister Carmen. Lulu would later say that up until that moment, she could barely tell a potato from a carrot.

Hélène Solomon, who was just recovering from typhus, was allowed to join the group after a prisoner doctor swore that she had only been suffering from flu. Viva was to have gone with them, but she had typhus and was in the *Revier*, where it seemed that she was holding her own.

Raisko, which consisted of an old schoolhouse surrounded by fields and greenhouses, lay some three kilometres from Birkenau. It was encircled by barbed wire, but not electrified, and there were no watchtowers with SS guards and guns. Caesar, who was afraid of contagion, as were all the SS, and whose own wife had died of typhus not long before, insisted that the women who worked for him were clean and healthy. After nearly three months of filth, the French women could not believe it when they were permitted to wash and were given clean new blouses and proper leather shoes; though the food was the same, the soup was thicker, and there were endless possibilities of 'organising' – Auschwitz's word for stealing – vegetables from the surrounding fields, where other prisoners were growing produce for the SS.

Until a new barracks was made ready for them, the women returned to Birkenau each night. The camp still lay under a crust of ice, and when the moon shone the barbed wire was picked out in frost. They tramped through a silent, still world, holding on to one another, so as not to slip. But then they moved into Raisko itself in which there were dormitories and each woman had her own bed, with a straw mattress. There were hot showers. The roll call, during which so many of their friends had died, was reduced to no more than a few minutes morning and evening. There were far fewer fleas. Caesar was more interested in getting results – which would keep him from a possible transfer to the eastern front – than in persecuting his staff. At times he treated the scientists among them almost as colleagues. Their ailments were even noted in the ledger of the Raisko hospital, where they were allowed to spend time when ill. When it got warmer, one of the SS guards, who told the women that unless he was soon transferred away from Auschwitz he was going to kill himself, let them bathe in a pond and wash their clothes, while he looked scrupulously away.

The work was not arduous. The more skilled among them, such as Marie-Elisa and Madeleine, were assigned to a young

German chemist called Ruth Weimann in the laboratory, where they divided their time between helping her with the chemistry for her dissertation, and ensuring that the results of their experiments appeared positive, the better to prolong Raisko's existence. The others worked in the kok-saghyz fields, sorted plants and acted as assistants. Occasionally, they were ordered to make funeral wreaths for SS guards who died of typhus.

On arriving, Marie-Elisa had discovered a friend and colleague from before the war, Claudette Bloch, who told her that several of the French men from the *Convoi des 45,000* were employed at Raisko as gardeners. As in Birkenau, the men had found ways of learning the news, and even of getting hold of newspapers, which they now left hidden in safe spots for the women. Using an atlas from 'Canada', concealed in an attic above the laboratory, Marie-Elisa, Charlotte and the others were able to follow the Nazi defeats on the eastern front.

When Caesar married Ruth Weimann, the women were ordered to make a duvet for the bridal pair, out of the feathers from the geese and ducks reared not far away for the SS. They took great pleasure in leaving in some of the sharper quills. For with the food and warmth had come a new taste for life. Women whose horizons had shrunk to an hourly preoccupation with survival found themselves once again wanting diversion. They began to barter, taught by the Polish women who had become skilled at negotiating for cabbages, potatoes and beans with the Russian prisoner gardeners. They discovered that extra bread, saved from their own rations, could be swapped for a lump of sugar, a packet of noodles, or even needles, thread and pens. To see their friends slowly come back to life, looking less haunted and skeletal, beginning to smile again, was a delight for all of them. When, one day, the SS came and confiscated everything from their barracks, the women gathered together and sang the Marseillaise, very softly, under their breaths. Next day they set about replacing everything they had lost.

On the pretext that the nearby Institute of Hygiene, where some of the French men were working, had more sophisticated equipment, and that they needed to centrifuge their latex samples, Marie-Elisa and Hélène hid tomatoes in their voluminous knickers and exchanged them for jam and even some blood, which they later made into blood sausage. It was very risky, for all such transactions were strictly forbidden, but it gave them a feeling that they were not entirely without power. It also inspired them to perform small acts of sabotage, selecting the weaker roots for propagation, mixing up the numbers of batches and treating the plants with chemicals to stunt their growth.

The women had become skilled at thieving. Charlotte Decock, who was sent to join the others in Raisko as cook for the SS, stole everything that she could lay her hands on – wine, flour, eggs, a jar of pickled pork – though getting rid of the jar afterwards proved almost impossible. All through the months at Birkenau, Charlotte Decock was one of the women who had remained most cheerful and optimistic; the others loved her and found her presence comforting.

In the evenings, sitting on their beds, the friends sewed and drew and even did embroidery, discussing how they might find ways of making borscht, and how delicious it would be if they could only get hold of some cream. They might have become bolder in their scavenging had Germaine Pican not been caught trying to smuggle onions back to their friends in Birkenau, and sent back there herself as punishment. Though he encouraged the women to do what they could to improve their surroundings and even once found sunglasses for those working in the fields, Caesar did not intervene over punishments. Nor did he save a young girl called Lily, who had a fiancé among the gardeners and who was shot when a note of his was intercepted. 'We are like plants full of life and sap, like plants wanting to grow and live,' the boy had written, 'and I cannot help thinking that these plants are not meant to live.'

Even at Raisko, however, the presence of the SS was constant and menacing. As the women's hair grew and was not immediately shaved off again, Marie-Elisa's hair grew back very curly. One of the SS guards eyed her suspiciously, saying that she looked to him very Jewish. No one gave her away.

One of their tormentors was Irma Grese, a farmer's daughter who had joined the SS at the age of 18 and arrived at Auschwitz at 19. Grese walked around the camp with a whip in her hand, smelling strongly of expensive scent. She was an exceptionally pretty girl, with large, very blue innocent eyes and an angelic face and she had plans to become a film star.

*   *   *

The fortunes of the women left behind in Birkenau were also about to take a sudden turn for the better.

Some time during the late spring, Marie-Claude, who was in the infirmary recovering from typhus, had overheard a conversation between a Polish doctor and an SS guard. The French women, said the guard, were not standing up well to the Polish climate; in fact, they seemed to be 'dying like flies'. It looked, he went on, as if 'they will all be transferred to Ravensbrück'. Though nothing of the kind was forthcoming, it was clear that the camp authorities were concerned about their non-Jewish French prisoners.

Towards the end of April, Emmanuel Fleury, a former communist city councillor in Paris now living underground in France, had received a telegram forwarded to him by fellow members of the Resistance. Originally addressed to her parents, it announced the death of his wife, Marie-Thérèse, from heart problems, in 'the Auschwitz hospital'. These 'death notices' were part of Auschwitz's grotesque bureaucracy. In theory at least, a secretary was appointed to each of the *Reviers* to note down the tattooed number of every corpse and record the cause of death in order to notify families. In practice, rats had often eaten the flesh where the numbers were tattooed, and many deaths were not recorded at all.

Marie-Thérèse had been assistant federal secretary of the French United Postal Federation and she had been active with her husband in the Resistance before being caught and sent to Romainville. Until the moment the telegram arrived, no one in France had known the fate of the 230 women who had left Compiègne together on 24 January 1943. There had been rumours about labour camps in the east, particularly after the notes slipped out through the cracks in the wooden cattle trucks reached their families, sent on by the railway workers who had found them lying by the tracks. But the *Nacht und Nebel* decree had ensured that there had been a terrifying silence about their whereabouts.

The telegram about Marie-Thérèse – sent in error by the German authorities – made its way to the French Resistance in London, where it was read out in the regular French-language broadcast over the BBC. Questions now began to be asked. Where in fact *had* all the women gone? Were many of them dead? And what was Mme Fleury doing in the Auschwitz hospital? What, precisely, was Auschwitz?

By the spring of 1943, much had already been said and written about the concentration camps in occupied Poland. Ever since the Wannsee conference of 15 senior Nazis in January 1942, stories had been circulating about the Nazi plans for a Final Solution for Europe's Jews, and about mass killing centres. Reports, based on information carried out by escaped prisoners, industrialists, travellers, workers, churchmen and Jewish organisations, had made their way to the Allied governments, to the Vatican and to the International Committee of the Red Cross in Geneva. And though, in October 1942, the ICRC had voted against the idea of issuing a public communiqué – saying that it would 'serve no purpose' and jeopardise their work with prisoners of war – by December of that year questions had been raised and statements made, both in London and in Washington. Even so, no military action was contemplated, the view being that all resources should be directed to ending the war. Bombers, dropping their loads on factories near Auschwitz had not been diverted to bomb the railway lines or the camp to which they led.

For the most part, the messages of fear and alarm that had reached the Allied leaders had spoken of Sobibor, Belzec and Treblinka as extermination centres where people were being gassed, but not Auschwitz, even though reports of Birkenau's gas chambers had been carried out to the Allies. The very size and nature of the camp, with its vast industrial complex and satellite factories, may have concealed its lethal intent. Auschwitz, it was said, was indeed a place of slave labour, but not of mass murder. The Jews deported on the trains from Drancy continued to be described as heading for 'an unknown destination, somewhere in Poland'.

What happened now was that the French families, whose 229 mothers, wives, sisters and daughters had been on the *Convoi des 31000* with Marie-Thérèse Fleury began to contact their local churches, the Red Cross and the Vichy government to ask for news. Some of these enquiries made their way to the Gestapo offices. A letter from Poupette and Marie Alizon's family spoke of Mme Alizon having died, 'crushed by despair', not knowing what had become of her two daughters. Bit by bit, other 'death notices' reached France from Auschwitz. Responding to the news of the deaths of nineteen women from Bordeaux and the Gironde, the Prefect announced that they had died 'because of poor conditions of hygiene and nutrition'. The truth was somewhat different: Aminthe Guillon had been caught in the murderous 'race' of 10 February, Elisabeth Dupeyron and Annette Epaud had been gassed, 20-year-old Aurore Pica had died of thirst and 21-year-old Andrée Tamisé had been beaten to death. Together, they left five children, the youngest Elisabeth's five-year-old daughter.

In France, the Front National de la Résistance collected all available facts and put out a bulletin, naming Danielle Casanova, Marie-Elisa Nordmann and a few others as having been on the train and now having vanished. Other reports circulated with a description of mass gassings. The story was picked up by a French correspondent in London called Fernand Grenier, who on 17 August broadcast at some length about the 'murder of these young French women', twenty-six of them widows of Resistance fighters, and insisting that Pétain and the Vichy government would have to take responsibility for their deaths.

He spoke of Maï Politzer, Hélène Solomon and Marie-Claude and gave a generally accurate picture of conditions in Auschwitz, but, unable to believe that his figures were right, changed the number of women for every tap of water from five thousand women to five hundred. 'This silence,' he concluded, 'must be broken.' Other language sections of the BBC picked up Grenier's story, which then also appeared in newspapers in Britain and the US. Hearing that Danielle was among the dead, a group of Parisian women wrote an open letter to Pétain. 'We wish to inform you that we hold you responsible for the death of these truly French women.'

No documents have ever been found in any French, Polish or German archive, or among the papers at Auschwitz, to explain what happened next. Was it because the US, USSR and Britain had announced that all those found guilty of war crimes would eventually be subject to 'terrible punishments'? Or that Himmler could no longer ignore the fact that in the case of defeat he would certainly be charged with war crimes? Or that, now that the place where the women were held was no longer a secret and the terrors of *Nacht und Nebel* no longer applied, orders had come from Berlin that no more French resisters were to be allowed to die?

Whatever the reason, Marie-Claude, to her terror, was suddenly summoned to the Gestapo office in the camp. Here, believing she was about to be punished for some misdemeanour, she was informed by an SS man called Schutz, who was known to like to attend gassings in person, that the International Committee of the Red Cross had been making enquiries about her, and that she was to be allowed to write a letter to her family. It was to be no longer than fifteen lines, written in German, and it was to contain no criticism of the conditions in which she was held. In fact, all the surviving French women, and all the men survivors of the *Convoi des 45000*, were also to be allowed to write letters to their families, provided someone translated them into German. What was more, they were to be permitted to receive parcels as well.

Better than this, the women were to be moved out of Block 25 and into quarantine in a barracks just outside the perimeter fence. There would be no more work in the factories and marshes, and no more roll calls for hours at dawn and dusk.

The surviving French women of the *Convoi* in Birkenau, after the departure of the group for Raisko, were now down to thirty-seven; most knew they were very close to death. The few young girls still alive looked ravaged and ageless. Hélène Bolleau weighed just 32 kilos; suffering from constant diarrhoea, she dragged herself around the camp wrapped in a filthy blanket. Simone was struggling to throw off a prolonged series of illnesses, having miraculously escaped the gas ovens when the *Revier* in which she was recuperating was cleared by the lorries collecting the sick: she got away by biting the hand of an SS guard and hiding among a group of women digging a ditch nearby. On the day of her 20th birthday, two of the French men prisoners gave her a little bag with a piece of soap and a small flask of scent.

*   *   *

The move to the quarantine block came too late, however, for Marie Alizon.

All through the early summer Marie, who had never got over her terrible hunger and cravings for food, had been growing weaker and weaker, exhausted by dysentery, her legs so swollen she could barely walk. She said sadly to Poupette, 'Maybe we didn't pray enough'. Soon she couldn't eat and her voice became that of a little girl. She clung on to Poupette. When she got an ear infection, she was moved into the *Revier*. The last time Poupette saw her sister she was lying naked under a filthy sheet and her lips were black. She was in a coma and her ears were full of pus; a rat had bitten her. Marie died a few days after her 22nd birthday. Poupette was devastated. She could not accept that the sister who had always looked after her, had been so good to everyone, was no longer there. Charlotte took her in her arms and held her tight. Marie-Claude managed to arrange for her to be transferred to Raisko, to join the team of biologists.

The change in the women's fortune also came too late for Viva Nenni. To the relief of her friends, and especially Charlotte, who had grown very close to her, Viva had seemed to recover from a particularly virulent attack of typhus. Then she fell ill again. When Charlotte went to see her in the *Revier*, she seemed almost unnaturally well, even if she had become so thin that her bones showed through her shoulders; her thick black curls were growing back and they talked about how pleased Viva's father, Pietro Nenni, must be at the news that the Allies had landed at Nettuno. Charlotte felt relieved. But suddenly, Viva told her that she was about to be sent back to France, where her sister was waiting for her. The delirium of typhus had set in. Soon she was unconscious. A few days later, she died. These deaths of friends to whom the women felt indissoluably bound, with whom they had endured so much, were almost too painful to bear.

And it came too late for the tall, aristocratic France Rondeaux, who had distracted herself when not praying by reciting recipes. France died of typhus, her skin slack over her emaciated body. She was at least spared the knowledge that her young daughter, at about this time, had died in a tragic accident in France.

* * *

Infinitely relieved by their change in fortune, the remaining women got together their one or two possessions and walked the couple of hundred yards to their new home just outside the barbed wire. Later they would all say that without this move, it was unlikely that any one of them would have survived. Hélène Fournier was so thin that she felt as if her thigh bones, which had so little flesh on them, were almost touching.

Now they got down to writing letters, devising codes and using historical references to try to convey to their families in France what had happened to them. Marie-Claude immediately sent news confirming the deaths of Danielle and Maï, using nicknames. 'I am very sad that Hortense [Danielle] has gone to her father [he had died in 1937]. I also think a lot about poor little Mimi [the nickname of Maï's son, now an orphan].' She wrote about Hades and Dante's Inferno, and said it was a bit 'as if Eurydice had received a letter'. She said that not only had she lost two teeth, but that, at the age of 31, she had fifty white hairs.

Betty wrote to her aunt saying that it was sad that Rosette [Blanc, founder of a branch of the Jeunes Filles de France] had also left with Hortense, but that she was happy to report that Pomme [Marie-Claude] was in good health. She added that she was delighted to hear that Monique [one of her own nicknames] was moving to another school, where she would be far happier.

Yvonne Noutari wrote to ask her sister whether there was any news of her husband Robert, arrested shortly before her. Her sister, in one of the first replies to reach the camp, answered that it was 'impossible to send news'. What she could not bring herself to write was that Robert had been executed by the Gestapo. When Yvonne wrote to her mother, saying 'Happy days will bloom again' – with the suggestion that the nightmare of the Nazis could not endure for ever – she was punished with one month in a disciplinary detail, which meant leaving for work at four in the morning and not returning until ten at night. Her friends saved extra bread from their rations to give her.

Learning from her example, the other women kept their letters very bland. Every letter that Lulu was able to write was about her son Paul, sending him her love, asking for photographs and news. 'I kiss you and little Paul from all my heart,' she wrote. 'It is hard for me to realise that he isn't a baby any more. I will

always regret these days in which I couldn't live with him . . .'
How much had he grown? she asked. What did he talk about?
What did he play with? About Auschwitz she said nothing.

In France, the letters were received and many of the references
understood. When Hélène Bolleau's aunt received a letter saying
that 'From now on, you will be my little mother', she understood
that Emma was dead. Some of the allusions however remained
puzzling. Why were the women asking for onions and garlic? (To
ward off scurvy.) What did Cécile mean when she wrote: 'don't
send any *oseilles* [sorrel]', which was French slang for money, but
which was translated by a friend in France for her family into
'lettuce'? And what could they possibly be saying when they
described a great many *pommes au four*, apples in the oven?

Complaints continued to be addressed by families to the authorities, and Aragon wrote a poem with the line: 'I salute you, Marie
of France of the hundred faces'. Parcels were quickly posted off
to Auschwitz, and some, though never all of the desperately needed
food, reached the women in their quarantine block, where it was
meticulously shared out. Hélène Bolleau's aunt sent a packet
containing oil, chocolate, biscuits, dried plums, sugar, jam, tuna,
cassoulet, mustard and onions. The taste of so many different
things, after so long, was extraordinary. When Betty received her
first parcel from her parents, she wept.

One day, while still in Raisko, Marie-Elisa received a pot
of honey. They had agreed that, when sharing out the contents of
their packets, the woman to whom it had been addressed would
be allowed to lick out anything that remained at the bottom of
a jar. Licking the pot, Marie-Elisa found a piece of paper stuck
along the bottom. Underneath was a photograph of her small
son. It was, she would later say, an incredible moment and from
this instant she knew she would survive and go home, because
she had to see her son again. Despite the risk of discovery and
punishment, for photographs were still forbidden, she found a
way of keeping it by her at all times. The other women shared
in her intense pleasure.

Some of the news from home, however, was unsettling. Poupette
discovered that her father, after the death of her mother, had
fallen in love with a much younger woman and was thinking of
marrying again. Simply being in touch with the outside world

again, after so long isolated in an existence infinitely remote from anything they had previously known and understood, but which they had learnt to navigate and adapt to, was in itself unnerving. The communication with home, said Marie-Claude, had served to remind them 'that there was also another world out there, of love and gentleness', and that was no bad thing because it was important not to allow oneself to become hard. But, she added, it also made them realise how very far away they were. It was a different world, and they had become different people.

Something of this came across to all of them the day that Olga Melin suddenly caught sight of her husband, working on the railway line in Birkenau. She dropped the vat of soup that she had been carrying and ran across to speak to him. When she returned, having by great good fortune not been seen by the SS, she told them that he was in Auschwitz because he had tried to escape from a prisoner of war camp. What about their divorce? the others asked, knowing that at the beginning of the war the two had decided to separate. 'We're getting back together,' Olga told them. The Melins' son, disabled from polio, was living with her mother. The Melins had helped Jews cross the demarcation line.

*　　*　　*

There was, however, one woman whose fate in Birkenau took a different turn. This was Dr Adelaïde Hautval, the psychiatrist from Alsace who had castigated the German soldiers whom she had seen mistreating a family of Jews. Adelaïde possessed a somewhat stern, reserved manner which had not brought her close to the other women, but the clarity of her moral stance did not desert her in Auschwitz, where she was widely respected and admired.

Not long after reaching the camp, Adelaïde was sent as doctor to the German infirmary block, where the 'asocials', the German criminal prisoners and the prostitutes, went when they fell ill. Though better provisioned than the other infirmary blocks, it was nonetheless menaced by enormous rats, so bold that they would attack the women patients. All the *Reviers* were a form of hell, with no soap, no clean sheets, very little water, and full of women with suppurating sores which would not heal.

Adelaïde did her best to help the other French women, by stealing medicines and food, though often she had nothing but a few aspirin to take them. When Paulette Prunières, a young colleague of Danielle's before the war, came down with pleurisy, she managed to get hold of some insulin, stolen for her by a Czech doctor. Adelaïde was tormented by having constantly to decide whom to save, whom to let die. 'One ampoule for a couple of hundred people,' she would write. 'How can one use this? Who should receive it? Toss a coin?' One day, a man working in 'Canada' brought her a box of medicines, stolen from the piles of possessions recently brought by a new train full of Jews. She hid it, and drew on the supplies secretly. But her hiding place was discovered by an SS doctor, who confiscated the drugs. Adelaïde cried with anger.

The patients in the German infirmary, perhaps disconcerted by her rigid ways, took against her and she would have been injured by them had it not been for the block elder, a prostitute with a strong sense of fairness, who protected her. When Adelaïde herself came down with typhus, it was this woman who looked after her. In her feverish nightmares, she dreamt about a man standing in front of an oven trying to lift her on to his spade and shouting 'I will show you how to die!' Some two and a half months after reaching Auschwitz, Adelaïde was informed that she was being transferred to the experimental block, to work as a gynaecologist. She would later explain that she agreed to go because she wanted to see for herself what went on there, and hoped to live to be able to describe it after the war was over. For the inmates of Auschwitz, the experimental blocks were places of rumour and nightmares; for the prisoner doctors, they were where the questions of compromise and complicity were at their most bald.

Nazi medical experiments lay at the heart of the long process of eugenic purification through medicine. From the summer of 1933, when a sterilisation law had identified a number of hereditary illnesses, among them schizophrenia, epilepsy and alcoholism, threatening to the purity of the German race, euthanasia programmes had been set up, foreshadowing the death camps, to select and exterminate those with mental or physical deformities. Once Auschwitz was running, it seemed the obvious place for ambitious doctors to extend their experimental work, not only on blood and drugs and surgical procedures, but on aspects of eugenics. Human flesh was far cheaper and more widely available than animals, and human guinea pigs were plentiful. 'Consumed material' could readily be replaced by 'fresh material' taken straight from the new transports. Marie-Claude, observing a long line of Greek Jews waiting to be used as experimental material, realised that they had no idea what was about to happen to them. 'But,' she would later say, in a brief, stark sentence, 'I knew.'

The most important experimental block was Block 10, in the main Auschwitz camp. Its windows were kept shuttered and barred, and all communication with the outside world was forbidden, which added to its sinister reputation; and it gave directly on to the courtyard of Block 11, against whose wall prisoners who had tried to escape were shot. Adelaïde could not avoid seeing these executions, or, later, parts of the bodies of those shot being amputated for SS researchers to dissect. Block 10 also acted as a bordello for the SS and privileged camp inmates, and it had a mascot, in the shape of a blond, blue-eyed six-year-old boy called Peter, who goose-stepped up and down at roll call, in imitation of the SS. It was here that Adelaïde was sent.

Block 10, with its four experimental operating rooms and its sophisticated X-ray equipment, was the domain of an SS brigadier-general from Upper Silesia called Professor Clauberg, a very short, bald, highly ambitious man who specialised in castration and sterilisation and who wore a Tyrolean hat and boots while he operated. Himmler had expressed a particular interest in his work, telling him that he wanted to know 'how long it would take to sterilise a thousand Jewesses'. Clauberg's guinea-pigs were all married Jewish women who had had children and were aged between 20 and 40, and they were selected straight from the trains, when they were given a vague promise that by agreeing they might be permitted to live. Much as they dreaded the operations, they dreaded even more the spectre of being transferred to Birkenau and the gas chambers.

Clauberg's experiments consisted in injecting a caustic substance straight into the cervix in order to obstruct the fallopian tubes. This procedure was extremely painful, causing high temperatures and inflammation, and those who survived were often mentally and physically scarred. It was not unusual for two male prisoners to be ordered to hold down the screaming women, whose cries could be heard several blocks away. Called on to certify whether the women had been so disturbed that they were 'incapable of work', which would have taken them immediately to the gas chambers, Adelaïde insisted that they would undoubtedly recover.

Since the women were not operated on when they were menstruating, she certified as often as she could that they were; even though the extremely malnourished women of Birkenau had long since stopped having any periods at all. She was finding the moral ambiguities of her work almost too painful to bear. To her horror, she had also learnt that when babies were born in the camp, they were drowned in a barrel by one of the 'green triangles', a German woman sent to Auschwitz because she had conducted abortions. Adelaïde was told that it took twenty minutes for a child to die. But when this German woman herself died, no one else could be found to do the job. So the babies lived, and soon died of starvation and neglect. To save the mothers, some of their friends became killers of their babies.

In May 1943 Josef Mengele arrived in Auschwitz to carry out his own experiments on eyes, heredity and race, using twins and dwarfs, selected, like the women, straight from the trains with the help of Drechsler and Taube. Mengele's obsession with creating a genetically superior race took the form of removing organs from twins, as well as blinding them or deliberately infecting them with fatal diseases in order to test out drugs. On being told that she was about to be sent to work with him, Adelaïde protested. 'Is this order definitive?' she asked. Yes, she was told, all orders were definitive.

Within Mengele's experimental block, she was forced to witness his own particular selections, the prisoners made to walk up and down naked before him: he sent some back into the wards, the others into a special room to await collection by the lorries that would take them to the gas chambers. While this was going on, Adelaïde and the other prisoner doctors were shut into a room, from where they could hear the cries of those being herded on to the lorries. Adelaïde wept. Elly, one of the nurses, said to her that as she saw it, there was not much difference between taking an active part in these selections, and sitting by passively and doing nothing. 'This is true,' Adelaïde would write. 'She is completely right. If we had more courage we would protest more.'

Later, she agonised over the 'grey area' inhabited by herself and others like her, caught up and complicit in these medical atrocities. What might have happened if she had interfered? 'A useless gesture? Perhaps, but that's not certain . . . A simple gesture can encourage others. But none of us set an example.'

There was another doctor working on racial theory. Horst Schumann was a tall, broad-shouldered and excessively brutal Nazi, whose area of interest lay in pre-cancerous conditions of the uterus, an interest shared by Auschwitz's chief SS medical officer, Dr Eduard Wirths, another tall man, with a sharp and menacing voice. Dr Schumann also removed ovaries to see whether X-rays had been effective in destroying tissue, sometimes burning the women severely in the process. He organised his operations as an assembly line, one prisoner immediately after another, a long chain of injured and crying women. One of the prisoner doctors, an Austrian called Dr Dering, refused to give anaesthetics to Jewish patients.

Also in May, an SS research scientist arrived at Birkenau to verify some racial theories of his own. He had women, of all ages, file naked before him while he took measurements. A number he directed to one side, telling them that he would be moving them from Birkenau to a better camp. Later, Adelaïde discovered that they had been shot, and their skeletons preserved and taken to an institute in Strasbourg for further study. Increasingly haunted by her job, she was forced to stand by while those whom he selected begged to be spared. It was, she said, like watching 'hunted animals'.

One day, a former professor of gynaecology from Cologne called Maximilian Samuel, deported to Auschwitz as a Jew and made assistant to Schumann, told Adelaïde that she was to assist at an experiment on a woman's uterus. She found Samuel's zeal for the work repugnant and despised his apparent inability to face reality. Having recently helped prepare a 17-year-old Greek girl for surgery, she had sworn that she would not do so again. She told him to inform Schumann that she would not work with him. Samuel reported her to the SS.

Wirths, to whom she was summoned, was not, by the standards of Auschwitz, a vicious man, and he had in fact made some attempts to improve the appalling conditions in which the prisoners lived. He asked Adelaïde whether she had not fully realised that Jewish women were very different from herself? Yes, she replied, there were indeed many people who were very different from herself, starting with Dr Wirths himself. She would assist at no more experiments. She now prepared herself for the inevitable, telling the others that she had never really expected to leave Auschwitz alive, and all that was left to her was 'to behave, for the rest of the short time that remains, as a human being'. She had made the gesture; found the courage. But even so, what worried her was that it simply meant that someone else would have to do what she refused to do, and that they would find it no less hard; while she was left with her 'good conscience'.

That evening, Orli, a medical assistant in the women's camp – a woman who had been a prisoner for many years and with whom Adelaïde had become friendly – told her that she had heard that a squad was coming next day to deal with the 'special cases', of which she was one. But Orli had a plan. She would give Adelaïde a strong sleeping draught, assign her a bed in the infirmary, and claim that she had died in the night, substituting a dead body in her place. The ruse worked. Adelaïde woke and was smuggled back to Birkenau. Later, she would tell another prisoner, 'I was fortunate enough to have higher values than life itself.'

* * *

The autumn brought no further deaths to the French women. A hundred and seventy-seven were dead, in a little over six months. Those who remained were determined, capable women, strong mentally as well as physically; it was no accident that all but a few of the survivors had been active politically, committed to shared beliefs in a better future, and accustomed to hardship and discipline. They were nearly all much the same age, in their late twenties and early thirties. Apart from Poupette and Simone, not one of the young girls was still alive; all the older women without exception were dead. Of the forty-seven women rounded up by Poinsot and his men in the Gironde and Charente, fewer than ten remained alive. Most of the *résistance intellectuelle* from Paris, almost all the printers and many of the young women who had handed out leaflets for the Jeunes Filles de France had perished.

There had been some changes in Auschwitz. After a scandal involving excessive pilfering of 'Canada' by the SS, Hoess had been replaced by a slightly less savage commandant. Arthur Liebehenschel set about curbing the corruption and transferring out of Auschwitz guards he regarded as too brutal. When the work commandos returned from the factories and marshes in the evenings, they brought fewer corpses back with them. Liebehenschel was particularly fond of music, and he liked to have an orchestra of women prisoners, many of them distinguished musicians in their former lives, playing on all possible occasions, dressed in matching pleated skirts and white blouses. The orchestra was ordered to play the work details in and out of camp morning and evening, tramping past in their rows of five to the sounds of Strauss and Offenbach.

In Raisko, the return to some small semblance of normality and physical health had brought with it a need to talk and to exchange stories, always taking care to avoid intimate and painful memories. 'We never spoke,' Charlotte would later say, 'of love.' They talked about what they would do after the war, spinning dreams that made them feel they might just still go home. Best was anything to do with literature or the theatre and when Claudette Bloch, Marie-Elisa's chemist friend, revealed that she knew Molière's *Le Malade imaginaire* almost by heart, the French women set about recreating the play, line by line, the memories coming back in fits and starts, scene by scene, with Charlotte directing and Cécile once again, as in Romainville, doing the costumes. Cécile had a sharp tongue, but she made the others laugh. Carmen found props; Lulu, who loved acting, took the part of Argan. Aprons were turned into the doctor's gown; tulle netting was borrowed from the laboratory for ruffles, and wood shavings were made into a wig. In the evenings, for an hour at the end of the day, the women rehearsed.

Then came the Sunday of the performance, attended by the whole block. 'It was magnificent,' Charlotte would write, 'because, for the space of two hours, while the smokestacks never stopped belching their smoke of human flesh, for two whole hours we believed in what we were doing.' After remaining silent for so long, the characters of plays and books had finally re-entered Charlotte's mind, and she entertained the others by describing them. Later she would say that she looked in vain for Madame Bovary, Anna Karenina and Rastignac, but that Proust returned to her.

On Christmas Eve, the women were permitted to stop work at four. Plans had been made for a dinner of celebration: women still alive despite all the odds celebrating the simple fact that they were not dead. They realised with delight that their hair had grown back a bit and they helped each other to wash it and brush the new tufts and strands that covered their heads. A few of the women had acquired stockings from 'Canada', and shirts had been 'organised' and cut up to make a clean white collar for each of them. With sheets as tablecloths, the refectory tables were formed into a horseshoe and decorated. Paper was crinkled into flowers, and the chemists had fashioned rouge and lipstick out of powders in the laboratory. Food, saved from the parcels from France and vegetables pilfered from the gardens were made into a feast of beans and cabbage, potatoes with onion sauce and poppy seeds. The women ate little, having lost the habit of food, but the sight of so much to eat made them cheerful. They drank sweet dark beer, stolen from the SS kitchens. After they had eaten, they turned out the lights, lit candles, and the Polish women sang hymns and ballads, saying to each other *Do domou*: back home. Presents were exchanged: a bar of soap, a rope woven into a belt, a teddy bear found near the gas chambers and exchanged for two onions.

* * *

Early in the New Year an SS guard appeared at Raisko with a list of names. On it were those of the French women, who were to return immediately to Birkenau. Extremely apprehensive, fearing that an order might have come to kill off the French prisoners, they packed a small cloth bag each, with a precious toothbrush and some soap. As they left the barracks, they began to sing the Marseillaise, which had marked every step of their journey. Loaded on to a cart, they went on singing, led by Carmen, who had a large repertoire of songs. When they saw the barbed wire and the smoking chimney stacks their hearts seemed to stop.

But the news was, as far as they could tell, good. A first party of French women was to leave for the camp of Ravensbrück, north of Berlin. Charlotte, Cécile, Poupette, Mado, Lulu, Carmen, Gilberte and Marie-Jeanne Pennec were told to undress while slightly cleaner clothes were found for them. Then, to their amazement, their original suitcases, with at least some of their possessions still inside, were returned to them, and they were asked to sign a form swearing not to describe what they had witnessed at Auschwitz. More surprising still, Taube, whose brutality had coloured many of their days, knelt down to fix Carmen's laces. As if in a dream, they were marched to the station, in their loose striped dresses and ill-fitting shoes, and put on to an ordinary train, where they looked out of the windows at ordinary people going about their lives as if Auschwitz had never existed. They noted with pleasure the degree of damage inflicted by Allied bombing on German towns. The train passed a column of tanks, a Panzer division heading for the eastern front. What surprised the women most was that they felt so little surprise at the luxury of their surroundings; like coats, left hanging behind a door, they had found their old selves, and it was as if they had never been away.

When they changed trains in Berlin, they found the city in ruins and felt 'nothing but pleasure'. The guards allowed them to go to the women's rest rooms, and there, for the first time in over a year, they saw themselves in a mirror. They stared with disbelief at their bony, haggard faces and straggling wisps of hair. They discussed trying to escape, but in their distinctive striped clothes felt there was little chance of success. And where would they have gone? They were herded on to a second train full of Gestapo officers in soft leather coats. Charlotte was touched and amazed when a young woman in their compartment with a little girl insisted that the French women take their places. It gave them a sense that there was still a world in which decency and pity existed.

The remaining French women were still in their quarantine block outside the fence of Birkenau when Hoess was reappointed commandant, in order to expedite the extermination of the Hungarian Jews, who from May arrived in their tens of thousands every day. There was now a new railway spur inside Birkenau itself, which led directly to the gas ovens. This meant that there was an assembly line of death, on a scale and at a speed never seen before. One night, Marie-Claude heard terrible cries; next morning she learnt that because the gas chambers had run out of Zyklon B pellets, the smaller children had been thrown directly on to the flames. 'When we tell people,' she said to the others, 'who will believe us?'

They were there when the gypsy family camp was finally liquidated, and those small children who had miraculously survived starvation were herded into the gas ovens with their parents. And they still had no news of their fate when an international commission visited Auschwitz and was effectively bamboozled about its true intent. After the commissioners left, the women were asked whether they wanted to go to work in Germany, but they refused, fearing a trap, and so were sent back inside Birkenau, to a wooden block just by the railway spur, where they were put to sewing crosses on to ordinary dresses, for Auschwitz had run out of striped material for the new arrivals. They sewed the crosses very loosely, hoping that the wearer might find the chance to escape. From their block they could watch the endless arrivals of Hungarian Jews, and heart-rending scenes when mothers were torn away from their children.

With summer, the garden of Hoess's house, where his children played with balls on the lawn, was full of roses, and in his window boxes grew begonias. Between the barbed-wire fence and the line of rose bushes lay the path leading to the crematoria, and all day long they could see the endless procession of stretchers carrying the dead to the ovens.

But then the day came when they too were put on to a train for Ravensbrück. Marie-Claude, Marie-Elisa, Adelaïde, Germaine Pican and Simone Sampaix were in the first group, followed a few days later by Germaine Renaudin and Hélène Solomon. They were forced to leave behind them one member of the *Convoi*, Marie-Jeanne Bauer, who had survived typhus and repeated abscesses but now had such bad conjunctivitis that the SS refused to let her leave; at one point, Marie-Jeanne had found herself sharing a bunk with four corpses. Her sense of loneliness and loss when the others left was overwhelming.

Of the women who had arrived at Birkenau with a sister, a mother or an aunt, there were almost no pairs left: Poupette had lost Marie, Hélène Bolleau had lost her mother Emma, Yolande her sister Aurore. Not one of the *Convoi* had died in Raisko, and only five during the spring and summer months the others had spent in the quarantine block. One of them was 17-year-old Sylviane Coupet, whom the others found covered in lice in the *Revier*, and whom Carmen kissed tenderly as she died. To Charlotte, who had accompanied her to see Sylviane, Carmen said: 'You kiss her too.' Looking at the skeletal body, with its sallow skin and lips covered with pinkish saliva, Charlotte drew back, appalled; ever afterwards, she felt ashamed when she remembered the moment.

The French women were now down to fifty-two. What was extraordinary was not that so many had died; but that so many had survived.

CHAPTER THIRTEEN

The disposables

The train bringing Charlotte, Poupette, Cécile and the others to Ravensbrück stopped at Fürstenberg station. From here they were marched seven kilometres through the flat wooded countryside of Mecklenburg, past dunes of almost white sand, until they reached a line of pretty cottages and a lake. 'It's less terrifying than electrified barbed wire,' Poupette said to the others. They saw ahead of them a high brick wall, an imposing stone building and a tall fence; entering the gates, which were guarded by SS men, they noted orderly rows of barracks, much like those at Birkenau, standing on an immense field of black clinker. There were no railway tracks leading to a crematorium, no trains delivering terrified families to the gas ovens, no signs of 'selections'. And there was water, a tap for every barracks, which meant that they could finally wash their clothes and drink as much as they wanted. 'Here we can live,' Mado remarked.

It was not, however, all it seemed, even if, in theory at least, Ravensbrück was a place of labour and not of extermination. Built on reclaimed marshland in 1939 as a camp for women to take members of the German Resistance, it had grown in a little over three years from twelve barracks to thirty-two. And it was still growing, as the Russians advanced from the east, overrunning German concentration camps and driving their inmates on long forced marches towards the interior of the Reich. The water that appeared so plentiful was contaminated by sewage and the over-spill of the factories that had sprung up in and around the camp. Each barracks already housed four times its theoretical maximum; blankets had run out; and fleas, as in Auschwitz, were endemic. No one ever got over the horror of the fleas. There were no spare socks and too few shoes, which meant that many of the women went barefoot; there were not enough spoons, and old tins doubled as bowls. The barracks, few of them with glass in the windows, remained well below freezing for much of the long northern winter; locals called the area 'Klein-Sibirien in Mecklenburg', the little Siberian Mecklenburg, on account of the glacial cold arriving from the Baltic.

After registration came showers, then a humiliating and insanitary gynaecological inspection, the doctor not bothering to change her rubber gloves from woman to woman. Ravensbrück had no striped dresses and they were given the clothes taken from the suitcases of new arrivals, with crosses painted clearly on the back and front. After this, they found themselves once again in the relative safety and ease of a quarantine barracks. The women were now, as Lulu wrote to her family, 'a little closer' to home.

Four weeks later, they were moved to a block which was already occupied by Russian women prisoners of war, who had refused to work in a German munitions factory and were being punished by being made to stand all day outside the barracks without food. When captured, these women had been described by the German propaganda office as 'Amazons' and hysterics, proof of what Bolshevism did to women. Many had arrived in Ravensbrück broken by forced marches.

The eight friends soon discovered other French women in the camp, among them acquaintances from the Resistance in France, from whom they learnt the lie of their confusing new land. Everywhere they looked there were women of different races, nationalities, religions and class, speaking dozens of different languages and dialects, and wearing, as in Birkenau, many combinations of distinguishing labels. Their own, as before, were the red triangles of political prisoners.

Ravensbrück, they heard, was ruled over by a commandant called Fritz Suhren, a man with a taste for drink, not very military in appearance but an able administrator and a particularly willing executioner of Soviet prisoners. Under him were some forty SS officials and several thousand guards, most of them women, either SS or auxiliaries drafted as part of the war effort, having been subjected to a mixture of threats and promises. Even kind and pleasant women, so it was said, took only a few days to become rough and vindictive. Ravensbrück was famous for its use of savage dogs. Those patrolling the perimeter fences were trained, on Himmler's orders, to tear to pieces anyone suspected of trying to escape.

By early 1944, the camp was home to some 20,000 women detainees. There were Germans who had opposed National Socialism, either because they were devout Christians or because they were communists; Jehovah's Witnesses, who had been told that they could be released, providing they forswore their beliefs; some five thousand *asociales*, prostitutes, criminals and abortionists; 'dangerous recidivists', in the form of Jews, Russians and Ukrainians, for whom the Reich decreed 'extermination through labour'; and women who had polluted the German race by marrying Jews. There were Italians, Yugoslavs, Spaniards, Norwegians, Albanians and a handful of Egyptians, Argentinians, Chinese, Greeks, British and two Americans. And there were the wives and daughters of Rotterdam's diamond merchants, along with scientists, professors, journalists, actresses and students from the whole of occupied Europe.

The largest group were the Poles, from the Polish Army and other different political factions, who, given their numerical superiority and their strong sense of discipline and comradeship, had managed to get themselves into the most important positions around the camp – the kitchens, the storerooms and the infirmaries. These they defended fiercely. Most despised, the French women were told, were the Russians, some of them elderly peasants, others doctors and teachers; and the French themselves, of whom there were now several thousand. They were regarded by the other nationalities as chronically undisciplined, and greatly resentful of the SS code of discipline.

The Polish women were said by the French to run the camp with 'extreme egotism, and a criminal lack of all social conscience', though by the time Charlotte and the first group of seven French friends reached Ravensbrück, a small number of well-educated German and Austrian women had secured places in the administrative offices. These were, for the most part, communists, and they looked after their own, which would prove useful to the group. Of the eight, only Poupette and Marie-Jeanne Pennec, who had guided people across the demarcation line, and was a solitary, secretive countrywoman who had kept many of them alive in Birkenau by foraging for food in the marshes, had no strong political beliefs.

There were also many gypsy women who, when the weather became warmer, could be seen wandering around the camp after dark, looking to exchange things they had found or stolen for extra rations of bread. Soon after arriving, Charlotte was offered the Larousse edition of Molière's *Le Misanthrope*. Back in their barracks, she read it aloud to the others, who each gave her a little bit of their bread, and then, ever frightened that she was losing her memory, she proceeded to learn it by heart, reciting the scenes to herself every day. Over the months, she had managed to bring back into her memory fifty-seven of the poems she had read and loved in her free life, and these too she recited to herself and to the others.

Attached to the main camp at Ravensbrück was a smaller one for men, where a number of Germans, Austrians and Poles, a few of them Jews, others wearing the pink triangles of homosexuals, were kept as a labour force for the constant building taking place in and around the camp. Here, among men working punishingly long hours, with rudimentary tools, not enough food and constantly punished, the mortality rate was extremely high.

*   *   *

When, in 1939, Ravensbrück had first opened, the camp was perceived as a place of re-education for 'polluters of race', prostitutes, recidivists and homosexuals. However, re-education had rapidly given way to slave labour as the needs of the German war economy grew, and by 1943, Ravensbrück was the hub for thirty-three satellite factory camps, producing everything from gunpowder to spare parts for Messerschmitts. Its position, in a relatively isolated area of lakes and forests, but with good rail connections, was ideal. As SS Gruppenführer Pohl, head of the Economic Office of the SS, explained, the Reich needed these women for 'their arms and their legs, because they must contribute to the great victory of the German people'. What

with the gassing of the Jews, the slaughter of the Russian prisoners of war, and the deaths from disease, starvation and
brutality among the slave labourers, there were constant fears
about running out of workers. As Pohl saw it, work was to be
'totally exhausting', and no one appeared to question how
sensible it was to make women weakened by hunger perform
until they collapsed jobs that were too taxing for them.

Within the camp itself, Siemens had a factory making spare
parts for telegraph, radio and precision tools. All these enterprises,
as in Birkenau, sent managers to inspect and select the women
they wanted. As Marie-Claude would later write, 'it was just like
a slave market. They felt the women's muscles, checked their state
of health, then pointed to the ones they liked.' After which the
women were again inspected, this time naked, by one of the camp
doctors. Those who proved 'feeble' were quickly returned, to be
swapped for better specimens.

It was not long before Charlotte and the others understood why
the women in the camp described Ravensbrück as 'l'enfer des
femmes', the women's hell. Overcrowding had turned the barracks
into a vision of the Inferno as seen by Renaissance painters, tier
upon tier of wooden boxes, filled with skeletal semi-naked women
in which even the most staunch were prey to terrible rages. To
survive meant to fight – for space, food, water. Nights were filled
with the noise of women groaning, quarrelling, snoring and yelping
with pain, as bony bodies touched the hard wooden slats.

Soon after being taken to their barracks Charlotte, Cécile and
the six French friends were put to sewing German military
uniforms, sitting as on a conveyor belt, doing twelve-hour shifts
in a hut without ventilation and with very little light. The women
there already, they noticed, were hunched and their sight had
suffered; they coughed constantly. The most unpleasant task,
which all dreaded, was unpicking the bloody uniforms of the
soldiers who had died on the eastern front. If the daily targets
were not reached, an SS woman called Binder threw herself on
the women, beating them about the head and arms in a frenzy
of fury.

One afternoon, orders came that all the women were to stop
work and stand in a line outside the hut. An SS doctor told them
to take off their shoes and stockings and hold up the hems of

their dresses. Hurriedly, Poupette and the other younger women formed up on the outer edges, shielding the older women in the middle. Orders were given to start walking round in a large circle. As they filed past, the doctor pulled out all those with swollen legs or feet deformed by oedema. With every circle, the ranks thinned. We walked, Charlotte would later say, 'like the damned upon the tympanums of cathedral portals'. Not one of the friends was pulled out; those who were learnt that they were to go to a 'fasting camp' nearby, but just what that entailed they could only guess.

Though not officially an extermination camp, the ethos of Ravensbrück was one of deprivation – of food, warmth, sleep and news. Everyone was hungry, obsessed with food, and afraid. In a world in which the unpredictable and unexpected reigned, there were no laces for shoes, but women were punished when their shoes fell off; no combs or scarves to hold back hair, but punishments if it was not pinned back. After the siren went at 3.30 in the morning, women had a few minutes in which to get ready for work, but there were no towels and no soap, and there were ten lavatories for a thousand women. As in Auschwitz, roll calls were times of ferocious cold and snarling dogs.

Not long after their arrival, two young French women from another barracks tried to escape. One of them, Odette Fabius, was caught and tortured. That day all the French women in the camp were ordered to spend the entire day on their knees on the sharp rough clinker, their hands held in the air, without moving. Many fainted.

Because of the overcrowding, the constant arrival of new inmates and the turmoil, it was sometimes possible to choose between being sent away to work in one of Ravensbrück's satellite camps and remaining among the *Verfügbaren*, the disposables. These were the women who, because they were sick, or frail, or *Nacht und Nebel*, or elderly, remained in the camp, often with no work to do but available for jobs that were both unpleasant and might lead to sudden round-ups. The worst of these was being harnessed to a steel roller, like a slave, and made to haul it over the rough earth to make new roads. But remaining in camp offered the possibility of finding a mushroom or some dandelions. The friends were growing skilled at avoiding work altogether, having decided that the way to conserve their dwindling strength was to hide – behind the blocks, in the latrines or in the rafters. Sometimes they concealed themselves among the *Schmuckstücke*,* Ravensbrück's *musulmans*, women who had lost all hope and energy and who drifted apathetically around the camp.

All they knew for certain was that the single most important thing in their lives now was to stay together, and that without the others none would survive. It was a terrible blow to all of them when Marie-Jeanne Pennec was suddenly sent off to work in a factory in Czechoslovakia. She had never been very close to any of them, remaining solitary and somewhat secretive, but all felt her departure as a terrible omen.

A drawing by Jeannette L'Herrminier in Ravensbrück

In the evenings, the seven who remained – Charlotte, Poupette, Cécile, Carmen, Gilberte, Lulu and Mado – gathered close together, pooling their rations, which were getting smaller all the time. The daily soup was now nothing but greenish-grey water, made of beets, white carrots and grasses, and they watched each ladle like hawks, to see which might contain a shred of meat. Dried vegetables had disappeared, and with them fats of any kind. Each woman received one soup spoon of jam and one small lump

---

* Literally 'pieces of jewellery', like *musulman*, a word never properly explained.

of cheese a week. The very occasional bit of sausage looked odd and seemed to glow in the dark. They were, quite literally, slowly starving to death. Often, now, they talked to each other about food, going over menus and recipes, dreaming of what they might one day eat again. But they also became resourceful and inventive, skilled at using little bits of wire or cloth or rubber to make combs and toothbrushes. None had quite lost the need to hold on to some vestige of physical pride and dignity, but it was becoming harder and harder to keep up the discipline of catching fleas, and there had been no change of underclothes in three months.

In Ravensbrück, Charlotte had discovered others who also longed to keep their minds alive. Among women reduced to skeletons, shuffling around in rags, a 'spoken newspaper' had taken shape, with news from the outside world, information about the camp, even poems, repeated and passed around from woman to woman. It was in this way that Charlotte heard of the Normandy landings in June, over which the entire camp rejoiced. National feast days were marked by small acts of celebration. Teachers gave classes in literature and history. Mathematicians drew problems in the sand. Discussion groups were started, on everything from raising rabbits to esoteric questions of philosophy. Despite the lack of books and paper, there was a huge hunger for knowledge, particularly the learning of languages, though very few women chose to learn German.

Whenever possible, the women sang. The Russians, with their haunting laments, proved the most popular, until Suhren forbade all singing of patriotic songs, after which they whistled, until that was forbidden too. Ordered to sing in German, they chanted '*Ja, Ja, Ja*' at the top of their voices. Even such minor acts of rebellion were exhilarating. On 14 July, the French women in Block 14 attached cockades the colours of the French flag to their dresses and sang the Marseillaise, until the SS fell on them with sticks. To survive, they instinctively knew, they had to remain human, and to be human was to remember that there was another world, of decency and culture and plenty, however painful the memories were.

Confined to the camp, the seven remaining friends decided that their job would be to brief all new women arriving on trains from France, finding ways of climbing into their barracks to instruct them on what to do and what to avoid. 'We told them,' Lulu would later explain, 'that they should never admit to being Jewish, that they should never say they were tired or ill, and that they should do everything they could to appear young and healthy. And we told them about the importance of looking after each other, which was the only way they were likely to survive.'

*   *   *

Early in August, arriving from Auschwitz in two separate groups, came all but one of the remaining survivors of the *Convoi des 31000*. Marie-Jeanne Bauer was too ill to be moved. As the cattle trucks pulled away, Marie-Claude remembered the day they had marched, singing, through the gates of Birkenau, nineteen months earlier, and thought of all the friends who had died. 'We had,' she said later, 'the feeling that we were leaving hell, and for the first time I felt a glimmer of hope that I would live to see the world again.' Fifty-one of them had now been transferred to Ravensbrück. The reunion between the friends felt like a celebration, for none had known they would ever see the others again, and Charlotte and the others quickly coached the newcomers in the art of surviving their surroundings. Ravensbrück had almost doubled in size since January, and more women were arriving every day. It was a confusing, chaotic place.

For some, arrival in Ravensbrück confirmed their worst fears. To her immense pleasure, Yolande found her mother Céleste Pica in the camp, but she had to tell her that 19-year-old Aurore was dead; and Céleste broke to her the news that her father, Attilio, had been executed by the Germans. What neither of them knew was that Yolande's husband Armand had been killed not long before while fighting with the Maquis. And Germaine Pican had to tell her friend Lucie Guérin, who had also recently arrived in Ravensbrück, that her 17-year-old daughter Claudine was dead.

Among the *Nacht und Nebel* prisoners were Marie-Elisa, Marie-Claude and Adelaïde, though their whereabouts were no longer in fact a secret. After the obligatory period in quarantine, they were sent to Block 32, to join the other secret prisoners from occupied Europe, many of them communist leaders, strong and capable women who were happy to take those they identified as possible future communists under their wing. Here they discovered Geneviève de Gaulle, niece to the general, the ethnographer Germaine Tillon and 20-year-old Annette Postel-Vinay, highly educated and forthright young French women brought straight to Ravensbrück from Paris after their capture for Resistance activities. Germaine Tillon's mother, arrested not long after her by the Gestapo, had recently arrived in Ravensbrück; she was a gentle and distinguished woman in her sixties.

These women had been in the camp some months, and had become skilled at navigating its pitfalls. They had news about the progress of the war and the approach of the Russian army, having persuaded an Austrian woman employed to clean the SS canteens to pass on any newspapers she found to a Czech friend who, in turn, passed them on to the French women. Annette, like Adelaïde, came from Alsace, and spoke German. At one end of the block were a number of elderly Russian women, so pious that they crossed themselves whenever they discovered a shred of rutabaga in the soup. One day Annette found a silk map hidden in the folds of a German uniform she was unpicking, after which they were able to follow the advance of the Allied troops. It gave them a sense that victory was possible.

Block 32 was also home to the survivors of Ravensbrück's lethal medical experiments, the *Kaninchen* or little rabbits, Polish girls whose legs had been 'treated' by Professor Gebhardt, President of the German Red Cross, Professor of Orthopaedic Surgery at Berlin University and former chief surgeon to the 1936 Olympics, whose private nursing home lay not far from the camp. Gebhardt had been summoned to care for Heydrich after he was shot, but had failed to save his life when the wound became infected with gas gangrene. On the eastern front, hundreds of German soldiers had died from gas gangrene, and there was a pressing need for a cure. In Ravensbrück, having been criticised for not using the new sulphonamide drugs on Heydrich and in order to redeem his reputation by proving that they would not have saved Heydrich's life, Gebhardt had removed muscles and bones from seventy-five Polish girls. He had then injected their wounds with tetanus, gangrene and streptococcus, before testing out different drugs.

When, after the first painful operation, the girls resisted a second, they were held down and operated on without anaesthetics, Gebhardt presiding in his military uniform and making no effort at cleanliness. Though initially lured into the operating theatre by promises that they would be released afterwards, none of the Polish girls had been freed. Five had died, six others had been shot, but the survivors could be seen limping around the camp, in considerable pain. In Block 32, the French women took care of them as best they could. The youngest was just 14. In Block 32 there was no thieving, and you could leave a piece of bread on your bunk and find it there later. The women kept their block clean and free of fleas, and shared their rations with those who had the least. It was, however, perfectly clear to everyone that the Germans intended no one in the block to survive and bear witness to their medical experiments.

* * *

The new French arrivals were distributed around various camp jobs by Hans Pflaum, the SS officer in charge of work details, a large, brutish man in his early twenties widely feared throughout the camp. Pflaum was often drunk. Some women were sent to haul coal from Fürstenberg to the furnaces heating the guards' villas; some went to work in the gardens, where they were sometimes spat on by the SS children; others cut down trees, shifted sand from the lake or joined Charlotte and Poupette and the others mending German uniforms. Occasionally one of them would be dispatched to unload wagons of iron or wood, arriving as loot from other countries.

Marie-Claude was sent first to the sand quarry, then moved to the *Revier* to act as secretary until she had an argument with a *kapo*, after which she was put to raking the paths in the camp, a job she much preferred. Hélène Bolleau was ordered to help a number of distinguished and important Austrian women, brought to Ravensbrück as hostages, who lived in the relative comfort of one of the privileged barracks; since they were allowed to receive parcels of food, they spurned the camp soup, and Hélène was able to take their rations back to her friends each evening. Betty once again found herself working as a nurse. What struck them all was that Ravensbrück, though indeed *l'enfer* (hell), felt very different from Birkenau. There, the primary goal had been to exterminate the inmates, with the majority being gassed as soon as they arrived, and the others worked to death; here they soon understood that the purpose was to run a successful commercial exercise, death being simply a by-product and not an end.

For the first time since leaving France nineteen months earlier they began to think that they had a real chance of surviving until the end of the war. But they knew, too, that to lower their guard would be fatal and that all the old rules that had saved them in Birkenau – cleanliness, wariness, a sense of humour, and close friendships – still applied. The friendship between them, stronger than anything they had known in their previous lives, had become their credo; it defined them.

In the evenings, after sharing their rations and eating them crouched on their bunks, the friends visited one another in their different barracks, swapping news and encouragement. They still never talked about their families, and particularly not their children, for it remained too painful. Not all had ever received a letter from home, and those who hadn't lived in a constant state of fear as to what might have befallen their families. Lulu, who had last seen Paul when he was 18 months old, at least had news that he was safe; but she was painfully conscious of how much of his infancy she had missed. In the occasional letter she was allowed to write, she begged for news of him. Though the letters were carefully bland, occasional cries from the heart came through. 'It is hard for me to realise,' she wrote one day, 'that he isn't a baby any more . . . I will always regret the days of his very young years in which I couldn't live next to him and with him.' Cécile and Germaine Pican had left little girls behind and could only wonder what the months of uncertainty about their mothers had done to them.

What the new arrivals discovered was that among the five thousand or so French women already in Ravensbrück all France was represented. About a quarter were theoretically 'criminals': these were prostitutes who had infected German soldiers with venereal diseases; and there were black marketeers, and women who had volunteered for German war work, then committed a crime. The rest were all 'politicals', though in some cases only because they were the sister or the concierge of a *résistant* wanted by the Gestapo, or had been denounced by a jealous neighbour. They found that those who came from recognised groups – the communists, the Catholic Bretons, the intellectual bourgeoisie – were team players, and the easiest to get on with. The very rich, the *tout Paris*, were the dirtiest and most unfriendly. But the French, as a national group, were more cohesive than the other nationalities, more prone to look after their own.

The lives of the new French inmates were immeasurably improved by the help of the German-speakers who had been able to secure positions in the various camp offices. One, whose job it was to sort through the vast piles of clothes arriving, as at Auschwitz, with every transport, had become skilled at smuggling sweaters under her clothes, going to work each morning naked under her thin dress. Another, who worked in the forest, brought back twigs, with which she made charcoal, which helped a little against dysentery. Each woman sewed herself a little bag out of scraps of material, in which she kept anything precious like a toothbrush and which she never let out of her sight.

Though the sulphonamide experiments – which had also been performed on male prisoners, brought from Sachsenhausen – were over by the time the women reached Ravensbrück, a number of sterilisation tests were still being conducted, and plans were being made to continue Professor Clauberg's work in Auschwitz. Adelaïde soon found herself summoned to the *Revier* where they were to take place. Once again, her manner glacial and appearing completely unemotional, as a friend later described her, she refused to have any part in the proceedings. 'My conviction is now certain,' she wrote. 'I won't follow orders any more. I will take as cover the abscesses on my legs, which won't heal, as a defence.' And, once again, she was lucky. Sent as doctor to another *Revier*, she set about saving lives.

It was not easy. By the summer of 1944, a military SS doctor called Percival Treite was in charge of Ravensbrück's medical services, a blond, correct but chilly surgeon, harsh but not sadistic, soon to be joined by Dr Adolf Winkelmann who came from Auschwitz. Winkelmann, who strode about the camp in his long brown leather coat, was much feared and hated; he sometimes rode a motorcycle and had a machine gun. The senior nurse was a large, hard, white-haired woman called Elisabeth Marschall. Together, they kept up a constant search for the very sick, women who were clearly dying, but taking too long over it, and who could be 'selected' and finished off with a lethal injection.

With the ever growing population of the camp and the inexorable spread of infectious diseases, long queues of severely malnourished, coughing, itching, shuffling, stinking women, their legs covered in suppurating sores, gathered outside the *Revier* every morning. What every woman feared most was being sent to Block 10, known as the cemetery, for it was here that women with TB were put, hundreds of women of dozens of nationalities crowded together with no treatment, for none was expected to live. Block 10 was presided over by Carmen Mori, one of the more vicious *kapos*, who frequently beat women until they were unconscious.

Faced with so many sick women and determined to protect them from Dr Winkelmann's selections, Adelaïde devised ways of falsifying the length of their illnesses, changed temperatures on charts, and discovered how to make a paste from the red pencils used in the *Reviers*, to put colour into the women's ashen cheeks. When Betty developed a phlegmon under her arm, which spread and became infected, Adelaïde and a Polish doctor operated – without anaesthetic – and showed her how to hold her arm during the SS medical inspections in such a way that the long scar did not show. And there was a wonderful day when a prisoner doctor, who happened to be working on unloading wagons bringing loot from Poland, came across a large medical chest full of drugs. He buried it in the sand and every day women passing that way returned with little stocks of medicine hidden in folds in their socks. For a while, many lives were saved. Once again, Adelaïde was haunted by the choices she had to make. 'I am integrated into a system that stems from the Devil . . .

We all take part in it in some way and I will always feel a sense of shame.'

In keeping with the premise instilled into every SS guard that the inmates of Ravensbrück were depraved and inferior, punishments for misdemeanours, however trivial, were ferocious. For attempting to escape, or striking a guard, women were shot, usually in the back of the head. For talking, not standing in orderly rows, moving too slowly, looking defiant or not understanding orders, prisoners were struck by the SS guards, who wore large silver rings with the death's head insignia, ideal for breaking teeth and noses. Or they were sentenced to lashes – with fifty death was probable, with seventy-five inevitable – carried out by *kapos*, who in return for volunteering for the job were given extra rations of food.

Most feared was the *Strafblock*, a prison within the camp, a bedlam of deranged women driven beyond the limits of endurance by the savagery of the guards and their dogs. A former kitchen maid of 24, Dorothea Binz, a pretty, blond young woman whose face was distorted by cruelty, and who had risen rapidly up through the ranks of the female SS, was in control of the *Strafblock*'s seventy-eight cells. Here, in water up to their ankles, languished women implicated in the July 1944 plot on Hitler's life. Binz was said to be the lover of Schutzhaftlager Edmund Bräuning, a huge and coarse man, responsible for order in the camp. It was Binz who conducted women into the punishment cage, where they could neither lie down nor stand up, and where they were left naked and without food. Binz used scissors with which to deal out blows. There was no woman in the camp who did not fear her. As she walked slowly down the rows of women assembled for the interminable roll calls, looking for culprits, the women trembled.

*　　*　　*

What happened now was precisely what the French women had long dreaded: they were split up. The first to go were Cécile, Poupette, Lulu and her sister Carmen – for them separation would not have been bearable – and Gilberte Tamisé, whose sister Andrée had been beaten to death in Birkenau. Called before Pflaum, they were informed that they were being sent to work in a factory making V1s and V2s at Beendorf in Lower Saxony. For Cécile, it meant being parted from Charlotte, to whom she had become very close.

Beendorf was an old salt mine lying 600 metres underground, and it was here, protected from Allied air raids, that the Germans were building their new weapons. Six hundred of the 2,500 women workers were inmates from concentration camps, two hundred of them French or Belgian. Lodged in a hangar three kilometres away and referred to as *Stücke* (pieces), they were marched after roll call each day to the mineshafts, to be carried down deep into the earth in cages. The vast cavern in which the factory had been built was reached across dark, perilous walkways, where it was hard, in ill-fitting clogs, not to trip over the rails laid to carry away the salt, and where the salt itself aggravated all scratches, wounds and open sores. In the immense echoing cave, the salt very white to the eye, the factory looked small.

The women worked twelve-hour shifts, six days a week, night and day, the day shift never seeing daylight. The friends found themselves attached to different groups. Poupette was put with Cécile, whose sharp tongue she had never liked. She befriended a little Jewish Hungarian girl called Véronique, who had been brought to Beendorf with her mother, who was now in the *Revier* dying. Véronique, who was nine, told Poupette that she was an only child, that she had lived in a big house in Budapest with her parents and a governess and that her father had been taken away by the Germans.

It was a measure of the women's toughness of spirit, and their sense of the approaching end to the war, that they immediately set about practising small acts of sabotage. Put to work on oil filters and assembling components, and given precise instructions, they did the opposite. Told to screw something tightly, they screwed it loosely; ordered to use only a small layer of grease, they spread it lavishly around. Much time was taken laboriously doing the same task again and again, screwing something up, then unscrewing it. Cécile made the holes for the screws just a little too big, so that the screws slipped through, until a German guard was detailed to watch over her continuously. Lulu gathered up some grains of salt and mixed them in with the grease. All the women found ways to drop the more fragile pieces and to spill their cans of oil. One month, seven of the ten completed motors burnt out before they left the factory.

Infuriated by the slow rate of progress, the German overseers tried to bribe the women to increase productivity. They brought in tempting extra food and tried to force them to take it, heaping it on to their arms. But the women refused and kept their arms tightly to their sides, though they were always hungry, their daily rations now little more than watery soup. When the next shift came on, word went down the line to refuse all inducements. 'We thus did all we could,' one of them wrote later, 'to be intelligently stupid and clumsy.'

It was not without risk. The machines were closely supervised and saboteurs were often hanged. The SS guards who had accompanied the women from Ravensbrück were as brutal as they had been in the camp. When Poupette washed her dress and left it to dry, borrowing another from a friend who was ill, she was discovered and beaten. A young German woman, caught talking to a male civilian worker, was so badly thrashed that her face was unrecognisable. During the autumn, fourteen German workers were shot, and their bodies tossed out in paper sacks.

Not long after their arrival, two Polish women escaped. That night, Cécile, Poupette and the others were made to run the three kilometres back to their barracks, where they were beaten and kicked by the SS and forced to spend the night outside, in the rain, without food. Next evening, having once again been made to run all the way back, they discovered that the two women had been caught. The elder was a large, gentle looking woman; the younger, her daughter-in-law, was very fair. They were terrified and trembling. The other women were made to stand and watch while the two captives were attacked; when they tried to get away, they were dragged back by their hair. Finally, they lay still. The others were now allowed to go to their bunks, leaving the bloody bodies on the floor surrounded by tufts of their brown and blond hair, pulled out at the roots. Later, they learnt that neither woman had died; but they disappeared and where they went no one could discover.

But the five friends remained strong. On 7 November, the anniversary of the Russian revolution, at an agreed moment they put down their tools and sang the Marseillaise. On 11 November, they stole coloured wires from the store and made flowers in the red, white and blue of the French flag, and sang again. Soon after their arrival at Beendorf, they had made contact with fellow communists and socialists by singing revolutionary songs, and some of the men, civilian workers drafted in to work in the factory, were able to smuggle in extra food. On Poupette's 20th birthday, she was given a pair of sandals by one man, a heart made of steel with her name engraved on it by another. Her friends all gave her part of their rations. One day, one of them managed to get hold of a length of cloth and had the idea of making brassières for all of them. But then they looked at themselves and realised that they had no need for brassières, having become as flat-chested as boys.

Hunger, for the women, took many forms. Some went over recipes in their minds, over and over again, savouring every ingredient. Others imagined themselves as empty sacks that nothing would ever fill. Starvation had eaten away not only the fat but the muscles of their bodies. The younger girls, having lost 10 or 20 kilos, looked like skeletons; the more corpulent found that their skin had lost all elasticity and hung in folds, their breasts sinking to their stomachs, their stomachs hanging over their genitals, the flesh of their upper arms and thighs covering their elbows and knees. Nails and hair no longer grew.

What haunted each surviving member of the *Convoi* was that at some point she might find herself alone, separated from all the others. Some time after the five were sent to Beendorf, Hélène Solomon, whose husband Jacques had edited *L'Université Libre* before being shot with Georges Politzer, was told that she was being sent as nurse to the Bosch factories near Berlin. Though transferred in the company of twenty other French women in Ravensbrück, to join 1,500 women making gas masks, she knew none of them. 'It was,' she said later, 'the only time I cried. For over two years, I had never been without my friends, mostly those like Betty and Charlotte whose husbands had also been shot.' She had lost Maï and Danielle in Birkenau, but the few survivors of the Parisian group of journalists, editors and printers had clung together, certain that only each other's warmth and protection could save them.

Now, leaving alone on the train for Berlin, Hélène felt desolate. Survival seemed unlikely.

* * *

In Ravensbrück itself, conditions were deteriorating. With ever more women arriving as concentration camps further east were evacuated and areas of occupied Europe liberated by the Allies, rations were cut. There was no room, very little water, only flickering supplies of electricity. Parcels of food and letters stopped. Every washroom and latrine was surrounded by a sticky mixture of mud and excrement, and since there was no place for bodies – one of the two crematoria had caught fire through overuse – it was not unusual to find corpses piled in heaps by the basins. One morning, one of the French women, arriving to wash herself, heard a prisoner at a basin, surrounded by bodies, singing to herself. The grotesque had become normal.

Though many of the new arrivals were quickly sent on to the satellite camps, requests for extra workers were diminishing and more and more inmates were to be seen wandering around the camp, wearing little more than rags. It made it easier for Charlotte, Cécile and the others to avoid being drafted into work details, but even so the SS were constantly on the lookout for able-bodied workers, and the women's hiding places were regularly discovered. Those caught malingering were punished. Charlotte narrowly avoided capture when the SS unexpectedly cordoned off the section of the camp in which she happened to be. She escaped by darting into a barracks and concealing herself in a narrow slit between the bunks. They all dreaded being conscripted into the group, which contained many French women, that was sent to cut clearings in the forest for hangars in which to conceal planes, and to flatten a plateau for an airstrip. The snow fell early; the women worked up to their ankles in freezing mud. There were many deaths.

Not long after their five friends had left for the salt mine at Beendorf, the others saw an enormous tent going up in a marshy dip at the far end of the camp perimeter. It had been delivered by the army and it stretched for about 50 metres. The tent remained empty, except for a very thin layer of straw strewn over the sharp clinker. But then women and children who had survived the destruction of the Warsaw ghetto began to arrive, and a number of exhausted, terrified and totally silent Hungarians, sent on from the massive deportations of Hungarian Jews to Auschwitz. Some weighed no more than 25 or 30 kilos, and their arms and legs were like sticks. Soon, there was no more space to lie down. Passing not far away, Charlotte and her friends observed that the women were without warm clothes, blankets or mattresses and that very little food or water was ever delivered to the tent. When cauldrons of soup were carried across, women scrambled and fought for a share, and those with children despaired of being able to keep them alive.

From the winter of 1941, it had been clear to the camp authorities that, to make Ravensbrück truly productive, the weak, elderly and sick women would have to be got rid of. The pattern was for a 'commission' of doctors to visit the infirmaries, inspect the patients – at a distance if they considered them infectious – and then recommend transfer for some to a 'nursing home' at Bernburg an der Saale – which was, in fact, a gas chamber. For those who preferred not to know, the euphemisms were reassuring. Just the same, most inmates referred to these departures as *transports noirs*, black transports, and it was hard to remain in ignorance when the women's glasses, clothes, toothbrushes and even false teeth were returned to Ravensbrück.

In October 1944, Suhren received orders from Himmler to step up the number of deaths to two thousand women a month. Pflaum became like a man possessed, chasing after women who tried to get away, catching them by their clothes and yanking them up by the scruff of the neck. In the *Revier*, Adelaïde and the other prisoner doctors redoubled their efforts to make their patients at least appear as if they were going to recover. Every kind of ancient remedy, remembered from grandparents, was tried out.

Ravensbrück's women prisoners, some of whom had been in the camp for several years, had become extremely resourceful. With the arrival of the Hungarian and Warsaw transports had come mountains of clothes, furs, household goods and even toys, and the women sorting them, though closely watched by the SS, had become skilled at every form of deception. Sweaters were the most prized item of clothing and once the striped dresses had run out, new prisoners were given one each, a large cross painted visibly on the front. In order to ensure that as many women as possible were warm, the sorters stole a pot of paint, and put crosses on every useful garment.

Towards Christmas, one of the transports brought a piano to Ravensbrück. Watching it being unloaded, a young Russian girl exclaimed, 'My God! If only I could be allowed to play.' The chief sorter that day, a German girl called Sophie, asked the SS guard in charge. He found the idea of a young Russian Jew able to play the piano absurd. But the piano was moved on to flat ground and the girl sat down. She was an accomplished pianist. All over the camp, as far as the notes reached, the women prisoners stopped what they were doing to listen.

This was the second Christmas the group of French women had spent in a German camp. Once again, they gave each other little presents that they had made, stolen or saved up. The news of the war, transmitted by the women working in the SS offices and translated into a dozen languages, was getting better all the time, and there were real hopes that it might be their last Christmas in captivity. A Christmas tree was brought from the forest and the women stole little bits of wire and thread and material from the factories with which to decorate it. Now, in the evenings, the French friends talked about how they would rebuild France, after the war, and how they would make certain that Germany was never strong again. A group of women in the camp put on a puppet show for the children who had arrived on a recent transport, and even the SS guards came to watch. Hungry, afraid, cold, the children stared; but they did not smile.

Still more women kept coming. Thick snow covered much of Germany and those whose journeys had involved forced marches, in ill-fitting clogs or barefoot, arrived with frostbite. Not one of the fifty-one friends had died during their months in Ravensbrück, but Simone Loche was gravely ill and being moved constantly from place to place around the camp to protect her from Pflaum's selections, Simone Sampaix had never been well since Birkenau and the only surviving Polish woman, of the six who had been on the *Convoi*, Julia Slusarczyk, had pleurisy and was being nursed by Adelaïde. Chaos in the vastly overcrowded camp, where the SS, faced with the increasing likelihood of German defeat, were growing palpably more anxious and irritable, was spreading. The question was how many of the group would survive the turmoil which was about to engulf them.

CHAPTER FOURTEEN

Pausing before the battle

By the winter of 1943, Ravensbrück had become home to children of all ages, some of them orphans, others sent to the camp with their mothers. Charlotte and her friends sometimes caught sight of little groups of them in the alleys between the barracks, playing games that mirrored the life of Ravensbrück: roll calls, punishments, SS guards, *kapos*. The children, observed one woman, had 'unlearnt how to laugh'. Cécile and Yvonne Noutari, who had left children of their own at home, were haunted by these frail, filthy, starving, wary children, often so emaciated that it was hard to tell whether they were boys or girls.

The first children to reach Ravensbrück had arrived with their mothers in the autumn of 1939. They were Sinti and Roma gypsies. Over the next five years, they were followed by Jewish children from the whole of occupied Europe, by Hungarian children sent on from Auschwitz, and by the child survivors of the Warsaw uprising, some 881 in all, it would later be said, from eighteen countries. Denied toys, given no books or lessons, they were obliged to endure the ordeal of the interminable roll calls, before spending their days lying on their bunks, waiting for their mothers to get back from work.

The children were always hungry. The arrival of the cauldron of thin soup caused fights to break out between the stronger ones. The younger were constantly to be found begging for food. One four-year-old girl, told that she would get a piece of bread if she danced, went on dancing right through an air raid. The French women, like many others in the camp, regularly gave them some of their own food, and did what they could to find them warm clothes and more to eat. When they reached the age of 12, the children had to join the work details and do twelve-hour shifts in the factories. Their diet was the same as their mothers', and almost totally lacking in vitamins. Child mortality was high. Yvonne had befriended the son of a Jewish doctor, a clever, well-educated little boy of seven whose parents had disappeared and who she found wandering miserably around the camp. Unlike the other French women, she talked constantly about her own two children, both younger than the Jewish boy, and what it would feel like to hold them in her arms again. She made Marie-Claude promise to come to her house to celebrate the next birthday of the younger one.

Adelaïde's old enemy, Dr Schumann, arrived from Auschwitz to continue his experiments in sterilisation. He chose 120 gypsy girls, some as young as eight. Once again he used X-rays, which caused appalling burns. Those who did not die soon disappeared from the camp.

In the first days of Ravensbrück, when the camp was still regarded as a place for re-education, pregnant women were allowed to give birth, after which their babies were handed over to the Nazis for adoption. When, in 1942, the nature of Ravensbrück changed and it became a work camp, pregnant women were forced to undergo abortions, sometimes as late as eight months. In 1943, when Dr Treite took over the medical services, the policy changed again. Now the women were allowed to give birth, but the newborn babies were drowned or strangled, often in full sight of their mothers.

At around the time the first eight French friends arrived in Ravensbrück, an announcement was made that babies would, henceforth, be allowed to live. But since no provision was made for either mother or child, both frequently died, of haemorrhages, infections and starvation. Mothers were left untended in unheated rooms, and the babies, for the most part naked, were soon covered in fleas. In the evenings, when mothers returned from the factories to feed them – if they had milk – they could see them turning grey and wizened before their eyes.

The fate of the babies was a constant source of anguish to many of the women in Ravensbrück. And when, in the autumn of 1944, Treite agreed that a special area, the *Kinderzimmer* (children's room) be set aside in Block 11, efforts were made to find nappies and milk for the newborn. Simone Loche, whose own son was four when she was arrested and deported, had been saved from the murderous Block 10 by her friends, and was smuggled into Block 11. Here she observed heartbreaking scenes. Babies whose mothers had no milk were fed a mixture of cow's milk and mashed grain from teats cut from the fingers of a doctor's surgical rubber glove, then swaddled and put to lie, in a row, on a bunk.

The babies were so weak and undernourished that they fed very slowly, and since there were not enough teats or bottles to go round, frantic mothers had to wait their turn, knowing that they might at any moment be summoned for roll call or departure to the factories before their own baby could be fed. Despite the efforts to steal and scrounge coal, the barracks, once the snows came in November and temperatures fell to below 30 degrees, were arctic. Since the mothers knew that if they put down one of their precious supplies of nappies, it would be stolen immediately, they dried them by carrying them around next to their skin. Only the most soiled were ever changed. Rats were constantly seen in the barracks.

One after another the babies died. Some lived a few hours, a few days, even a month. Marie-José Chombart, who had started her medical studies before joining the Resistance, was put to work in Block 11, and was able to describe to Marie-Claude and the French *Nacht und Nebel* women how she had to undress the babies who died, wrap them in rags, then carry them down to the morgue to join the piles of dead and naked women lying there. 'It is terrible,' she wrote in notes kept at the time and hidden, 'these little soft white bodies, I hate to touch them . . . Every day, the places of the dead are taken by new deaths . . . I have the feeling that I am descending, day after day, down a staircase that never seems to end.' In her evidence to a war crimes tribunal after the war, she estimated the number of babies born in Ravensbrück at somewhere between 500 and 550. Almost none survived.

*   *   *

There were now some 45,000 women in Ravensbrück and as the confused, violent, filthy camp kept filling, its barracks so crammed that there was nowhere for anyone to sleep, its basins and latrines blocked and overflowing, so the SS guards withdrew further and further into their own quarters, effectively leaving power in the hands of the *kapos*. There were constant air bombardments. Some women were so weak that they could not lift the watery bowls of soup to their mouths. Others kept fighting – for food, for space, for warm clothes. The camp seethed with rumours. The thirty-nine remaining French friends kept up a constant check on each others' whereabouts.

Towards the end of January 1945, the *Jugendlager* – a youth camp built in 1941 for juvenile offenders two kilometres from Ravensbrück, part of the programme of cleansing Germany of 'degenerates' – was emptied and made ready for new occupants. To it were sent the sick and the elderly from Ravensbrück, lured by the promise of no roll calls and better conditions. Adelaïde was ordered to draw up lists of women who might benefit from the change, which she conscientiously did until she discovered where they were going. After this, she told her patients to sit up straight, tidy their hair, appear as youthful and strong as they could, and to turn down all blandishments to move.

At first, those who volunteered to make the move were delighted with their new surroundings in a clearing of pine trees, agreeable after the scorched appearance of Ravensbrück, where no blade of grass grew. But soon they found themselves in another kind of hell. There were no blankets in the *Jugendlager*, no mattresses and it was snowing hard. Put on half-rations, the 3,672 women taken there over the next few weeks were left standing outside for five or six hours every day. Aimée Doridat, the woman whose leg had been amputated in Auschwitz after she fell from a ladder and her fracture became gangrenous, was caught and sent to the *Jugendlager*. Her friends were all despairing of her return when a compassionate *kapo* unexpectedly brought her back to Ravensbrück. To wander about on one leg was to invite death and the others joined forces to hide her.

When Suhren complained that the women in the *Jugendlager* were still not dying fast enough, their warm clothes were taken away as well as their shoes, and they stood barefoot, in cotton dresses, in the snow. Passing nearby one day, Marie-Claude saw what she took to be an enormous pile of steaming manure; it was a few minutes before she realised that it came from the women inside the *Jugendlager*, for whom the 50-metre walk to the latrines across the slime had become too much. Every morning, lorries arrived to collect the naked bodies of the fifty or so who had died in the night. What was so extraordinary was that more did not die.

To speed up the rate of deaths still further, a small gas chamber was opened in a converted storeroom near the crematorium. A systematic programme of extermination began. Dr Winkelmann, helped by Greta Bösel, a woman much feared for her sudden, brutal attacks, did the rounds of the various infirmaries every day, going through the motions of inspecting temperature charts and medical records, the patients ordered to hold up their dresses to show the state of their feet and ankles. By some names, a mark was made. Later, lorries arrived and the designated women, those with TB or suppurating sores, or who seemed to have lost their wits, were herded out in their nightshirts and roughly loaded on to the back.

The women left behind watched and listened in silence. The journey took about six minutes. They could hear the sound of the motors being switched off by the gas chamber. Then the empty lorries returned. Next morning, at roll call, the wind brought waves of gluey, thick smoke. All the women learnt to dread this sinister shuttle of lorries. In the camp offices, the files of the women who had been removed were marked 'departure for convalescence', with the destination given as the nursing home of Mittweida, a euphemism quickly known to all. Every day, the list of the gassed grew longer. As a further absurdity, Marie-Elisa found herself as chemist analysing the urine of sick prisoners, as if they might be treated, when in fact all were destined to be destroyed.

The Allies were advancing and the SS, suddenly faced with not knowing what to do with so many ravaged human skeletons, were becoming increasingly nervous. They killed even more, even faster. In Block 10, an SS nurse called Schwester Maria offered powders to women who could not sleep and those who took them seldom woke up. A second gas chamber, referred to by the SS as the 'new laundry', was being built, but meanwhile some of the sick women were taken behind the crematorium and shot in the back of the head. Suhren, it was said, attended executions. Pflaum, known to the women as the 'rat catcher' or the 'cattle merchant', was tireless in his round-ups, hurling himself in what looked like rugger tackles at the legs of frantic women trying to escape. Pflaum, too, took his turn making selections in the *Jugendlager*. But it was the SS nurse Elisabeth Marschall who personally supervised the emptying of the barracks. The women and children were sent to Belsen. The thirty-two remaining babies were gassed at Ravensbrück.

Towards the end of January 1945, the first of some seven thousand women arrived from Auschwitz, which they had left shortly before the liberating Red Army had arrived. Many of them were in a state of complete collapse, having walked most of the way through snow and ice, the stronger carrying the weaker between them, incessantly hounded by SS guards with whips and snapped at by their dogs. Hundreds of these walking cadavers died along the way and their bodies were left lining the roads. The last convoy, with three thousand women on board, spent twenty-four hours parked in the open before being allowed into the camp.

Marie-Jeanne Bauer was left behind. She had endured the lonely autumn in Birkenau, missing her companions. When the Red Army arrived she was looked after by Soviet doctors and nurses. But there was more horror to come. One evening a soldier entered the kitchens where she was working, having just learnt that his entire family had been killed by the Germans. He was drunk. Taking out his pistol and mistaking Marie-Jeanne for a German, he shot her. The bullet passed close to her aorta and emerged under the shoulder blade. She survived, and managed to prevent the soldier from being executed. Though it would be many months before she was able to set off for France, one of the French friends, at least, had survived to tell their story.

*   *   *

What was now clear to Charlotte, Marie-Claude, Adelaïde and the others still in Ravensbrück was that a race was on, with the Germans bent on destroying all possible evidence of the atrocities, and the prisoners determined to survive until the liberation which they sensed could not be far away. In this last battle for survival, renewed efforts were made to protect and save each other. Never had the French women felt greater resolve not to die, but to defeat their jailers: it gave them a last burst of strength, a shared purpose. The ethnographer, Germaine Tillon, could do nothing for her mother, Emilie, who one day was taken off to the *Jugendlager* and not seen again. But when 20-year-old Hélène Bolleau broke her leg, slipping on the ice by the kitchens under the weight of a cauldron of soup, the group closed in to help her.

Adelaïde and another prisoner doctor fashioned splints out of pieces of wood and held them in place with paper bandages, and then her friends carried her back to the barracks and hid her in a gap just below the rafters. Hélène was a fighter. Back in the days when she had helped her father, then taken over his role in the Resistance after his arrest, she had always been strong. Now she concentrated on staying alive, one day at a time.

Solidarity and mutual help now extended well beyond the small band of friends. When the French women were collectively punished for some misdemeanour by being denied all food for three Sundays in a row, they received so much bread from the other women in the camp that they could not eat it all; being full, not craving more, was a sensation they had totally forgotten. Women suspected of being in danger of a selection were hidden behind the coal bins, in the cellars beneath the kitchen, or in among the typhus cases, where the SS never ventured. Marie-Claude, learning that three of their Austrian friends were to be executed, managed to swap their numbers in the office where she worked for those of women who were already dead. Since they had come to Ravensbrück from Auschwitz and had tattoos on their arms, she found prisoner doctors to scrape them off, to make them look like infected abscesses. It was, she would later say, a heartbreaking question of 'triage, trying to save those who might survive'. But she could do nothing to save four young French girls, two of whom had been parachuted by the Allied secret services into France, the other two the radio operator and liaison officer waiting for them, who were taken out into the woods one afternoon and shot.

The rescue of the surviving *Kaninchen*, the maimed little Polish girls who had been earmarked for extermination, involved the resources not only of the French women in Block 32, but many others in the camp. When it became known that their turn had come, women working in the administrative offices arranged for the electricity of the camp to be turned off for several hours, thereby delaying the roll call. The others used the time to spirit the girls away into hiding places all over the camp. None was ever found; all survived.

With the approach of the Allies had come an intense desire to document what would later be called the *univers concentrationnaire*. Some information had already been recorded and smuggled out by resourceful Polish women, writing between the lines of letters with urine, which became visible under a warm iron. But Germaine Tillon and Marie-Claude were determined to record accurate facts, dates, names, deaths, illnesses, the brutality of the guards, the amount of money looted by the SS. They began to keep diaries and notes. Both felt driven by rage and sheer determination to tell the world all that they had witnessed. Germaine, mourning her mother, would say that though she had lost all 'visceral desire to live', her fury and her desire to see the Germans punished kept her going.

Annette Postel-Vinay, who worked in the textile factory, was able to steal paper; a Czech friend in the building office, ink. With this, tiny notes were written, so small as to be barely legible to the naked eye, and then hidden behind a loose plank above their bunks. As the days passed, and the camp became more chaotic and murderous, the two women moved around, avoiding Pflaum and his men, feverishly collecting data. What they could not write down, they memorised.

* * *

Now began what was in some ways the most perilous period in the long odyssey of the French women friends. With the Allies advancing from all directions, and conflicting orders reaching the camp commandants from Berlin, a wind of uncertainty spread through the concentration camps. What was to be done with these hundreds of thousands of prisoners, all in various stages of malnutrition and sickness? How dispose of so many living testimonials to atrocities? In Auschwitz, before leaving, the SS had bombed the gas chambers and set fire to mountains of documents chronicling five years of mass murder. Because the SS had kept meticulous records, noting down, in minute detail, every element of the camps and their inmates, the question now, with German defeat imminent, was how to get rid of so much evidence.

Early in March, the French friends learnt that they were to be transferred to the camp of Mauthausen, together with the other remaining *Nacht und Nebel* French women, in all, 585 women of all nationalities. Thirty-three joined a convoy of cattle trucks that left Ravensbrück on 2 March. Among them were Marie-Elisa, Germaine Pican and Madeleine Dissoubray. But several of the friends had to be left behind. Simone Loche was now so ill that no one believed she could survive till liberation. Mado Doiret was working in the Siemens factory. Hélène Bolleau's broken leg made any transport too dangerous. Betty, Julia Slusarczyk and Simone Sampaix were all in the *Revier*, while Aimée Doridat, whose amputated leg made daily life extremely precarious, was in hiding. To look after them, Adelaïde, Charlotte and Marie-Claude arranged to stay behind. The parting from the others was extremely painful.

The camp of Mauthausen near Linz in Austria had been built in the summer of 1938, soon after the *Anschluss*, on a bluff above the Danube. From afar it looked like a medieval fortified castle, made out of blocks of granite, with bastions and towers and surrounded by dense forest. In some ways the worst of all the concentration camps – as opposed to the extermination camps – Mauthausen had worked to death countless thousands of Soviet prisoners of war, captured Allied airmen, political detainees, Jews, gypsies and priests in the nearby stone quarry. Here they had cut and hauled vast blocks up a 'stairs of death' for the public buildings planned by Hitler for Nuremberg and Berlin. Even by Nazi standards, the regime was harsh; when, in 1941, Himmler and Heydrich had ranked the camps according to the severity of treatment and danger to the prisoners, only Mauthausen had come out in the third, and worst, category. No one who was sent to Mauthausen, so it was said, would ever emerge alive. And though never designated an extermination camp, as at Ravensbrück a small gas chamber had been built to dispose of those too feeble or too disobedient.

The thirty-three French women had reached the limits of what they could endure when they finally reached Mauthausen on 7 March. The journey had been appalling, the train constantly stopping during bombardments, and the last bit had been done on foot, walking all night by the light of the moon through silent, deserted villages; those too weak to walk were pulled out and shot, their bodies left by the roadside. Eighteen of the 585 women who started out had died on the way. There was an agonising moment when a young woman holding one child in her arms and pulling another by the hand, staggering and faltering at every step, was suddenly yanked out of the line by an SS guard and shot dead. Silently, the other women picked up the small children and walked on.

On reaching Mauthausen, Marie-Elisa and the others were led to a barracks, where they caught sight of a group of men they had known in France during their time in the Resistance. Telling them how hungry they were, having had almost no food for five days, they were surprised when not one offered to find them something to eat. They were then taken to a shower room, had their genitals doused in disinfectant with a brush, and given men's clothes to put on. The women were so thin and shrunken that the trousers and jackets fell off them. The moment they reappeared, their male comrades hurried over and handed them bits of bread, and pieces of string with which to tie on their clothes. 'Why didn't you give us the bread before?' asked Madeleine. 'Because we assumed that you were being taken straight to the gas chamber,' the men replied.

Conditions in the barracks were little better than those in the tent at Ravensbrück: no mattresses, no blankets, only the floor to sleep on. Marie-Elisa was sent off to work as a nurse in the *Revier*, where there were many cases of TB, but only medicines for a fraction of them.

Then, on 21 March, something terrible happened. Most of the French women had been taken to clear the rubble from the station at Amstetten, partially destroyed in an American bombing raid. While they were digging through the twisted rails and cement, the bombers returned. A hundred of the women were killed. Among them were three of the French friends: Charlotte Decock, the much-loved cook from Raisko, who had stolen food from the SS kitchens for her companions; Olga Melin, who left a 15-year-old disabled son, and who had been planning to return to her husband and patch up their marriage; and Yvonne Noutari, the young mother who had talked so often and with such longing of her two small children. Yvonne did not die at once, but lay in great pain all night. Having felt so close to the moment when she might see her children again, she clung desperately to life. But next day she could fight no longer.

For the others, these deaths were profoundly upsetting. As Cécile said, so close did each of the women feel to the others, that to die oneself would be no worse than to see one of the others die. Every day now, the survivors wondered who might go next. It was impossible not to feel constantly afraid, the *Nacht und Nebel* prisoners especially, because they had so clearly understood that the German plan was to exterminate them all.

But the war for those in Mauthausen was nearing its end. On 22 April, the thirty remaining women were summoned to the offices, ordered to stand in rows of five, and informed that they were to have a shower. For survivors of Auschwitz, showers meant only one thing. But standing nearby were some of the men they knew, and they learnt that a number of Red Cross lorries had arrived to evacuate the French. They found it inconceivable. Even stranger, when the SS handed out mouldy bread for the women to take with them on their journey, the Red Cross officers ordered the Germans to replace it with their own better bread – and the SS obeyed. Slowly, uncertain and apprehensive, the women approached the lorries and climbed on board. It was later that they discovered that their lives had been saved only because the telephone lines were down and Hitler's message that the women were to be liquidated had not come through. They were alive, Marie-Elisa, Madeleine, Simone, the two Germaines and the others; and they were on their way home, through a country in ruins and under bombardment. But what they would find when they got there, and how they would feel, none of them knew.

*   *   *

The Mauthausen group was lucky: the end of their war came quickly. The others did not fare so well.

In Oranienburg, Hélène Solomon was working in the Bosch factory when it was bombed. The barracks caught fire. The inmates were ordered to form up into lines, keeping to their national groups, and marched out, the men in front, the women behind. The SS guards set a course, with the Russians to the east, the Americans to the west. Those too weak to keep up were shot. It began to snow. Hélène had brought a blanket and wrapped it around her shoulders. For twelve days they kept walking, mostly at night, stopping from time to time to rest in barns, but there was almost nothing to eat, and, day by day, more women died.

One morning, they realised that the SS had disappeared. Hélène and some of the other French women went ahead and found a group of French soldiers, who gave them some food and took them in carts to an American encampment in a former holiday centre for the Hitler Youth. Hélène was given a glass of schnapps. It was her first taste of alcohol in over three years. Later, the French women returned to the others waiting in the forest, and as they walked, they sang the Marseillaise. When the liberating troops considered it safe, they were driven by truck to Lille, where the Red Cross and some French officers were waiting for them. Hélène had survived to see liberation. She weighed just 35 kilos.

In Beendorf, Cécile, Poupette, Lulu, Carmen and Gilberte decided to refuse to descend into the salt mine if news came of the imminent arrival of the Allies; what they feared was being locked in and left to die. On 10 April, orders were suddenly given to get on to a train for Neuengamme, 180 kilometres away. There were five thousand prisoners on the train, so tightly wedged in that the women took turns lying, sitting and standing. Among them were a number of *kapos*. The little group of friends clung together. There was again almost nothing to eat and fights broke out. The *kapos*, who, having been better fed in Ravensbrück were considerably stronger than the other women, wrapped the weakest and sickest prisoners in blankets and sat on them, suffocating them, then tipped their bodies out on to the tracks. During the frequent stops, the women were forced to bury the many corpses of the dead, after which they looked for grass shoots to eat.

One night, when the train was stopped, all the Russian prisoners of war in one car escaped. The SS raked the train with their machine guns, then selected three hundred men and shot them. After five days, the remaining men on the train were unloaded and the train travelled on, in fits and starts. The women could hear the bombing getting closer. Occasionally they were shunted into a siding, to let a train of German soldiers by. Poupette's sandals were stolen while she slept. She was now barefoot.

When, after twelve days, the train reached the camp of Neuengamme, they discovered that it had been evacuated that morning, and that some of the last inmates had been put on to a boat, the *Cap Arcona*, in the Bay of Lübeck. Unaware that the ship contained survivors from the concentration camps, and believing it to be full of escaping officers from the SS, the Royal Airforce bombed it. Many of the SS guards on board were able to escape, but the prisoners were locked below, and just 350 of the 4,500 on board survived. At Neuengamme, the French friends were joined by Mado Doiret, who had still been working in the Siemens factory when it was liberated by the Red Cross. Her reunion with her friends was saddened by the bitter news that awaited her. Her brother Roger, who had joined the Maquis before being caught and deported from France to a concentration camp, was one of the men drowned in the *Cap Arcona*. Her cousin Serge, who had also been in Neuengamme, had died just a few days before her arrival.

The women deportees, the five French friends among them, were put back on the train, which crawled on. They had eaten nothing but a little sugar, some raw noodles and some grass for twelve days, and many had died; but the group of friends, now, with Mado, six, were alive. Two days later, they reached a camp near Hamburg. The military police guarding the camp told Cécile and the others: 'None of this is our fault, don't blame us.' The noise of the bombing was very close. Poupette, still barefoot, was ordered to dig graves, and spent her days carrying corpses. The women, starving, thirsty, filthy, their legs covered in sores, their clothes in rags, were suddenly informed that they were to be handed over to the Red Cross. At first, they felt nothing. Then, Poupette would later say, there was an 'explosion of joy. We sang. We shouted out the words from half-remembered songs'. Put back on a train, they travelled until four the next afternoon, when it stopped in the middle of the countryside. They could see Red Cross ambulances waiting. Silently, warily, one behind the other, they climbed down and approached. A Red Cross official gave them cigarettes.

After this came yet another train, to Copenhagen. Each woman was given a little box with white bread, butter, cheese, jam and a piece of chocolate. They ate slowly, in silence. Copenhagen station was full of staring, friendly crowds, who pressed more food on them. Their clothes were burnt, their bodies disinfected, and they were given new clothes. Then came a ferry to Malmö, and another train to Stockholm. On the last night, the train paused and, sitting there in the dark, remembering all they had been through, they realised at last that they were, indeed, free.

They sang the Marseillaise, as they had sung it so often before to mark the stages of their long ordeal, and it seemed right to sing it now, when it was over. They were alive, and they were going home, emaciated, haunted, grieving for their dead companions, but alive. 'It was,' Poupette would say, 'an incredible feeling. And then we just sat silently, waiting. It was like the pause before a battle.'

*　　*　　*

The end, for those still left in Ravensbrück – Charlotte, Marie-Claude, Adelaïde, Hélène, Betty, Julia and Simone – came suddenly.

For some time now, discussions had been taking place between Count Bernadotte of the Swedish Red Cross, Norbert Masur, Sweden's representative to the World Jewish Congress, and Himmler who, against Hitler's wishes, hoped to negotiate a separate peace. An earlier deal with Musy, ex-president of the Swiss Confederation, to evacuate a number of Jews from Theresienstadt, had angered Hitler and negotiations were tricky. However, Bernadotte pressed on, and early in April the first group of sick women was evacuated from Ravensbrück; on the 7th a number of Norwegian and Danish women followed.

By now, the camp had descended into chaos. Orders were given, then countermanded. Groups were lined up ready to depart to other camps, then told that they were not leaving. Commandos no longer set off for the factories. There was very little water and virtually no food. Marie-Claude noted in her diary that rats were everywhere, eating the bodies of the dead that lay around the camp. The SS themselves were erratic, at times behaving harshly, at others almost fawning on the prisoners, anxious about the coming end to the war. One day, in anticipation of a visit by the International Committee of the Red Cross, Suhren ordered that all the *Schmuckstücke,* the women who looked more like corpses than human beings, be locked up in the latrines and kept out of sight. Hélène Bolleau was in the *Revier* that day and she watched as the nurses hid all the more skeletal and wretched women behind curtains at the far end of the barracks. When an ICRC official appeared and spoke to her, Hélène urged them to examine the whole place more thoroughly. The SS doctor showing him around hurried him away. 'No, no, you mustn't go there, there are highly contagious typhus cases.' The ICRC man obeyed.

A few Canadian Red Cross parcels reached the camp. Late that night, when the others were asleep, Charlotte made herself a cup of coffee from the packet in her box. There was no hot water, so she made it with cold, stirring in spoon after spoon of the powder, wanting her first cup after so long to be truly delicious. When she tasted it, she found it bitter and disappointing. She realised, she wrote later, that remembered delights are not easily recaptured. 'I would have to get used to pleasures all over again.' That night her heart beat so wildly from the caffeine that she thought she was dying. Next morning, she and the others sat dipping their fingers into the tins of butter, very slowly licking them, then tried the peanut butter, which many had not seen before.

Simone Loche was very ill and growing weaker all the time; Betty, Julia and Simone Sampaix were frail; but the others redoubled their efforts at avoiding detection by the SS. They had become extremely skilled at choosing their hiding places and when, during the interminable roll calls that continued day after day, the guards walked up and down the lines, pulling out the sicker women, they had mastered the technique of appearing strong and healthy. The selections for the gas chamber continued, and Rudolf Hoess, having left Auschwitz well before the arrival of the Red Army, arrived one day to inspect the building of the second chamber. Often, now, the selections took the form of manhunts, the women chased around the camp while they tried frantically to hide.

One day, seven French women were pulled out of the line. Locked in a barracks to await transport to the gas chamber, they managed to escape. When the SS realised they were missing they announced that all the remaining French women would be 'selected', if the seven did not give themselves up. The seven returned. Their friends watched in horror as one cried out: 'I'm 34 years old. I have three children to bring up. I don't want to die.' That night, they listened to the sound of the lorries taking the women to the gas chamber, and they could hear the cries of the women as the SS men beat them and they begged for mercy.

One afternoon not long afterwards, while Adelaïde was in the *Revier*, she heard the sound of lorries approaching. A nurse appeared and began to call out names. Adelaïde fled, feeling that she could no longer bear to be witness to so many deaths. But when she returned later, expecting a row of empty beds, she found the women still there, the order for their gassing having been cancelled. She understood that such was the chaos that anything was now possible. 'I realised,' she said later, 'that the time had come for me to fight.'

On 23 April, orders were given for all the remaining 488 French, 231 Belgian and 34 Dutch women in Ravensbrück to line up. It was four o'clock in the morning and, standing with Simone, Betty, Julia and Marie-Claude, Charlotte saw SS guards with machine guns take up positions by the gate. The women were searched. Germaine Tillon managed to hide a roll of photographs of the little *Kaninchen* with their mutilated legs in an empty tin of milk powder. As they stood there, a group of ragged, shrunken, staggering women appeared out of the dark from the direction of the *Jugendlager*: they were heading for the gas chamber.

The five friends clung to each other; the moment had come and they knew they were about to die. Having for so long feared death, Charlotte felt completely calm. Instructions were shouted out to begin walking towards the gate. The SS pointed their machine guns. But they did not fire. The lines of women, in silence, walked out. There was a man in a khaki uniform waiting for them, with a Red Cross band on his arm. 'You are French?' he asked. 'I am taking you to Sweden.' No one moved.

Then, very slowly, still in silence, they climbed on to the white lorries waiting on the road; those barely able to walk were gently helped. They had longed for this moment, certain that they would feel an overwhelming sensation of joy. Instead, they felt flat. Before the lorries moved off, one of the women called out that they should observe a moment of silence for all their friends who had died at Ravensbrück. Several of the women wept. Charlotte remembered that 23 April was the date when she had first walked home with Georges Dudach after class; and it was also the date on which she had said goodbye to him in La Santé.

They drove, in slow convoy, along roads clogged with fleeing people, past ruined houses, through Kiel where the very earth seemed to have been turned over by the shelling. Young German boys threw stones at the lorries. Among the French women was 20-year-old Madeleine Aylmer, who had given birth to a girl a month earlier and who had somehow managed to avoid Pflaum's round-ups of the pregnant women and nursing mothers and their babies. In the confusion of the moment, she had succeeded, with the help of the others, in smuggling her baby out under her dress. The little girl was one of only a handful of babies to survive. As the lorries crossed the border into Denmark, the French women began to sing. There were banners welcoming them. Charlotte thought how incredibly beautiful everything looked.

*   *   *

Of the original group of French friends on the *Convoi* there now remained in Ravensbrück only Hélène Bolleau, with her broken leg, Simone Loche, who was growing weaker, and Adelaïde and Marie-Claude, who had insisted on remaining behind to be with them. During the night of 27 April most of the SS guards disappeared, cutting off the supplies of water and electricity and making bonfires of the camp records as they left. The convoy taking Suhren and his wife in one car, his deputy in another in advance of the liberating Allied troops, drove past a final forced march of women leaving the camp. Many of the women were so weak that they could barely stagger, but they clutched their Red Cross parcels to them. Suhren's last orders were to bury the dead, so that their graves 'looked neat'.

There had been rumours that the Germans would blow up Ravensbrück before they left, but nothing happened. 'The camp looks abandoned and filthy,' Marie-Claude wrote in her diary. Some of the *Schmuckstücke*, she noted, had rallied, and were sitting by the gates, eating the Red Cross tins of food, looking as if they were having a picnic. She could hear the bombing getting closer all the time, but 'such are the horrors of this camp that it is hard to feel a sense of joy that the end is near'. Not until she saw the first Red Army soldier would that come.

Bit by bit, Adelaïde, Marie-Claude and a number of doctors who had remained behind began to take charge of the sick. They moved the dying women into the infirmary, Marie-Claude noting that they looked like scraps of rubbish. They drew up lists of names for the next Red Cross evacuation, and they directed the stronger women to cook what little there was to eat and to start clearing up the camp. The *Schmuckstücke* continued to wander aimlessly around, defying any attempt to organise them, and Marie-Claude told them that they would not be fed unless they helped. There were also 260 elderly German nuns, who had spent over ten years in various concentration camps for saying they believed that Hitler was the Antichrist. The much-hated Dorothea Binz, one of the very few SS still in the camp, appeared to ask for food. It was refused.

Adelaïde and Marie-Claude went to visit the nearby men's camp, where they found four hundred dying men, and about four hundred others, many French among them, who were clearly not far from death. They had had no food or water for eight days.

'It is simply atrocious,' Marie-Claude wrote. 'They no longer look like men but like haggard ghosts, driven out of their minds by pain, hunger and thirst. No one, no one could ever describe this sight; no one could believe us.' They fetched some of the stronger women and between them carried the dying men to one of the abandoned SS barracks.

At 11.30 on the morning of 30 April, the first Red Army soldiers were spotted approaching through the trees. Later, the liberators would say that the camp could be smelt from three kilometres away, and that when they saw the filth, the piles of human remains and the living skeletons, they felt extreme pity, but also revulsion. 'Seeing the first motorcyclist,' Marie-Claude wrote, 'my eyes were filled with tears, tears of joy this time. I thought of the tears of rage that I had shed when I saw the first German motorcyclist in the Place de l'Opéra in June 1940.' They were followed by soldiers from an infantry brigade, then by officers in cars. 'The camp has gone mad . . . everyone wants to see them, to talk to them,' Marie-Claude wrote, adding crisply that in the excitement they seemed to have forgotten that there was work to be done.

The Red Army commanding officer was polite and asked precise questions about conditions in the camp; then he arranged for supplies of food and medicines and left a number of doctors to help care for the sick. A Russian doctor put Hélène Bolleau's leg in a cast and she was now able to hobble around the camp. Before leaving, the commanding officer directed that the German inhabitants of the surrounding villages be forcibly brought to the camp to help. Adelaïde found herself walking down the line of German civilians, looking for women to assist with the nursing, thinking of the way the German industrialists had gone down the lines of women prisoners, not so long before, selecting women to work in their factories. The Russians were both welcomed and feared. There were stories of some of the women who had been sent off with the SS to other camps, had escaped along the way, then been raped by the advancing Red Army.

Going to look for mattresses in the abandoned villas of the SS guards outside the camp gates, Marie-Claude discovered one of the men prisoners, asleep under an enormous pink silk eiderdown. She observed with some pleasure that the SS villas had been ransacked. She experienced an overwhelming longing to go home. Looking at the sky and the lake, she felt 'drunk on freedom. I think,' she wrote, 'that when I first go home I will want to spend some time alone in the mountains.'

Another day, passing Suhren's abandoned villa with a friend, she went in and saw a piano. Her companion sat down to play. Marie-Claude felt rising in her 'a cloud of long suppressed desire', a wave of pleasure in hearing something that she had for so long been deprived of. They finished by playing old French songs and the inevitable Marseillaise. That night she could not sleep for an intense feeling of 'fullness'.

By 3 May, when Adelaïde and Marie-Claude went round the camp with a doctor, a photographer and a Russian officer, to document what Ravensbrück had been, the place was much changed. The water and electricity were back on, and the Russians had arranged for thirty cows and a hundred chickens to be brought in, along with some horses. There was now milk for breakfast, butter to have with bread, meat and onions for lunch. Some French soldiers had visited the camp, bringing news from France, much of it depressing. A French general called Allard arrived one day, seeking to find out what had happened to his wife, who had been deported to Ravensbrück early in the war. Marie-Claude had to tell him that she had been gassed. Allard told her that the liberation committee in Paris had been a 'scandal', and that the left and the right were arguing fiercely. What she minded most, Marie-Claude wrote in her diary, was the fact that so many of the best men were dead, having died for their country, while so many of the worst, the collaborators, were alive and in positions of power. With the old values gone, and no new ones in place, how could a moral crisis be avoided? There were some days when she dreaded the thought of the political battles to come.

Simone Loche was clearly fading and Adelaïde had almost abandoned all hope of saving her when a Russian doctor, saying that there was one chance in a hundred that it would work, proposed operating on her. Since there were no general anaesthetics available, he gave her a local, and then operated, after which Marie-Claude gave blood for a transfusion. Awake, but not in pain, Simone thought that she would die, but felt pleased that she had at least lived to see liberation. After the operation, her temperature stayed high. Marie-Claude felt wretched. 'It's terrible to watch over someone so dear to you, and see them diminish day by day.' But Simone rallied. The day came when she was evacuated by the Red Cross to Berlin, and from there flown to Paris, where she would spend many months in a hospital at Créteil.

Marie-Claude and Adelaïde stayed at Ravensbrück until mid-June, watching their patients grow stronger and more recognisable as human beings as their hair grew back and their bodies filled out. Turning down General Allard's invitation to fly back to Paris with him, Marie-Claude felt overwhelmed with a longing for it all to be over, but determined to stay long enough to help the Russian Commission document what had taken place at Ravensbrück. Writing to the Communist leader, Maurice Thorez and telling him what had befallen the 113 Communist women on the *Convoi*, she apologised for her stilted style, saying that it was the first proper letter that she had written in French for almost three years.

Adelaïde had moved into a former SS barracks with a piano, and on 17 May Marie-Claude spent her first night outside the camp perimeter, in a room overlooking the lake, with a real bed, sheets and a pillow. She tried to dwell as little as possible on what might await her at home, for she still had no news of her family or of Pierre Villon, her companion. When the last of the Red Cross lorries came to collect the remaining sick women, and there were some who would clearly die before they reached home, she felt how sad it was to die now, having survived so much.

At last, their patients gone, she and Adelaïde set off for home. 'This passage of darkness to light,' Adelaïde wrote, 'cannot be expressed in words.' Later she would write that when 'life took on its colours and was so often disappointing, it was good to remember the infinite privilege of having experienced such a moment of joy'.

*   *   *

Forty-nine of the 230 French women, thirty-four of them communists, who had left Paris twenty-nine months earlier on the *Convoi des 31000*, had lived to see the end of the war. A hundred and eighty-one of their friends and companions had died, of typhus, brutality, starvation, gassing; some had been beaten to death, others had simply given up. Not one who had been over the age of 44, and very few of the youngest, were still alive. Danielle, Maï, Aminthe and Yvette Guillon, Raymonde Sergent, Madeleine Zani and Viva Nenni were all dead, and there were dozens of young children who would now learn that they were orphans, both their mothers and their fathers murdered by the Nazis. It was through the women reaching France again that many families would finally know that their mothers, daughters and wives were not coming home.

Some of the survivors of the *Convoi* reached France on their own, after wandering journeys across countries chaotic with refugees and returning prisoners of war. Others came home in small groups. Ten of the friends found themselves together in Sweden. Mado's sister, who worked for a Swedish doctor, arranged for them to stay with a senator in a house in the country, where they were slowly nursed back to health. Lulu and her sister Carmen were there – the only two sisters to have survived – and Cécile, Betty, Hélène Bolleau and Simone Sampaix. Simone, the plump young girl who had smiled so warmly out of the photograph taken in Romainville, weighed just 23 kilos. They were fed cream, fish, cheese and fresh vegetables, though it took a while for their mouths and teeth not to ache from the unaccustomed food, and at first they ate only a teaspoon at a time. 'It was,' wrote Hélène, 'one good thing after another.' From time to time they were asked to answer questions about Ravensbrück put to them by reporters or the Swedish government. 'We are in a little paradise,' Betty wrote to her parents. 'I need this after such terrible hardship.' She complained of amnesia and anxiety, but her arm, which doctors feared she might lose the use of as a result of the infected abscess, was slowly getting better.

Later, they were put on a plane to Paris. Charlotte could feel only loss and uncertainty. She had an overpowering sensation that from now on, for the rest of her life, she would be alone, and that no one, ever, would take the place of her lost companions. 'As time gathered speed,' she wrote later, 'they became diaphanous, more and more translucent, losing their colours and their forms . . . Only their voices remained, but even they began to fade as Paris grew closer . . . When we arrived, I could no longer recognise them. Was I alive to have an afterwards, to know what afterwards meant?'

CHAPTER FIFTEEN

Slipping into the shadows

It was not long after Charlotte Delbo came home to Paris that she began to write about the German camps. Much of it was in verse. 'I've come back from another world,' she wrote,

> to this world
> I had not left
> and I know not
> which one is real . . .
> As far as I am concerned
> I'm still there
> dying there
> a little more each day
> dying over again
> the death of those who died . . .
> I have returned
> from a world beyond knowledge
> and now must unlearn
> for otherwise I clearly see
> I can no longer live.

Her words could have been written by any one of the forty-nine survivors of the *Convoi des 31000*, for each shared the same sense of alienation, loss and loneliness. In their two years and three months in the German camps they had been too cold, too frightened, too ill, too hungry, too dirty and too sad. They had witnessed both the worst and the best that life had to offer, cruelty, sadism, brutality, betrayal, thievery, but also generosity and self-lessness. Their reserves of strength and character had been pushed to the very far limits of endurance and every notion of humanity had been challenged.

An ambivalence marked them all. They no longer felt themselves to be the same people and, looking back at the young women they had once been, full of hope and confidence and excitement, they marvelled at how innocent and trusting they had been. There was no innocence left, in any of them; and they would not find it again.

Having lived so intensely together, depending on each other to stay alive, they were now forced apart: by geography, by families, by a world whose rules and ways they had forgotten and which, physically weak, quickly exhausted, prematurely aged, they had to learn again. When, later, they met, they admitted to one another that the return to France in the early summer of 1945 had proved as hard and as unhappy as anything they had known. Return, they said, was a time of 'shadowy places, silences and things not said'.

*   *   *

The art deco Hotel Lutétia on the boulevard Raspail in Paris, home to the Abwehr for the four years of German occupation, had been turned into a reception centre for returning deportees. Because no one had a clear idea of the numbers involved, nor of the state of health of those coming back from the concentration camps, conditions in the former hotel were chaotic. There were doctors and Red Cross officials on hand, representatives from the government and journalists, and in the halls and lobbies had been posted photographs and lists of names of the missing. Arriving by plane or train in little groups, the friends found themselves surrounded by anxious families holding photographs of lost relatives, desperate for news of survivors, begging them to look at the pictures and see if they could recognise the faces. Madeleine Dissoubray, put into a room with four strangers, was constantly disturbed by knocks on the door, frantic parents outside searching for lost sons and daughters, women for their husbands, men for their wives.

Lulu arrived at the Lutétia a few days before her sister Carmen. She had been able to telephone her husband Georges, who had been wounded trying to escape from a prisoner of war camp and had been repatriated early. Lulu reached home in time for Paul's fifth birthday. She took him some sweets; they were the first that he had ever eaten. She had left a baby, and returned to find a little boy who did not know her.

Gilberte Tamisé – putting off the moment when she would have to send a telegram to her father in Bordeaux, telling him that though she had survived, her younger sister Andrée was 'dead – found herself alone in the Lutétia. Some of her friends had already left to join their families, others had not yet been repatriated. That night she dreamt of freedom, but waking in an empty room, alone for the first time in nearly three years, her immediate thought was 'Is this really freedom, this intolerable solitude, this room, this exhaustion?' How was she going to answer the question 'And Andrée? what did you do with Andrée?' What if her father, too, were dead? And how would she explain to the Lapeyrade family that Berthe had died in the marshes at Birkenau, and that she, Charlotte, Viva, Lulu and Carmen had carried her body back to the camp for the evening roll call? How tell Charlotte Lescure's young son that she had seen his mother beaten to death by a *kapo*? Overwhelmed by a sense of aloneness and bewilderment, aching for Lulu and Carmen and Charlotte, she went back to bed and slept. This time she dreamt of being back among her friends and felt 'comforted, reassured, warmed'.

Finally driven from her room by hunger, Gilberte stood in the corridor watching, waiting, wondering where to go. She felt afraid, inadequate. Seeing her there, so uncertain and wary, a man approached and told her he had just come from Mauthausen. Coaxing her along, urging her to try to face up to going home, he steered her gently to the dining room, then to the telegram office, then to the desk where there were vouchers for travel. More than anything else, she felt like crying. He brought her food, helped her fill in the forms, wiped her face softly with his handkerchief. Later that evening, she travelled south to Bordeaux, with others who had returned from the camps. Her father was waiting for her on the platform. He looked stooped and tired. He did not ask her about Andrée: he knew already. At home, Gilberte found Andrée's things in her room, just as she had left them. Everything felt to her sharp, threatening; she had a sensation of being wounded, as if covered in bruises.

Germaine Pican, reaching the Lutétia, stood in the lobby, searching with her eyes among the crowds for some member of her family. There was no one. She caught sight of a journalist she had known before the war. She asked him if he knew where her father was. 'He's dead,' the man told her. However, her two daughters were alive and waiting for her at home. André, her husband, had been shot by the Germans, a fact that she had known in Romainville but that she now had to come to terms with, to make a new life for herself and the girls. But first she needed to find where André was buried and she spent her first weeks back in France checking through the records in different municipalities. She recognised the body that was eventually dug up by the jacket, a lock of hair and a gold tooth.

Germaine Renaudin, also standing in the lobby of the Lutétia, did not recognise the tall young man who approached her. The boy who three years earlier had been a slender child was now an adult, and when the telegram informing the family that Germaine was alive had reached the farm where he was working, Tony had borrowed the train fare from the farmer, walked 12 kilometres to the nearest station and gone to Paris to wait for his mother. Germaine seemed to him lost and distracted, her body curiously swollen and blotchy from the typhus she was still not quite free of.

Together, they took part in a parade of returned prisoners of war and deportees on 1 May, marching with many of the former concentration camp inmates wearing the striped clothes in which they had come home. Then they took the train home. The whole village turned out to welcome Germaine, and there was a chair waiting for her in case she felt tired during the speeches. She said very little. In the months that followed, her hair went entirely white; but in time it grew back black.

And so, in ones and twos and little groups, the forty-nine women came home. The last to come was Marie-Jeanne Bauer, repatriated from Auschwitz via Odessa. No one was waiting for her. Her building had been bombed, her apartment looted, and she learnt that her brother had been executed. She was dazed, exhausted and had lost the sight of her right eye; she was still testing positive for typhus. Her strongest feeling was that everything they had been through, she and the other women, all their sacrifices, had been for nothing.

Fourteen of the forty-nine returning women were widows, their husbands shot by the Nazis or dead in the concentration camps. It was on reaching France again, the war over, that the deaths finally hit the women. Hélène Solomon knew perfectly well that Jacques was dead: she had said goodbye to him in Romainville, before he was taken to Mont-Valérien and shot. But without really realising it, she had clung to the idea that he would somehow be there waiting for her if ever she did manage to return. Now, suddenly, the full force of his loss overwhelmed her. 'I thought I would go mad,' she said later. 'For a long time, I was hardly able to speak.'

Sixteen of the returning women – among them Lulu, the two Germaines, Marie-Elisa and Cécile – had children waiting for them, and twenty-two children were now reunited with their mothers. But fifty-three mothers had failed to come home, and they left seventy-five orphans between them.

Seven-year-old Michel Politzer would not see his mother again, nor three-year-old Pierre Zani, nor Claude Epaud, whose mother Annette had run L'Ancre Coloniale in La Rochelle, nor Yvonne Noutari's two young children, whom she had talked about with such love and longing in Birkenau. In Saint-Martin-Le-Beau, 12-year-old Gisèle Sergent kept waiting and hoping. Had her mother not promised she would come home? One day, standing in the village grocery, she overheard a stranger tell the owner that Mme Sergent was dead. Even then, she found it hard to believe. Her mother had returned twice from the German prisons: why would she not do so again? And Rosa Floch's parents would never see their young daughter again; her mother's last glimpse of her was finishing the washing up before going off to school on a cold December morning in 1942.

Louise Loquet's daughter, who at the age of 15 had helped her mother with the spelling of the tracts for the Resistance, returned to the Lutétia day after day, hoping for news. She showed every returned deportee her mother's picture, begging them to try to remember something. It was only in December 1946, happening to meet Marie-Claude, that she heard that her mother was dead; and even then, no one had seen her die.

And it was not only children who stood and waited. Yvonne Noutari's mother went to the station in Bordeaux every day for many weeks. The last news she had heard was that Yvonne had survived Auschwitz. She was quite sure that her daughter had simply been delayed. It was only much later that she learnt that Yvonne had been killed during the bombing of Amstetten, just six weeks before the German surrender.

What each of the survivors was now faced with was the question of how they would remake their lives, and how they would convey to their families what they had been through. Auschwitz and Ravensbrück, as Marie-Claude had remarked, were so extreme, so incomprehensible, so unfamiliar an experience, that the women doubted that they possessed the words to describe them, even if people wanted to hear; which, as it turned out, not many did.

* * *

Long before the end of the war, the French government in exile in Algiers had been planning for the return to France of those deported or made prisoner by the Germans. Henri Frenay, founder of one of the main Resistance movements, Combat, had been appointed head of a Commissariat aux Prisonniers et Déportés, men and women he grouped together under the words *les absents*. At that stage, neither he nor anyone else knew just what to expect. He had figures for prisoners of war, put at 950,000, and numbers for those who had been sent as part of the Service de Travail Obligatoire to work in Germany – 650,000 – but he had no idea at all as to how many resisters, Jews, gypsies, homosexuals or people deemed hostile to the Nazis had been put on trains and deported to the east. When asked for a figure, he would say that it probably lay somewhere between 40,000 and 160,000. What worried him more was a repeat of the chaos that followed the First World War, when liberated prisoners of war coming home brought with them the Spanish flu, which by the time it spent itself had killed more people across Europe than the war itself.

As it happened, Frenay's figures for those deported from France were not far out. But what made them so terrible was what they soon revealed. Of France's 75,721 deported Jews, the *déportés raciaux*, not many more than 2,500 came home. The *politiques* had fared somewhat better: 40,760 of 86,827, a little less than half, returned. All, to some extent, were in a bad way. Though reports of conditions in the camps had been reaching France for many months, they had been largely suppressed, not least in order not to alarm families. And though the photographs from Bergen-Belsen, liberated by the British on 15 April, did just precede the men and women in their striped clothes who disembarked at the Gare de l'Est or got off planes at Le Bourget, there had been very little time to take stock of what they had been through. The reality, with its new vocabulary of persecution, proved profoundly shocking.

Among those greeting the first concentration and extermination camp survivors at the Gare de l'Est was Janet Flanner, recently returned correspondent for the *New Yorker*. 'Their faces,' she wrote, 'were gray-green, which seemed to see but not to take in.' Others spoke of bald heads, waxen complexions and shrunken faces 'reminiscent of those little human heads modelled by primitive tribes'. Some were too frail to stand up. The crowds welcoming them home had brought with them spring flowers to present to the skeletal, wary men and women; when the bunches of lilac fell from their 'inert' hands, they left a purple carpet on the platform and 'the perfume of the trampled flowers mingled with the stench of illness and dirt'. The returning deportees sang the Marseillaise in low, croaking voices; some of the onlookers wept.

It was, however, all considerably more complicated than simply repatriating these particular *absents* and looking after them. The question was how what they had been through should be acknowledged and, most crucially, how France should deal with the collaborators responsible for what had happened to them, and to France itself. Who was actually culpable? How many French men and women had spent the four years of occupation in Primo Levi's 'grey zone' of ambiguity between victims and persecutors? Who was to be punished? The French police who had carried out the Germans' bidding, implementing anti-Semitic ordinances, rounding up and torturing suspects before turning them over to the Nazis? The French judges who had presided over the courts sentencing resisters to death? The French train drivers of the SNCF who transported the deportees on the first stage to the camps? Their bosses, who charged the German occupiers so much per head for every person carried? The 700, 000 members of the civil service, without whom France could not have continued to function under

German rule? The cleaning ladies who had worked in the German administrative offices? And what about those who had gone over to the Resistance only in the final months of the war, the *résistants de la dernière heure*? Millions of French men and women had far exceeded the 'correct manner' towards the occupier as laid down in the terms of the armistice: were they all to be punished?

Even before the Allied forces had crossed the Channel in June 1944 and embarked on the liberation of Europe, an *épuration sauvage*, a savage purge, of *collabos* had seen the summary execution by French partisans of 5,238 members of Darlan Page's Milice, informers, collaborators and over-zealous policemen. Some 20,000 French women, the *tondues* who were said to have become too friendly with the occupiers, had their heads shaved. The French government in exile, arriving to take over from Vichy, had been extremely conscious of the need for justice to be seen to be done, for the guilty to be punished and publicly humiliated. The Communists in particular, referring to themselves as *le parti des fusillés*, the executed, and claiming that 90,000 patriots had been shot by the Germans – the true figure was later put at around nine thousand – were demanding widespread purges.

But de Gaulle – anxious to see France reinstated as a major power, fearful of excessive American influence, conscious of the need for a united France and for the French, traumatised by four years of occupation, to put the war behind them – was reluctant to dwell too much on the collaborators and their victims. The time had come to celebrate heroes, not hunt down those he called 'miserable specimens'. 'Assez de cadavres! Assez de suppliciés!', a publisher said to a survivor from Mauthausen, Maurice Delfieu, who proposed to write his memoirs. Thanks to the glorious exploits of the Resistance, the French, by their own efforts, had been rehabilitated. 'Paris martyrisé!', declared de Gaulle, entering the capital. 'Mais Paris libéré! Libéré par lui-meme! avec l'appui et le concours de la France entière . . . la vraie France . . . la France éternelle . . .' The days of tears were over; those 'of glory' had returned. Assuming control in Paris, the general and his colleagues decreed that the most guilty among the collaborators should rapidly be brought to trial and punished with the utmost severity, though not in a spirit of revenge; and that, soon afterwards, France should forgive and move on.

Working day and night under an avalanche of papers, prosecutors considered untainted by the occupation assembled dossiers on 311,000 suspected collaborators and presented them to various courts of justice. A large number of documents was conveniently found to have mysteriously disappeared. Sixty thousand cases were shelved. Of the rest, just over three-quarters of those charged were found guilty. Seven hundred and sixty-four people were executed and 46,145 sentenced to 'national degradation' which meant that they lost voting rights, were banned from membership of a union and from a number of professions and that they forfeited medals, decorations, honours and pensions.

Like other European countries, France had no adequate legislation to deal with the crimes of occupation. The charge, for many of those tried, was of having threatened the liberty and equality of the country by providing 'intelligence to the enemy', or of having committed a new 'crime of collaboration', something between treason and acceptance of the occupiers. France, divided and ambivalent, did not incorporate crimes against humanity into French law until 1964. It would be the 1980s before Klaus Barbie, the 'butcher of Lyon', was brought to trial. Both Maurice Papon and René Bousquet, responsible as secretary-general of the Vichy police for the deportation of many thousands of Jews from the free zone, lived until the 1990s as free men.

* * *

The forty-nine survivors of the *Convoi des 31000* arrived home in time for Betty Langlois to give evidence at the trial of Commissioner Fernand David, the Paris head of the Brigades Spéciales who had sent so many of the women to Auschwitz and so many of their husbands to their deaths. Charlotte, Cécile, Mado, Maï and Danielle were all among his victims; because of him and his men, Charlotte had lost her husband, Betty her lover. Looking at him across the courtroom, Betty kept wondering why he did not recognise her, when she had his features so indelibly stamped on her mind. In the dock, David argued that he personally had never seen anyone tortured, that he had only obeyed orders, and that if any one of his men had been a little rough, well, it never went as far as actual violence. The judge referred to him as the 'Parisian Himmler'.

The jury deliberated for seventeen minutes; when they returned a verdict of guilty the entire courtroom rose up and clapped. On 5 May, David was shot, together with his dapper boss Lucien Rottée, whose position at the head of the Renseignements Généraux had been so lethal to the Resistance. Across France, five thousand policemen were suspended, and ten members of the Paris Brigades Spéciales were executed. But France needed magistrates and policemen, and many others avoided punishment. Rottée's nephew René Hénoque, chief of the second Paris Brigade Spéciales, condemned *in absentia* for the deaths of 216 executed resisters, escaped and died many years later of old age in Brussels. Cécile, returning to the 11th arrondissement in Paris, was approached by the policeman she knew had given her away. He put out his hand and smiled. She turned her back on him.

Almost no woman from the Gironde or Charente on the *Convoi* had survived to give evidence against Poinsot, the head of the Brigades Spéciales responsible, so it was charged, for the death in deportation of 1,560 Jews and nine hundred *politiques*, for the execution of 285 men, and for torture so extreme people were 'literally massacred'. Aminthe Guillon and her daughter-in-law Yvette were dead, and their husbands had been shot at Souge; neither Madeleine Zani, nor Jeanne Souques, nor Marguerite Valina had lived to come home.

Poinsot, who at the end of August 1944 had slipped away from France to Germany in one of twelve cars commandeered for himself and his associates, was recognised and arrested in Switzerland and handed over to the French police. His wife was picked up a few days later at Dijon station, with a million francs and a fortune in other currencies. Poinsot narrowly escaped being lynched when the prison in which he was held was mobbed. On 12 June 1945, he appeared before the court in Moulins. The most damning piece of evidence against him was a list written in red ink, in his own hand, with the names of those he had sent to their deaths. Poinsot was shot at Riom on 12 July. Ferdinand Vincent, the informer who had given away Annette Epaud, the Guillons and many others, went before a firing squad in 1949.

Some of the harshest criticism for behaviour during the occupation was levelled at the writers and journalists who had extolled the virtues and policies of the Nazis. In September 1944, the

Comité Nationale des Écrivains, which Charlotte's husband Georges Dudach along with Georges Politzer had helped set up, had drawn up a first blacklist of twelve writers perceived as collaborators. Later, the list grew to 158 names. In the event, forty-four were charged and Robert Brasillach and Jean Luchaire were executed; Drieu la Rochelle managed to commit suicide on his third attempt. As with the political leaders, no one could quite agree on the severity of the judgments. Mauriac, worried that too much *épuration* would pollute the new French state before it had time to govern, acted as an apostle for reconciliation and pardon, while Camus began by urging the French to move straight from resistance to 'revolution' and to treat collaborators harshly. Later he tempered his views and said that the very word *épuration* had become odious to him.

It was generally agreed, however, that a great many prominent writers had sat out the occupation in shameful silence and inaction, and it would long be remembered that Simone de Beauvoir worked for a while for Radio Nationale under the Germans, and that Sartre had been happy to replace a Jewish professor of philosophy who was dismissed from his post under the anti-Semitic edicts. There were eulogies to the editors of *Lettres Françaises* shot at Mont-Valérien.

Pétain's trial, which opened on 23 July 1945 and lasted three weeks, was less a legal hearing than a ceremonial condemnation of all that Vichy had stood for. In the dock, Pétain remained largely silent, not least because the 89-year-old *maréchal* was becoming increasingly senile. He was sentenced to death by firing squad but de Gaulle commuted the sentence to life imprisonment; Pétain was sent to the Ile d'Yeu in the Atlantic, where he died, entirely senile, six years later. On 16 October 1946, Pierre Laval, Prime Minister of Vichy France, having attempted but failed to commit suicide by taking cyanide, was executed. At neither trial was there much talk of the deportation of the Jews.

Across liberated Europe and in the four zones of Allied occupation in Germany many other trials were under way. Long before the end of the war, the Allies had announced that anyone who had taken part in war crimes would be tried and punished, and on 26 June 1945 a conference was called in London for the purpose of reaching an agreement on how precisely the major war criminals were to be prosecuted. It was not made easier by the animosity between negotiators and the bitter disagreements over legal traditions, but on 8 August a London Charter, setting out the statutory basis for an International Military Tribunal was agreed on. The crucial legal innovation was a category of 'crimes against humanity', to be applied not only to murder and to extermination but to a wide variety of other acts.

The first and most important tribunal opened at Nuremberg on 20 November 1945. There were twenty-two leading Nazis in the dock; there should have been twenty-four, but Gustav Krupp, the Nazi industrialist, was ill and Robert Ley, the head of the German Labour Front, committed suicide before the trial began. The hope, as expressed by the American Counsel for the Prosecution, Telford Taylor, was that justice would prevail, and also that the truth, 'why and how these things happened' would emerge. The nature and gravity of the offences lay at the far limits of human experience, and all present were conscious of how hard it would be to bring the holocaust into the courtroom in a way that did honour to the catastrophe that had taken place. 'The wrongs which we seek to condemn and punish,' said Taylor, 'have been so calculated, so malignant, and so devastating that civilisation cannot tolerate their being ignored, because it cannot survive their being repeated.' Almost hardest to address was the question of where the line should be drawn between legitimate and illegitimate violence in time of war.

Marie-Claude was the only survivor of the *Convoi des 31000* to be called as witness at Nuremberg. She appeared on the 44th day of the trial, on Monday, 28 January 1946. Dignified and articulate, her fair hair wound in a plait around her head, she described, in firm, clear sentences, what she had seen and experienced in Birkenau and Ravensbrück. She answered questions about her arrest in Paris, her friends and colleagues shot by the Germans, her months in La Santé prison; then she talked about the journey from Romainville to Auschwitz, the roll calls, the brutality of the guards, the gas chambers. She used the word *nous*, us, because she was speaking, she said, not just for herself but for the 229 women deported with her. She talked about Alice Viterbo, the singer with only one leg, who had fallen in 'the race' and begged Danielle to give her poison before she was driven away to her death.

Marie-Claude Vaillant-Couturier, giving evidence at Nuremberg

Occasionally Marie-Claude was stopped and told to speak more slowly, for the interpreters were having trouble keeping up with her. Later she would say that, sitting in the witness box, looking across at Göring, Keitel, Dönitz and von Ribbentrop, she thought to herself: 'Look at me, because in my eyes you will see hundreds of thousands of eyes staring at you, and in my voice you will hear hundreds of thousands of voices accusing you.' Staring at their faces and their expressions, she marvelled at how ordinary they looked. She had returned to France, Marie-Claude said, with a deep hatred of Fascism, whether French or German, and she considered the men in the dock to be monsters, and as such 'to be done away with'. She was appalled and upset when, on the first morning, Dr Hans Marx, one of the lawyers for the defence, asked her how she could explain the fact that she had been subjected to such horror and hardship, and yet was able to return in such apparent good health. Her reply was terse: she had been home over a year. Ten of the twenty-two men in the dock were eventually hanged; the firing squad was deemed too dignified an end for them.

The London Charter served as a basis for subsequent Allied and German trials. Over five thousand people were convicted in allied courts and about the same number in German ones. Safeguards from the Anglo-American legal traditions ensured the right to counsel, presumption of innocence and convictions based upon proof beyond all reasonable doubt, but there were complaints of victors' justice. And there was not always sufficient evidence to convict the clearly guilty. In the dock, in courts all over Europe, those charged argued that they had only obeyed orders, that they had been under duress themselves and that they were victims of mistaken identity.

On trial in Warsaw, Rudolf Hoess, commandant of Auschwitz, struck the court by the calm with which he described the gas chambers, explaining, with technical precision, the process of asphyxiation and how roughly a third of the people died at once, while the others 'staggered about and began to scream and struggle for air'. Asked whether it was true that some two and a half million people had gone to their deaths in Auschwitz, he replied that he thought the figure was nearer to one and a half. In his memoirs, written while he was in prison awaiting trial, he noted that the public would never regard him as anything but a 'bloodthirsty beast . . . cruel, sadistic and a mass murderer', and that no one would ever understand that he, too, had a 'heart and that he was not evil'. Hoess was hanged at Auschwitz on 15 April 1947, in front of the villa in whose gardens Charlotte had watched his children play.

Many, but not all, of the people whose brutality had dominated and destroyed the lives of the women from the *Convoi* were brought to justice. Mengele, the doctor whose experiments Adelaïde Hautval had refused to assist in, slipped away and was never caught. Dr Schumann, who had X-rayed young men and women and burned them beyond recovery, went to work in Africa and died, a free man, in 1983. Dr Clauberg, who had performed his sterilisation operations in his military uniform, died in a prison cell, in mysterious circumstances, in August 1957. Dr Treite, head of the medical services at Ravensbrück, committed suicide. Dr Winkelmann, who had made selections for the gas chamber with such relish, died before his sentence could be carried out. Dr Caesar, the botanist at Raisko, avoided prison altogether and set up a laundry business. General Karl Oberg and Helmut Knochen, the SS officers who between them had rounded up, tortured, shot and deported countless thousands of French men, women and children during the four years of occupation were condemned to death, but their sentences were commuted. They were freed in 1962.

But Hans Pflaum, the murderous guard in Ravensbrück, who had cornered escaping women with rugby tackles, and Adolf Taube, the bull-like tormenter in Birkenau were both executed, as were Elisabeth Marschall and Dorothea Binz, who had clubbed sick and frail women to death. It would be said that many of those sentenced to die were hanged in such a way that they were slowly strangled to death. But what became of the vicious Margot Drechsler, known to the inmates as 'Death' and at whose hands the women had suffered so repeatedly in Birkenau, no one ever discovered.

After the Allied High Command lifted the remaining restrictions on German courts in 1955 a kind of amnesty fever broke out. Sentences were commuted, convictions overturned, prosecutions lifted. In France, 40,000 people went to prison for collaboration; in 1948, there were only 13,000 still inside, and by 1965 all were free.

The last of the *Convoi*'s women to testify was Adelaïde, called to give evidence against Dr Dering, the Polish prisoner gynaecologist in Auschwitz, whom she had so often observed ingratiating himself with the Nazi doctors. In 1964, in London, Dering sued the American writer Leon Uris for libel, after Uris wrote in his novel *Exodus* that Dering had performed 17,000 sterilisations on prisoners without anaesthetic. In the event, the jury ruled in Dering's favour and he was awarded a halfpenny in damages, but the court made its feelings clear by the decision that he was to pay the costs himself.

In his summing up, Lord Justice Lawton referred to Adelaïde as 'one of the most courageous and remarkable women who has ever testified before a British court'. When, the following year, Israel proposed to confer on her a medal as one of the Righteous Among the Nations, she refused to accept it, saying that everything that she had done in Auschwitz and Ravensbrück was only natural, logical and born of a 'moral obligation'. She came back from the camps, she would say, obsessed with the fear that the Nazis would go unexposed and unpunished, and that only some superhuman force, some extraordinary feat of determination, would really be able to bring to an end the 'negation of every human and spiritual value' demonstrated by the Nazis. The French gave her a *Légion d'honneur*.

*   *   *

It was no accident that the women from the *Convoi* called to testify at war crimes trials were Marie-Claude, Adelaïde and Betty. All three were strong, determined, combative women who had survived in part because of a ferocious desire to see the Nazis and the French collaborators punished. But France was not altogether in the mood to hear what they had to say; and the men and women who had returned from the camps were not, for the most part, well enough, either physically or mentally, to make their voices heard. De Gaulle, pushing his myth of France as a country of united resisters betrayed by a handful of traitors, needed collective amnesia. The gaunt, sickly deportees were an unwelcome reminder that in five weeks the Germans had crushed what had been considered one of the finest armies in the world; and that, during four years of occupation, it was the French themselves who had rounded up and interned Jews and resisters, before sending them to their death in Poland.

There was, however, no avoiding the fact that the deportees had to be acknowledged and rewarded. Arriving home, each man and woman – providing they could prove that they were French, which excluded the many thousands of non-French Jews, Polish resisters, Spanish refugees, all those who had made France their home and fought in the Resistance but never taken French nationality – received 5,000 francs, extra food rations and a long paid holiday. But there were acrimonious debates about who precisely was a *résistant* and much squabbling over the relative entitlements of *politiques* and *raciales*. It was not until 1948 that two statutes, one for each category, with different degrees of recognition and pensions, depending on sickness and invalidity, were finally made law; even then, the *politiques*, deemed fighters and not victims, fared better.

Of the 40,760 *résistants politiques* who came home, 8,872 were women. It said much about the way that the women's role in the Resistance was perceived in France that of the 1,053 people eventually made *Compagnons de la Libération* – the highest honour – only six were women. In keeping with de Gaulle's image of a heroic band of fighters, true resisters were portrayed in the public eye as armed men, carrying out acts of sabotage or engaging in combat with the enemy. The parts played by women – messengers, couriers, printers, distributors of banned literature, providers of safe houses – did not seem quite heroic enough. And among the women themselves there was a tendency to belittle what they had done, to say that it had been no more than what they always did, as women. Returning to France, most of them slipped back into the shadows.

One of the few who was not forgotten was Danielle Casanova, quickly celebrated as a new Joan of Arc, a martyred communist heroine, the supreme patriot and symbol of resistance. Babies and streets were named after her and her picture put on to medallions and posters. For a while, it was thought best that her husband Laurent should not confess to having married someone else, but appear as devoting his life to the cult of his dead wife.

Even before they left the camps, some of the French deportees had discussed the formation, when they got home, of *amicales*, associations which would bring survivors together and lobby for their rights. Marie-Claude and Madeleine Dechavassine took leading roles in starting an Amicale des Déportés d'Auschwitz, Birkenau et des Camps de Haute-Silésie, and by October 1945 a Fédération Nationale des Déportés et Internés Résistants et Patriotes had been formed, with rooms in the rue Leroux in Paris where the Gestapo had once had offices. Many of the concerns revolved around the health of the deportees, who suffered from what became known as the *syndrome des déportés*; this included chronic exhaustion, digestive problems and depression.*

The people left out from nearly all the deliberations, however, were the Jews, of whom only a fraction of those deported returned. In part because so few came back and in part because the extermination camps of Poland had been largely destroyed by the

---

* Within ten years, a third of all survivors had died.

departing Germans, and in any case now lay within the Soviet zone of occupation, the early stories of the death camps were written not by the Jews but by the communists. But it was more complicated than this. Simone Veil, deported as a Jew with her family, would later say that the surviving resisters were quick to scorn and marginalise Jewish survivors. 'They, they had fought against the Nazis. We, we were nothing.' Neither de Gaulle nor anyone else was keen to admit that much of France had not only tolerated anti-Semitism and xenophobia but actually anticipated German wishes in identifying and deporting Jews.

It would be the early 1970s before there was any serious re-evaluation of what were called *les années noires*, the black years. Marcel Ophüls four-hour film of life under Vichy, *Le Chagrin et la pitié*, with its clear message that there had been few resisters and many collaborators, was made for television at the end of the 1960s, but not shown on it until 1981. By then Beate and Serge Klarsfeld had published their monumental study on the deportation of the Jews from France, listing every name and every train; and Claude Lanzmann was at work on *Shoah*, his nine-hour film about Germany and the Jews. It would take a foreign historian, Marcus Paxton, to publish the first authoritative work on Vichy and the Jews, and many years before Vichy was judged guilty of crimes against humanity.*

For the time being, in the austere winter of 1945–46, the French were more concerned with food, politics and the weather. Women had failed to win the vote after the First World War, but 1944 brought female suffrage and some small improvements to their economic and social rights, though they were for the most part folded back into the French family, along with other vulnerable groups like children. Laws on abortion and contraception were in fact strengthened. Women were enfranchised in time to help vote into power de Gaulle as President in November, but, as Marie-Claude had feared, there were deep divisions between the political parties. The Communists won 159 seats and were now the largest party in France but de Gaulle remained extremely

---

* In 1980 a poll of French people aged between 18 and 44 revealed that 34 per cent did not think that the existence of gas chambers had been clearly proven.

reluctant to give them ministerial posts. The eventual compromise would last just a few months. Unable to unite the country behind him, de Gaulle resigned as head of government in January 1946, but went on calling for national reconciliation, saying that the Communists were to blame for the growing sense of political disillusionment.

The winter was bitterly cold. The franc had plummeted and it was said that France was now eighty-four times poorer than in 1914. The economy was bankrupt and the country was being kept afloat on American aid and loans. There was very little to eat and the cost of rationed goods soared. Parisians complained that they were colder than at any time during the occupation. Because of a lack of plaster in the hospitals, there was nothing with which to mend bones weakened by years of poor nutrition and broken by falls on the ice.

Factories were idle, their equipment and machinery having been dismantled and shipped back to Germany by the occupiers; there was very little fertiliser, timber or coal. Seven and a half thousand bridges were down and the shortage of salt meant that pigs were not killed for *charcuterie*. The Allied forces, on their way across France during 1944 and 1945, had consumed scarce food, vandalised, looted and raped, and their destructiveness and rapaciousness was everywhere compared to that of the German soldiers. Caen, Le Havre and Saint-Lô had been reduced to rubble; five million people, many more than after the First World War, were homeless. In the *New Yorker*, Janet Flanner described the clatter of wooden soles on Parisian cobbles, and the way that the students in the Sorbonne went to their classes wrapped in thick ski clothes. But if the grocery shelves were bare, the theatres were packed. Edith Piaf, the singer so loved by Georgette Rostaing, was performing at Giro's nightclub. A new lightness was in the air, a desire for pleasure and enjoyment, and people compared it to the heady days of the Directoire, after the bleakness and terror of the 1789 revolution. 'Paris is not gay,' wrote Janet Flanner. 'It is restless, anxious, cantankerous.' But, she added, it was 'convalescent'.

*   *   *

There were many things that the forty-nine women found hard when they got home. There was, first of all, a feeling of guilt, that they should have survived when so many of their friends had died. This was particularly hard for Félicienne Bierge, one of the very few women from the Gironde or Charente to return, who felt it her duty to tell families how their dead mothers, sisters and daughters had died. There were eighteen calls and visits to make; Félicienne was a timid, reserved woman and found the task almost impossibly distressing.

Families had become strangers, children altered beyond all recognition and wary of these unfamiliar women who claimed to be their mothers. Marie-Elisa found her small son Francis well, but learnt that her brother had died in Bergen-Belsen and that her friend France Bloch, with whom she had made explosives for the Resistance in Paris, had been executed in Hamburg, her head cut off with an axe. She also received confirmation of what she had feared: that her mother, having admitted to being Jewish, had indeed been gassed in Auschwitz. Hélène Bolleau, whose broken leg was still mending, returned to Royan to find the city in ruins, her home bombed, her grandfather dead, her grandmother injured; she had watched her mother die from dehydration in Birkenau, desperately trying to get some water from the ruts in the earth left by a passing cart.

Many came home feeling that they carried with them what David Rousset, another camp survivor, would call 'gangrene', the whole terrifying, shocking ordeal that lived on to haunt survivors. 'I no longer had the right to be unhappy,' wrote one woman, 'but there existed no pleasure or joy capable of compensating for the suffering I had been through. I came back bringing the camp with me, and yet I felt totally alone.' Having survived the unsurvivable in order to return, the idyllic world of kindness and ease they had held and nursed in their minds quickly seemed little more than an illusion. Life was flat, empty. The women thought of themselves as travellers in another land, no longer quite like other people. Having so badly wanted to live, they found they no longer cared whether they did so or not. They had told themselves that in the camps they had endured the whole gamut of misfortune, and that now they were entitled to happiness. But happiness eluded them.

Most found they could not bear to sleep alone, and dragged a mattress into their parents' rooms; unable to digest anything but bland food, their teeth missing or sore, they ate little mouthfuls out of teaspoons. They flinched if anyone made a sudden movement, as if to ward off a blow, and they avoided striped materials. They found they could no longer cry at funerals, having seen so many people die. They worried that they looked peculiar and behaved oddly, and were ashamed of their missing teeth. Brutalised and starved for over two years, they found it almost impossibly hard to relearn how to live in a world not governed by force and cunning. They felt irritable, distracted. A few were obsessed with the need to confront the men who had betrayed them. Germaine Renaudin and her husband went to Bordeaux to look for the two policemen who had tortured her in the Fort du Hâ. Both men had died in the war. Charlotte tracked down the men of the Brigades Spéciales who had arrested her and Dudach: she was told that they had both fought against the Germans during the liberation – *Résistants de la dernière heure* – and were thus immune from prosecution.

What all the women found almost hardest was how to find the words to describe what they had been through. Having imagined telling their families exactly what it had been like, they now fell silent. Often, as it turned out, the families did not really want to hear: the stories were too unbearable to listen to. 'It wasn't food we wanted,' Cécile would say. 'It was talk. But no one wanted to listen.' When she returned to work for her former employer in the fur business, a Jew who had survived the Parisian round-ups, he made it clear that he wanted to hear nothing about the camps. Strangers asked questions, then quickly changed the subject and began to recount the hardships of their own war. At a village fête, soon after her return, Hélène Bolleau talked a little about the camps. A farmer interrupted. 'It can't be true. If it was, you wouldn't have survived.' She cried for three days; then she stopped talking. It was Hélène who later told the others that she had met a woman who, seeing the numbers tattooed on her arm, said: 'Oh, is that where you write your phone numbers? Or is it the new fashion?'

Charlotte arrived back in Paris with the feeling that she had indeed survived, not as herself, but as a ghost, floating in a world that in some way did not exist. When she tried to read a book, she was filled with a curious sensation that she could see through the words to emptiness and banality. With all subtlety gone, there seemed to be no gradations of shade or light, and the world was stripped of all mystery. It was, she would say, a period of 'prolonged absence', devoid of taste, colour, smell and sounds. And then, very slowly, things gained definition. One day, she picked up a book and began to read again.

Poupette, acutely conscious that she had survived while her sister Marie had died, arrived back in Rennes to find that her father was about to remarry. She was 20 and felt inexpressibly old. Her new stepmother, not much older in years than herself, had assumed the two girls were dead and turned their bedrooms into extra guest rooms for the hotel. 'It was only at that moment that I really realised that I no longer had a sister,' Poupette would say. 'Return was wretched, sordid, a pile of shabby details.' Like the other women, she found the loss of the intense friendship and intimacy that had bound them together extremely painful.

Not feeling wanted, disliking her stepmother, she soon married one of the survivors of the Johnny network.* She had two daughters, but nothing in her life seemed to work out and when her father died she sold the hotel – her stepmother had long since moved away – and went to run a small business in Buenos Aires. 'For years,' she would say, 'I behaved as if all was well, but inside I lived in a fog of unhappiness.' But she went on reading and learning, faithful to her promise to herself that if she returned alive, she would discover for herself all the things that Charlotte, Maï, Danielle and Marie-Claude had talked about. Later, Poupette would anger the other survivors by writing a memoir, in which she gave the names of five of the seven dwarfs to the women who had been with her in the salt mine in Beendorf. Cécile, whom she had never much liked, was called *Grincheuse,* Grumpy.

Simone, not yet 21 when she came home, learnt that of all the young men and girls who had picnicked and trained together in

---

* Of the 120 men and women who had worked for Johnny, twenty-eight had been killed by the Germans.

the Bois de Boulogne and fought alongside each other in the Battaillons de la Jeunesse, only one boy had survived. Simone's younger brother Pierre found her curiously unchanged until she slept in the room next to his, and he heard her crying out night after night in her sleep. A first marriage, to another survivor of the camps, failed; a second brought a son and happiness. But Simone, the pretty, plump schoolgirl whose smiling photograph was taken in Romainville, came home physically broken. In the years that followed, she had seventeen operations. The dream she had had in Auschwitz, about being driven by hunger to cut a piece of flesh from a living horse, which then cried, continued to haunt her.

Many of the women married quickly, often choosing men who had been in the Resistance themselves. Betty met a former member of the Spanish Brigades who had been in Mauthausen; they had a son and moved to live in Morocco. Hélène Bolleau married, determined to have children, to prove that 'the Germans had not destroyed me'. But there were long spells when she was too depressed to look after them, and they had to go to her parents-in-law. Germaine Renaudin found herself pregnant – her husband returned from a prisoner of war camp soon after she got home – but she did not want the baby. There were days when she was 'absent', and she feared that she could never look after anyone again. In the event, a son was born and she called him Daniel, after Danielle Casanova, and then a daughter. Germaine too had nightmares, crying out, again and again, 'les chiens! les chiens!' (the dogs, the dogs).

It was not only the women who found life so hard in 1945. Their children were confused and upset. This applied both to those whose mothers returned and those who had only a letter or a final parting to remember them by. Many grew up torn between a desire not to be overwhelmed by their mothers' stories, yet at the same time needing not to forget the memories so crucial to their identities. No one was quite sure which train would bring Félicienne Bierge back to Bordeaux, so her uncle and grandfather met every train. Her son had been four when he last saw his mother. He went with them to the station, but did not recognise the woman who eventually arrived. Not knowing what to do, he put out his hand and said, 'Bonjour, madame'. He would never forget the fact that when Félicienne discovered that her husband had been shot at Souge, she said that had she known, she would not have tried so hard to survive.

Some grandparents and surviving husbands found it easier not to tell children where their mothers had gone. Jaunay and his sisters waited, day after day, for news of their mother, Germaine, who had been part of a *passeur* network in and around Amboise, all of them denounced and arrested in the summer of 1942 and not one of whom returned. Their father said nothing. Germaine's name was never mentioned. The weeks, then the months, passed. Finally Jaunay's sister went to friends and found out the truth. But his father refused to speak about their mother and never referred to her again. All his life, Jaunay lived with the pale memory of a woman who had loved him, and at the age of 80 he still found it impossible to talk of her without crying.

Pierre Zani, who was 18 months old when his mother was taken away, was brought up by grandparents and aunts who blamed his father for his mother's arrest. As a boy, he hated the way that the children of parents who had died in the Resistance were singled out at school. For ever afterwards, though he had no conscious memory of his mother, he felt her absence like a hole in his life, a gap that nothing could fill up.

Claude Epaud was 15 when he was told that his mother Annette would not be coming home. He lived with his aunts in a family of close brothers and sisters who treated him as their own. It was years later, talking to Marie-Claude, that he discovered that his mother had been put on to a lorry and taken to the gas chambers after she had given water to the dying women in Block 25 at Birkenau, and that, as she was being driven away, she had called out to the others 'Look after my son'. And it was not until after the death of his father, when he discovered among his papers the little drawing done of him as a boy that his mother had held on to and then given to Félicienne Bierge, that he realised that she had kept his picture by her through all her months in Birkenau. Félicienne had looked after it and after the war given it to his father. He put the drawing up above his desk, so that he could look at it every day. Annette Epaud was made a 'Righteous Among the Nations'.

Georgette Rostaing's daughter Pierrette, who remembered her as a laughing, loving mother, always singing, always dressed up and in high heels, who took her with her when she went to hear Edith Piaf sing, grew up consumed with longing to find out what had happened to her. Her grandparents, with whom she lived, spoke little, existing in a state of grief, having lost not only Georgette but her brother Pierre, who some said had been beaten to death by an SS guard during the evacuation of the Dora camp at Nordhausen, and others that he had been locked up with others in a barn and burnt. Pierrette would later say that after the war she never once saw her grandfather smile.

Knowing that Cécile had returned, she contacted her and asked to see her; but Cécile refused, telling her only much later that she had been unable to bear such things at the time. Cécile herself did not find return easy. Her daughter was eight when she left, 11 when she came home, a tall, very thin, unhappy child who had been intensely miserable in the household in which she had been put to spend the war. She was possessive of her mother and jealous and difficult when Cécile met and married a survivor from Mauthausen. The girl decided she did not want to live with her mother again. 'If I am honest,' said Cécile later, 'I would have to say that I never got her back.' For twenty years, Cécile kept having the same nightmare. An SS guard, carrying a revolver, was coming up the stairs to kill her. It only stopped, she said, when, in her dream, she told the man, 'I don't care if you shoot me.'

And the sense of loss, of unfinished business, of confusion over feelings, went on down the generations. Adrienne Hardenberg, who had helped her printer husband in the Resistance and died in Birkenau, had left behind a daughter, Yolande, who had been sent to live with comrades in the Communist Party. At the end of the war, the child, now a teenager, learnt that her parents were dead. Moved from family to family, never doing well at school, considered a secretive, unstable girl, Yolande died after a botched abortion at home. Only then did her family discover that she had left another baby, a girl called Catherine, with a wet nurse. Catherine grew up with another communist family and it was not until her adoptive mother died, many years later, that she began to put together the story of her grandmother's life.

Reluctant to talk to their children – though less so to their grand-children – the forty-nine women kept in touch with one another, and as they grew older they met more often, either in ones and twos or at the reunions which increasingly came to mark days of

A reunion of some of the survivors in 1945: among them Gilberte, Mado, Betty, Cécile, Lulu and Carmen

commemoration. Charlotte, Cécile, Carmen and Lulu, though scat-tered between Geneva, Paris, Brittany and Bordeaux, remained the closest of friends. Often their conversations began with memories of incidents in the camps that had made them laugh, or had good endings: days when some bit of luck had befallen them, or the way that Charlotte, recounting the story of her arrest, would change the colour of the skirt she wore each time she retold the story. But then the mood would grow sombre and they would begin to talk about the women who had died.

Sometimes they talked about why they had survived, what it was in their particular story or character that enabled them to live, whether it was their optimistic nature, or because they had been able to use their skills as women, caring for others. In the end, they always came back to the same two reasons: they had lived because each of them had been incredibly lucky, and because of the friendship between them, which had protected them and made it easier to withstand the barbarity. They had learnt, they would say, the full meaning of friendship, a commitment to each other that went far deeper than individual liking or disliking; and they now felt wiser, in some indefinable way, because they had understood the depths to which human beings can sink and equally the heights to which it is possible to rise.

They would tell each other that for all its extreme horror, the experience had made them more receptive, more interested in the world around them, more conscious of the suffering of others, though they worried that they were not true witnesses, in Primo Levi's sense, in that only their dead friends, the *sommersi*, the drowned, could really bear witness to the full horror. And they would agree that there were times when the past and the memory of the camps was more real to them than the world about them. Many suffered from poor health, exhaustion, bad eyesight and such terrible nightmares that they fought against going to sleep. They felt, and looked, far older than their years. Lulu told the others that she could not stop dreaming that she smelt burning flesh and bones, and that it was months before she could bear the taste of coffee again. Charlotte longed for the first year of return to end, so that she would no longer be able to say to herself: 'a year ago, at this time . . .'

Even when they were not able to meet, the survivors continued to feel bound to each other in ways that did not weaken with time. There remained a familiarity between them, a sense of openness and ease that they shared with no one else. When Germaine Renaudin died, Carmen, Lulu and Charlotte met on the train on the way to the funeral. Joined by other survivors from the *Convoi*, whom they had not met in some years, they found themselves instantly relating not to the faces and figures they saw before them, but to the women they had known in the camps. They fell back, as Charlotte would say, into conversations in which there was 'no effort to be made, no constraints, not even that of common politeness. Between us, it's us.' It was a kind of closeness that required no keeping up.

And, as the years passed, many of the women made new lives, saying they often felt that they had to do all the things that those who had died had not been able to do. As in Birkenau and

Ravensbrück, those with strong political commitments, a cause in which to believe, found it easier. Marie-Claude and Hélène Solomon both went into politics; Marie-Elisa Nordmann returned to her research laboratory. Adelaïde Hautval did not go back to her job as psychiatrist but became a school doctor in a suburb of Paris, where she baked cakes for the local children. Haunted by the need to document the medical experiments in the camps, she wrote detailed notes of what she had witnessed. They were not published until after her death; she committed suicide after the death of an elderly friend with whom she had shared her house. As with Primo Levi and Bruno Bettelheim, surviving the horror, in the end, may have proved too hard.

*　　*　　*

In the late 1940s, Charlotte Delbo sat down and wrote a book about Auschwitz. She had come back to Paris with bad headaches, high temperatures and toothache, suffering from nightmares in which death kept fastening upon her; she spent many months in a sanatorium in Switzerland before rejoining Louis Jouvet at the Athenée theatre. It was only on her return from Poland that she discovered that her youngest brother had died in a concentration camp. Without money or a flat of her own, she moved to Geneva to work for the UN where her knowledge of languages brought her a good salary. She did not complain, but she sometimes wondered whether she had not fled post-war France too heedlessly. 'It's not a life for a woman alone, exile,' she wrote sadly to Jouvet. Having written her account of the camps while convalescing, she decided to put it to the side for twenty years, to see whether it stood the test of time and really conveyed what it had all been like. She wanted her style to be so plain, so transparent that nothing came between the reader and his understanding.

In one form or another, in verse and prose and dialogue, Charlotte spent the rest of her life writing about the camps. She put down a long account to Jouvet in the form of a letter, invoking Eurydice; but she never sent it, and Jouvet died. In her book *Auschwitz and After*, made up of three shorter books, published separately only in the early 1970s, she spoke of having two selves, an Auschwitz self, and an after-Auschwitz self, like a snake shedding its skin in order to gain a new one; always, she feared that the skin might grow thin, crack and that the camps would get hold of her again. Only, unlike a snake's skin, her skin of Auschwitz memory, so deeply etched that she could forget no part of it, did not disappear. 'I live,' she wrote, 'alongside it. Auschwitz is there, unalterable, precise, but enveloped in the skin of memory.'

There were thus two kinds of memory: the now, which she called 'ordinary' memory, and the 'me of then' which was *la mémoire profonde*, deep memory, the memory of the senses. The first allowed her to see Auschwitz as part of a narrative, something that had happened and ended, and it made going on possible. The second condemned her to feel that Auschwitz was never, and would never be, over. The thinking, ordinary memory allowed her to transmit the facts; the feeling memory enabled her to convey a glimpse of the unimaginable anguish that accompanied them. Like Paul Celan and Primo Levi, she used careful, stark words, beautifully balanced and without embellishment, in order to touch the reader by appealing to the senses. She wanted, she would say, to carry her readers into Auschwitz with her, to make it as real for them as it had been, and would always be, for her.

Charlotte remained close to many of the women from the *Convoi*, and at some point decided to take down and record, in brief biographical notes, the story of every one of the 230 women. It was when talking to Madeleine Doiret, Mado, that she pinned down in words the essence of what Birkenau and Ravensbrück had meant to them. Mado, who was 22 when she had been sent to Birkenau, told Charlotte that when her first baby was born after the war, she was overwhelmed by a feeling of immense happiness, but that almost at once she was invaded by the ghosts of the women who had died without knowing this particular delight. 'The silky water of my joy,' she explained, 'changed to sticky mud, sooty snow, fetid marshes.'

Then she went on: 'The life we wanted to find again, when we used to say "if I return" was to have been large, majestic, full of colour. Isn't it our fault that the life we resumed proved so tasteless, shabby, trivial, thieving, that our hopes were mutilated, our best intentions destroyed?' Her husband, she said, was sensitive, thoughtful, and wanted her to forget, and she did not want to hurt his feelings. But all she could think was that to forget would be an act of betrayal. She thought of them all, of Viva and Danielle and Raymonde and Annette, all the time and for the most part she felt closer to those she went on thinking of as 'real ones, our real comrades'. So she had decided not to talk any more about Auschwitz. 'Looking at me, one would think that I'm alive . . . I'm not alive. I died in Auschwitz, but no one knows it.'

Appendix: the women

In 2008, when I started work on this book, there were seven women still alive from the *Convoi des 31000*. They were:

Simone Alizon (Poupette). b. 24 February 1925 and the youngest of the survivors. Poupette married and had two daughters and was awarded the *Légion d'honneur*. She returned to live in Rennes.

Cécile Charua, the *Cygne d'Enghien*. b. 18 July 1915. After the war, Cécile remarried and had two sons. She lives near them, in Brittany.

Madeleine Dissoubray. b. 25 November 1917. Madeleine came back from Ravensbrück, married, had two children, and a career in education. She remained close to the Resistance organisations.

Madeleine Langlois (Betty), *Ongles Rouges*. b. 23 May 1914. After the war, Betty married, had a son and went to live in Morocco. She spent the last years of her life in Paris, where she died in 2009.

Geneviève Pakula. b. 22 December 1922. Originally Polish, Geneviève returned from the camps to France, married, had a daughter and became a dressmaker. She was awarded the *Légion d'honneur*.

Gilberte Tamisé. b. 3 February 1912. Gilberte's younger sister, Andrée, died in Auschwitz. Gilberte came back to Bordeaux and looked after her father. She died in 2009.

Lulu Thévenin. b. 16 July 1917 in Marseilles. She and her sister **Carmen** both came home – the only pair of sisters to do so. Lulu found her husband and her son Paul waiting and returned to her work with the Communist Party. She died in 2009.

There was not always very much that I was able to find out about the other **42 women** from the *Convoi* who survived the war, but who died in the years that followed. They returned to families that had been broken up, houses that had been bombed or ransacked, children who no longer knew them. Many had husbands and lovers who had been shot by the Germans. Some married again. Some of the single women married and had children. Nearly all suffered from continuing bad health – arthritis, heart problems, skin disorders, the lingering effects of typhus. They got tired quickly and had bouts of depression. Few, very few, found the life of happiness they had dreamt about.

Marie-Jeanne Bauer. b. 14 July 1913 in Saint-Affrique, remained in Auschwitz until liberation. Returned to find her house bombed, her husband and brother executed. In the camps she had lost the sight of one eye.

Antoinette Besseyre. b. 7 July 1919 in Brittany. Antoinette's communist husband had been shot by the Germans. She remarried but felt too ill, with recurrent symptoms of typhus, to have children.

Félicienne Bierge. b. 9 June 1914 in Spain but grew up in Bordeaux. Félicienne's husband had been shot by the Germans, but she returned to her son, remarried, and had one daughter.

Claudine Blateau. b. 23 March 1911 in Niort. Claudine returned to find that her husband had been shot by the Germans, but her two children were waiting for her. She remarried.

Hélène Bolleau. b. 6 April 1924 in Royan. Hélène's mother Emma had died in Auschwitz and her father had been shot by the Germans. She returned, at the age of 21, married and had children. But her health was always poor and she suffered from depression.

Marie-Louise Colombain. b. 12 April 1920 in Paris. Marie-Louise came home to learn that her husband had died in Mauthausen. She remarried, and had three children.

Marguerite Corringer. b. 15 June 1902 in Paris. Marguerite had been a lady's maid and housekeeper before the war. Her husband, a communist, was shot by the Germans. She returned ill, with arthritis and osteoporosis.

Madeleine Dechavassine. b. 1900 in the Ardennes. Madeleine returned to her work as a chemical engineer but never married. She retired in 1960 and lived alone.

Alida Delasalle. b. 23 July 1907 in Fécamp. Alida's health was destroyed in the camps. She returned with pericarditis, nephritis, sclerosis and rheumatism, and she had lost her teeth and part of her hearing. She was not well enough to work again. Her husband had been shot by the Germans.

Charlotte Delbo. b. 10 August 1913 in Seine-et-Oise. Returned to a job in Geneva with the UN and to write poetry, plays and memoirs of the camps. Her husband had been shot by the Germans and she did not remarry.

Madeleine Doiret (Mado). b. 2 November 1920 in Ivry. Mado was only 24 when she returned. She married and had one son. She went back to work as a secretary, but was forced to retire early because of spinal problems. She remained haunted by those who did not survive.

Aimée Doridat. b. 14 March 1905 in Nancy. Aimée was deported with her sister-in-law Olga Godefroy, who did not return. Aimée's leg was amputated in Birkenau. When she returned home she found her husband and children waiting for her, and was awarded the *Légion d'honneur*.

Germaine Drapon. b. 1 January 1903 in Charente. Took in wanted communists. Returned to find husband, freed from Oranienburg, and her daughter. Their house had been bombed, but they were together.

Marie-Jeanne Dupont. b. 11 March 1921 in Douai. Aged 24 when she returned, Marie-Jeanne married and had two children, but her health was constantly bad.

Mitzy Ferry. b. 6 March 1918 in the Vosges. Mitzy returned to settle in the Midi and bring up her son. But her health was always poor and she had many abdominal operations.

Hélène Fournier. b. 23 December 1904 in Indre-et-Loire. The only survivor from the Tours region, Hélène returned to find her husband and daughter. She was awarded the *Légion d'honneur*.

Yolande Gili. b. 7 March 1922 in the Moselle where her Italian immigrant parents had settled. Her father and husband had both been shot by the Germans, and her sister Aurore Pica did not return from the camps, but Yolande came back to her son, and remarried. Her health was extremely poor.

Adelaïde Hautval. b. 1 January 1906 in the Rhine basin. One of the last women to be repatriated, she returned to become a school doctor. She was awarded the *Légion d'honneur* for her devotion to her comrades in the camps.

Thérèse Lamboy. b. 25 July 1918. Details of her life unknown, beyond the fact that she had one child; and that she survived.

Fernande Laurent. b. 31 December 1902 in Nantes. Fernande returned to file a complaint against the family who had denounced her. She found her husband and children waiting for her but her health was extremely bad; she suffered from heart trouble, bronchitis and phlebitis.

Marcelle Lemasson. b. 28 November 1909 in Saintes. Reunited with her husband, who had survived Mauthausen, she had one son, but suffered from back problems and a bad heart.

Simone Loche. b. 27 October 1913 in Loire-Inférieure. She returned to her husband and small son, and was slowly nursed back to health.

Louise Losserand. b. 23 February 1904 in Paris. Louise's husband had been shot by the Germans. Although she remarried, she was never able to resume her work as a furrier.

Louise Magadur. b. 21 April 1899 in Finistère. The eldest of the survivors to return, Louise reopened her beauty parlour. But the dog bites to her legs never healed properly, and she had terrible nightmares.

Lucie Mansuy. b. 3 June 1915 in the Vosges. Lucie's husband had died in the Spanish Civil War, and her lover was killed by the Germans. She returned to find that her house had been stripped. She became a machine cutter, but suffered from terrible nightmares.

Henriette Mauvais. b. 22 October 1906 in Vitry-sur-Seine. Henriette returned to her husband and two daughters and went on to have twins. She worked as a shorthand typist.

Marthe Meynard. b. 29 March 1912 in Angoulême. Marthe's husband died in Mauthausen. Her only son, who was three when his parents were deported, committed suicide in 1973, leaving four children.

Lucienne Michaud. b. 4 April 1923 in Creusot. Lucienne married her fiancé from before the war, had two children, and took a job in a travel agency.

Marcelle Mourot. b. 31 July 1918 in Doubs. After the war Marcelle married another resister and had two children. She underwent numerous ear operations.

Marie-Elisa Nordmann. b. 4 November 1910 in Paris. Marie-Elisa, whose mother had died in Birkenau, returned to her son and her scientific career. She remarried and had three more children. She was awarded the *Légion d'honneur*.

Marie-Jeanne Pennec. b. 9 July 1909 in Rennes. Marie-Jeanne returned to her son, but had constant troubles with him, and when he moved to Indochina she suffered a nervous depression, tried to commit suicide and had a lobotomy.

Germaine Pican. b. 10 October 1901 in Rouen. Germaine's husband André had been shot by the Germans but she returned to her two daughters. She remained a member of the Communist Party. The elder of the two girls, affected by the war and the loss of her father, died two years later.

Germaine Pirou. b. 9 March 1918 in Finistère. In 1956, Germaine married an Austrian who had joined the Foreign Legion. They had one son, and took a job managing an estate. She was one of the very few survivors to live a happy life.

Renée Pitiot. b. 17 November 1921 in Paris. Renée's husband had been shot by the Germans at the age of 22. She remarried and had three daughters, but died young of kidney failure.

Paulette Prunières. b. 13 November 1918 in Paris. Paulette married and had two children but she was frequently ill.

Germaine Renaudin. b. 22 March 1906 in Meurthe-et-Moselle. A Catholic and a communist, Germaine returned to her husband, son and two daughters and had two more children. She died of cancer in 1968.

Simone Sampaix. b. 14 June 1924 in Sedan. Simone was 20 when she returned. She married twice and had one son, but her health never recovered.

Jeanne Serre (Carmen). b. July 1919, in Algeria. Carmen married and had three children. She suffered from ill health but remained a militant communist.

Julia Slusarczyk. b. 26 April 1902 in Poland. Julia never knew why she had been arrested. She returned to Paris to find her pork butcher business destroyed and her companion very ill. Her own health never recovered.

Hélène Solomon. b. 25 May 1909 in Paris. Hélène's husband Jacques was shot by the Germans. She returned to become a Deputy in the French parliament, and to work in scientific research. She remarried, but had no children and her health was always poor.

Marie-Claude Vaillant-Couturier. b. 3 November 1912 in Paris. Widowed before the war, Marie-Claude returned to remarry her companion, Pierre Villon. She became a Communist Deputy and had a distinguished career. She was awarded the *Légion d'honneur*.

Rolande Vandaële. b. 18 April 1918 in Paris. Rolande was deported with her mother Charlotte Douillot and aunt Henriette L'Huillier, neither of whom returned. After the war she was reunited with her postman husband and had one son. But she remained fearful and haunted.

And the women who did not come home:

Jeanne Alexandre. Cantal. Transported weapons for the Resistance. She was 31 when she died of typhus in February 1943. Left one son.

Marie Alizon. Rennes. Lodged resisters. Aged 22 when she died of dysentery and acute inflammation of the ear in June 1943. (Sister, Poupette, survived.)

Josée Alonso. Spanish, came to France as a four-year-old. Nursed and looked after wounded resisters. Divorced with two sons. Aged 32 when she was beaten by SS and died of pneumonia in February 1943.

Hélène Antoine. Vosges. Textile worker, one son. Hid weapons. Husband shot. Died spring 1943 at the age of 44. Cause unknown.

Yvonne B. Indre-et-Loire. Farmer's wife. Denounced – wrongly – for concealing weapons. Husband prisoner of war. Because pregnant, could have avoided deportation but child not her husband's and too embarrassed to say. Taken in 'the race', 10 February 1943, at the age of 26.

Gabrielle Bergin. Bourges. Kept cafe near the Cher, helped escaped prisoners and Jews cross demarcation line. Denounced by husband's mistress. She was 50 when she died in March 1943. Cause unknown.

Eugenia Beskine. Russian. Aged 54, she was caught in 'the race' on 10 February 1943.

Antoinette Bibault. Sarthe. Suspected of betraying thirty members of the Resistance. 39 when died in bunk ten days after reaching Birkenau. Husband died in Mauthausen, brother in Buchenwald.

Rosette Blanc. Pyrénées-Orientales. Communist and liaison officer for the intellectual Resistance in Paris. She was 23 when she died of typhus in April 1943.

Yvonne Blech. Brest. Editor, married to writer René Blech. Both communists and part of the intellectual Resistance. Died of dysentery on 11 March 1943, aged 36.

Emma Bolleau. Royan. With husband Roger and daughter Hélène created first FTP group in Charente-Maritime. Arrested taking food to Hélène in prison. Held on for fifty-two days. Died of dysentery and dehydration on 20 March 1943 aged 42. (Roger executed; Hélène returned.)

Josée Bonenfant. Paris. Seamstress. Died end of February 1943, cause unknown. Left one 10-year-old daughter.

Yvonne Bonnard. Very little known about her. One evening after roll call fell in mud and died. She was 45.

Léona Bouillard. Ardennes. With contractor husband denounced for distributing tracts. Husband died in Oranienburg. Died three days after reaching Birkenau during roll call, at the age of 57.

Alice Boulet. Saône-et-Loire. Communist and liaison officer in Paris for National Front. Died of dysentery in March 1943 at the age of 28. Husband died in Wilhemshafen.

Sophie Brabander and her daughter **Hélène**. Polish émigrées living in Paris. Belonged with husband to Monika network. Together with son Romuald, all on train from Compiègne. Sophie was caught in 'the race' of 10 February 1943 aged 55. Hélène died of typhus on 12 May 1943, aged 20.

Georgette Bret. Gironde. Hid and distributed clandestine material with husband, militant communist with armed Resistance. Continued work after he was executed by Germans. Died of typhus on 20 May 1943, at the age of 27. Left one 10-year-old daughter.

Simone Brugal. Saint-Denis. Hairdresser on transatlantic liner. Four sons by Jewish cavalry officer, then married fishmonger. No apparent Resistance activities. Died beginning of February 1943 at the age of 45. No known cause. Father of sons gassed at Auschwitz.

Marcelle Bureau. Charente-Maritime. Involved with BOLLEAU family network. Died, aged 20, of typhus on 16 April 1943.

Alice Cailbault. Paris. Had farm with husband in Charente and involved with Guillon/Valina network. Betrayed by Vincent. Daughter Andrée took over farm and Resistance activities. Died on 8 March 1943 aged 36, with legs so swollen she could not walk.

Germaine Cantelaube. Paris. Stored tracts and took part in Resistance activities in Bordeaux. After husband shot, continued to shelter resisters. When interrogated by Poinsot, spat in his face. Died of dysentery on 31 March 1943, aged 35.

Yvonne Carré. Montceau-les-Mines. Active with husband in FTP in Losserand network. Husband executed. Died of gangrene from SS dog bite March 1943 at the age of 45.

Danielle Casanova. Ajaccio. Dentist. Founder of JFdeF and active in National Front, Young Communists and intellectual Resistance in Paris. Died of typhus on 9 May 1943 at the age of 34. Posthumously awarded the *Légion d'honneur*.

Hélène Castera. Gironde. With husband and three sons, active in the Resistance in and around Bègles. Died of dysentery at the beginning of March 1943, at the age of 45, without knowing that two of her sons had been executed by the Gestapo. Her husband died in Mauthausen.

Yvonne Cavé. Montrouge. Neither she nor her husband, a cardboard-maker, concealed their antipathy to the Germans, and they listened to Radio London. Died end of February 1943, from acute nephritis. Someone had stolen her shoes and she had to go barefoot during four hours of roll call in the snow. She was 46. Her husband died in Oranienburg.

Camille Champion. Finistère. Ran boarding house, but no known Resistance activities. Picked up with husband in Pican/Politzer round-up. Died of typhus in April 1943 aged 44. Husband executed by Germans. Left one son.

Marie Chaux. Tain-l'Hermitage. Widowed and ran boarding house. Arrested for keeping husband's service revolver, but suspected of lodging resisters. Taken to Block 25 on 3 February 1943 after saying she could not tolerate roll calls; probably gassed. She was 67.

Marguerite Chavaroc. Quimper. With her husband in the Johnny network (see ALIZON). Died of dysentery in the middle of March 1943, aged 48. Husband survived Oranienburg.

Renée Cossin. Amiens. Working for the communist Underground, became liaison officer between the two zones, then active with women protestors in Picardy. Died in *Revier* of dysentery and oedema in April 1943, aged 29. Left two children, aged 11 and six.

Suzanne Costentin. Deux-Sèvres. Schoolteacher and skilled leather worker. Caught carrying tract relating fate of those shot at Châteaubriant. Beaten so badly she could not move; gangrene set in. Died March 1943 at the age of 49.

Yvonne Courtillat. Morbihan. Nurse's aide working near the river Cher, across which she conducted Jews and resisters from the occupied to the free zone. Denounced. Among the first to die, but no one witnessed death. She was 32. Left a 12-year-old son and a 10-year-old daughter.

Jeanne Couteau. Paris. Working as a cook in Tours when arrested for distributing tracts. Died of typhus at the beginning of April 1943 aged 42.

Madeleine Damous. Indre. She and her husband were communists working with the FTP. Died in March 1943 after being so violently beaten by a *kapo* that she could not see. She was just 30. Her husband was shot by the Germans. They had no children.

Viva Daubeuf. Ancona. Daughter of the Italian Socialist leader Pietro Nenni. Helped printer husband prepare clandestine publications. When husband arrested, could have escaped, but stayed to take him food and cigarettes. Died of typhus on 26 April 1943 aged 29. Husband executed by the Germans.

Simone David. Evreux. Collected funds and distributed propaganda material for the National Front while waiting to emigrate. Turned herself in to prevent father being taken hostage. Died of typhus at the end of May, aged 21. Husband and brother-in-law shot by Germans, and his wife committed suicide. Other brother-in-law released because father of eight children, but died soon after in an accident.

Charlotte Decock. Haute-Vienne. Taken as hostage for her husband, who was in the Resistance. Died in the bombardment of Amstetten in March 1945. She was 44.

Rachel Deniau. Indre-et-Loire. Post office worker who helped people across the demarcation line (see JAUNAY, LAURILLOU, GABB). Died, aged 53, in *Revier*. Left two children.

Charlotte Douillot and her sister **Henriette L'Huillier.** (See also ROLANDE VANDAELE, Charlotte's daughter.) Paris. Rounded up when followed by police tracking Charlotte's communist resister husband. Charlotte died of dysentery on 11 March 1943, aged 43. Henriette died of typhus on 23 March 1943, aged 39. Both their husbands were shot by the Germans. Henriette left one son.

Marie Dubois. Beaune. Ran cafe that was meeting place for resisters and letter drop. Died on 10 February 1943, in Block 25, after raising her hand to say she could no longer tolerate roll calls. She was 52.

Marie-Louise Ducros. Gironde. Together with husband stored gunpowder and grenades and sheltered resisters. Died 28 February 1943, aged 40. Left four children.

Elisabeth Dupeyron. Bordeaux. Active in GUILLONS/VALINA network. Gassed on 15 November 1943 at the age of 29. Left two children, aged 10 and five. Husband shot by the Germans.

Charlotte Dupuis. Yonne. Ran farm with brother while keeping cache of weapons for the Resistance and sheltering fighters. Died of dysentery on 8 March 1943, aged 49. Brother survived Mauthausen.

Noémie Durand and her sister, **Rachel Fernandez.** Haute-Vienne. After trade unionist husband shot by the Germans, Noémie became the representative of the National Front for Charente, arranging liaisons for FTP and distributing tracts. Widowed sister Rachel arrested with her. Noémie died on 22 February 1943 after being caught in 'the race' and taken to the gas chamber. She was 53. Rachel died of dysentery on 1 March 1943, aged 48. Their mother arrested with them but freed; died, insane, in 1943.

Simone Eiffes. Paris. Assistant to a Paris tailor, by whom she had a baby. No Resistance activities but caught when visiting members of the Bataillons de la Jeunesse (see SAMPAIX). Died of typhus in May 1943. She was 22. Daughter brought up by grandmother.

Yvonne Emorine. Montceau-les-Mines. Dressmaker. With husband organised groups in Charente and Gironde. Caught in the PICAN round-up. Died on 26 February 1942 at the age of 30; cause not known. Husband tortured to death, though Germans claimed that he had committed suicide. Left six-year-old daughter.

Annette Epaud. La Rochelle. Kept cafe, lodged resisters and distributed clandestine tracts. Denounced by Vincent. Gassed on 22 February 1943, at the age of 42, after giving water to woman begging for a drink. Left 13-year-old son.

Gabrielle Ethis, and her niece **Henriette Pizzoli.** Romainville. Gabrielle and her husband sheltered German communists who had fled Germany when Hitler came to power. Henriette, a cardboard-maker, was suspected of supplying them with black market supplies. Gabrielle died immediately on reaching Birkenau; she was 47. Henriette, who was 23, died of typhus in June 1943. She left one daughter.

Lucienne Ferre. Seine-et-Oise. Hairdresser and member of Danielle

CASANOVA's JFdeF. Young and unstable, suspected of denouncing a large number of comrades. Died at the age of 20 from frostbite on 5 March 1943

Yvette Feuillet. Paris. Glassblower and member of JFdeF. Liaison officer with the intellectual Resistance. Died on 8 July 1943 from typhus at the age of 23.

Marie-Thérèse Fleury. Paris. Helped set up a Resistance organisation within the postal service, the PTT, where she was adjunct federal treasurer. The notice of her death, on 16 April 1943, from 'myocardial deficiency', alerted France to the fate of the 230 deportees. She was 35 and left an eight-year-old daughter.

Rosa Floch. Eure. Schoolgirl and the youngest woman on the train. Caught painting Vs on the walls of her school. Died at the beginning of March 1943 at the age of 17. Cause not known.

Marcelle Fuglesang. Norwegian by birth. Studied nursing in Paris and converted to Catholicism. Doing social work with families of prisoners of war in Charleville, helped escaped prisoners cross border into Switzlerland. Died at the age of 40 of dysentery in March 1943. Croix de Guerre, Medal of the Resistance. *Légion d'honneur.*

Marie Gabb. Amboise. Belonged to network passing letters to the unoccupied zone. (See JAUNAY, DENIAU.) First to die, the day of arrival in Birkenau, on 27 January 1943. She was 51.

Madeleine Galesloot. Belgium. With her Dutch husband, worked with Underground printing presses in Paris. Died of dysentery in March 1943, at the age of 34. Her husband was executed by the Germans.

Yvonne Gallois. Eure-et-Loir. Cook in Paris when involved with young man who took part in an armed attack on the Germans. No one witnessed her death. She was 21.

Suzanne Gascard. Rueil-Malmaison. Married young, had a daughter, and became wet nurse to a baby she adopted after her mother disappeared. Kept and distributed tracts until denounced by a neighbour. Died of dysentery at the end of February 1943 at the age of 41. Posthumously awarded the Croix de Guerre with palm leaf and the Medal of the Resistance.

Laure Gatet. Dordogne. A pharmacologist collecting information for the Resistance. Died of dysentery, aged 29, on 15 February 1943.

Raymonde Georges. Transported weapons, supplied partisans, liaison officer for the armed Resistance. (See SAMPAIX.) Caught when revolver fell out of knapsack on train. Died at 26 of dysentery in March 1943.

Sophie Gigand, and her daughter Andrée. Aisne. Together with husband and children, Sophie stored weapons and distributed tracts. Sophie was caught in 'the race' on 10 February 1943. She was 45. No one witnessed 21-year-old Andrée's death. Husband and son survived deportation.

Germaine Girard. Paris. Nothing known of her life except that she died in March 1943 in the *Revier*, at the age of 39.

Renée Girard. Paris. Bookkeeper, parliamentary secretary and journalist.

Militant communist and agent for the National Front. Died – no known cause – end of April 1943. She was 58. An orphan, she had no family and there was no one to notify.

Olga Godefroy. Nancy. Member of large communist family of resisters. (See DORIDAT.) Died aged 37 on 26 February 1943 after *kapo* broke her spinal column with a cudgel.

Marcelle Gourmelon. Paris. Became agent for armed Resistance as kitchen worker in Luftwaffe camp. Stored weapons and explosives. Died of typhus in July 1943 at the age of 19. Her mother, arrested with her and sent to Romainville, was freed.

Cica Goutayer. Allier. Helped resisters cross demarcation line near Tours. Denounced by BIBAULT. Died in *Revier* at the beginning of April 1943, at the age of 42. Husband died in deportation. Left 16-year-old son.

Jeanne Grandperret. Jura. Painter on enamel. Working with husband in Paris, took in escapers sent to them by Resistance network. Died in *Revier* on 1 March 1943, at the age of 46.

Claudine Guérin. Seine-Inférieure. Schoolgirl. Liaison for local Resistance. Died of typhus on 25 April 1943, shortly before her 18th birthday.

Aminthe Guillon and her daughter-in-law **Yvette.** Charente. Family of farmers, communists, members of the FTP. Stored weapons. Denounced by Vincent. (See VALINA.) Aminthe was caught in 'the race' on 10 February 1943; she was 58. Yvette, aged 32, died of gangrene on 16 March 1943. Prosper, Aminthe's husband, and Jean, her son were executed by the Germans.

Jeanne Guyot. Argenteuil. Husband, who had printing press, printed anti-German tracts. Jeanne, not politically active, was arrested with him. She was 32. No one witnessed her death. Husband executed with group of printers. Left a boy of nine, a girl of eight.

Adrienne Hardenberg. Saint-Quentin. Cutter, married to a photoengraver who worked for the clandestine *L'Humanité*. She was 36. No one witnessed her death. Husband executed by the Germans. Left a daughter, aged 13.

Hélène Hascoët. Finistère. Dressmaker in Paris. Sheltered Jewish friends. Died of infected lesions, dehydration and dysentery at the age of 32 on 9 March 1943.

Violette Hebrard. Paris. Worked for an insurance company. With husband, militant communist, printed clandestine *L'Humanité*. No one witnessed death, in April 1943. She was 33. Husband died in deportation.

Lucette Herbassier. Tours. Kept bar where she hid clandestine publications. Died of haemorrhage, at the age of 28. Left 10-year-old son.

Jeanne Herschel. Grew up in Switzerland, England and the US. No Resistance activities known; concealed fact that she was Jewish. No one witnessed death in the middle of February 1943. She was 31.

Jeanne Hervé. Côtes-du-Nord. Housekeeper, waitress. Denounced Jews and black marketeers and finally taken in by police. Ostracised by other women. Died, at the age of 42, in the middle of February 1943, of acute nephritis.

Marguerite Houdart. Verdun. With her printer husband in Paris, sold paper to Resistance, but were not active politically themselves. Caught in round-up of printers and husband executed. Died on 10 May 1943, probably of typhus, her body devoured by rats. Left 14-year-old daughter.

Jeanne Humbert. Blénod-les-Toul. Husband took part in sabotage attacks on the railways and Jeanne transported the weapons. Died, at the end of March 1943, badly beaten by an SS guard, then sent to the gas chamber. She was 28. She left two children, aged three and five.

Anna Jacquat. Luxembourg. With French husband, ran a cafe near the station of Charleville, and worked with Marcelle FUGLESANG supplying provisions to escaped prisoners. No one witnessed her death. She was 46 and left a son of 16 and a daughter of 14.

Germaine Jaunay. Indre-et-Loire. Lived at the border between the two zones and helped resisters cross the demarcation line. Denounced along with niece (see DENIAU). Christened by other women 'the philosopher' because always even tempered. Died in the *Revier* on 5 April 1943, at the age of 44. She left four children under 15.

Marie-Louise Jourdan. Paris. Kept a dry-cleaning shop which became meeting place for Resistance. Caught in the PICAN round-up. Died of typhus in April 1943, aged 44.

Suzanne Juhem. Geneva. Raised in Paris and became a dressmaker. Involved with militant communist, but not believed to be political herself. Died of dysentery in March 1943 at the age of 32.

Irina Karchewska. Poland. Emigrated to France with husband in 1920s and kept a restaurant-grocery in Paris. Hid Poles trying to reach London. Died of dysentery, at the age of 43, on 30 April 1943.

Léa Kerisit. Vienne. Nurse, involved with chain helping prisoners of war attempting to reach free zone. Bludgeoned to death in April 1943 at the age of 47. She left three grown-up sons.

Karolina Konefal and **Anna Nizinska.** Two Polish peasant girls who arrived in Paris shortly before their arrest. Suspected of belonging to the Monika network. Karolina died in March 1943, having been beaten, thrown into a stream and soaked by an SS officer; she was 22. There were no witnesses to 25-year-old Anna's death.

Eugénie Korzeniowska. Lublin. Came to France in 1931 to teach children of Polish miners. Probably connected to the Monika network. Caught in 'the race' on 10 February 1943. She had bad hip problems and walked with a limp. She was 41.

Marguerite Kotlerewsky. Secretary on *France-Soir* from the Auvergne when married a Russian émigré Jew. Denounced. Died on 26 February 1943, at the age of 40, having lost all will to live when her daughter Gisèle, deported with her, was whipped by Taube and died. Left another daughter. Son, Léon, also deported, never returned.

Lina Kuhn. Paris. Member of the Johnny network (see ALIZON). Died at about the age of 35 at the beginning of March 1943, probably of typhus.

Georgette Lacabanne. A dressmaker from Bordeaux who sheltered resisters. Died in the *Revier* on 8 March 1943, at the age of 32. She left an 11-year-old daughter and a three-year-old son.

Madeleine Laffitte. Maine-et-Loire. Worked in a spinning mill. Became liaison agent for the Front National and was arrested during the round-up of the CADRAS network. Died of dysentery, at the age of 29 at the end of November 1943.

Gisele Laguesse. Poitiers. With her husband, a teacher, acted as liaison between the Front National leadership and the regions, printed tracts, transcribed broadcasts from London. Died of dysentery and from being beaten on 11 March 1943 at the age of 28. She said goodbye to her husband when he was taken from Romainville and shot.

Léa Lambert. Ardennes. Cook and housekeeper in Charleville and helped Marcelle FUGLESANG smuggle escaped prisoners to Switzerland (see also JACQUAT). Died soon after arrival, in the middle of March 1943 at the age of 50. On hearing the news, her husband cursed the Germans, was overheard, arrested, deported and died in Dachau.

Fabienne Landy. Loire-et-Cher. Stenographer and member of the Communist Party, she worked for the Front National and typed tracts. Died of a lethal injection of formol after blisters spread and became infected on 25 February 1943. She was 21.

Berthe Lapeyrade and her sister-in-law **Charlotte Lescure.** Lot-et-Garonne. With their husbands, stored propaganda material and sheltered *résistants*. Berthe died in the marshes at the beginning of March 1943, at the age of 47; Charlotte was caught in 'the race' on 10 February 1943, but her friends managed to save her. A few weeks later, she was beaten to death. She was 40. Both their husbands were also killed.

Suzanne Lasne. Paris. Drawn into the Resistance with Louise Magadur and worked for the FTP. Arrested with the names of Jeanne ALEXANDRE, Marie-Louise COLOMBAIN and Angele MERCIER, all of whom were caught in the net. Died in the *Revier*, consumed with guilt, on 14 March 1943. She was 19.

Marcelle Laurillou. Indre-et-Loire. Part of a Resistance chain of *passeurs* in Amboise. Died of dysentery around 20 April 1943 at the age of 28. She left two children, aged seven and nine.

Louise Lavigne. Vienne. Worked in a factory making clogs. When her brother was arrested, she and her husband took over his work for the Front National in Poitiers. Beaten to death with a revolver by an SS officer around 25 March 1943. Left two daughters, aged seven and two. Husband executed; brother died in Auschwitz. She was 39.

Lucienne Lebreton. Paris. Concierge. Denounced as a communist. Died at the end of March 1943, in the *Revier*, at the age of 38.

Angèle Leduc. Roubaix. Worked as cashier in her husband's butcher shop in Paris. Probably denounced for listening to Radio London. Died from oedema, her legs so badly swollen that she could not walk, in March 1943, at the age of 51.

Elisabeth Le Port. Lorient. Teacher and leader in the Front National. Denounced by a pupil who saw the tracts and stencils on her desk. Died at the age of 23 on 14 March 1943 from dysentery.

Marguerite Lermite. Nantes. Teacher. With her husband, distributed clandestine tracts. There were no witnesses to her death at the end of February 1943. She left a four-year-old son. Her husband also died in Auschwitz, probably gassed.

Marie Lesage. Doville. Ran a cafe on the outskirts of Cherbourg and hid Resistance fighters. No witness to her death early in February 1943. She was 45.

Sophie Licht. Moselle. Married to a Jew, and possibly denounced for listening to the BBC. Died at the age of 37 of typhus. Her husband was shot by the SS during the evacuation of Buchenwald. Her children, 10-year-old Denise and four-year-old Jean-Paul, were deported from Drancy to Auschwitz and gassed on arrival.

Yvonne Llucia. Oran. Very little known about her beyond the fact that she died, at the age of 32, in March 1943. Her mother refused to accept her death.

Alice Loeb. Paris. Chemist. Active communist. Managed to escape a selection on 20 February 1943, but died after roll call next day. She was 52.

Louise Loquet. Morbihan. Orphaned at eight, and brought up her three brothers, sole survivors of thirteen children. Operated stitching machine for a printing shop and with her husband composed and typed tracts. No one witnessed her death soon after arrival at Birkenau. She was 42. She left a daughter aged 17.

Yvonne Loriou. Charente-Maritime. Secretary. Wrote secret letters about the Resistance to her brother, a prisoner of war in Germany. Died, on 8 March 1943, of erysipelas. She was 41.

Suzanne Maillard. Somme. With her husband sheltered resisters and transmission radios. Died of typhus in mid-April 1943. She was 49. She left a 13-year-old son.

Yvette Marival. Indre-et-Loire. With her husband, she was a member of the Communist Party and joined the Front National. Denounced by a member of her network who talked under torture. No one witnessed her death.

Luz Martos. A refugee from Spain, she and her French husband joined the Resistance in Paris. Fell in the mud and gave up and died early in February 1943. She was 37.

Germaine Maurice. Indre-et-Loire. Helped father as a *passeur* across the demarcation line (see KERISIT). Died of pneumonia on 23 February 1943. She was 24. Her father died in the deportation.

Olga Melin. Pont-Sainte-Maxence. Craftswoman. With her brother, helped Jews escape across the demarcation line. Killed in the bombing near Mauthausen on 21 March 1945, aged 29. She left a son with polio.

Angèle Mercier. Seine-et-Marne. Managed hotel in Paris. Liaison agent.

Died at the beginning of March 1943 at the age of 33. Cause of death unknown.

Georgette Mesmer. Besançon. Part of a chain helping prisoners of war reach Switzerland. She died, aged 29, of dysentery, leaving a son.

Suzanne Meugnot. Almost nothing known about her, beyond the fact that she was born in April 1896 and died early in February 1943.

Renée Michaux. La Rochelle. Member of the JFdeF and under the name 'Marcelle' organised local groups of the Front National in the Gironde. Died of dysentery in mid-April 1943. She was 23. Her companion, André Sautel, was tortured and hanged himself.

Simone Miternique. Eure-et-Loir. Part of a chain of *passeurs*, taking Jews and resisters from Paris to the demarcation line. Died in 'the race' on 10 February 1943. She was 36 and left a son.

Gisèle Mollet. Paris. Maid in a hotel. Caught helping communist boyfriend distribute tracts. Badly beaten by SS. Died in the first half of August 1943, at the age of 23.

Suzanne Momon. Paris. Worker in a paint factory. Mother of Gilbert Brustlein of the Bataillons de la Jeunesse. No witness to her death in February 1943 at the age of 46. She left two children.

Denise Moret. Haute-Vienne. Never knew why she was picked up. Died soon after reaching Birkenau at the age of 25; no witnesses. Left a four-year-old daughter.

Madeleine Morin and her mother **Marie-Louise Morin.** Paris. The two women ran a beauty salon, where Jews collected false IDs. Madeleine died of typhus at the end of April 1943; she was 21. There were no witnesses to the death of Marie-Louise, towards the end of February 1943.

Marie-Louise Moru. Morbihan. Worked in a canning factory as a packer. Helped young people flee to the free zone to join the French navy. Died at the age of 17 in the *Revier* in March 1943.

Madeleine Normand. Charente. With her husband ran a small farm, hid resisters and helped them across the demarcation line. Beaten to death on 23 February 1943. She was 45. Her husband was executed by the Germans. Her mother died of grief and worry the day the *Convoi* left for Auschwitz.

Yvonne Noutari. Gironde. With her husband member of the Front National and sheltered resisters. Killed in the bombing near Mauthausen on 2 August 1944. She was 28. Her husband was executed by the Germans. They left two children.

Toussainte Oppici. Marseilles. Nothing known about her beyond the fact that she ran a restaurant and that she died of typhus at the end of April 1943, leaving an adolescent son. She was 37.

Anne-Marie Ostrowska. Rhineland. Married Jewish Polish refugee. Caught illegally crossing the demarcation line. Died in the marshes at the beginning of April 1943, at the age of 42. Her husband died in the camps; her son, deported to Auschwitz, survived, as did her daughter.

Lucienne Palluy. Paris. Stenographer. Became liaison officer for the FTP and transported powder and explosives. Died of dysentery at the end of February 1943 at the age of 33.

Yvonne Pateau. Vendée. With her husband – who was also her first cousin – had a small farm and hid weapons stolen from the quarry at Jonzac. Died at the beginning of February 1943 at the age of 42 of acute nephritis. Her husband was executed by the Germans. They left a five-year-old son.

Lucie Pecheux. Nièvre. Worked in Paris for a clothing manufacturer and collected funds for the Resistance. Died in the *Revier* around the middle of February 1943 at the age of 37, leaving an 18-year-old daughter.

Aurore Pica. Moselle. Evacuated to Gironde with her family, worked with the Resistance gathering information, procuring passes, assisting in theft of weapons. Died on 28 April 1943 of thirst. She was 19. Her sister Yolande GILI survived.

Yvonne Picard. Athens. Came to Paris to teach philosophy at the Sorbonne, where she joined the Resistance. Died of dysentery, at the age of 22, on 9 March 1943.

Suzanne Pierre. Meurthe-et-Moselle. Not connected to any official Resistance group, but worked with friends to blow up a canal lock. No one witnessed her death in August 1943. She was 31.

Juliette Poirier. Maine-et-Loire. No one knows why she was arrested and no one saw her die. She was 24. She left an eight-year-old son.

Maï Politzer. Biarritz. Midwife. Worked with the intellectual Resistance in Paris. Died of typhus on 6 March 1943. Her husband Georges was shot by the Germans. She left an eight-year-old son.

Pauline Pomies. Toulouse. Laundress. With her husband, sheltered resisters. Caught in 'the race' on 10 February 1943. She was 62. She left a daughter.

Line Porcher. Eure-et-Loir. Widow, and communist, who hid typewriter for tracts. Probably gassed in February 1943 at the age of 63.

Delphine Presset. Nimes. Not connected to the Resistance but caught in a sweep in Bordeaux. No one witnessed her death in February 1943. She was 42.

Marie-Thérèse Puyoou. Basses-Pyrénées. Ran a co-operative and sheltered members of the Resistance. Died in the *Revier* on 31 March 1943. She was 46. She left two daughters, aged 17 and 10.

Jacqueline Quatremaire. Orne. Secretary. Worked with Front National in Paris. Died of TB on 24 February 1943. She was 24.

Paula Rabeaux. Saumur. Worked making funerary ornaments. With husband part of Resistance in Bordeaux area. Died, her tongue so swollen she could not eat or breathe, in March 1943, at the age of 31. Her husband was shot by the Germans.

Constance Rappenau. Yonne. Ran restaurant used by Resistance. Caught in 'the race' on 10 February 1943. She was 63. She left one son.

Germaine Renaud. Seine-et-Oise. Ran a clandestine printing press. Beaten to death by *kapos*. She was 24.

Marguerite Richier, and her daughters, **Odette** and **Armande.** Paris. Members of the Front National. Marguerite was caught in 'the race' on 10 February 1943. She was 62. There were no witnesses to the deaths of Odette, aged 31, or Armande, 26.

Anne Richon. Lot-et-Garonne. Knitted sweaters. With son and husband worked for the FTP. Died of oedema on 21 March 1943. She was 44. Her husband was shot by the Germans. Her son survived.

France Rondeaux. Normandy. Helped aviators and Jews escape. Died of typhus, at the age of 41, in May 1943.

Georgette Rostaing. Ivry-sur-Seine. Militant communist who hid resisters and weapons. No one witnessed her death in March 1943. She was 31. She left one daughter.

Félicia Rostkowska. Poland. Came to France to teach the children of Polish miners and joined the Monika network. No one witnessed her death. She was 34.

Denise Roucayrol. Tarn. Hospital aide and worked with the FTP. Died of typhus in April 1943 at the age of 33.

Suzanne Roze. Seine-Inférieure. Communist and shop steward, and liaison officer for the Resistance. Died from a severe beating by an SS guard in February 1943. She was 38.

Esterina Ruju. Nothing known about her beyond the fact that she died at the end of March 1943, aged 58.

Léonie Sabail. Châtellerault. Office manager. With husband sheltered resisters. Died in the *Revier* on March 1943. She was 53. Her husband was shot by the Germans. She left one daughter and one son.

Anna Sabot. Alsace. No one witnessed her death or learnt anything about her. She was 44.

Berthe Sabourault. Charente. Started beauty salon and with her husband worked for the FTP. Died of typhus in April 1943 at the age of 38. Her husband died in Mauthausen. She left one son.

Raymonde Salez. Lilas. Member of the Young Communists and took part in armed attacks. No one witnessed her death. She was 23.

Henriette Schmidt. Essert. Worked with Danielle Casanova in the JFdeF and with DALLIDET network. Died in the *Revier* on 14 March 1943. She was 30.

Antoine Seibert. Paris. Nurse's aide. Worked with FTP. Death not witnessed. She was 43.

Léonie Seignolle. Paris. Nothing known of either her life or her death.

Raymonde Sergent. Indre-et-Loir. Cafe owner who helped people cross the demarcation line. Died at the end of March 1943 from oedema at the age of 39. She left a 12-year-old daughter.

Yvonne Souchaud. Tours. Worked with the Front National. Died of dysentery in March 1943 at the age of 45.

Jeanne Souques. Gironde. Helped husband run laundry. Delivered tracts, and hid typewriter. Died of typhus on 1 April 1943. She was 48. Her husband survived Mauthausen.

Marguerite Stora and her niece, **Sylviane Coupet.** La Manche. Marguerite had no known activities in the Resistance, but married to a Jew. Swore at the Germans who came to arrest him. Died in the *Revier* in March 1943 at the age of 47. Sylviane, whom she regarded as her daughter, died in the *Revier* in August 1943; she was not quite 18.

Andrée Tamisé. Bordeaux. Helped type and print tracts and formed student group with sister GILBERTE (who survived). Died on 8 March 1943 of pulmonary congestion; she was 21.

Jeanne Thiebault. Meurthe-et-Moselle. Specialised worker for Citroën, no known work for the Resistance. No one witnessed her death. She was 33.

Marguerite Valina. Charente-Maritime. Sheltered members of the Resistance and hid weapons. Caught in the Poinsot sweep (see GUILLONS). Died end of February 1943 in the *Revier*. Her husband was executed by the Germans. She left a son of 17, a daughter of 14 and a son aged eight.

Théodora van Dam and her daughter **Reyna.** Netherlands. With her husband belonged to a chain helping Dutch resisters escape to England. Caught in 'the race' on 10 February 1943. She was 60. Reyna did not want to leave her mother and both were gassed. She was 19. Another daughter survived.

Jakoba van der Lee. Netherlands. Lecturer at the School of Oriental Studies. Wistfully predicted Hitler's defeat. Caught in 'the race' on 10 February 1943. She was 54.

Alice Varailhon. Charente-Maritime. Lodged Resistance members and acted as liaison officer. Shot by SS for protesting about the death of a child on 11 March 1943. She was 45.

Alice Viterbo. Egypt. Singer at the Paris Opéra. Caught in 'the race' on 10 February 1943 at the age of 47.

Madeleine Zani. Meurthe-et-Moselle. Sheltered hunted resisters in Bordeaux. No witnesses to her death. She was 27 and left one son, aged three.

Source notes

Preface

1   **Over the next two weeks:** Police archives, Paris. Affaire Pican BS2 Carton 6; Pican, Cadras, Politzer et autres GB129 BS2–37; GB 65 BS–17.

4   **In the early 1960s:** see Charlotte Delbo, *Qui rapportera les paroles?* (Paris, 2001)

Part One

Chapter One

11   **What surprised:** see Alistair Horne, *To Lose a Battle: France 1940* (London, 1969); Roger Langeron, *Paris: Juin 1940* (Paris, 1946).

14   **Hitler, who paid:** Rod Kenward, *France and the French since 1900* (London, 2005), p. 243.

14   **a wonderful new toy:** Dominique Veillon, *Fashion under the Occupation* (Oxford, 2002), p. 22.

16   **Long before they reached Paris:** see Pierre Bourget, *Histoire secrète de l'occupation de Paris* (Paris, 1970); Jacques Delarue, *Histoire de la Gestapo* (Paris, 1962).

18   **From his sumptuous embassy:** see Gilles Ragache and Jean-Robert Ragache, *La Vie quotidienne des écrivains et artistes sous l'occupation 1940–1944* (Paris, 1988).

19   **At the time of the 1789 revolution:** Stéphane Courtois, Denis Peschanski and Adam Rayski, *Le Sang des étrangers* (Paris, 1989), p. 19.

19   **In early August:** see Gérard Walter, *La Vie à Paris sous l'occupation* (Paris, 1960).

21   **Parisians were advised:** Richard Cobb, *French and Germans, Germans and French* (London, 1983), p. 128.

SOURCE NOTES

Chapter Two

24 **The first acts:** see Henri Amouroux, *La Vie des français sous l'occupation* (Paris, 1990); Albrecht Betz and Stephan Martens, *Les Intellectuels et l'occupation* (Paris, 2004).

25 **There was, however:** see Stéphane Courtois and Marc Lazar, *L'Histoire du Parti Communiste Français* (Paris, 1995); Tony Judt, *Marxism and the French Left* (Oxford, 1986); Annie Kriegel, *The French Communists: Profile of a People* (Chicago, 1972).

26 **One of these young idealists:** Cécile Charua. Conversation with author.

29 **While Cécile was busy:** Betty Langlois. Conversation with author.

31 **'As Heydrich ...':** Roger Bourderon and Ivan Avakoumovitch, *Détruire le PCF* (Paris, 1988).

32 **In the 1930s:** Herbert R. Lottman, *The Left Bank* (Boston, 1982), p. 151.

33 **'Alas,' remarked:** see Tony Judt, *Past Imperfect: French Intellectuals 1944–1956* (Oxford, 1992); Piers Brendon, *The Dark Valley* (2000).

33 **Other writers:** see Jean Guéhénno, *Journal des Années Noires* 1940–1944 (Paris, 1947).

35 **Despite the presence:** see Henri Noguères, *Histoire de la résistance en France de 1940 à 1945* (Paris, 1967).

37 **One of these was:** see Charlotte Delbo, *Auschwitz and After* (New Haven, 1970).

38 **Fascinated by the theatre:** Fonds Jouvet, Bibliothèque Nationale, Paris.

40 **The couturière:** Veillon, *Fashion*, p. 31.

40 **For the most part:** Cobb, *French and Germans*, p. 100.

41 **For all this:** see Betz and Martens, *Les Intellechuels*.

Chapter Three

43 **Dozens of Vichy:** Archives Nationales AJ72/257 Reports of Prefects in Occupied France; Nina Kunz, 'Les Françaises dans la résistance', Mainz, 2003.

44 **Sport, the Vichy:** Margaret Collins-Weitz, *Sisters in the Resistance* (New York, 1995), p. 56.

44 **Since laxity of morals:** see Veillon, *Fashion*.

50 **Not far from Mado:** Pierrette Rostaing. Conversation with author.

52 **Another household:** Paul Thévenin and Christiane Fillatre. Conversations with author.

55 **As dawn broke:** see Courtois and Lazar, *Histoire*, p. 119.

56 **To it came:** see Jean-Marie Berlière and Franck Liaigre, *Le Sang des communistes* (Paris, 2004).

57 **Among the first:** Frédéric Blanc. Conversation with author. Also the unpublished memoir by Simone Sampaix.

57 **The new young:** see Maroussia Naitchenko, *Une Fille en guerre* (Paris, 2003).

59   **Many spoke Yiddish:** see Albert Ouzoulias, *Les Bataillons de la Jeunesse* (Paris, 1972); Marie Granet, *Les Jeunes dans la résistance* (Paris, 1985).

59   **The attack had:** see Hervé Villeré, *L'Affaire de la Section Spéciale* (Paris, 1973).

60   **The German response:** see Louis Oury, *Rue du Roi-Albert – Les Otages de Nantes, Chateaubriand et Bordeaux* (Paulin, 1997).

61   **As Pétain remarked:** Bourderon and Avakoumovitch, *Archives*, p. 154.

Chapter Four

64   **A silent, dour:** see Oury, *Rue du Roi-Albert*.

65   **As the Parisian resisters:** Jean Jérôme, *Les Clandestins 1940–1944* (Paris, 1986).

66   **The Picans had:** recorded interview 4AV812 Archives Départementales du Val-de-Marne.

67   **Not far away:** Madeleine Dissoubray. Conversation with author.

70   **De Gaulle, however:** Ouzoulias, *Les Bataillons*, p. 132.

70   **For the Germans:** Claudine Cardon-Hamet, *Mille Otages pour Auschwitz* (Paris, 1997), p. 83.

70   **With a broken:** Noguères, *Histoire*, p. 152.

71   **But for the most part:** see Primo Levi, *The Drowned and the Saved* (London, 1988).

72   **By the summer:** see Berlière and Liaigre, *Le Sang*.

74   **Look elegant and coquettish:** see Alain Guérin, *Chronique de la résistance* (Paris, 2000).

75   **The first anti-Semitic:** see Michael Marius and Robert Paxton, *Vichy France and the Jews* (London, 1981).

75   **In any case:** see Halimi, *La Délation*.

77   **Returning across the line:** see Elsa Triolet, *Ce n'était qu'un passage de ligne* (Paris, 1945).

77   **He was back in Paris:** see Anne Simonin, *Les Editions de Minuit* (Paris, 1994).

80   **Everything seemed:** see Albert Ouzoulias, *Les Fils de la nuit* (Paris 1975).

Chapter Five

87   **It was in early:** Gisèle Jaffredo. Conversation with author.

91   **The first escape:** see Sara Helm, *A Life in Secrets* (London, 2005).

92   **As a child:** Simone Alizon. Conversation with author.

Chapter Six

97   **By now, however:** Police archives, Paris. BS2 Carton 6.
99   **Better than the people:** see Frédéric Couderc, *Les Renseignements Généraux sous l'occupation* (Paris, 1992).
100 **Once Madeleine:** Police archives, Paris. BS2 Cartons 6 & 37.
101 **Charlotte Delbo was:** Mme Riera-Collet. Conversation with author.
107 **Commissioner David:** see Claude Angeli and Paul Gillet, *Debout Partisans!* (Paris, 1970).
108 **Otto von Stulpnägel:** see Ernst Junger, *Journal de guerre et d'occupation 1939–1948* (Paris, 1965).
109 **When it came to:** see Serge Klarsfeld, *Memorial to the Jews Deported from France* 1942–1944 (New York, 1983).
112 **Appalled by the sentences:** Police archives, Paris. BS2 Carton 9. Affaire Brodfeld.
115 **One was:** Police archives, Paris. GB129; BS2–37.
116 **Among the first:** see Klarsfeld, *Memorial*.
117 **Most of the executions:** see Arsène Tchakarian, *Les Fusillés de Mont-Valérien* (Nanterre, 1995).
117 **A German soldier:** Guérin, *Chronique*, p. 509.
117 **A modest, quiet:** see R. Closset, *L'Aumonier de l'enfer* (Paris, 1965).

Chapter Seven

121 **By early February:** see Maurice Rajsfus, *La Police de Vichy* (Paris, 1995).
122 **The Germans had not:** see Raphaël Delpart, *Les Convois de la Honte* (Paris, 2005).
123 **One of the people:** see Adelaïde Hautval, *Medizin gegen de Menschlichkeit* (Berlin, 2008).
126 **Towards the middle:** Police archives, Paris. GB102; BS2–10.
128 **From his repeated:** Police archives, Paris. GB50. L'Affaire Tintelin.
130 **Crucial to:** Police archives, Paris. GB65bis; BS1–17.

Chapter Eight

133 **But the long stretch:** Archives Départementales de la Gironde. Individual files 1400, 3009, 3025bis; VR199; see also René Terrisse, *A la Botte de l'occupant* (Bordeaux, 1988).
134 **Born in 1907:** Archives Départementales de la Gironde, SC493.
136 **Nearby Bègles:** Mme Vignac. Conversation with author.
137 **Aminthe and Prosper:** Hervé Guillon. Conversation with author; Michel Bainaud. Conversation with author.
140 **Hélène was an only:** Archives du Val-de-Marne. 4AV 788–90.
141 **Not far away:** Claude Epaud. Conversation with author.

142 **One of these was:** Tony Renaudin. Conversation with author.

143 **And there was:** Pierre Zani. Conversation with author.

144 **Some time after her arrival:** Archives Départementales de la Gironde, SC456.

144 **In April 1942:** See Michel Slitinsky, *La Résistance en Gironde* (Bordeaux, n.d.).

149 **By the end of October:** Archives Départementales de la Gironde, VRAC 707.

Chapter Nine

151 **The fort at Romainville:** see Thomas Fontaine, *Les Oubliés de Romainville* (Paris, 2005).

151 **The first of:** accounts taken from conversations with Cécile Charua, Simone Alizon and Betty Langlois; and memoirs left by Charlotte Delbo and Marie-Claude Vaillant-Couturier.

169 **Not long before:** see Jamine Ponty, *Les Polonais du Nord* (Paris, 1995); Karel Bartosek, René Gallissot and Denis Peschanski, *De l'Exil à la résistance* (Paris, 1989). See also archives of the Sikorski Museum in London and the Polish Institute in Paris.

170 **The entire Brabander:** see files in the Memorial de la Shoah, Paris.

175 **Of the 230:** see Charlotte Delbo, *Le Convoi du 24 janvier* (Paris, 1965).

Part Two

Much of the material for the second part of the book comes from conversations with Cécile Charua, Betty Langlois, Madeleine Dissoubray and Simone Alizon, and from their papers and letters; from talks with the descendants and relations of the women on the train; and from unpublished memoirs left by survivors.

Chapters Ten and Eleven

184 **In the summer of 1941:** see Yisrael Gutman and Michael Berenbaum, *Anatomy of the Auschwitz Death Camp* (Washington, DC, 1998); Robert Jan van Pelt and Deborah Dwork, *Auschwitz 1270 to the Present* (New Haven, 1996).

185 **As he would later:** see Rudolf Hoess, *Commandant of Auschwitz* (London, 1959).

187 **By early 1943:** see Diarmuid Jeffreys, *Hell's Cartel* (London, 2008).

189 **Later, Primo Levi:** see *The Drowned and the Saved*.

Chapter Twelve

220 **Their own particular:** see Myra Goldenberg, 'Different Horrors, Same Hell', in Roger Gottlieb ed., *Thinking the Unthinkable* (New York, 1970).

222 **Caesar was more interested:** Auschwitz Archives. APMA-B ; V46 p. 55.

227 **The story was picked:** see Fernand Grenier. *C'était ainsi. . .* (Paris, 1959).

233 **Nazi medical experiments:** see Robert Jay Lifton, *The Nazi Doctors* (London, 1986); Hautval, *Medizin gegen de Menschlichkeit* (Berlin, 2008)

237 **She now prepared:** see Lore Shelley, ed. *Criminal Experiments on Human Beings in Auschwitz and War Research Laboratories* (San Francisco, 1991).

Chapter Thirteen

243 **It was not, however:** see Bernhard Strebel, *Ravensbrück. Un Complexe Concentrationnaire* (Paderborn, 2003).

245 **The Polish women:** Germaine Tillion, *Ravensbrück* (Paris, 1973), p. 54.

248 **Not long after:** see Charlotte Serre, *De Fresnes à Ravensbrück* (Paris, 1982).

251 **Among the Nacht:** Annette Posnay-Vittel. Conversation with author.

260 **One day, one of them:** see Raymonde Guyon-Belot, *Le Sel de la mine* (Paris, 1990).

261 **Not long after:** Marie-Claude Vaillant-Couturier, evidence to Nuremberg.

Chapter Fourteen

267 **One after another:** Geneviève de Gaulle, evidence to Nuremberg.

271 **Women suspected of:** see Marie-Claude Vaillant-Couturier, Unpublished diary; Keith Mant, 'The Medical Services in the Concentration Camp of Ravensbrück', *Medico-Legal Journal.* Vol. 18.

272 **With the approach:** see David Rousset, *L'Univers concentrationnaire* (Paris, 1946).

278 **For some time now:** see Comte Bernadotte, *La Fin* (Lausanne, 1945).

280 **One day, seven:** Mme Hommel, testimony, Ravensbrück Archives TH401.

Chapter Fifteen

288 **Much of it:** see Delbo, *Auschwitz and After.*

291 **Germaine Renaudin:** Tony Renaudin. Conversation with author.

292 **In Saint-Martin:** Gisèle Jaffredo. Conversation with author.

294 **Among those greeting:** see Janet Flanner, *Paris Journal 1944–1965* (London, 1966); Antony Beevor and Artemis Cooper, *Paris after the Liberation, 1944–1949* (London, 1994).

295 **Even before:** see Jean-Marie Berlière and Franck Liaigre, *Liquider les Traîtres* (Paris, 2007).

296 **Like other European:** see Patricia Heberer and Jürgen Matthaus, *Atrocities on Trial* (London, 2008).

297 **Poinsot, who at:** Trial documents in the Archives Départementales de L'Allier; see also Dominique Lormier, *Bordeaux brûle-t-il?* (Bordeaux, 1998).

298 **It was generally:** see Tony Judt, *The Burden of Responsibility* (Chicago, 1998).

299 **Marie-Claude was:** see testimony in Marcel Ophüls, *Memory of Justice* (film, 1976); Marie-Claude Vaillant-Couturier, evidence to Nuremberg, 28 January 1946.

301 **On trial in Warsaw:** see Jeremy Dixon, *Commanders of Auschwitz* (Atglen, 2005).

305 **But it was more complicated:** see Simone Veil, *Une Vie* (Paris, 2007).

311 **Pierre Zani, who:** Conversation with author.

311 **Claude Epaud:** Conversation with author.

311 **Georgette Rostaing's daughter:** Pierrette Rostaing. Conversation with author.

312 **And the sense of loss:** Catherine Hardenberg. Conversation with author.

314 **When Germaine:** See Delbo, *Auschwitz and After*.

List of illustrations

The maps were drawn by Reginald Piggott.

Every effort has been made to trace or contact all copyright holders, and the publishers will be pleased to correct any omissions brought to their notice at the earliest opportunity.

Bibliography

Primary sources

The most important material for this book came from interviews with survivors and their families, from the works by Charlotte Delbo, and from unpublished memoirs and letters.

Before her death in 2009, I visited Betty Langlois several times at her flat in Paris. I also spoke at some length to Cécile Charua, Madeleine Dissoubray and Poupette Alizon. The other four women, still alive when I began work, were not well enough to see me. However, the families of many of the women who formed part of the *Convoi des 31000* agreed to talk to me, to give me letters and papers and unpublished memoirs.

When Charlotte Delbo returned to France in 1945, she wrote the first of what would become three memoirs of her months in Birkenau and Ravensbrück, but then put it aside for twenty years. Published as a single volume, *Auschwitz et àpres*, in the 1970s, it has been in print ever since. From then until her death in 1985, Delbo continued to write about the camps – in verse, plays and essays. Most important for this book was *Le Convoi du 24 Janvier*, in which she drew together biographical notes on her companions. This book was crucial in my search for the women and their families.

The following women of the *Convoi* wrote memoirs:

Alizon, Simone, *L'Exercise de vivre*, Paris, 1996.

Borras, Christiane, *Cécile, une 31000, communiste, déportée à Auschwitz-Birkenau*, Domont, 2006.

Delbo, Charlotte, *Le Convoi du 24 janvier*, Paris, 1965.

Delbo, Charlotte, *Auschwitz et après*, 3 vols (Paris 1970–71).

Delbo, Charlotte, *Spèctres, mes compagnons*, Lausanne, 1977.

Delbo, Charlotte, *Une Scène jouée dans la mémoire*, and *Qui rapportera les paroles?*, Paris, 2001.

Hautval, Adelaïde, *Medizin gegen de Menschlichkeit*, Berlin, 2008.

Sampaix, Simone, Unpublished memoir 1941–1945.

Vaillant-Couturier, Marie-Claude, *Mes 27 Mois entre Auschwitz et Ravensbrück*, Paris, 1946.

Vaillant-Couturier, Marie-Claude, Unpublished diary.

Two other sources provided important material:

Lazaroo, Gilbert and Peyrotte, Claude-Alice, Interviews on tape with Hélène Bolleau, Lulu Thévenin and Germaine Pican.

Quény, Marion, 'Un Cas d'exception: 230 femmes françaises déportées à Auschwitz-Birkenau en janvier 1943 par mesure de repression: le Convoi du 24 janvier,' thesis for the Université Charles de Gaulle 3, June, 2004.

Manuscript sources

Invaluable documents on the Resistance, the resisters, the Brigades Spéciales, France under occupation, deportations, and the German occupiers are to be found in CARAN, the Archives Nationales in Paris (series 72AJ45; 72AJ69; 72AJ78), the Archives Départementales of the Gironde, the Archives Départementales de l'Allier, the Archives Départementales de Indre-et-Loire, the Archives Départementales du Val-de-Marne, the Archives de la Préfecture de Police, Paris: Cartons des Brigades Spéciales, Dossiers individuels des 31000 et de leurs maris ou compagnons constitués par les Renseignements Généraux; the Bureau des Anciens Combattants in Caen, Dossiers des Personnes rentrés de Déportation; the Memorial de la Shoah, Paris; Musée de la Résistance et de la Déportation, Besançon, Fonds Marie-Claude Vaillant-Couturier; Sikorski archives, London.

I translated all the primary material quoted myself.

Secondary sources

The Second World War in German-occupied France, the deportations of Jews and resisters to the extermination and concentration camps in the east, and life inside Birkenau, Auschwitz and Ravensbrück have all been extensively written about in memoirs, histories and academic journals. The following is a brief selection of those most frequently consulted for this book.

Added, Serge, Le Théâtre dans les années de Vichy. Paris, 1992.

Alary, Eric, La Ligne de démarcation. Paris, 2003.

Alary, Eric, Les Français au quotidien. Paris, 2006.

Alary, Eric, Un Procès sous l'Occupation au Palais Bourbon. Mars 1942. Paris, n.d.

Alcan, Louise, Le Temps ecartelé. St-Jean-de-Maurienne, 1980.

Amicale de Ravensbrück et Association des Déportées et Internées de la Résistance, Les Françaises à Ravensbrück. Paris, 1965.

Amouroux, Henri, La Vie des Français sous l'occupation. Paris, 1990.

Avon, Robert, Histoire de l'épuration. Paris, 1967.

Aziz, Philippe, Le Livre noir de la trahison. Histoire de la Gestapo en France. Paris, 1984.

Bartosek, Karel, Gallissot, René and Peschanski, Denis, De l'Exil à la *résistance. Réfugiés et immigrés de l'Europe centrale en France 1933–1945.* Paris, 1989.

Beevor, Antony and Cooper, Artemis, *Paris after the Liberation, 1944–1949.* London, 1994.

Bellanger, Claude, *La Presse clandestine 1940–1944.* Paris, 1961.

Berlière, Jean-Marie and Laurent Chabrun, *Les Policiers français sous l'occupation.* Paris, 2001.

Berlière, Jean-Marie and Liaigre, Franck, *Le Sang des Communistes. Les Bataillons de la Jeunesse dans la lutte armée.* Paris, 2004.

Berlière, Jean-Marie and Liaigre, Franck, *Liquider les traîtres. La Face cachée du PCF. 1941–1943.* Paris, 2007.

Bernadotte, Comte, *La Fin.* Lausanne, 1945.

Besser, Jean-Pierre and Ponty, Thomas, *Les Fusillés. Répression et exécution pendant l'occupation. 1940–1944.* Paris, 2006.

Bettelheim, Bruno, *The Informed Heart.*

Bettelheim, Bruno, *Surviving the Holocaust.*

Betz, Albrecht and Martens, Stephan, *Les Intellectuels et l'occupation.* Paris, 2004.

Blumenson, Martin, *Le Réseau du Musée de l'Homme.* Paris, 1977.

Bourdel, Philippe, *La Grande Débâcle de la collaboration. 1944–1948.* Paris, 2007.

Bourderon, Roger and Avakoumovitch, Ivan, *Détruire le PCF – Archives de l'Etat Français et l'Occupant Hitlérien 1940–1944.* Paris, 1988.

Bourget, Pierre, *Histoire secrète de l'occupation de Paris.* Paris, 1970.

Breton, Catherine, 'Mémoires d'avenir,' doctoral thesis, Nanterre-Paris X, 1994.

Cardon-Hamet, Claudine, *Mille Otages pour Auschwitz. Le Convoi du 6 Juillet 1942.* Paris, 1997.

Chombart de Lauwe, Marie-Jo, *Toute une Vie de résistance.* Paris, 1998.

Closset, R., *L'Aumonier de l'enfer: Franz Stock.* Paris, 1965.

Cobb, Richard, *French and Germans, Germans and French.* London, 1983.

Cohen, Elie A., *Human Behaviour in the Concentration Camp.* London, 1954.

Collins-Weitz, Margaret, *Sisters in the Resistance. How Women Fought to Free France 1940–1945.* New York, 1995.

Couderc, Frédéric, *Les Renseignements Généraux sous L'occupation.* Paris, 1992.

Courtois, Stéphane and Lazar, Marc, *Histoire du Parti Communiste Français.* Paris, 1995.

Courtois, Stéphane, Peschanski, Denis and Rayski, Adam, *Le Sang des étrangers: les immigrés de la MOI dans la résistance.* Paris, 1989.

Dabitch, Christophe, *24 Octobre 1941. Bordeaux. Les 50 Otages – un assassinat politique.* Montreuil-Bellay, 1999.

Debû-Bridel, Jacques, ed. *La Résistance intellectuelle.* Paris, 1970.

Delarue, Jacques, *Histoire de la Gestapo.* Paris, 1962.

Delpart, Raphaël, *Les Convois de la honte*. Paris, 2005.

Dixon, Jeremy, *Commanders of Auschwitz*. Atglen, PA, 2005.

Durand, Pierre, *Danielle Casanova, L'indomptable*. Paris, 1990.

Fabre, Marc-André, *Dans les prisons de Vichy*. Paris, 1944.

Flanner, Janet, *Paris Journal 1944–1965*. London, 1966.

Fontaine, Thomas, *Les Oubliés de Romainville*. Paris, 2005.

La France de 1945: Résistances, retours, renaissances. Actes de Colloque de Caen 17–19 Maï 1995. Caen, 1996

Furet, François, *The Passing of an Illusion*. Chicago, 1999.

Gaillard-Menant, Sundy, 'Résister à l'occupation, Résister à Auschwitz, Résister à l'oubli: la mémoire des femmes. De Charlotte Delbo, du Convoi du 24 Janvier 1943', Thesis, Université-Sorbonne Panthéon, 1999.

Gilzmer, Mechtild, Levisse-Touzé, Christine and Martens, Stephan, *Les Femmes dans la résistance en France*. Paris, 2003.

Gottlieb, Roger S., ed. *Thinking the Unthinkable: Meanings of the Holocaust*, New York, 1970.

Granet, Marie, *Les Jeunes dans la résistance. 20 ans en 1940*. Paris, 1985.

Grenier, Fernand, *C'était ainsi . . .* Paris, 1959.

Gresh, Sylviane, *Les Veilleuses*. Paris, 1996.

Guéhenno, Jean, *Journal des années noires 1940–1944*. Paris, 1947.

Guérin, Alain, *Chronique de la résistance*. Paris, 2000.

Gutman, Yisrael and Berenbaum, Michael, *Anatomy of the Auschwitz Death Camp*. Washington, DC, 1998.

Guyon-Belot, Raymonde, *Le Sel de la mine*. Paris, 1990.

Halimi, André, *La Délation sous l'occupation*. Paris, 1983.

Hamelin, France, *Femmes dans la nuit 1939–1944*. Paris, 1988.

Hardman, Anna, *Women and the Holocaust*. Holocaust Educational Trust Research Papers. Vol 1. No 3, 1999/2000.

Heberer, Patricia and Matthaus, Jürgen, *Atrocities on Trial. Historical Perspectives and the Politics of Prosecuting War Crimes*. London, 2008.

Heller, Gerhard, *Un Allemand à Paris 1940–1944*. Paris, 1981.

Helm, Sara, *A Life in Secrets*. London, 2005.

Higonnet, Margaret Randolph et al., eds, *Behind the Lines: Gender and the Two World Wars*. New Haven, 1987.

Hill, Mavis M. and Lewis, L. Norman, *Auschwitz in England*. London, 1965.

Hitchcock, William, *Liberation: Europe 1945*. London, 2008.

Hoess, Rudolf, *Commandant of Auschwitz*. London, 1959.

Horne, Alistair, *To Lose a Battle. France 1940*. London, 1969.

Hughes, H. Stuart, *The Obstructed Path. French Social Thought in the Years of Desperation. 1930–1960*. London, 2002.

Jeffreys, Diarmuid, *Hell's Cartel. IG Farben and the Making of Hitler's War Machine*. London, 2008.

Jérôme, Jean, *Les Clandestins 1940–1944*. Paris, 1986.

Josse, Raymond, 'La Naissance de la résistance étudiante à Paris,' *Revue d'histoire de la deuxième guerre mondiale* (Paris, July 1962), No.47.

Judt, Tony, *Marxism and the French Left*. Oxford, 1986.

Judt, Tony, *Past Imperfect: French Intellectuals 1944–1956*. Oxford, 1992.

Judt, Tony, *The Burden of Responsibility*. Chicago, 1998.

Junger, Ernst, *Journal de guerre et d'occupation 1939–1948*. Paris, 1965.

Kaufmann, Dorothy, *Edith Thomas: A Passion for Resistance*. London, 2004.

Kedward, H.R., *Occupied France. Collaboration and Resistance 1940–1944*. Oxford, 1985.

Kenward, Rod, *France and the French since 1900*. London, 2005.

Klarsfeld, Serge, *Le Livre des otages*. Paris, 1979.

Klarsfeld, Serge, *Memorial to the Jews deported from France 1942–1944*. New York, 1983.

Kogon, Eugen, *The Theory and Practice of Hell. The German Concentration Camps and the System behind them*. New York, 1979.

Kriegel, Annie, *The French Communists: Profile of a People*. Chicago, 1972.

Kunz, Nina, 'Les Françaises dans la résistance,' Diplomarbeit über das Thema, Johannes Gutenberg-Universität, Mainz, 2003.

Lallam, Sandra, Maitrisse d'Histoire Contemporaine. Paris 1V Sorbonne. 1999–2000.

Langbein, Hermann, *People in Auschwitz*. London, 2004.

Langeron, Roger, *Paris: Juin 1940*. Paris, 1946.

Laroche, Gaston and Matline, Boris, *On les nommait les Etrangers. Les Immigrés dans la résistance*. Paris, 1965.

Levi, Primo, *The Drowned and the Saved*. London, 1988.

Lifton, Robert Jay, *The Nazi Doctors. Medical Killing and the Psychology of Genocide*. London, 1986.

Livre-Mémorial des deportés de France par mesure de repression 1940–1941, 4 vols. La Fondation pour la Mémoire de la Déportation. Paris, 2004.

Lottman, Herbert R., *The Left Bank. Writers, Artists and Politics from the Popular Front to the Cold War*. Boston, 1982.

Marius, Michael and Paxton, Robert, *Vichy France and the Jews*. London, 1981.

Marius, Michael, *The Nuremberg War Crimes Trial*. London, 1997.

Marnham, Patrick, *The Death of Jean Moulin*. London, 2001.

Michel, Henri, *Paris Allemand*. Paris, 1981.

Michel, Henri, *Paris Résistant*. Paris, 1982.

Milhaud, G., *Raymond Losserand 1903–1942*. Paris, 1949.

Morris, Alan, *Collaboration and Resistance Reviewed. Writers in the Mode Rétro in Post-Gaullist France.* New York, 1992.

Naitchenko, Maroussia, *Une Fille en guerre.* Paris, 2003.

Noguères, Henri, *Histoire de la résistance en France de 1940 à 1945,* 5 vols. Paris, 1967.

Novick, Peter, *The Resistance versus Vichy. The Purge of Collaborators in Liberated France.* London, 1958.

Ouzoulias, Albert, *Les Bataillons de la Jeunesse. Les Jeunes dans la résistance.* Paris, 1972.

Ouzoulias, Albert, *Les Fils de la nuit.* Paris, 1975.

Pendas, Devin O., *The Frankfurt Auschwitz Trial 1963–1965. Genocide, History and the Limits of the Law.* Cambridge, 2006.

Pollak, Michael, *L'Expérience concentrationnaire.* Paris, 1990.

Ponty, Janine, *Les Polonais du Nord ou la mémoire des corons.* Paris, 1995.

Pozner, Vladimir, *Descente aux enfers. Récits de deportés et de SS d'Auschwitz.* Paris, 1980.

Prost, Antoine, ed., *La Résistance: Une Histoire sociale.* Paris, 1997.

Ragache, Gilles and Ragache, Jean-Robert, *La Vie quotidienne des écrivains et des artistes sous l'occupation 1940–1944.* Paris, 1988.

Rajsfus, Maurice, *La Police de Vichy.* Paris, 1995.

Rayski, Adam, *The Choices of the Jews under Vichy.* Notre-Dame, 2005.

Rémy, *La Ligne de démarcation,* 6 vols. Paris, 1964.

'La Résistance et les français', *Les Cahiers de l'IHTP,* No. 37 (Paris, Dec. 1997).

Richet, Charles and Mons, Antonin, *Pathologie de la déportation.* Paris, 1958.

Rioux, Jean-Pierre, Prost, Antoine and Azéma, Jean-Pierre, *Les Communistes français de Munich à Chateaubriand 1938–1941.* Paris, 1987.

Rossi, A., *La Guerre des papillons. Quatre ans de politique communiste 1940–1944.* Paris, 1954.

Rossiter, Margaret L., *Women in the Resistance.* New York, 1986.

Rousset, David, *L'Univers concentrationnaire.* Paris, 1946.

Serre, Charlotte, *De Fresnes à Ravensbrück.* Paris, 1982.

Shelley, Lore, ed., *Criminal Experiments on Human Beings in Auschwitz and War Research Laboratories.* San Francisco, 1991.

Shelley, Lore, ed., *Auschwitz – The Nazi Civilisation, Twenty-three Women Prisoners' Accounts.* London, 1992.

Simonin, Anne, *Les Editions de Minuit. Le Devoir et l'insoumission.* Paris, 1994.

Slitinsky, Michel, *La Résistance en Gironde.* Bordeaux, n.d.

Souleau, Philippe, *La Ligne de démarcation en Gironde 1940–1944.* Perigieux, 1998.

Strebel, Bernhard, *Ravensbrück. Un Complexe concentrationnaire.* Paderborn, 2003.

Szmaglewska, Seweryna, *Smoke over Birkenau*. New York, 1947.

Tchakarian, Arsène, *Les Fusillés de Mont-Valérien*. Nanterre, 1995.

Témoignages sur Auschwitz. Edition de l'Amicale de déportées d'Auschwitz. Paris, n.d.

Terrisse, René, *A la Botte de l'occupant*. Bordeaux, 1988.

Terrisse, René, *Face aux Peletons Nazis*. Bordeaux, 2000.

Thatcher, Nicole, *A Literary Analysis of Charlotte Delbo's Concentration Camp Representation*. New York, 2000.

Thatcher, Nicole, *Charlotte Delbo: Une Voix singulière*. Paris, 2003.

Thibault, Laurence, ed., *Les Femmes et la résistance*. Cahiers de la Résistance, Paris, 2006.

Tillion, Charles, *On Chantait Rouge*. Paris, 1977.

Tillion, Germaine, *Ravensbrück*. Paris, 1973.

Veillon, Dominque, *Le Temps des restrictions en France 1939–1949*. Paris, 1996.

Veillon, Dominique, *Fashion under the Occupation*. Oxford, 2002.

Vercors, *Le Silence de la mer*. Paris, 1945.

Vercors, *La Bataille de Silence*. Paris, 1967.

Vidalenc, Jean, *L'Exode de mai–juin 1940*. Paris, 1957.

Villeré, Hervé, *L'Affaire de la Section Spéciale*. Paris, 1973.

Villon, Pierre, *Résistant de la première heure*. Paris, 1983.

Vinen, Richard, *The Unfree French: Life under the Occupation*. London, 2006.

Walter, Gerard, *La Vie à Paris sous l'occupation*. Paris, 1960.

Wieviorka, Annette, *Ils étaient Juifs, resistants, communistes*. Paris, 1986.

Wieviorka, Annette, *Déportation et génocide. Entre la mémoire et l'oubli*. Paris, 1992.

Acknowledgements

My thanks, first and foremost, go to the four survivors of the *Convoi* who were kind enough to see and talk to me: Simone Alizon (Poupette), Cécile Borras (Charua), Madeleine Jegouzo (Betty Langlois) and Madeleine Odru Dissoubray. Their long interviews with me and their kind permission to quote from their letters and papers made this book possible. By the same token, I wish to thank Catherine Benainous, Frédéric Blanc, Claude Epaud, Jaunay, Yves Jegouzo, Catherine Kestemberg-Hardenberg, Tony Renaudin, Pierrette Rostaing, Gisèle Sergent Jaffredo, Paul Thévenin, Christine Umido, Michelle Vignac and Pierre Zani for talking to me about their mothers and for letting me see unpublished letters and memoirs. Christiane Fillatre generously talked to me about her sisters, Lulu and Carmen, and Hervé Guillon about his grandparents. Frédéric Blanc very kindly allowed me to read the unpublished diary written by his mother, Simone Sampaix.

In the course of my research I was helped by the following people; I would like to thank them all very much for their time, generosity and encouragement: Michel Bainaud, Rosine Crémieux, Fernand Devaux, Catherine Dubois, Claudine Ducastel, M.R.D. Foot, Trudy Gold, Roger Hommet, Freddy Knoller, Pierre Labate, Gilbert Lazaroo, Christine Levisse-Touzé, Mme Marchelidon, Stefan Martens, André Montagne, Claude-Alice Peyrotte, Marion Quény, Claudine Riera-Collet, Bernard Strebel, Rita Thalmann and Mala Tribich. Claudine Riera-Collet, friend and executor of Charlotte Delbo, gave me advice and kind permission to draw on Delbo's works.

Much of the material for this book comes from archives held by a wide number of libraries and institutions. I should in particular like to thank the following individuals and the staffs of their libraries: M. Roland-Boisseau and the AFMD in Bordeaux; L'Amicale de Ravensbrück, Paris; M. Laux and the Archives Départementales de la Gironde; Mme LeClerc and the Archives Départementales de Indre-et-Loire; Laurence Bourgade and the Archives Départementales du Val de Marne; Cyrille Lequellec and the Fondation pour la Mémoire de la Déportation; L'Association des Deportés, Internés de la Résistance; L'Association Mémoire Vive des Transports des 45000 et 31000; Mme Rutkowski and the Bibliothèque

ACKNOWLEDGEMENTS

Polonaise in Paris; Patrick Le Boeuf and the Bibliothèque Nationale, Rue de Richelieu; Arnaud Boulligny and the Bureau des Archives des Victimes des Conflits Contemporains, Caen; CARAN; Le Centre Jean Moulin; Le Comité des Fusillés de Souge; Mme Baron and Mme Micheline of the Fédération Nationale des Déportés et Internés Résistants et Patriots (FNDIRP); The Holocaust Survivors Centre, Hendon; Christine Levisse-Touzé and the Mémorial du Maréchal Leclerc de Hautecloque de la Libération de Paris; Le Mémorial de la Shoah in Paris; Wojciech Plosa and Symon Kowalski of the Muzeum Oswiecim-Brzrzinka; the French Ministère de La Défense: the Musée de l'Histoire Vive at Montreuil; Marie-Claire Ruet and the Musée de la Résistance et de la Déportation, Besançon; Xavier Aumale and the Musée de la Résistance Nationale at Champigny-sur-Marne; the Sikorski Museum, London; Cordula Hundertmark, Monika Herzog and Dr Insa Eschebach of the Ravensbrück archives.

Christina Meier and Monika Liro helped me with the Polish and German research: for which I thank them very much.

And I should like to thank all the friends who, through their hospitality and willingness to travel with me, made this book happen: Catherine and Olivier Beressi, Anne Chisholm, Karin Demorest, Virginia Duigan, Hubert Faure, Annie Nairn, Kathy van Praag, Patricia Williams, Lyn and Carlos Windmann. Ingrid von Rosenberg and Gerd Stratman not only travelled with me to Ravensbrück and Auschwitz but found material that I would never have seen.

Once again, I would warmly like to thank my editors, Jennifer Barth, Poppy Hampson and Penelope Hoare, my agent, Clare Alexander, and Helen Smith for the index.

For the lines from Charlotte Delbo, *Auschwitz and After*, translated by Rosette Lamar, on p.288, I would like to thank Claudine Riera-Collet and the Charlotte Delbo literary estate.

The lines by Louis Aragon on p.231 are from the *Collected Poems* published by Gallimard.

The lines by Paul Éluard on p.80 are from his poem 'Courage', from his book *Au Rendez-vous Allemand*, Editions de Minuit, France, 1944. Author's translation.

Index